"This highly accessible book captures—better than any other I know currently available in English—the key debates currently taking place in Japan as it searches for a new sense of identity following the triple disasters of earthquake, tsunami and nuclear meltdown which befell the country on 11 March 2011. It should go straight on the reading list of anyone teaching courses on contemporary Japan."

Roger Goodman, *Nissan Professor of Modern Japanese Studies, University of Oxford, UK*

"From immigration and demographics to Okinawa and the changing role of the Supreme Court, this collection of essays provides a fresh and comprehensive guide to a society that is changing more than widely recognised. Kingston has gathered a collection of essays that shun cliché in favour of rational discussion."

David Pilling, *Asia Editor, Financial Times*

"This timely collection by cutting-edge scholars of East Asia covers many of the key issues in Japanese domestic society and international relations. The readable and informative essays take us beyond the mass media stereotypes, making it a valuable tool for students, teachers, journalists, and general readers seeking a deeper understanding of Japan today."

Jordan Sand, *Associate Professor of Japanese History, Georgetown University, USA*

"In a post-earthquake, tsunami and radiation Japan, many of the assumptions we had about Japan, even those we had felt were chronically problematic, have been directly challenged. This volume is an important collection that allows us to explore that challenge, both in our understanding of what is distinct to a rapidly changing Japan in itself, but also as a way for us to engage in comparative research on a number of dynamics that are characteristic to post-industrial society in Asia and around the world. Hugely valuable for current research and a great teaching tool for advanced students."

David Slater, *Sophia University Faculty of Liberal Arts, Japan*

Critical Issues in Contemporary Japan

This book provides undergraduate and graduate students with an interdisciplinary compendium written by a number of leading specialists on contemporary Japan. Chapters reflect the standards of rigorous scholarly work, but also exceed them in their accessibility of language and engagement with concerns relevant to non-specialists. The probing analysis of key debates and issues confronting Japan make this ideal for college courses and an essential reference work on Japan/Asia for libraries.

This book encompasses a range of disciplines in the social sciences and thus will be useful for a variety of courses including Comparative Politics, Media Studies, Anthropology, Sociology, Asian Studies, International Relations, Public Policy, Health Care, Education, Judicial Reform, Gender and Minority Studies. The strength of this volume is in the collective efforts of accomplished experts providing in-depth analysis and up-to-date comprehensive coverage of Japan in the 21st century. Students will gain the analytical insights and information necessary to assess the challenges that confront the Japanese people, policy makers and private- and public-sector institutions.

Key issues covered in this volume include:

- Rapidly aging society
- Changing employment system
- Energy policy—nuclear and renewable
- Gender discrimination
- Immigration
- Ethnic minorities
- Trade policy
- Civil society
- Rural Japan
- Okinawa
- Post-3/11 tsunami, earthquake, nuclear meltdown developments
- Internationalization
- Sino–Japanese relations
- East Asia's divisive history

Jeff Kingston is Professor of History and Director of Asian Studies at Temple University, Japan. He is the author of *Japan's Quiet Transformation* (2004) and *Contemporary Japan* (2011).

Critical Issues in Contemporary Japan

Edited by
Jeff Kingston

LONDON AND NEW YORK

First published 2014
by Routledge
2 Park Square, Milton Park, Abingdon, Oxon OX14 4RN

and by Routledge
711 Third Avenue, New York, NY 10017

Routledge is an imprint of the Taylor & Francis Group, an informa business

British Library Cataloguing in Publication Data
A catalogue record for this book is available from the British Library

Library of Congress Cataloging in Publication Data
Critical issues in contemporary Japan / edited by Jeff Kingston.
p. cm
Includes bibliographical references and index.
1. Japan–Politics and government–1989- 2. Japan–Social conditions–1989- 3. Japan–Economic conditions–1989- 4. Japan–Foreign relations. I. Kingston, Jeff, 1957- editor of compilation.
DS891.C75 2013
320.60952–dc23
2013020891

ISBN: 978-0-415-85744-4 (hbk)
ISBN: 978-0-415-85745-1 (pbk)
ISBN: 978-0-203-79759-4 (ebk)

Typeset in Bembo
by Taylor & Francis Books

Printed and bound in Great Britain by
TJ International Ltd, Padstow, Cornwall

Contents

Illustrations

Figures

Tables

Maps

Contributors

Daniel P. Aldrich is an Associate Professor of Political Science at Purdue University who has been a Visiting Scholar at the University of Tokyo's Law Faculty in Japan, an Advanced Research Fellow at Harvard University's Program on US–Japan Relations. He has published two books, *Site Fights* (2008) and *Building Resilience* (2012), and more than 80 peer-reviewed articles, book chapters, reviews, and op-eds. His research has been funded by grants from the Abe Foundation, IIE Fulbright Foundation, the National Science Foundation, the Reischauer Institute at Harvard University, the Weatherhead Center for International Affairs, and Harvard's Center for European Studies.

Robert Aspinall, DPhil, received his doctorate from St Antony's College, Oxford. He is a Professor in the Department of Social Systems, Shiga University, and author of *Teachers' Unions and the Politics of Education in Japan* (SUNY, 2001) and *International Education Policy in Japan in an Age of Globalisation and Risk* (Brill, 2013).

Tina Burrett is an Assistant Professor of International Relations at Temple University, Japan. She holds a PhD in Political Science from the University of Cambridge. Her publications include *Television and Presidential Power in Putin's Russia* (Routledge, 2011).

Kyle Cleveland is a sociologist and administrator at Temple University's Japan Campus in Tokyo. As the founding Director of TUJ's Institute of Contemporary Asian Studies, he has supervised special programs in Japanese popular culture and visual media studies, organized a lecture series, and produced symposia related to contemporary political issues. Through the Wakai Project, he organizes a series of events in which scholars, activists, and students from various universities collaborate to address how globalization is affecting youth culture in Japan. His research focuses on youth politics, popular culture and trans-global ethnic identity.

Andrew DeWit is Professor in Rikkyo University's School of Policy Studies, and holds a PhD in the political economy of Japan (University of British Columbia, 1997). He is lead researcher for a five-year (2010–15) Japanese government-funded project on the political economy of the feed-in tariff. He has published extensively on renewable energy including (with Kaneko Masaru and Iida Tetsunari) "Fukushima and the Political Economy of Power Policy in Japan," in Jeff Kingston (ed.) *Natural Disaster and Nuclear Crisis in Japan: Response and Recovery after Japan's 3/11* (Nissan Institute, 2012).

Alexis Dudden is Professor of History at the University of Connecticut. She is author of *Troubled Apologies Among Japan, Korea, and the United States* (Columbia, 2008). Her current research focuses on the modern history of oceans and islands in Northeast Asia.

Robert Dujarric is Director of the Institute of Contemporary Asian Studies, Temple University, Japan Campus, in Tokyo. He is a former Council on Foreign Relations (Hitachi) International Affairs Fellow. He has worked in North America, Europe, and Asia in finance and policy research. He was raised in Paris and New York. He is a graduate of Harvard College and holds an MBA from Yale University. He has published several books and articles, including *America's Inadvertent Empire* (with William E. Odom, Yale, 2004). For more information, visit www.tuj.ac.jp/icas/the-institute/staff/

Aurelia George Mulgan is Professor of Politics in the School of Humanities and Social Sciences, University of New South Wales, Canberra, Australia. She is the author of a number of books including *The Politics of Agriculture in Japan* (Routledge, 2000), *Japan's Failed Revolution: Koizumi and the Politics of Economic Reform* (Asia-Pacific Press, 2002) and *Power and Pork: A Japanese Political Life* (ANU E-Press, 2006). In 2001 she won an Ohira Memorial Prize for *The Politics of Agriculture in Japan*, and in 2010 the Toshiba Prize from the British Association of Japanese Studies.

Sachiko Horiguchi is an Assistant Professor of Anthropology at Temple University, Japan Campus. She earned her DPhil in Social Anthropology from the University of Oxford. Her main research interests lie in the social and medical anthropology of Japanese society and culture, with particular focus on youth mental health issues in contemporary Japan. Her recent works include a chapter in *A Sociology of Japanese Youth* (Routledge, 2012), entitled "Hikikomori: How Private Isolation Caught the Public Eye."

Tin Tin Htun teaches gender and minority issues at Temple University, Japan Campus and Chuo University in Japan. She did her PhD in social psychology on gender and leadership orientation in Japan at Tsukuba University. She is currently researching the identity of minorities in Japan and gender discrimination in Burma.

Jeff Kingston is Professor of History and author of *Contemporary Japan* (Wiley, 2013, 2nd edition) and *Japan's Quiet Transformation* (Routledge, 2004), and editor of *Natural Disaster and Nuclear Crisis in Japan* (Routledge, 2012). He is Director of Asian Studies, Temple University, Japan.

David Leheny (PhD, Cornell, 1998) is the Henry Wendt III '55 Professor of East Asian Studies at Princeton University. He is the author of *Think Global, Fear Local: Sex, Violence, and Anxiety in Contemporary Japan* (Cornell University Press, 2006) and *The Rules of Play: National Identity and the Shaping of Japanese Leisure* (Cornell University Press, 2003), as well as co-editor (with Kay Warren) of *Japanese Aid and the Construction of Global Development: Inescapable Solutions* (Routledge, 2010).

Dr. David McNeill has been a foreign correspondent in Japan since 2001 and writes for *The Irish Times*, *The Independent*, *The Economist* and *The Chronicle of Higher Education*, and helps coordinate the e-journal Japanfocus.org. He previously taught at universities in Ireland, Britain and China, and currently teaches a course on media and politics at Sophia University in Tokyo. He is a former board member of the Foreign Correspondents' Club of Japan and co-author of *Strong in the Rain: Surviving Japan's Earthquake, Tsunami and Nuclear Disaster.*

John Mock is a social anthropologist who has lived and worked in the United States and Japan. After being 'retired' from the University of Tsukuba, he now teaches at Temple University, Japan. He is author of *Culture, Community and Change in a Sapporo Neighborhood 1925–88: Hanayama* (Edwin Mellen Press, 1999).

Akihiro Ogawa is an Associate Professor of Japanese Studies at Stockholm University, Sweden. His research interest is political anthropology, focusing on civil society in Japan and East Asia. He is the author of the award-winning book *The Failure of Civil Society? The Third Sector and the State in Contemporary Japan* (SUNY Press, 2009).

Lawrence Repeta is a Professor at Meiji University Faculty of Law, Tokyo. He has served as a lawyer, business executive, and law professor in Japan and the United States. The primary focus of his advocacy and research is transparency in government. He serves on the board of directors of Information Clearinghouse Japan, a nongovernmental organization devoted to promoting open government in Japan (www.clearing-house.org). He has written widely on Japanese law issues, especially related to constitutional rights. In 2011 his writings appeared in the *Washington University Law Journal* (lawreview.wustl.edu/in-print/vol-886/), in the *Routledge Handbook of Japanese Culture and Society* (edited by Victoria Bestor and Theodore C. Bestor), and in other publications. He is a graduate of the University of Washington School of Law and member of the Washington State Bar Association.

Sven Saaler is Associate Professor of Modern Japanese History at Sophia University in Tokyo. He was formerly Head of the Humanities Section of the German Institute for Japanese Studies (DIJ) and Associate Professor at the University of Tokyo. He has written a monograph on history debates in Japan (*Politics, Memory and Public Opinion*, 2005) and articles on the history textbook controversy, the Yasukuni question and the historical development and significance of pan-Asianism. He co-edited *Pan-Asianism in Modern Japanese History* (with J. Victor Koschmann, Routledge, 2007), *The Power of Memory in Modern Japan* (with Wolfgang Schwentker, Global Oriental, 2008) and *Pan-Asianism: A Documentary History* (with Christopher W.A. Szpilman, Rowman & Littlefield, 2011). He is also co-author of *Impressions of an Imperial Envoy. Karl von Eisendecher in Meiji Japan* (in German and Japanese, 2007) and of *Under Eagle Eyes: Lithographs, Drawings and Photographs from the Prussian Expedition to Japan, 1860–61* (in German, Japanese and English, 2011). His research also has been translated into Korean, Chinese and French.

Paul J. Scalise is a Japan Society for the Promotion of Science (JSPS) Foreign Research Fellow at the Institute of Social Science, University of Tokyo, and Non-Resident Fellow at the Institute of Contemporary Asian Studies, Temple University, Japan Campus. He received his DPhil in comparative political economy from the University of Oxford. He publishes extensively on public policy, agenda-setting and decision-making processes in Japanese and comparative energy politics. His research has been funded by grants from the Toshiba International Foundation, the Japan

Foundation Endowment Committee, the Social Science Research Council, and elsewhere.

Mark Selden is a Coordinator of *The Asia-Pacific Journal: Japan Focus* (japanfocus.org) and a Senior Research Associate in the East Asia Program at Cornell University. He is a specialist on the modern and contemporary geopolitics, political economy and history of China, Japan and the Asia-Pacific. His books include *China in Revolution: The Yenan Way Revisited*; *Chinese Village, Socialist State*; *Censoring History: Citizenship and Memory in Japan, Germany and the United States*; and *Chinese Society: Change, Conflict and Resistance.*

Arthur Stockwin was born in Great Britain, has a first degree in Philosophy, Politics and Economics from the University of Oxford and a doctorate in International Relations from the Australian National University, Canberra. Between 1964 and 1981 he taught in the Department of Political Science of the Australian National University. Between 1982 and his retirement in 2003, he was Nissan Professor of Modern Japanese Studies and Director of the Nissan Institute of Japanese Studies at the University of Oxford. In 1994–95 he was President of the British Association of Japanese Studies. He is now an Emeritus Fellow of St Antony's College, University of Oxford. His publications include: *The Japanese Socialist Party and Neutralism* (1968), *Japan and Australia in the Seventies* (editor, 1973), *Dynamic and Immobilist Politics in Japan* (editor and part author, 1988), *Dictionary of the Modern Politics of Japan* (2003), *Collected Writings of J.A.A. Stockwin: The Politics and Political Environment of Japan* (2004), *Governing Japan: Divided Politics in a Resurgent Economy* (4th revised edition, 2008) and *Japanese Foreign Policy and Understanding Japanese Politics: The Writings of J.A.A. Stockwin* (2012).

Ayumi Takenaka is an Associate Professor of Sociology at Bryn Mawr College. She currently works on immigrants' social mobility in comparative perspective and the relationship between geographical mobility and social inequality in Japan. Her recent publications include: "How Contexts of Reception Matter: Comparing Peruvian Migrants' Economic Trajectories in Japan and the U.S.," *International Migration*, 2012 (with K. Paerregaard); "Negative Assimilation: How Immigrants Achieve Economic Mobility in Japan," Discussion Paper No. 293, Economic and Social Research Institute, Cabinet Office of the Government of Japan, 2013 (with N. Nakamuro and K. Ishida).

Matthew J. Wilson is currently the Associate Dean for Academic Affairs and Professor of Law at the University of Wyoming College of Law. Before joining the University of Wyoming, Wilson spent over six years serving as Senior Associate Dean and General Counsel of Temple University's 3,000-student campus in Tokyo, Japan. He is a recognized expert in Japanese law, comparative law, international business and international dispute resolution, and has published extensively in these areas. Wilson also has significant legal practice experience. As legal counsel to US and Japanese entities, Professor Wilson's legal activities have encompassed complex international litigation, intellectual property litigation and transactions, cyberspace law, employment law, as well as general corporate matters. He also has extensive business experience working in Japan and the Pacific. Professor Wilson speaks frequently in the United States and Asia on transnational and domestic US legal matters. He is fluent in Japanese.

Introduction

Jeff Kingston

Why should we study Japan? The world's third-largest economy plays a key role in the rising Asia story as a crucial trading partner and investor, competing for resources, markets and geopolitical influence. Japan remains, however, poorly understood, with limited recognition of its fundamental strengths and enormous contributions to regional stability and global development. Despite two decades of sluggish growth, the "declining Japan" story has been overstated, a narrative that overlooks its still enormous economic heft. It is the world's top creditor nation; many of its companies are world leaders in their sectors; it is at the cutting edge of technological innovation, especially in the renewable energy and environmental industries; its soft power and fashion trends appeal to youth the world over; and there is considerable capacity for reform despite institutional inertia and conservative inclinations. It is, however, a nation going through a 21st-century identity crisis. The halcyon days of the economic miracle in the 1950s–1960s and triumphalist dreams of a Pax Nipponica prevalent in the late 1980s have faded into history as clouds gather on the horizon.

Knowing more about Japan is important because what happens here matters a great deal, especially to Asia, the world's most dynamic and populous region. Japan is the fulcrum of the burgeoning Asian economy and regional supply chain, a fact underscored in the aftermath of the 3/11 disaster as assembly factories in China and South Korea shut down because the flow of high-tech specialty widgets produced in Japan's tsunami-devastated northeast was suddenly interrupted—and with typical efficiency restored far sooner than anyone expected.

In the early 2013 cycle of media coverage, the "Japan in demise" narrative has given way to more euphoric coverage; *The Economist* cover, for example, depicted Shinzo Abe as Superman (*The Economist*, May 18, 2013). "Abenomics" vaulted into the global lexicon in 2013, symbolizing a new policy dynamism aimed at reviving the economy. The Bank of Japan's bold monetary easing took global markets and media by storm, transforming the national reputation for cautious consensus. However, as we discuss in the chapters to follow, the narrative is far more complex and interesting than the current fascination with a booming stock market suggests.

In fact, recent jubilation has only partially dispelled the malaise that haunts contemporary Japan. There is no shortage of doom and gloom stories in a country where the young are said to have no dreams, women are marginalized, jobs and families are less stable, and traditions seem in retreat. The negative fiscal and economic consequences of a rapidly aging society also weigh heavily on perceptions about Japan's future. Eclipsed by China in the early 21st century, worried that Japan-bashing (trade friction in the 1980s) has given way to Japan-passing (US prioritization of China), some Japanese also feel anxious about the shifting geopolitics of Asia and underappreciated by Washington. Can Japan regain its mojo?

Crises beget action, albeit not always apt. The lost decades of economic stagnation and apparent policy drift in the 1990s and 2000s, the rise of China and the shocking disasters of March 11, 2011—tsunami and nuclear—have become catalysts for renovation. In a remarkable and rare political comeback, Prime Minister Shinzo Abe (2006–07, 2012–) strode back onto the national stage for the second time at the end of 2012, riding a wave of voter disillusionment over the Democratic Party of Japan's (DPJ) mostly broken promises and inept governance. The DPJ had gained control of both houses of the Diet (national parliament) in 2009, interrupting the Liberal Democratic Party's (LDP) near monopoly on political power since 1955. The DPJ promised to focus on improving people's lives and rectify a gamut of social problems, but disappointed supporters because it never got traction on its reform agenda. In addition, tensions with China escalated sharply in 2012 due to the government's decision to nationalize disputed islands in the East China Sea, making national security a major campaign issue that played to the LDP's advantage.

As a result, the business-friendly, conservative LDP regained power and implemented Abenomics, including huge increases in the money supply and debt-financed public works spending. The LDP has long favored such spending, which helps explain why Japan's public debt-to-gross domestic product (GDP) ratio reached an incredible 240% as of 2013. The twin monetary and fiscal stimuli are designed to provide an opening for "structural reforms"—an expansive concept that ranges from promoting trade liberalization, ending utility monopolies and sweeping deregulation, to improving women's status, education and boosting immigration, among other proposals.

Making headway on this agenda will be difficult and contentious, but this is the litmus test of whether Abenomics is a chimera of reform or can really deliver sustainable growth. Is it a quick fix delivering fleeting and limited gains only benefitting financiers and construction firms, or can it deliver on its inflation and investment targets and promised restructuring while improving productivity and competitiveness, boosting wages, narrowing income disparities and expanding good jobs? With nearly one quarter of the population aged 65 or over mostly living on fixed incomes and more than one third of the workforce mired in low-paid, non-regular jobs, Abenomics appears to be an inadequate and risky remedy. Unlike in the United States where individual retirement accounts are closely tied to stock market performance, relatively few Japanese households own stocks and thus do not directly benefit from a rising Nikkei index. The impact on bond markets may be destabilizing and higher interest rates will raise public debt-servicing costs while burdening homeowners with higher mortgage payments. Due to the yen's sharp depreciation, consumers are paying higher prices for fuel and food while producers are squeezed by higher costs for imported inputs. The stakes are very high and whether the gamble pays off will have a considerable impact on Japan's economic prospects. Yet, there is much more to be understood about the return of the LDP than the current business news, because Japan's future very much depends on its past and overcoming obstacles to regional reconciliation.

Japan remains a nation where prominent political leaders, especially in the LDP, are still struggling to come to terms with wartime history and as a result regional ties remain fraught because the past keeps haunting the present. Overall, nationalist sentiments among Japanese seem relatively muted compared to East Asian neighbors.

However, uncertainties about Japan's future and the prospects of Chinese hegemony have aroused patriotic passions among some while expanding support for Abe's agenda of remaking Japan by revising its pacifist Constitution. Abe's supporters call this a sensible policy of nurturing civic nationalism, stressing that Japan lives in a dangerous neighborhood and should unshackle its armed forces. Critics oppose sacrificing this iconic symbol of post-World War II Japan's redemption and worry that constitutional revision will roil the region and erode civil liberties.

Battles over the Constitution are also battles over the past. The contenders are a vocal and now ascendant minority who deny or minimize Japan's wartime atrocities, justify its actions and feel it has been unfairly singled out for criticism, versus the majority who believe it is important for the nation to assume the burdens of history and express contrition about the unjustifiable devastation caused by Japan's imperialist rampage across Asia (1931–45). Contemporary nationalists are eager to turn the page on this history, but most Japanese still think there are important lessons to be learned from Japan's authoritarian era of militarism, aggression and political repression at home. Some Japanese resent how the neighbors use the past to badger and belittle Japan, and keep it squirming uncomfortably on the hook of history despite numerous apologies and efforts at restitution. However, others understand that Japan has handed the hammer of history to victims of Japanese aggression precisely because of incomplete acknowledgement of responsibility and inadequate expressions of contrition. To some extent Japan has tried to accept responsibility and atone for its misdeeds, but conservatives like PM Abe have actively repudiated such gestures of reconciliation and repeatedly voice views that reignite Japan's history problem. Reinterpreting this tragic history while seeking dignity in denial or blurring war memory and responsibility tramples on the dignity of the nations that suffered most from Japan's depredations and remains a dead end for regional relations in East Asia. Where are the extraordinary acts and sites of memory that have redeemed Germany in the eyes of former adversaries and facilitated its reintegration in Europe? Japan's unequivocal acceptance by East Asian neighbors is unattainable, but this is no excuse for avoiding a forthright reckoning and grand gestures of atonement. There are possibilities and benefits of pursuing reconciliation that will remain unrealized in the absence of a more remarkable remembering and sincere remorse.

Many Japanese people are often quite introspective and critical of national shortcomings. While many also take pride in their society, they tend to be reticent about tooting their own horn; the value of modesty and understatement is deeply ingrained and endearingly so. However, perhaps this is also one reason Japan remains an enigmatic society: there are few Japanese businessmen, politicians or public intellectuals who command attention on the international stage and can influence knowledge and opinions about Japan.

Moreover, few non-specialists have the time to peel back the layers behind the headlines or probe beneath prevailing stereotypes to understand what may seem puzzling or inscrutable. Hence the purpose of this book, geared towards a broad audience of readers with an interest in knowing more about a nation of consequence, a country both fundamentally similar to and yet profoundly different from other advanced industrialized nations, facing a litany of challenges familiar to us all. In this collection, we assume no prior knowledge about Japan. Our aim is to challenge assumptions and facile impressions while imparting the perceptions of experts about their subjects in a succinct and accessible style. We do not presume to present a "Japanese" view of their world, but rather offer a diverse range of critical analyses about key issues that take on prevailing monolithic representations that are at odds with Japan's evident diversity.

Everywhere one goes "the Japanese" is a frequent refrain, as if 127 million people all march to the same beat and sing from the same hymnal. Japanese themselves frequently reinforce this homogenized image by relying on monolithic terms. We understand that stereotyping and generalizations can be a convenient shorthand, but one that can be misleading and reinforce dubious assumptions. Our aim is not to dismiss the cohesiveness of Japanese society, or to overstate how diverse it is or overlook pressures to conform, but rather to suggest that readers bear in mind that *Japan* as a unifying and unvarying idea is not consistently evident in reality.

While China grabs the most attention, Japan is a leading economic and military power in Asia and boasts the region's highest standard of living despite recent travails. Japan can take pride in a robust democracy and relatively egalitarian society. Japan has not overcome its environmental challenges, but they are relatively mild compared to the rest of Asia's problems of pollution and urban congestion. In Japan, violent crimes are rare and random attacks targeting religious, ethnic or sexual minorities are virtually unheard of. While the rapid aging of the population certainly poses various policy challenges, it is a useful reminder that Japanese enjoy the greatest longevity in Asia, owing much to good medical care and universal health insurance. Japan's varied and innovative policy responses to these problems represent an important model and inspiration for other nations that are or will be facing similar problems. Moreover, with the exception of South Korea, no other Asian nation comes close to Japan in terms of soft power, from its huge anime industry to its Michelin-renowned restaurants. However, it is also an archipelago vulnerable to natural disaster, regularly experiencing powerful earthquakes, typhoons and, on occasion, massive tsunami.

In March 2011, as the world looked on in horror at the tsunami devastation wrought on communities along the nation's northeast coast, it saw what social cohesion looks like. Japanese survivors demonstrated a dignity and gutsiness under duress that commanded our admiration. People who lost everything valuable in their lives somehow managed to persevere and set about restoring a semblance of normalcy to a world ripped asunder. However, the slow recovery in the region means that the natural disaster has become a symbol of government dysfunction and the failure of political leaders to put aside party squabbles and prioritize the public interest. The ongoing problems besetting the decontamination and decommissioning of Fukushima's ruined reactors help explain lingering grassroots anxieties about the safety of nuclear power even as the government is pushing for rapid resumption of nuclear power generation and selling reactors abroad. Although there has been considerable speculation that 3/11 might be a watershed in modern Japanese history, these hopes mainly have been unrealized as attention faded, what initially seemed urgent was overtaken by other priorities and policies settled back into familiar ruts.

In September 2013 Tokyo was awarded the 2020 Summer Olympics for the third time, owing much to PM Abe's reassurances that the problem of radiation leaks into the ocean and management of toxic water at Fukushima was under control. In 1940 the games were cancelled due to Japan's escalating aggression in China. In 1964, hosting the Olympics signaled Japan's reacceptance into the international community, showcasing Japan's recovery from war devastation and sparking robust economic growth and innovation. On the eve of the games Japan's high-speed rail service, the shinkansen (bullet train), commenced operations, associating Japan with cutting edge technologies and reliability; the safety record is unblemished. The slogan of the 2020 games is Discover Tomorrow, expressing hope that the nation will be fully recovered from the 3/11 disasters and signaling that visitors will encounter not only Japan's rich culture and warm hospitality, but also its continued economic and technological vibrancy. The message is unabashed boosterism- Japan is Back-countering gloomy assessments about the nation's prospects.

Whither Japan? This is a recurring question/theme that defies simple answers or firm predictions, but it is a particularly pressing issue in 21st-century Japan and constitutes a common thread in our chapters. We examine how citizens, parties, civic organizations, social movements, business and bureaucratic institutions are contesting and promoting competing agendas that are shaping emerging realities and future outcomes. This is why our endeavor is a valuable resource for comprehending a Japan in flux, where ongoing significant and sometimes sweeping transformations face significant obstacles that may divert, dilute or otherwise stymie anticipated consequences. These trajectories of change are not onward and upward, and in Japan are often gradual, incremental and zigzagging.

Naturally we think that Japan matters for many reasons and we believe that scholarly assessments of this complex society deserve more prominence in public discourse. Media coverage is very useful to get a quick understanding of the new issue of the moment, but often lacks the contextual perspective that helps promote deeper appreciation of what is going on and what it portends. Journalists based in Japan are often exceptionally knowledgeable, but editors back home need stories to which domestic audiences can relate and prefer attention-grabbing headlines. Hence the tendency to hype the weird or whacky and analyze Japan in terms of cultural stereotypes. Observed Japan often relies on tropes about how the traditional shapes the contemporary world. Culture and tradition do matter, but the nuances are not easily conveyed in the television sound bite or 600-word story produced on a tight deadline. There are also far fewer international journalists based in Japan compared to a decade ago, meaning that in-depth knowledge is often lacking and discussions of Japan are more prone to caricature.

The idea motivating this project was to assemble a group of scholars, both eminent and rising, and ask them to write about their subject as succinctly and engagingly as possible, with a minimum of the usual academic paraphernalia, targeting an audience of non-specialists and students. We are not trying to provide simple answers to the complexities of contemporary Japan, but to avoid the pitfalls of excessive problematizing and jargon in academic work that inhibits clear writing and often leaves many readers in the dark and in despair. The 22 chapters here deliver an encompassing and scrutinizing analysis of contemporary Japan that we believe is imperative to understanding what is going on here in the early 21st century and where it is going. The authors present fresh thinking about how to interpret Japan's post-World War II trajectories and simultaneous transformations while reminding us about elements of continuity and persistence. We are a diverse group of scholars from eight countries, representing an array of social science disciplines: political science (seven), history (four), anthropology (three), sociology (three), law (two), public policy (one) and business (one). As such, our book delivers an interdisciplinary and critical interpretation based on extensive and ongoing research, working and living experiences in Japan.

The book is organized into five sections by thematic content: political environment; nuclear and renewable energy; international dynamics; social dilemmas; and reforming Japan. These subject areas help clarify what is indispensable to understanding the urgent issues with which Japanese people and their government are grappling and what they bode for the future.

The first section, on political environment, includes five chapters that examine politics from different angles: the party system, trade, the judiciary, civil society and the media. This is a story mostly of party dysfunction and fragmentation, policy immobilism, ossified institutions, cooptation and missed opportunities interrupted by spurts of concerted action and sweeping reform.

The second section, on nuclear and renewable energy, revisits and updates the controversies, policy considerations and divisive perspectives about which the same four authors wrote in *Natural Disaster and Nuclear Crisis in Japan* (Routledge, 2012); we still have our disagreements.

The third section, on international dynamics, focuses on Japan's international relations and how they remain hostage to history. The chapters feature Japan's troubled relations with China, Korea and Russia, assessment of the historical context that underlies these contemporary disputes, and the problems involving the US military presence on Okinawa.

The fourth section, on social dilemmas, includes six chapters that evaluate salient issues confronting Japanese society. It is difficult to comprehensively examine such a sprawling and fascinating subject, but these probing essays cover a lot of ground and engage many of the ongoing debates in Japan. We elucidate topics ranging from an aging and shrinking population, immigration, minorities and the status of women, to mental health care, school violence and rural depopulation.

Finally, the last section presents three chapters about reform discourse within Japan and about Japan. Although popular perceptions focus on gridlock and missed opportunities, Japan's legal system has embarked on an ambitious agenda of reforms aimed at transforming it from a nation featuring the *rule by law* to a nation of the *rule of law*; this is a work in progress. While Japan may not live up to the expectations and aspirations of many observers, we conclude this volume by questioning some of the assumptions that drive the heated discourse about what ails Japan.

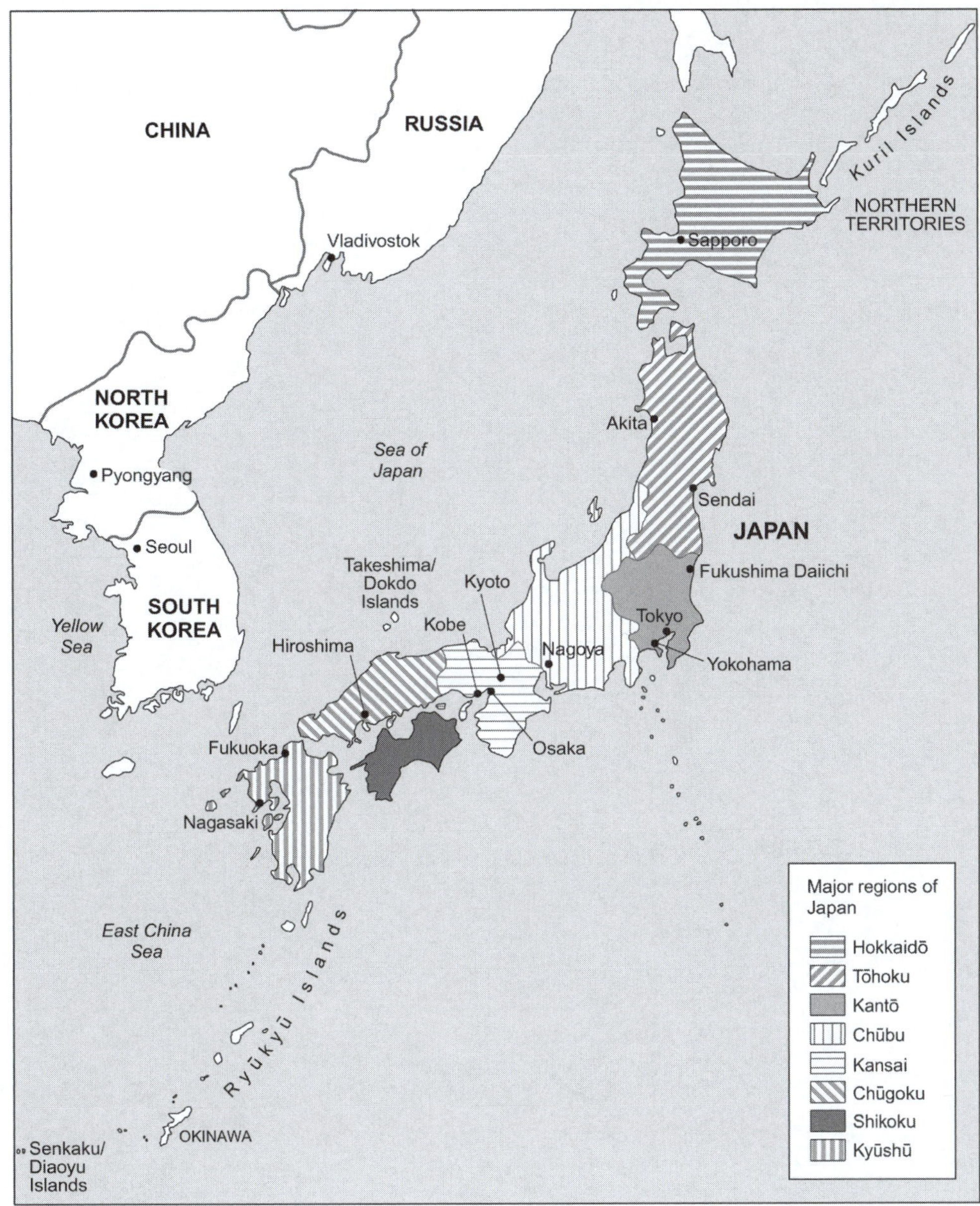

Map 1 Map of Japan

Part I

Political environment

1 Japanese politics

Mainstream or exotic?

Arthur Stockwin

Introduction

The politics of Japan is often regarded, particularly in Western media, as obscure and radically difficult to understand, presenting conceptual difficulties far greater than those of political systems closer to home. A young BBC journalist once told me that whenever some aspect of Japanese politics came up, the news room entered a mode of collective panic, and journalists would search frantically for a conceptual peg on which to hang a coherent argument about the limited facts at their disposal. In my experience these pegs would often turn out to be clichés of dubious value, such as that "Japan is a consensus society," or that "politics in Japan is governed by questions of face."

In contrast, many political scientists, taking their cue from economics, tend to shun explanations dependent on essentialist reasoning, or what are assumed to be "cultural" characteristics of a given population. It is intriguing to compare two works in English on the Japanese political system, published 18 years apart: J. Mark Ramseyer and Frances McCall Rosenbluth, *Japan's Political Marketplace* (Ramseyer and Rosenbluth 1993), and Ellis S. Krauss and Robert J. Pekkanen, *The Rise and Fall of Japan's LDP* (Krauss and Pekkanen 2011). The two books develop contrasting—even diametrically opposed—arguments concerning the dynamics of Japanese party politics.

Ramseyer and Rosenbluth rest their analysis on a "principal-agent" variant of rational choice theory, and maintain that reforming the Lower House electoral system from a single non-transferable vote in multi-member districts to a mixed system based predominantly on single-member districts, would inevitably lead to a drastic upheaval in the way parties behaved, so that factions (*habatsu*), personal support machines (*kōenkai*), the powerful Liberal Democratic Party (LDP) Policy Affairs Research Council (*seimu chōsakai*), and other elements, would rapidly decline once the particular set of incentives embodied in the old electoral system were removed.

Krauss and Pekkanen, by contrast, able to reflect on several years of experience under the new electoral system, and using historical institutionalism, argue on the basis of detailed research that the effects of the electoral reform in 1994 were far less drastic, and far slower to appear, than had been predicted by Ramseyer and Rosenbluth, even though at the same time they were curiously deferential to the writers of the earlier book (Stockwin 2012).

A comparison of the two books, therefore, reveals a major theoretical and empirical gulf between them, so that we find here a major controversy in the English-language literature on Japanese politics. Yet on one issue it is impossible to insert a sheet of tracing paper between their respective arguments.

In the words of Ramseyer and Rosenbluth:

> [n]ot so long ago, scholars began their accounts of Japanese politics by invoking the peculiarities of Japanese culture … Scholars lavished praise on the [cultural] theories and elaborated them in essays about Japan's need for consensus, about its rejection of individualism and open conflict, about its Confucian fascination with loyalty, and about its patriarchal legacy. To their credit, many Japan specialists eventually recognised the circularity of much of this work.
>
> (Ramseyer and Rosenbluth 1993, 2)

Krauss and Pekkanen would presumably agree with this opinion. Writing of *habatsu*, they express their skepticism about "culture" as an explanatory variable in the following terms: "[c]ultural determinist explanations for the factions have often been made, but they are not sustainable in the face of the transformation of the factions over the first postwar decades … [T]he culturalist claims [are] trying to explain change with a constant" (Krauss and Pekkanen 2011, 266).

Culture, however, is a highly contested area because the term attracts contrasting definitions. On the one hand, many political scientists assume that "cultural" means essentialist, unquantifiable and very slow to change. Given this definition, they reasonably reject most "cultural" explanations as spurious at worst and only marginally useful at best. Social anthropologists, however, favor a quite different type of definition, based on the view that culture is changeable and contingent. The following definition is by Brian McVeigh: "[Culture is] 'something learned', or more specifically, the arts, beliefs, customs, socio-political institutions, and all other products of human creation and thought developed by a group of people at a particular time that is learned" (McVeigh 1998, 16).

If we adopt a concept of culture along these lines, then we may be able to reintroduce the factor of culture into political analysis. We shall return to this in the final section of this chapter, but meanwhile, we need to examine why "culturalist" explanations of Japanese society and politics have acquired such a bad name.

The *Nihonjinron* controversies

Reluctance to take "culture" seriously owes much to the frontal attack launched in the early 1980s by scholars based in Australia and elsewhere on the literary and (pseudo-?) scholarly genre popular at that time in Japan known as *Nihonjinron*, which is roughly translated as "what it means to be Japanese." Prominent among these writers were Sugimoto Yoshio and Ross Mouer, both Australian-based sociologists whose approach was firmly rooted in American social science of that period. Their best-known work, published in 1986, was *Images of Japanese Society* (Mouer and Sugimoto 1986).

Another anti-culturalist writer of the same period, once again Australian but long resident in Italy, was Peter Dale, whose 1986 book *The Myth of Japanese Uniqueness* achieved a *succès de scandale* (Dale 1986). He shared similar perceptions of Japanese society to those of Sugimoto and Mouer, but applying a quite different methodology, Dale being a multilingual literary scholar steeped in European and East Asian cultures, classical and modern. He defined the *Nihonjinron* in a broad sense as:

> … works of cultural nationalism concerned with the ostensible "uniqueness" of Japan in any aspect, and which are hostile to both individual experience and the

> notion of internal socio-historical diversity … What we are dealing with is not a national "mentality", … but rather a fictional mentality constructed by innumerable thinkers and writers over a considerable length of time, through whose lens, due to the impact of constant discussion and exposure, the people often tend to interpret their world.
>
> (Dale 1986, v–vi)

Mouer and Sugimoto worked with various Japanese scholars, in particular the sociologist Befu Harumi, whose "Critique of the Group Model of Japanese Society" became a classic of the genre (Befu 1980). There is an interesting passage in his article, where Befu argues that the cultural uniqueness assumption of many *Nihonjinron* writers was a denial of the relevance of social class analysis to Japanese society:

> Since the group model of Japanese society is predicated on the absence of conflict and on the presence of harmony, a model of society that assumes inherent conflict is not acceptable. The denial of the existence of social classes in Japan is suspect regardless of whether one adopts an objective or a subjective definition of social class.
>
> (Befu 1980, 34)

It is clear from this passage (and from many other possible citations) that the culturalist versus anti-culturalist controversies in the 1980s had strong political overtones. Those who wrote, often expansively and with enthusiasm, about the inherently harmonious and non-conflictual character of Japanese society, were easily portrayed as conservative or reactionary by those whose political instincts were further to the left. Few of the anti-culturalist writers were specifically Marxist (though we should remember that Marxist concepts were still often to be found in intellectual writings of the period), but they rightly perceived that conflict was a powerful driver within the political process and that change without conflict was likely to be still born, in Japan as elsewhere.

Prominent among the targets of anti-culturalist attack was Nakane Chie, a social anthropologist at Tokyo University. Her book *Japanese Society* was widely read during the 1970s and was distributed by Japanese embassies in various countries (I believe in a cut-down version) as a key to understanding how Japanese society worked (Nakane 1970). Her analysis presented a rigid and unvarying hierarchical model of vertical loyalties. Another target was the social psychologist Doi Takeo, who popularized the notion of *amae*—roughly meaning a pervasive psychological desire to presume upon another's benevolence—as key to comprehending social interaction in Japan (Doi 1971). There was good reason for believing that these writers' theories were conservative in implication.

Remembering these often passionate controversies after 30 years, within what is now a far more turbulent and somber politico-economic environment, it seems extraordinary that so many writers should have been seriously arguing in the 1970s and 1980s that the Japanese were a unique people whose society worked according to principles of harmony, hierarchy, consensus and sacrifice of the individual for the good of the whole (whereas most other countries, particularly those in the "West," exhibited characteristics contrary to those principles).

Insights from history

It remains theoretically possible that Japanese society and politics have changed so much over three decades that what was reasonable then is absurd today, and there may be some truth in this. Nevertheless, the critics could marshal powerful arguments to show that political manipulation by dominant national power structures were at work in the formulation of such culturalist literature, and indeed that this may have stemmed from the political dominance of a particular set of forces between the 1950s and the 1980s. By contrast, a recent 80-year history of pre-war Japanese political history from 1857 to 1937 by a leading historian of modern Japan, Banno Junji, shows that for many years before the war the politics of Japan was extremely fragmented rather than extremely cohesive. In a passage towards the end of the book, he writes:

> … [T]he greatest reason why Japan entered the Age of Breakdown (*hōkai no jidai*, 1937–45), was that the domestic rulers were split in multiple directions, and were unable to control foreign relations. This situation of multiple divisions had deepened over the five years from 1932, and it developed into one of divisions without winners … Leaders who might have restructured the political system so as to stop the Japan-China war in its tracks, and then avoid war between Japan, Britain and America, essentially did not exist.
>
> (Banno 2012a, 442)

Cyclical politics in Japan?

If the politics of Japan can manifest extreme fragmentation at certain periods and extreme solidarity at other periods, this suggests at the very least that narrow interpretations of Japan as a "consensus society" prevalent in the 1970s only painted half of the picture—or perhaps missed the point altogether. Scrutiny of both pre-war and post-war political trends suggests that there have been periods of common purpose and energy, when the population was effectively energized through the actions of a relatively united political, bureaucratic and commercial elite, towards widely accepted goals of national development, but there have also been periods where the system has performed badly and narrow interests have torpedoed any serious attempts to pull Japan out of a mire of political fragmentation, lack of effective leadership and consequent stagnation. The three decades or so following the Meiji Restoration of 1868 and a similar period following the 1945 defeat are examples of the former, while we can find examples of the latter in the 1930s and over the two decades 1993–2013. Another way of looking at this is to say that both types of period have seen attempts at radical systemic reform, but while some have succeeded, others have failed.

Banno adopts what might be interpreted as a cyclical approach to modern Japanese political history, dividing his book into six "ages," namely the Age of Reform (1857–63), Age of Revolution (1863–71), Age of Construction (1871–80), Age of Enforcement (1880–93), Age of Reorganization (1894–1924), and Age of Crisis (1925–37). He deliberately refrains from covering what he calls the Age of Breakdown, lasting from 1937 to 1945, for the following reason:

> As for the eight years that were to follow [1937], those prepared to express dissent in the political parties, bureaucracy, financial world, the world of labor, among

> critics and academics, were nowhere to be found, and above all, it was the "Age of Breakdown." I lack the ability to describe this "Age of Breakdown" in which those expressing dissent had been extinguished.
>
> (Banno 2012a, 442)

What Banno was expressing here was not despair at the pluralistic elements he had identified in the "Age of Crisis," but rather at the *consequences* of fragmentation and sectionalism leading inexorably to a semi-totalitarian state, imposed in an Orwellian pursuit of mindless war. In a series of newspaper articles after the book was published in 2012, he ventured also into post-war history and hinted at a cyclical view of Japanese modern history. Developing a series of parallels between the various "ages" traversed by Japan from the Bakumatsu period to the 1930s and political history from 1945 into the 21st century, he argued (writing in 2012, after the Tōhoku disasters and with the Democratic Party of Japan, DPJ, still in power) that Japan had in certain senses entered an "Age of Breakdown":

> Concerning politics, leaders who were supposed to lead Japan to recovery following the Great Eastern Japan Earthquake Disaster, were divided all ways and rendered inadequate, just like their predecessors in early Shōwa who embarked on the Japan–China war, so that both politics and society were in meltdown. This is the "Age of Breakdown."
>
> (Banno 2012c, 2)

Some observers would not agree that the reaction of the Kan government to the natural and man-made disasters of March 11, 2013 was as hopeless as this. For instance, according to Curtis, "[b]y any comparative measure, the Kan government's response to the triple catastrophe of earthquake, tsunami and nuclear breakdown was not as awful as his critics made it out to be ... It was far better than the way the Bush Administration dealt with the aftermath of Hurricane Katrina and compares favourably to how other governments have responded to disaster situations" (Curtis 2012, 25). Nevertheless, Banno is surely right about the dysfunctional nature of the party political system as a whole in the second decade of the 21st century.

Single-party dominance or alternation in power?

One central aspect of the debate about this dysfunctionality is the appropriateness of a two-party alternating government in Japanese social and political conditions. When asked by an interviewer on the *Asahi Shimbun* whether Japan should keep such a system, Banno replied firmly in the negative: "I think that a system of two major parties does not fit Japan. The period before the war during which the *Seiyūkai* and the *Minseitō* alternated in power was not very successful" (Banno 2012b).

Now the present writer argued on several occasions both before and after the change of government in September 2009 that single-party government was stultifying and eventually incapable of new thinking, whereas it was desirable to have a system in which alternation in power was a realistic possibility, in Japan as elsewhere. For instance:

> Most crucially, perhaps, a single party that may be seen as a congeries of special interests remains in power as though by right. Until alternation in office becomes a

> real, not a theoretical, possibility, the reforms emerging in the new millennium will not be complete.
>
> (Stockwin 2008, 155)

This difference of opinion, however, is much less important than it appears at first. Let us continue the passage from Banno's interview in the *Asahi*, cited above:

> If parties do not have convictions, a two-party system will not work. For instance, party X may advocate social welfare and helping people, whereas party Y proclaims competition and personal responsibility. In this respect Japanese parties are weak. Therefore, when the *Seiyūkai* and the *Minseitō* were trying to create points of difference between them, they moved from one extreme to another, and every time the government changed, policies switched 180 degrees. Between the DPJ and the LDP, on the other hand, differences have disappeared.
>
> (Banno 2012b)

As a condition for creating a system based on parties having conviction, he argues that Japan needed a social democratic party that would work towards a fully functioning welfare state, and maintained that one great weakness of the former Japan Socialist Party under Doi Takako in the late 1980s and early 1990s, was that in opposing tax rises (specifically consumption tax), she implicitly deprived future governments of the necessary revenue to create a welfare state worthy of the name.

We may add that among the reasons for the failure of the DPJ government (2009–12) were the party's recent origin (it was founded in 1996, then re-constituted in 1998), and its lack of clear identity, being composed of a number of politically disparate groups. This second point is consistent with Banno's argument that Japanese parties tend towards fragmentation. However, it is highly arguable that the key DPJ problem was its failure to appeal to the electorate on the basis of a clear progressive commitment to the creation of a welfare state, *and then follow through with real policy initiatives to that end*. By 2012, under the third DPJ prime minister, Noda Yoshihiko, it had become difficult to discover any real policy differences between the DPJ and the LDP, though that did not inhibit the most uncompromising political rivalry between them. In the Lower House general elections of December 16, 2012, even though many voters deserted the incumbent DPJ for the opposition LDP, the percentage of the total votes cast in the proportional representation blocs (the best measure of party preference) for those two parties combined was only 43.28% (LDP 27.79%, DPJ 15.49%), while the rest of the votes went to a variety of other parties.

Two questions remain: if it is correct to say that a two-party alternating system—given the character of Japanese parties—is inappropriate for Japanese conditions, are those conditions endemic and culturally determined, or contingent and subject to change over relatively long periods of time? The second question is whether if two-party alternation is eliminated, then a return to single-party dominance is likely to create more acceptable results. The evidence on the first question seems to point to a factor of surprisingly long-term continuity. Moreover, this cannot be explained by the electoral system, since quite different electoral systems were in place during the two periods. On the second question, the answer would appear to be ambiguous, given that such a system accompanied long periods of both rapid economic growth and economic stagnation between 1955 and 2009.

Putting these two concerns together, it seems reasonable to argue that there are endemic and deep-seated problems in the ways in which party politics operates in Japanese conditions. If two-party alternation does not work properly, and single-party dominance works well in some periods but badly in others, then what are the underlying causes of such poor performance?

Endemic problems of political parties

Even though conditions in Japanese economy and society have changed enormously over the past three decades, political parties have failed to accomplish the kind of structural reform that would enable them to react effectively to contemporary circumstances. The analysis of a leading political commentator, Sasaki Takeshi, is significant in this regard. Responding to a question from an *Asahi* journalist about political confusion and "politics in which nothing can be decided" (*kimerarenai seiji*), Sasaki spoke as follows:

> The common feature [in periods of political confusion] is that political parties do not function in terms of their organisation. They have tried, through political reform, to change from politics centered on individual politicians to politics based on the party. But they have not been able to reform. Politicians have not worked out how to manage political parties. In a word, they have given up [*ichigon de ieba, kore ni tsukiru*].
>
> (Sasaki 2012)

If this is correct, however, how can we explain the long and broadly effective management of the economy under LDP governments up to the late 1980s when poor economic control contributed to the formation of an unsustainable boom? Sasaki provides the following answer:

> The LDP previously maintained internal order within the party by factions and money. Another aspect is that they made adjustments working to a long time-scale. In other words, with the regime lasting over the long term, balance could be maintained on the principle that "I will repay this debt after several years." But when a change of government occurred, the time axis became unusable, and it became unusable as money and factions were rendered inoperative.
>
> (Sasaki 2012)

It did not, however, follow from this, according to Sasaki, that all would be well if the LDP simply returned to its old methods. The party, in opposition, had had plenty of time to reform itself, but had succumbed to the temptation merely to take advantage of mistakes by the DPJ government, and such reforms as the LDP had put in place were half measures (Sasaki 2012).

Leadership

If political parties have performed below expectations in Japanese conditions, what about the factor of leadership? Some observers have regarded leadership as the missing factor in Japanese politics, or at the very least argue that Japan suffers from a leadership deficit. Famous indeed is Karel van Wolferen's dictum that "there is no place where, as Harry Truman would have said, the buck stops. In Japan, the buck keeps circulating" (van Wolferen 1989, 5).

The question is, however, why should this be so, if it is indeed the case? First of all, as frequently pointed out (not least by the present writer), prime ministers succeed each other more frequently in Japan than in many other comparable political systems. In the 67.5 years between August 1945 and March 2013, 33 men became prime minister, two of them (Yoshida Shigeru in the early post-war period and Abe Shinzō very recently) holding the position twice with an interval between their two terms in office. This is comparable with Italy, but nearly three times more than the United Kingdom (12 men and one woman over the same period), or Australia (11 men and one woman). While the LDP was in power institutional factors were important, since the position of party president was contested every two years and the incumbent could not be guaranteed renewal, even though he was automatically prime minister if the party was in office. Indeed, the faction system guaranteed that the incumbent would be challenged every time a party presidential election was held. There were a few significant exceptions to the two-year tenure rule, including Yoshida Shigeru (1946–47 and 1948–54, most of whose tenure was under exceptional Occupation conditions), Satō Eisaku (1964–72, three of whose factional rivals died within a year of his taking office), Nakasone Yasuhiro (1982–87) and Koizumi Junichirō (2001–06). The link between length of tenure and performance is shown by the fact that all four were unusually activist and agenda-driven leaders (admittedly, a few with shorter tenure were active too).

Even so, when we compare this with prime ministerial tenure before the war, when the system was very different, and the prime minister did not have to be a member of the Diet (national parliament), we find that changes of prime minister were even more frequent than after 1945. Between Takahashi Korekiyo in 1921 and Konoe Fumimaro in 1937 there were no fewer than 15 prime ministers, none of whom lasted more than two years, and some much less than a year.

This suggests that something more than institutional factors was involved. Indeed, it is becoming difficult to avoid the conclusion that the heyday of LDP dominance in post-war Japan—roughly the late 1950s to the late 1980s—was an exceptionally stable period in which mechanisms were in place to lock most of the powerful organized interests into the system. It can hardly be a coincidence that it was also a period in which the economy was growing rapidly and producing revenue surpluses for distribution (for some years also the LDP received funds from American government sources). If we take prime ministerial tenure as our criterion, in the 30 years between the accession of Kishi Nobusuke in 1957 and the resignation of Nakasone Yasuhiro in 1987, the average length of tenure of a prime minister was 41 months, or three years and five months. Admittedly this figure was boosted by the exceptionally long period in office of Satō Eisaku, but in that 30-year period only one prime minister (Ōhira Masayoshi) fell below two years (19 months), and his tenure was ended in 1980 by the passage of a no-confidence motion against his government followed by his death during the subsequent electoral campaign.

By contrast, the six men who were prime minister between the resignation of Koizumi Junichirō in September 2006 and the defeat of Noda Yoshihiko in December 2013 had an average tenure of 12.33 months, or just over a year.

Though we are well aware of the enormous number of variables that should ideally be taken into account here, there seems to be *prima facie* evidence that over the

90 years between the early 1920s and the early 2010s, with the exception of the period between the 1950s and the 1980s, the norm has been for short-term governments, many of them desperately trying to survive in a no-holds-barred situation of perpetual conflict of interest between different factions and pressure groups, and lacking the political cement that would create long-term stability. The LDP in its glory period found out how to provide such cement, but this was premised on the dominance of a single party, with the serious erosion of democratic principles to which that inevitably led. When two-party competitive politics began to emerge from the late 1990s, much of the cement was scraped away, and the "natural anarchic state" of Japanese politics once again took over. This proved particularly debilitating for the untried DPJ that took over power in September 2009.

Bureaucracy

One cliché about Japanese politics is that decision making has been controlled by government officials rather than by politicians. According to this, politicians spend their time engaging in factional disputes and cultivating their personal political machines at district level, while bureaucrats actually make the decisions. The classic statement of this position (which I have slightly caricatured here) is that of Chalmers Johnson in his *MITI and the Japanese Miracle* (1982).

Bureaucratic supremacy, however, though reasonably apposite as a description of civil service influence during the heyday of LDP dominance between the 1950s and 1980s, has been seriously eroded since. An important stage in a complex process was reached in 2001 when reforms to the structure of central government were instituted, and much more power was placed in the hands of the prime minister. This was done through the creation of the Cabinet Office (*naikakufu*) and by increasing political control with the introduction of deputy ministers and others to boost the decision-making resources available to the prime minister. Koizumi, who became prime minister a few weeks after the reforms were implemented, made good use of the increased powers available to him to rescue the beleaguered banking system and to implement his pet project of privatizing the postal services (especially the huge postal savings bank). The main purpose of this reform was to promote his neo-liberal agenda of market efficiency and to break the hold of special interests over the national economy. The culmination of his campaign over the postal services occurred when he faced down postal privatization rebels within his own party and spectacularly won the Lower House general elections of September 2005, having expelled the rebels from the LDP and promoted alternative candidates in their place.

Whatever the merits and demerits of Koizumi's initiatives, his successors Abe Shinzō, Fukuda Yasuo and Asō Tarō, following at annual intervals from September 2006, quickly lost the momentum he had established, and rapidly forfeited much of the support that he had built up by his activism. The impression that they gave (especially Abe) was of wanting to return to outdated nationalist themes from the 1950s and 1960s, rather than of solving the pressing economic and social problems that really worried the electorate. Not surprisingly, just four years after Koizumi had led the LDP to electoral victory in September 2005, the party was defeated in the general elections of August 30, 2009, and for the first time in more than half a century an opposition party replaced the LDP in government with a clear majority in the House of Representatives.

The loss of political momentum after Koizumi was reflected in what we may regard as a reprieve for the bureaucracy, as government officials could return to their "comfort zone" of exercising power in conjunction with vested interests, as they had done in the heyday of LDP power up to the 1980s. The DPJ, however, came to office in 2009 with the express intention of imposing political control and establishing a genuine "Westminster model" under which politicians made decisions on policy and government officials gave advice and implemented decisions but did not make policy. An important aspect of this was the practice whereby the non-elected heads of government ministries and agencies would meet weekly prior to cabinet meetings in order to arrive at a common position on issues to be put to Cabinet, so that cabinet meetings had little effective substance. These meetings of top bureaucrats were called "Meetings of Permanent Vice-Ministers," or *jimu jikan kaigi*. Under the new government, such meetings were squeezed out of the system (though they had already become less significant under previous governments).

The problem, however, for the DPJ was that in attacking bureaucratic dominance they risked alienating officials upon whose advice they needed to rely. This problem became particularly acute following the disasters of March 11, 2011. In the end, the government's determination to reconfigure relations between the political and bureaucratic worlds was a casualty of the multifarious problems that it faced, so that by the time of its electoral defeat in December 2012, relations between DPJ politicians and government officials differed little from those obtaining when the LDP had been in power. The DPJ, while in power, was notably less successful than Koizumi had been in establishing policy-making mechanisms that could reduce bureaucratic power, even though the long-term impact of Koizumi's neo-liberal reforms had been a significant factor in alienating the electorate from the LDP and handing victory to the DPJ in August 2009.

"Twisted Diet" (*nejire kokkai*)

One further factor has contributed to political crisis in Japan and to the difficulties facing serious reformers. It relates to the blocking power of the House of Councilors (Upper House).

After the elected House of Councilors replaced the non-elected House of Peers under the 1947 Constitution, it was seen for many years as a pale shadow of its more powerful counterpart, the House of Representatives. Most ministers were appointed from the Lower House, and since the LDP commanded a majority in both houses, it was unlikely that the House of Councilors would attempt to block bills sent to it from the House of Representatives. Unlike the Lower House, members of the Upper House were elected on a fixed term of six years (half renewed every three years), and the government was not able to dissolve it, as it could the Lower House. However, when for the first time, in 1989, the LDP lost control of the House of Councilors, that House found itself temptingly able to block legislation. Moreover, given the different electoral cycles of the two houses, a government with a majority in the House of Representatives could well lack the opportunity to campaign to restore its majority in the House of Councilors. This was especially so given that only half the Upper House members were renewed every three years.

Since 2000 there have been two episodes of a "twisted Diet," in which the government controls the House of Representatives but not the House of Councilors. The first was under an LDP administration between July 2007 and its demise in September 2009, and the second under the DPJ administration between July 2010 and its defeat in December 2012. Article 59 of the current Constitution provides that: "A bill which is passed by the House of Representatives, and upon which the House of Councilors makes a decision different from that of the House of Representatives, becomes a law when passed a second time by the House of Representatives by a majority of two-thirds or more of the members present."

In other words, a government that can command a two-thirds majority in the Lower House can overturn a veto in the Upper House. This, though, is a high fence to clear, and even when the condition is fulfilled, governments (as in the case of the Fukuda government between 2007 and 2008) have been reluctant to overturn an Upper House rejection. This may be because of a disinclination to impose what used to be called the "tyranny of the majority." The second instance of a "twisted Diet" was particularly debilitating. When in July 2010 the DPJ lost its majority in the House of Councilors, following the debacle over relocating the Futenma marine base in Okinawa and the consequent resignation of Hatoyama Yukio as prime minister, the DPJ in government and the LDP in opposition engaged in fierce conflict, in which the Westminster-type conventions of a "loyal opposition" disappeared from view. Even following the Tōhoku catastrophes in March 2011, after a brief political truce, uncompromising hostility to the government on the part of the opposition became normal, as manifested in the scheming by the LDP to force the resignation of Prime Minister Kan Naoto, conducted throughout the summer of 2011. In effect, throughout this period, a combination of government ineffectiveness and opposition intransigence stifled any real hope there might have been for successful reform, so that by 2012 the DPJ government, now led by Noda Yoshihiko, adopted policies indistinguishable from the LDP.

In a lecture given in London in 2012, the popular and often maverick LDP politician Kōno Tarō spoke frankly about the dysfunctional aspects of contemporary party competition, stressing in particular the mindlessness of whichever party happened to be in opposition using the Upper House to block tax bills coming to it from the Lower House. He also stressed the lack of institutional cohesion evident within both major parties, and held that on policy towards economic deregulation, immigration and agriculture, each major party was divided down the middle (Kōno 2012).

Whether the second Abe Cabinet that emerged, following LDP victory, from the general elections of December 2012, will behave in the traditional LDP fashion of allowing public- and private-sector vested interests to dominate policy making, or rationalize the political system so as to centre policy making on the prime minister and Cabinet, remains to be seen.

Conclusions: mainstream and "exotic" features of Japanese politics

Use of the word "exotic" easily brings to mind the sins of "Orientalism" pilloried by Edward Said (1978). It also might suggest that we are falling into the trap set by *Nihonjinron* writings of assuming total incompatibility between Japanese and non-Japanese (especially "Western") institutions and practices. This is not our intention.

The principal dilemma that we have been seeking to address is the following: Japanese political institutions and practices since the Meiji period have been consciously based on models largely derived from Western countries, and yet in so many instances these institutions and practices turn out to be radically different from the models from which they are derived. This emphatically does not mean that the ways things work in Japan are inferior to the ways in which they work in the countries from which they were derived. It is not a matter of better or worse, but of different.

This takes us to the question of whether these differences stem from the way institutions and practices have developed over time, the outcomes of power struggles, or socio-economic factors impinging on politics, or whether we need to look for something deeper. At this point we are brought up against the "culture" variable that was so much discredited by the *Nihonjinron* literature, and concerning which Ramseyer and Rosenbluth on the one hand, and Krauss and Pekkanen on the other, found themselves united in rejecting, while disagreeing on so much else.

The evidence outlined in this chapter suggests that there is a "default position" in Japanese politics—that of party fragmentation, weak central leadership and networks of privileged interests. This has endured over many decades before and after the Asia-Pacific War, despite radical institutional change. At times, a more cohesive system emerges, but this is the exception, not the rule.

Returning to McVeigh's contingent definition of culture, namely something learned at a particular time and circumstances but historically embedded, we may conclude that explanation needs to go beyond institutional and quantifiable analysis and reach down into less easily measured but crucial areas.

As far as reforming the political system is concerned, we concur with Banno's judgment that a two-party system with indistinguishable parties cannot work well. The answer, however, is not a return to single-party dominance, but rather to have a party of the Left confronting a party of the Right. Expressing it slightly differently, Kōno (2012) said that politics should center on rivalry between two parties, one liberalizing the economy and promoting economic growth and the other pushing for redistribution and fairness.

Bibliography

Banno Junji (2012a) *Nihon kindai shi* (Japan's Modern History), Chikuma Shinsho.

——(2012b) Interview in *Asahi Shimbun*, June 20.

——(2012c) Interview in *Nishi Nihon Shimbun*, December 6: 2.

Befu, Harumi (1980) "Critique of the Group Model of Japanese Society," in Ross Mouer and Yoshio Sugimoto (eds) "Japanese Society: Reappraisals and New Directions," Special Issue of *Social Analysis* (Adelaide), No. 5/6, December.

Curtis, Gerald (2012) "Tohoku Diary: Reportage on the Tohoku Disaster," in Jeff Kingston (ed.) *Natural Disaster and Nuclear Crisis in Japan*, Abingdon and New York: Routledge, 15–32.

Dale, Peter N. (1986) *The Myth of Japanese Uniqueness*, London: Routledge.

Doi, Takeo (1971) *The Anatomy of Dependence*, Tokyo: Kodansha.

Johnson, Chalmers (1982) *MITI and the Japanese Miracle: The Growth of Industrial Policy, 1925–1975*, Stanford, CA: Stanford University Press.

Kōno Tarō (2012) Lecture in series "Political Leadership in the UK and Japan," Daiwa Foundation Japan House, London, April 24.

Krauss, Ellis S. and Pekkanen, Robert J. (2011) *The Rise and Fall of the LDP: Political Party Organizations as Historical Institutions*, Ithaca, NY: Cornell University Press.

McVeigh, Brian J. (1998) *The Nature of the Japanese State: Rationality and Rituality*, London and New York: Routledge.

Mouer, Ross and Sugimoto Yoshio (1986) *Images of Japanese Society*, London and New York: Routledge and Kegan Paul.

Nakane, Chie (1970) *Japanese Society*, London: Weidenfeld and Nicolson.

Ramseyer, J. Mark and Rosenbluth, Frances McCall (1993) *Japan's Political Marketplace*, Cambridge, MA and London: Harvard University Press.

Said, Edward (1978) *Orientalism*, New York: Vintage Books.

Sasaki Takeshi (2012) Interview with *Asahi Shimbun*, June 26.

Stockwin, J.A.A. (2008) *Governing Japan: Divided Politics in a Growth Economy*, Malden, MA and Oxford: Blackwell, 4th edn.

——(2012) "Review of *The Rise and Fall of Japan's LDP*," *Journal of Japanese Studies* 38(1): 199–204.

van Wolferen, Karel (1989) *The Enigma of Japanese Power*, London: Macmillan.

2 The politics of trade policy

Aurelia George Mulgan

Trade politics in Japan provides a classic illustration of structural immobilism in the policy-making system. Despite major transitions in party governments, the relative powers, roles and policy positions of the institutions and actors involved, as well as the central issues, have altered little over the years. The main impetus for change has come from outside—from Japan's trading partners—in multilateral, regional and bilateral trade negotiations. Even then, the degree of market opening for politically sensitive items, especially rice, has been limited and has required substantial compensation for domestic producers.

This chapter will outline these long-standing features of trade politics with examples drawn primarily from Democratic Party of Japan (DPJ) administrations in 2009–12 and more recently from the administration of the Liberal Democratic Party (LDP) Prime Minister Abe Shinzō.

Japanese trade policy: an overview

The degree to which Japan should open its markets in international trade negotiations is the central and most controversial issue in trade policy. Initially negotiations to liberalize trade were conducted under the auspices of the General Agreement on Tariffs and Trade (GATT), which Japan joined in 1955. It was a major player in the multilateral trade negotiations leading to the GATT Uruguay Round agreements in 1994. On January 1, 1995, when the World Trade Organization (WTO) replaced the GATT, Japan officially became a WTO member.

In the early 2000s Japan adopted a multi-layered trade policy, opening up the possibility of participation in bilateral and trilateral free trade agreements (FTAs) and economic partnership agreements (EPAs),[1] and in regional trade agreements (RTAs) as well as in the so-called Doha Round of multilateral trade negotiations conducted under WTO auspices. Since 2002, Japan has signed bilateral EPAs with 12 countries, chiefly in Southeast Asia, as well as with the Association of Southeast Asian Nations (ASEAN) in 2008. Negotiations have begun on several others such as with Australia, Mongolia and Canada, while pre-negotiations are taking place on a Japan–China–South Korea FTA and the first steps towards a Japan–EU EPA are continuing.

Japan is also actively engaged in promoting RTAs in East Asia and in the Asia-Pacific. In April 2006 it announced a proposal for an East Asian Economic Partnership Agreement, also known as the Comprehensive Economic Partnership for East Asia (CEPEA), consisting of the current members of the East Asia Summit, namely the ASEAN+6 (the members of ASEAN plus Japan, China, South Korea, India, Australia and New Zealand). In November 2012, Japan participated in the launch of negotiations for a Regional Comprehensive Economic Partnership (RCEP) encompassing the membership of ASEAN+6. Since 2010, the option of Japan's joining the Trans-Pacific Economic Partnership (TPP) has also come to the fore as a trade policy option. Both the RCEP and TPP have wider significance for Japan as possible stepping stones to a Free Trade Area of the Asia-Pacific (FTAAP), a wide-ranging free trade zone involving all 21 member countries of the Asia-Pacific Economic Community (APEC) committed to abolishing all barriers to economic relations amongst member states.

An additional emerging element in Japan's trade policy is the strategic dimension. The TPP and RCEP present very real geopolitical and security alternatives to Japan. The United States is the dominant player in the TPP, which presently excludes China, while the RCEP is likely to be dominated by China and excludes the United States. Hence Japan's pursuit of regional trade partnerships has implications not only for its trade relations but also for its security relations. If the TPP is successfully extended to include Japan, while excluding China, it will strengthen the Japan–United States security alliance and help to sustain US political and trade leadership in the Asia-Pacific region. On the other hand, if the RCEP proves to be the dominant trade partnership, including Japan but excluding the United States, it will promote the formation of a China-centered economic zone and thus help to consolidate China's economic and trade leadership in the region. Japan's choice of free trade partnerships thus potentially adds not only its economic heft as the world's third largest economy but also its strategic weight to the realization of wider US and Chinese goals relating to the balance of power in East Asia. Hitherto in the background because of constraints from domestic politics, this strategic dimension is likely to become more dominant in Japan's trade policy thinking.

Politicization of trade policy issues

Trade policy formation in Japan has long been highly politicized because of the likely impact of market opening on Japan's internationally uncompetitive farm sector. Agriculture dominates the political debate on trade policy, while the farm lobby and its political allies in the Diet (national parliament) remain the principal stumbling block to agreements to liberalize trade. Despite the 1994 Uruguay Round agreements and 13 EPAs that Japan has signed, it has declined to remove tariffs on around 840 items (roughly 10% of all imported goods), mainly agricultural. Some so-called "sensitive" farm products still shelter behind very high tariff walls such as 778% for rice, 360% for butter, 328% for raw sugar, 252% for wheat and 256% for barley.

The possibility of participating in the TPP negotiations has politicized Japan's trade policy debate to an even greater degree. The TPP represents an "extreme" FTA because it aims to achieve trade liberalization with no exceptions in principle. Its specific objective is the complete abolition of tariffs within 10 years. It also aims to deepen relations between nations not just in trade but also in other economic aspects by widening the scope of potential liberalization to a number of other sectors and markets. A total of 21 areas are under discussion in the negotiations, including the trade in services, conditions for foreign investment as well as policies that come under the broad heading of regulatory issues, which are increasingly important in an international trade context such as intellectual property rights, government procurement, technical standards and regulations, competition policy, labor standards and environmental policy.

The essential issues involved in the TPP thus go well beyond border protection with implications extending to a host of Japanese regulatory and business systems. Opponents of the TPP in Japan argue that not only is it an "extreme FTA" but it also entails "extreme structural reform" (Mitsuhashi 2011), reflecting its nature as a very broad agreement covering a host of tariff and non-tariff barriers.

The structure of Japan's trade politics

Pro-trade government leaders

Japanese governments, including prime ministers, have been strong advocates of international trade agreements. Adopting a whole-of-government approach, they have prioritized the national interest over protectionist interests, seeing trade as integral to economic growth (George Mulgan 2008). The policy manifesto of the new DPJ government, which came to power in September 2009, envisaged Japan playing a proactive role in liberalizing trade and investment, promoting FTAs and EPAs with other Asia-Pacific countries and, in particular, promoting negotiations for the conclusion of an FTA with the United States (Sugawara 2010).

In the early months after its inauguration, the administration of Prime Minister Hatoyama Yukio agreed to work closely with the United States in reviving the stalled Doha Round and promoting EPAs. Its "new development strategy" adopted in late 2009 contained a commitment to establishing an FTAAP. In early 2010, Prime Minister Hatoyama again gave his commitment to promoting international trade negotiations including FTAs. Shortly afterwards, his government resumed stalled negotiations on an EPA/FTA with Australia.

The Kan administration (2010–11) adopted a similarly proactive free trade agenda (George Mulgan 2011a). Its *Basic Policy on Comprehensive Economic Partnerships* declared the government's resolve "to 'open up the country' … and promote high-level economic partnerships with major trading powers … [and to embrace the principle of subjecting] all goods to negotiations for trade liberalization" (Ministry of Foreign Affairs 2010). Prime Minister Kan Naoto elevated participation in the TPP to his signature policy under the slogan "Opening up the country in the Heisei era" (*Heisei no kaikoku*—Heisei is the reign name associated with current Emperor Akihito).

The Noda administration, inaugurated in September 2011, also expressed firm support for Japan negotiating its way into the TPP, arguing that the Asia-Pacific region would be an "engine of growth" for the global economy and that there would be "benefits for Japan from forming high-level economic partnerships" (*Daily Yomiuri Online* 2011). Prime Minister Noda Yoshihiko saw the TPP as the first step towards attaining the goal of realizing an FTAAP by 2020, with 75% of Japan's exports bound for prospective FTAAP states (Fujimori 2011).

The LDP's manifesto of November 2012 reiterated its commitment to free trade as a pillar of Japan's foreign trade policy and declared the usual support for a revived Doha Round as well as actively promoting EPAs/FTAs and RTAs. Although the LDP's commitment to free trade was more conditional than the DPJ's,[2] Prime Minister Abe expressed his commitment to making a quick decision on entering the TPP negotiations early in his administration.

Despite the generally proactive and positive stance of Japanese government leaders on pursuing international agreements to liberalize trade, the pace of market opening has been incremental at best. The chief obstacles to trade reform have been a divided bureaucracy, politically well organized and entrenched protectionist interests, and institutionalized opposition from ruling party politicians, who have acted directly to block their own government's trade policy initiatives from within the policy making process. These factors are responsible for the structural immobilism that has characterized this sector of government policy making. As a result, trade negotiations involving Japan have often taken years to complete, with the results falling far short of the levels of trade liberalization desired by Japan's trading partners.

A divided bureaucracy

Unresolved divisions within the Japanese bureaucracy on trade policy have consistently stalled progress on market opening. The main divide falls between the Ministry of Agriculture, Forestry and Fisheries (MAFF) and the Ministry of Economy, Trade and Industry (METI). MAFF is fixated on protecting agriculture while METI wants to promote free trade in order to expand Japan's industrial exports (Tsujihiro 2010). Both positions reflect the long tradition of ministries representing the interests of the domestic industries within their administrative bailiwicks.

When the Kan government announced its pro-TPP stance, MAFF and METI came up with different mathematical formulas to calculate the costs and benefits to the national economy of concluding the TPP and criticized each other's numbers as "too big" (*Yomiuri Shimbun* 2013). METI estimated that if Japan joined the TPP, internationally competitive Japanese industries such as car and electronics manufacturers would increase their exports and as a result the nation's gross domestic product (GDP) would rise by ¥10.5 trillion and 812,000 jobs would be created (Tsujihiro 2010). METI also estimated that abolishing tariffs would result in savings of ¥70 billion in tariffs on 1.56 million cars exported to the United States where the tariff was 2.5% (*Asahi Shimbun* 2011). On the other hand, the MAFF published its estimate showing that if Japan joined the TPP, GDP would decrease by ¥7.9 trillion yen owing to a fall in agricultural production, with a loss of 3.4 million jobs (Kuno and Naoi 2012).

Into this divided bureaucracy stepped the Cabinet Office, issuing an official government projection that TPP membership would boost Japan's real GDP by 0.54% (¥2.7 trillion) over a period of 10 years (Komine 2011). If losses were subtracted from the profits gained through TPP participation, there would be a ¥2.4–¥3.2 trillion increase in GDP, a calculation that many specialists regarded as "neutral and adequate" (Tsujihiro 2010). However, the Cabinet Office's estimate simply became one of the competing projections on the likely impact of the TPP on the Japanese economy.

Weak top-down coordination in a vertically divided bureaucracy blocked resolution of these differences on trade policy. Not even the Ministry of Foreign Affairs (MOFA), which consistently argues from the position of enhancing Japan's foreign relations through trade, is able to override the deep divisions in the ministries representing their respective domestic industries.

In the new Abe administration, METI Minister Motegi Toshimitsu sought to circumvent this problem by proposing a unified estimate of the impact on the Japanese economy of participating in the TPP. He revealed that he and MAFF Minister Hayashi Yoshimasa had "decided to work together … MAFF Minister Hayashi is not a spokesperson for MAFF's interests. We have similar opinions" (*Jiji Tsūshin* 2013). This was a significant development given how clashes between the two ministries had stymied progress on the TPP issue in the past. The Economic Revitalization Headquarters set up by Prime Minister Abe to formulate an economic growth strategy for his administration then took over the task of issuing the unified government estimate compiled by the Cabinet Secretariat showing that Japan's participation in the TPP would push up real GDP by ¥3.2 trillion over 10 years (*Asahi Shimbun* 2013).

Protectionist interest groups

Japan's agricultural cooperative organization (JA, or Japan Agriculture), which represents the majority of Japanese farmers, has a long history of using its organizational and electoral clout to block the liberalization of agricultural markets. The possibility of Japan's participating in the TPP negotiations has precipitated a sustained and vociferous campaign from JA, which has seized the opportunity "to strengthen organizational unity by inciting a sense of crisis among agriculture-related personnel" (Tsujihiro 2010). JA argues that tariff abolition on agricultural imports will lead to an influx of cheap farm products, which will destroy Japanese agriculture.

JA's peak organization, JA-Zenchū, launched an offensive against participation in the TPP talks as soon as Prime Minister Kan announced his desire for Japan to join the negotiations (*Mainichi Shimbun* 2011). The Kan administration certainly "flinched in the face of its intimidation" (Tsujihiro 2010). One of its tactics was to organize the collection of 10 million signatures on a petition requesting that the government not participate in the TPP negotiations. JA-Zenchū successfully obtained 11,668,809 signatures, delivering the petition to Prime Minister Noda on the eve of the APEC meeting in November 2011 when he was hoping to announce Japan's participation in the TPP negotiations. JA-Zenchū also listed 363 Diet members as supporting the petition: 235 from the Lower House (members of nine parties including 99 from the DPJ and 93 from the LDP and seven Independents), and 128 from the Upper House including 26 from the DPJ and 73 from the LDP.[3]

In order to magnify the effectiveness of its campaign, JA-Zenchū joined forces with a range of other primary industry groups, including forestry and fisheries cooperatives, as well as consumer groups and housewives' organizations taking a firm stand against TPP participation. These groups shared concerns relating to food safety, food self-sufficiency and the health care system. The office of a Network to Protect Japan's Food, Livelihood and Lives against the TPP formed in January 2011 by agriculture, forestry, fisheries and consumer groups set up in the JA building in Tokyo with JA-Zenchū's assistance.

In addition, JA-Zenchū involved groups within the medical and construction industries in its anti-TPP offensive (Yamashita 2012). A senior official from METI criticized JA-Zenchū for this tactic, saying: "Agricultural cooperatives are fanning anxiety about the TPP by inciting other industry circles" (*Mainichi Shimbun* 2011, 1). The Japan Medical Association (JMA) opposed the introduction of so-called "market fundamentalism" into Japan's medical services and feared the collapse of the public health insurance system if the ban on mixed medical services were removed[4] and profit-making companies (including foreign companies) were permitted to enter the medical services sector.

For the Japanese construction industry, concerns arose regarding the potential impact on rules for placing orders for public works projects, with the possibility of foreign businesses participating in bids for public works. JA-Zenchū officials even visited factories in Tokyo where small businesses were concentrated, explaining to them that an influx of cheap labor would harm local workers and cause regional economies to collapse (*Mainichi Shimbun* 2011, 1). The prospect of Japan joining the TPP thus provoked "unprecedented levels of lobbying among special interest groups and the politicians" (Kuno and Naoi 2012, 5).

Institutionalized opposition from within the ruling parties

Pro-farmer politicians in the ruling parties remain the most important political barrier to Japanese trade liberalization from within the policy process. They operate in both formal party policy committees and informal party lobby groups.

In the DPJ's Policy Research Council (PRC), newly re-established and reinvigorated by the Kan and Noda governments, the primary committee concerned with trade policy was initially the Project Team for Examining How to Deal with APEC, EPAs and FTAs. Its position on the TPP was directly reflected in the Kan administration's November 2010 *Basic Policy on Comprehensive Economic Partnerships*, which restricted the government to gathering further information on the TPP and commencing prior consultations with TPP member countries, whilst postponing an actual decision on joining the talks. This committee was replaced in the Noda administration by the Economic Partnership Project Team, which likewise put the brakes on Japan's entry into the TPP talks, restricting the prime minister merely to entering into "consultations *toward* participating in the TPP negotiations with the countries concerned" (Prime Minister of Japan and his Cabinet 2011, emphasis added).

Supplementing the activities of the DPJ's formal policy committees and frequently operating within them was an informal lobby group of around 100 members called the "Association to Think Carefully About the TPP" (the so-called "cautious faction," or *shinchōha*). Its strong anti-TPP stance was another factor constraining Prime Minister Noda's eagerness to announce Japan's participation in the TPP negotiations at the November 2011 APEC meeting in Hawaii.

In blocking these prime ministerial trade initiatives, the PRC's trade committees effectively revived the LDP's convention of prior screening and approval of government policy by the ruling party and thus its de facto veto power. This "government-versus-party" phenomenon had traditionally worked to limit the power of the political executive including the prime minister, with the result that it often failed to get its policy initiatives through the policy-making process (George Mulgan 2011b).

The LDP was just as divided as the DPJ on the TPP issue. Concerned LDP Diet members established their own informal "Group that Demands Immediate Withdrawal from TPP Participation" in October 2011, which adopted a resolution opposing participation. The LDP's Comprehensive Agricultural Policy and Trade Investigation Committee within the LDP's Policy Affairs Research Council (PARC) adopted a resolution against the TPP on the same day (Nenbutsu and Okazaki 2011).

Over 160 LDP Diet members with support bases in rural areas subsequently won seats in the December 2012 Lower House election with endorsement from political organizations affiliated with JA. Indeed, JA based its decisions on whom it would recommend in the election on candidates' positions on the TPP (George Mulgan 2013). With the Upper House election due in July 2013, JA also stepped up its pressure on LDP politicians to prevent the Abe administration from announcing participation in the TPP negotiations. Three PARC agricultural committees—the Agriculture, Fishery and Forestry Strategy Investigation Committee and its Agriculture, Forestry and Fisheries Trade Countermeasures Committee together with the Agriculture and Forestry Division—dealt with the TPP issue, as did the Regional Diplomacy and Economic Partnership Investigation Committee, which became the primary venue for discussing the TPP within the party. In addition, the "Group that Demands Immediate Withdrawal from TPP Participation," to which more than 60% of the LDP's Diet members belonged, mobilized as a separate intra-party lobby group.

Diet members representing rural and regional constituencies find it difficult to oppose JA out of fear of losing farmers' votes. The concern is particularly strong in close battles in the single-seat districts of the Lower House, where "even a small number of agricultural votes may determine the results of the election" (Yamashita 2012). Election candidates standing in the 31 single-member prefectural constituencies in the Upper House are swayed by similar considerations. Farmers remain an important electoral constituency. In 2010, voters resident in commercial farm households numbered 5.5 million voters, which was 5.3% of the total national electorate (George Mulgan 2013).

Compensating farmers

The reality of agrarian power in Japan has made agricultural trade liberalization politically impossible without generous support and compensation for farmers. The enunciation of market opening policies has always been coupled with measures to promote farming and support domestic producers.

The DPJ's approach was to compensate farmers with direct income subsidies in order to counterbalance the prospective fall in their incomes caused by tariff abolition and lower agricultural prices. The Kan government established a Headquarters to Promote the Revival of the Food, Agriculture, Forestry, and Fishery Industries in November 2010 in order to facilitate international trade agreements by undertaking appropriate domestic agricultural reforms formulated as a "revival" plan for agriculture. Its objective was to promote free trade and domestic agriculture simultaneously.

The Noda government adopted the same approach. Its *Basic Policy and Action Plan for the Revitalization of Our Country's Food and Agriculture, Forestry and Fisheries* sought "to realize sustainable agricultural, forestry and fisheries industries that are compatible with high levels of economic partnership" (Kokka Senryaku Shitsu 2011). Once again, the policy was designed to strike a balance between supporting market opening and developing domestic agriculture (Isozumi 2011). It outlined a series of measures such as promoting the farm household income compensation scheme, scale-expansion of farming and turning agriculture into a "sixth" industry[5] as part of a strategy to strengthen agriculture's structure and competitiveness. Prime Minister Noda said at the government's "Headquarters for the Revitalization of Food, Agriculture, Forestry and Fisheries," which drew up the plan, "We need to manage both economic partnerships (such as the TPP) and the revitalization of agriculture" (Yamashita 2011).

The Abe government's approach was essentially a carbon copy of the Kan and Noda administrations, combining policies to support farmers with those to expand agricultural exports and strengthen cooperation between the agricultural, commercial and industrial worlds. The cost was rumored to be around ¥10 trillion over 10 years, following the earlier pattern of ¥6 trillion when the LDP government at the time signed the Uruguay Round Agreement on Agriculture (URAA) in 1994 (Andō and Chō 2013).

In practical terms, these plans were all designed to lay the groundwork for trade liberalization with policies to promote the ability of the farm sector to deal with the impact of agricultural market opening. In political terms, they were designed to reduce opposition from the farm lobby to the prospect of increased competition in the domestic market from farm imports. However, in entering the TPP negotiations, the Abe administration still demanded exemptions from tariff elimination for key agricultural products such as rice and beef in keeping with the pattern of limited market opening for politically sensitive items.

The role of external pressure

One force with impetus to break through the structural immobilism of the trade policy-making system and the power of vested interests opposed to market opening has been external pressure (*gaiatsu*) arising from international trade negotiations (Davis and Oh 2007). It has been most effective when it has aligned with internal pressure (*naiatsu*), particularly from big business interests seeking to expand internationally competitive exports (George Mulgan 2012). In the face of concerted and well organized opposition from agricultural interests and their representatives in the ruling party, big business finds it difficult to sway governments to their point of view. Agricultural trade policy remains an area where vertical divisions in the bureaucracy tend to neutralize the views of big business, thus undermining the force of cross-sectoral liberalization pressures. For these reasons, although Japan's export industries are extremely influential, in specific policy domains their views do not necessarily prevail.

The Japan Business Federation (Nippon Keidanren) has spearheaded the drive to promote Japan's trade liberalization process. In mid-April 2011, Keidanren released its *Proposals for Japan's Trade Strategy*, calling for Japan to "pursue a proactive and strategic trade policy" (Nippon Keidanren 2011), including a proactive approach to concluding the WTO Doha Round and promoting "the conclusion of EPAs with the United States, China, and the EU … through the frameworks of the TPP, ASEAN+6, and Japan-EU EIA [Economic Integration Agreement]" (Nippon Keidanren 2011). Keidanren Chairman Yonekura Hiromasa frequently reiterated that "Japan should promptly join the TPP negotiations" (JA-Zenchū 2011b).

Other business leaders and lobby organizations support Keidanren's free trade advocacy. The vice-chairman of the Japan Association of Corporate Executives (Keizai Dōyūkai) and chairman of its economic partnership committee stated, "I believe that the TPP and other economic partnerships bring three benefits: boosting Japan's international competitiveness as a country, preventing industrial hollowing out and setting fair rules between countries" (Fujimori 2011, 13). Manufacturers, especially those in cars, electronics and electronic components have warned that South Korea's successful negotiation of FTAs with Europe and the United States (and prospectively with China), will put Japanese exporters at a competitive disadvantage in these markets.

On the TPP, American *gaiatsu* has successfully targeted access to particular Japanese markets in the prior consultation process, extracting concessions as the price of its approval for Japan's entry into the formal negotiations (George Mulgan 2012). As a result, Japan has relaxed the age restrictions on imported beef from the United States; Japan Post Insurance Co., under the wing of government-backed Japan Post, has decided to call off its entry into the cancer insurance market; and there has been discussion of relaxing some import procedures for motor vehicles (George Mulgan 2012). A proposal for setting up a special framework for importing a certain set volume of rice from the United States has also been floated in government circles (*Nihon Keizai Shimbun* 2013).

Changing the trade policy-making process

Breaking through the structural immobilism in trade policy making helped to deliver policy change on the TPP under the Abe administration in 2013. In an attempt to limit the role of the party's policy committees, Abe first secured the agreement of LDP executives to entrust him with the TPP decision, bypassing opposition from within the ranks of LDP Diet members backed by JA. The reaction from the LDP's agricultural groups was to demand that the government and prime minister listen to the party's opinions and deal with the matter in accordance with the LDP's tradition of emphasizing discussions within the party (*Nihon Nōgyō Shimbun* 2013a).

However, Prime Minister Abe took control of a newly established task force called the TPP Affairs Committee, which he chaired and which became the "main battlefield" for discussions and for coordinating the views of party members on the TPP (*Nihon Nōgyō Shimbun* 2013b). It replaced the party committees previously examining the TPP issue. The key innovation provided by the new committee was its unification of the party and government streams of policy making, thus overcoming the customary structural divide between the two institutions. Moreover, its main focus was compensation for individual sectors subject to market opening and the list of items to be exempted from tariff elimination in the TPP talks, thus catering to anti-trade vested interests. In this way, the prime minister was able to outmaneuver the farm lobby and its political allies within the LDP whilst simultaneously offering reassurances that his government would properly protect vulnerable sectors.

The prime minister then overcame the vertically divided bureaucracy by gathering together a staff of full-time TPP specialists representing a cross-section of ministries in the Prime Minister's Office. These key adjustments to the policy-making process, which allowed Prime Minister Abe to exert his policy leadership, was the breakthrough needed to facilitate Japan's entry into the TPP negotiations, a policy triumph that had eluded his two predecessors since June 2010.

Conclusion

Since 2009, a succession of prime ministers have sought to advance Japan's trade and economic prospects through participation in bilateral, regional and multilateral agreements to liberalize trade. However, despite their proactive trade policies, on the defining trade issue of the moment—whether or not Japan should join the TPP negotiations—a vertically divided bureaucracy, well mobilized protectionist interest groups and ruling party politicians responding to pressure from special interests as well as to electoral incentives, stalled a series of key trade policy decisions. In an attempt to overcome the structural immobilism in the trade policy-making system, Prime Minister Abe modified the policy process as a way of delivering the key breakthrough on the TPP, heralding Japan's entry into the talks. Although joining the TPP negotiations represented a political risk for the Abe administration given the impending Upper

House election in July 2013, the prime minister was motivated by a strong desire to use trade to boost Japan's economic growth by absorbing overseas demand for Japanese goods and services. Moreover, in Abe's view, signing on to the TPP had the added bonus of drawing Japan closer to the United States, thus contributing to the nation's security and also to stability in the Asia-Pacific region.

The decision to participate in the TPP negotiations exacted the usual political price of generous compensation to affected groups as well as the prospect of limited concessions in terms of access to key Japanese markets, including for farm products. Thus, while an element of dynamism might have been injected into domestic trade policy-making, it was not matched by evidence of any dramatic change in Japan's posture of minimalist concessions in international trade negotiations.

Notes

1 The 13 bilateral trade agreements that Japan has signed to date are called "EPAs" because "they cover various elements beyond tariff elimination, such as customs procedure cooperation; technical regulations, standards, and conformity assessment; investment; trade in services; movement of natural persons; energy and mineral resource development cooperation; intellectual property rights; government procurement; and control of anti-competitive activities" (Hiratsuka *et al.* 2009).

2 It laid down specific qualifications in the areas of agriculture, forestry and fisheries, for example, and affirmed the need to maintain border measures it regarded as necessary. In the case of the TPP, the conditions it set were absolutely specific: it would oppose participation in the negotiations as long as they were premised on "tariff abolition without exceptions" (Jimintō 2012, 19). It also itemized a further five restrictions relating to rejection of numerical targets for imports of manufactured products such as cars, protecting the universal health care system, protecting food safety standards, not accepting the Investor State Dispute Settlement (ISDS) clause that violated national sovereignty, and taking Japanese characteristics into account in relation to government procurement and financial services (Jimintō 2012, 19). These were all markets and systems that the LDP wanted to protect.

3 These figures were obtained by counting names on lists of signatories from different political parties who signed the JA-Zenchū petition, which were compiled by JA-Zenchū and published on November 1, 2011 (JA-Zenchū 2011a).

4 Under a mixed medical services system, there would be two different systems for medical bills in hospitals: one for treatment covered by medical insurance and another for treatment not covered, the risk being that the existing universal health insurance system would collapse as resources moved to more profitable areas of medical services.

5 The notion of a "sixth" industry is reached by multiplying industrial sectors—primary x secondary x tertiary. If successfully implemented, it would mean more Japanese farms selling directly to consumers, processing farm products, undertaking agri-tourism, and increasing exports of agricultural products to China and other Asian markets, such as fruit, beef, Chinese yams, chicken, rice, chestnuts, peaches, grapes, pears and mandarin oranges.

Bibliography

Andō, T. and Chō, Y. (2013) "TPP kōshō de nōgyō kaikaku ni gōhō, Nichi Bei shunō kaidan" (Go sign for agricultural reforms with TPP negotiations, Japan-US summit meeting), *Nikkei Business Online*, March 4, business.nikkeibp.co.jp/article/topics/20130228/244331/?rt=nocnt (accessed March 4, 2013).

Asahi Shimbun (2011) "TPP kōka '2.7 chō en' GDP, 10 nenkan de Naikakufu shisan" (The TPP will boost GDP by "2.7 trillion yen" in ten years, Cabinet Office conducts trial calculations), October 26: 4.

——(2013) "Shushō, TPP kōshō sanka o hyōmei, Kaigō sanka wa 7 gatsu ka 9 gatsu ka" (Prime Minister announces participation in the TPP negotiations, participation in meetings likely to start in July or September), March 15, www.asahi.com/politics/update/0315/TKY201303150235.html (accessed March 16, 2013).

Daily Yomiuri Online (2011) "Noda Keen on TPP Participation, Prime Minister also Committed to Prompt Resolution of Futenma Issue," October 19, www.yomiuri.co.jp/dy/national/T111018005521.htm (accessed September 16, 2012).

Davis, C. and Oh, J. (2007) "Repeal of the Rice Laws in Japan: The Role of International Pressure to Overcome Vested Interests," *Comparative Politics* 40(1), October: 21–40.

Fujimori, Y. (2011) "TPP kōshō sanka, kokueki yūsen, ima sugu ketsudan o, Fujimori Yoshiaki-shi (kikō)" (Prioritize national interests and make a decision now on TPP negotiation participation, contribution by Yoshiaki Fujimori), *Yomiuri Shimbun*, October 26: 13.

George Mulgan, A. (2008) "Japan's FTA Politics and the Problem of Agricultural Trade Liberalisation," *Australian Journal of International Affairs* 62(2), June: 164–78.

——(2011a) "No Longer the 'Reactive State': Japan's New Trade Activism," *Asie. Visions* 38, Paris, Institute Français des Relations Internationales, May, www.ifri.org/downloads/asievisions38agmulgan.pdf (accessed September 16, 2012).

——(2011b) "The Politics of Economic Reform," in Alisa Gaunder (ed.) *Handbook of Japanese Politics*, London and New York: Routledge, 261–72.

——(2012) "Can Trade Talks Drive Reform in Japan," *Current History* 111: 241–43.

——(2013) "Farmers, Agricultural Policies and the Election," in Robert Pekkanen, Steven Reed and Ethan Scheiner (eds) *Japan Decides*, New York: Palgrave Macmillan, 213–24.

Hiratsuka, D., Sato, H. and Isono, I. (2009) *Impacts of Free Trade Agreements on Business Activity in Asia: The Case of Japan*, Working Paper No. 143, Asian Development Bank Institute, 31 July, www.adbi.org/working-paper/2009/07/31/3254.fta.japan/japans.fta.status/ (accessed August 27, 2012).

Isozumi, T. (2011) "Nōgyō shien saku chikara busoku, Saisei kihon hōshin zaigen ni fumikomazu" (Agricultural support policies inadequate, the basic policies for revival do not touch on fund sources), *Yomiuri Shimbun*, October 21: 9.

JA-Zenchū (2011a) "'TPP kōshō sanka hantai no kokkai seigan' zen kokkai giin no kahan ga sandō" (The majority of Diet members support the "petition to the Diet opposing participation in the TPP negotiation"), *JA-Zenchū Puresu Ririisu*, November 1, www.zenchu-ja.or.jp/release/pdf/1320139260.pdf (accessed September 16, 2012).

——(2011b) "Keidanren kaichō to JA-Zenchū kaichō no kondankai gaiyō ni tsuite" (On the summary of the roundtable conference between Keidanren chairman and JA-Zenchū chairman), *JA-Zenchū* Puresu Ririisu, November 9, www.zenchu-ja.or.jp/pdf/press/1320833274.pdf (accessed July 3, 2013).

Jiji Tsūshin (2013) "TPP no eikyō de tōitsu shisan=konran kaihi e sakutei—Motegi Keisansō" (Unified trial calculation on the impact of the TPP=formulation to avoid confusion—METI Minister Motegi), January 12, headlines.yahoo.co.jp/hl?a=20130112-00000055-jij-pol (accessed March 4, 2013).

Jimintō (2012) "Jimintō senkyo kōyaku (An), Seiken kōyaku" (LDP election promises (draft), administration pledges), *J-Fuairu2012*, November 21, www.jimin.jp/policy/pamphlet/pdf/j_file2012.pdf (accessed February 28, 2013).

Kokka Senryaku Shitsu (Decision of the Headquarters for the Revitalization of Food, Agriculture, Forestry and Fisheries) (2011) *Waga Kuni no Shoku to Nōrinsuisangyō no Saizei no tame no Kihon Hōshin-Kōdō Keikaku* (Basic policy and action plan for the revitalization of our country's food and agriculture, forestry and fishing industries), October 25, www.npu.go.jp/policy/policy05/pdf/20111025/siryo1.pdf (accessed September 16, 2012).

Komine, T. (2011) "Hontō ni jūyō na no wa TPP ni kanyū shita ato no senryaku, TPP wa bōkoku no seisaku ka kyūkoku no seisaku ka (chū)" (What is really important is the strategy after we join the TPP. Is the TPP a policy that will ruin or save the country? (Part 2)), *Nikkei*

Bijinesu Online, November 7, business.nikkeibp.co.jp/article/money/20111104/223611/ (accessed September 16, 2012).

Kuno, A. and Naoi, M. (2012) *Framing Business Interests: How Campaigns Affect Firms' Positions on Preferential Trade Agreements*, Version 2.1: April, www.princeton.edu/politics/about/file-repository/public/FramingBusiness_Princeton_April16.pdf (accessed September 18, 2012).

Mainichi Shimbun (2011) "Fūun TPP:/jō (sono ichi) Hantairon kakudai, kokuron o nibun, JA ga sendō, Rōso Nichii mo kyōtō" (TPP in turmoil: (part 1): Arguments against the TPP spreads and splits national opinion, JA takes the lead and labor unions and Japan Medical Association work together), October 25: 1.

Ministry of Foreign Affairs (Ministerial Committee on Comprehensive Economic Partnerships) (2010) *Basic Policy on Comprehensive Economic Partnerships*, 6 November, www.mofa.go.jp/policy/economy/fta/policy20101106.html (accessed September 13, 2012).

Mitsuhashi, T. (2011) "Kōzu 'seizōgyō vs. nōgyō' no mekuramashi kōka, Mondai wa '24 bun no 2' ni waishōka, nokori 22 kōmoku no giron o kīta koto ga aru ka" (The deceptive effect of the "manufacturing industry VS agriculture" picture, the problem is trivialized to "2/24"; have you heard any discussions about the remaining 22 items?) *Nikkei Business Online*, 7 March, business.nikkeibp.co.jp/article/topics/20110303/218708/ (accessed September 13, 2012).

Nenbutsu, A. and Okazaki, D. (2011) "TPP: Ji Kō, hantairon ni ikioi, tōmen wa Minshu o yōsumi" (TPP: opposition gains momentum in LDP and Kōmeitō, two parties to wait and see what the DPJ does), *Mainichi Shimbun*, October 26: 5.

Nihon Keizai Shimbun (2013) "TPP kyū kasoku (1) Kome igai 'seiiki' chiisaku" (TPP gains rapid momentum (1) "Sanctuaries" other than rice become smaller), February 26: 5.

Nihon Nōgyō Shimbun (2013a) "TPP de Jimin ga kaigō handan ichinin dekinu, Jōhō kaiji, kokumin giron uttae" (LDP holds meeting in regard to TPP, judgment cannot be entrusted [to the Prime Minister], appeals made for information disclosure and national discussion), February 27, www.agrinews.co.jp/modules/pico/index.php?content_id=19431 (accessed February 27, 2013).

——(2013b) "TPP taisaku iinkai ga shidō, Shushō no handan zairyō teigen, Jimin" (TPP Affairs Committee makes a start, the committee will provide information for the prime minister to make the judgment, LDP), March 6, www.agrinews.co.jp/modules/pico/index.php?content_id=19592 (accessed March 6, 2013).

Nippon Keidanren (2011) *Proposals for Japan's Trade Strategy*, April 19, www.keidanren.or.jp/english/policy/2011/030/proposal.html#part1 (accessed September 13, 2012).

Prime Minister of Japan and his Cabinet (speeches and statements by prime minister) (2011) *Press Conference by Prime Minister Yoshihiko Noda*, November 11, www.kantei.go.jp/foreign/noda/statement/201111/11kaiken_e.html (accessed November 12, 2012).

Sugawara, J. (2010) *Japan's Trade Policy at the Crossroads: The Hatoyama Administration's Agenda*, Mizuho Research Paper 24, Tokyo: Mizuho Research Institute, March, www.mizuho-ri.co.jp/publication/research/pdf/rp/MRP1003.pdf (accessed September 13, 2012).

Tsujihiro, M. (2010) "Kaikoku ka sakoku ka—TPP ga tou 'kono kuni no katachi'" (Will Japan open up or become isolated? The TPP calls into question "the shape of the country"), *Diamond Online*, 117, November 18, diamond.jp/articles/-/10104 (accessed September 18, 2012).

Yamashita, K. (2011) "Shin no nōsei kaikaku no tame no 3 suteppu, Seifu no kihon hōshin de wa TPP ni sanka shiyō ga shimai ga nōgyō wa shukushō suitai suru shika nai" (The three steps to true agricultural administration reform. Under the government's [current] basic policy, agriculture has no choice but to decline regardless of whether or not Japan participates in the TPP), *Nikkei Bijinesu Online*, November 1, business.nikkeibp.co.jp/article/manage/20111031/223506/?ST=world (accessed September 18, 2012).

——(2012) "Yamashita Kazuhito Kyanon Gurōbaru Senryaku Kenkyūjo kenkyū shukan, 'TPP no ronten, TPP obake no shōtai' ni tsuite iken kōkan" ("Canon Institute for Global Studies Senior Fellow Kazuhito Yamashita, An opinion exchange on 'the points at issue regarding the TPP, and the true character of the TPP-ghost'"), Japan Institute for National Fundamentals/

Kokka Kihon Mondai Kenkyūjo, January, jinf.jp/news/archives/6888 (accessed September 18, 2012).

Yomiuri Shimbun (2013) "TPP eikyō, Keisan Nōsui barabara shisan yame seifu de" (Separate trial calculations on the impact of the TPP conducted by METI and MAFF to be discontinued and replaced by calculations by the government), January 13: 9.

3 Limiting fundamental rights protection in Japan

The role of the Supreme Court

Lawrence Repeta

Japan's Constitution is a progressive document that declares protection for a long list of individual rights against violation by government authority. To assess whether the Constitution succeeds in achieving this goal, we must consider the role played by Japan's Supreme Court. The Court holds final authority to judge cases involving conflicts between individuals who assert beliefs or engage in behavior unacceptable to government authorities and government efforts to impose discipline against them. The Court is also charged with the constitutional mandate to prohibit discrimination against individuals or groups on the basis of race, gender and other classifications. Japan's progress toward achieving a free and open society relies heavily on the Court's work in these areas.

In this chapter, we examine rulings of the Court in cases that feature conflicts between individuals and the state. To begin, we consider a landmark case in which the Court ruled in favor of a minority group that claimed to be victims of discrimination. Many commentators have expressed the hope that this judgment suggests the Court will take a more proactive stance in upholding individual rights in the future.

The children's case

On June 4, 2008, the Supreme Court of Japan rendered a startling decision. Responding to a petition filed on behalf of 10 children of mixed parentage, the Court ruled that a provision of Japan's Nationality Law that barred them from citizenship violated Japan's constitutional guarantee of equal treatment. The Court's decision opened the door to citizenship not only for the 10 plaintiffs, but for thousands of people in similar circumstances (Supreme Court 2008b).

Editorials labeled the decision epoch-making and said it was symbolic of bigger changes taking place in Japanese society. Legal commentators said the decision was historic because Japan's Supreme Court so rarely rules in favor of individuals who claim that a law or government action violates their rights guaranteed in Japan's Constitution. Some said that this was indicative of bigger changes taking place at the Court, which appeared to be at long last stepping forward to assert its power as the final bastion (*saigo no toride*) of human rights protection in Japan's legal system.

The 10 children were all the offspring of Filipino mothers and Japanese fathers. Their parents were not married to each other and the Japanese fathers had not recognized paternity until after the children were born. Under an odd provision of Japan's Nationality Law, this lack of timely recognition by their fathers disqualified the children from citizenship.[1] If the fathers had come forward before the births or if they had

Figure 3.1 Celebrating a courthouse victory that opened the door to citizenship for thousands
Source: (Photo: Kyodo News)

subsequently married the children's mothers, the children's names could have been entered into the fathers' family registries and they would be citizens of Japan. The law's discriminatory treatment was illustrated most clearly by the case of two sisters, one 14 and the other six years old. Although they were both born in Japan to the same parents, one qualified for Japanese citizenship and the other did not. The father had recognized paternity for the younger child prior to birth, but not for her older sister.

Although the case was filed on behalf of 10 children, it is believed that many thousands of people, young and old, were in the same situation. Like the petitioners in this case, some were born in Japan and had known no other home. Others had been born in the Philippines or in other countries and had never set foot in Japan. By invalidating Article 3(1) of the Nationality Law, the Court removed a barrier to citizenship for all of these people.

Judicial review

Article 88 of Japan's Constitution declares that the Constitution itself is the supreme law of the land. Several articles guarantee fundamental human rights, such as freedom of speech and religion, against governmental interference. Article 14 includes a non-discrimination rule, which reads "All of the people are equal under the law and there shall be no discrimination in political, economic or social relations because of race, creed, sex, social status or family origin."[2] In the case of the 10 children, the Supreme Court decided there is no rational basis for the difference in treatment between individuals who met the Nationality Law standard and those who did not. Accordingly, the Court struck down the statute as an unconstitutional violation of Article 14.

The source of the Court's power to act in a case like this is Article 81, which declares that the Supreme Court has the power to determine the constitutionality of any "law, order, regulation or official act." This power to review the actions of other agencies of government is usually called "judicial review" (*shihõ shinsaken*). Along with the words of the Constitution itself, the Court's exercise of judicial review provides the people's most important protection against government abuse of power.

The Court's decision in the children's case was especially significant because it was rendered by the Court's so-called "grand bench" comprising all 15 justices. Nearly all cases that reach the Supreme Court are resolved through judgments issued by one of the Court's three "petty benches" comprising five justices each. Ordinarily, the grand bench is convened only in cases that raise important constitutional questions. In many years, the grand bench accepts no more than one or two cases.

The primary reason observers described the Court's decision as historic is the extreme scarcity of cases in which Japan's Supreme Court has exercised its power to declare government action unlawful. Since the Court was first seated in August 1947, it has overruled government action in just a handful of cases. The Court's reluctance to act has disappointed many scholars and advocates of individual rights.[3] In standard American terms, the Court's attitude would be described as highly deferential in its review of government action.

Before examining specific cases, we will briefly consider the nature of the Constitution itself.

Popular sovereignty and universal rights

The Preamble to Japan's Constitution begins with the words:

> We, the Japanese people … do proclaim that sovereign power resides with the people and do firmly establish this Constitution. Government is a sacred trust of the people, the authority for which is derived from the people, the powers of which are exercised by the representatives of the people, and the benefits of which are enjoyed by the people.

These are the words of revolution. Under the Meiji Constitution, the people were subjects of a divine emperor. The people's "rights" were not guaranteed by the Constitution, but subject to limitations imposed by government. That the people are not mere subjects of an emperor but are themselves sovereign, and that the Constitution protects their fundamental rights from improper actions of government were radical ideas in the Japan of 1947, the year the new Constitution took effect. The guns had fallen silent only two years before and little more than a year had passed since January 1, 1946, the day the emperor formally renounced divinity (Takemae 2002).

Japan's Constitution was born in an era when the world was embracing a new understanding of human rights. It took effect on May 3, 1947, just two years after creation of the United Nations (UN) and one year before adoption of the Universal Declaration of Human Rights by the UN General Assembly. The Universal Declaration is an exhaustive catalog of individual rights that has come to define the common aspiration of societies all over the world. The list of individual rights in Japan's Constitution closely tracks the Universal Declaration and various human rights treaties subsequently ratified by the Diet. By adopting this Constitution, Japan joined the global movement toward expanded recognition of fundamental human rights.

However, it is much easier to write inspirational statements of grand ideals than it is to enforce them. To achieve their goals, the reformers who produced Japan's Constitution had to deliver more than just words—they had to create institutions with the power and inclination to enforce the human rights it proclaimed. Their answer to this problem was to create a new Supreme Court and system of lower courts and entrust them with the power of judicial review described above. When cases involving government violations of individual rights or other abuses of power by other government agencies were brought before the courts, it would be the judges' duty to correct them. The success of this scheme, however, required a major change in the role played by judges in Japan's legal system.

The reluctance of Japan's Supreme Court to make this change and exercise its new power means that the protection or lack of protection for individual rights is often left to the discretion of other agencies of government, including the police and the prosecutors' office. This is why the Court's forthright action in the children's case caused so much excitement in Japan's legal community.

Has the Court changed?

The judgment in the children's case is of special interest because it was not alone. It followed several other notable decisions in recent years in which the Supreme Court exercised its power to declare laws or acts of government unconstitutional. In response to these decisions, commentators began to ask whether the Supreme Court had changed (Sato *et al.* 2009; Yamaguchi and Miyaji 2011).

Voting rights and elections

In another decision rendered by the Court's full complement of 15 justices, in 2005 the Court ruled in favor of a group of Japanese plaintiffs who reside outside Japan and were denied the same opportunity to vote as their fellow citizens in Japan. According to published estimates, nearly 1 million Japanese live abroad and as many as 720,000 may benefit from the Court's ruling.

Fifty-three Japanese voters living in eight countries filed a lawsuit challenging the 1996 elections. In a partial response, the Diet amended the law in 1998 to enable expatriate Japanese to vote for a political party in the proportional representation component of Japan's hybrid electoral system, but they remained ineligible to vote for candidates in single seat districts.[4]

In its September 14, 2005 decision, the Court held that the Diet (national parliament) had unconstitutionally violated its obligations by failing to adopt a statute that would enable the plaintiffs fully to exercise their right to vote (Supreme Court 2005b).

The notion that the legislature had violated its constitutional obligations by *failing to act* was without precedent. The Court even ordered the government to make nominal payments to the plaintiffs.

The Court has displayed its greatest zeal in enforcing constitutional standards when policing national elections. Malapportionment of electoral districts has plagued Japan throughout the post-war era, with rural voters enjoying disproportionately high representation. The Supreme Court first ruled a national election unconstitutional in 1976 and has done so again most recently in 2011 and 2012, ruling that elections for both Houses of the Diet violate Article 14 and other provisions of the Constitution.

Despite its repeated admonitions to the Diet to pass legislation rectifying these imbalances, however, the Court has been unable to craft a remedy. Although it declared elections unconstitutional, or "in a state of unconstitutionality," the Court has not declared them invalid. So the Diet has been able to go about its business without adjusting electoral districts to meet the Court's concerns. The battle continues, with national election results, including the December 2012 elections that brought Prime Minister Abe and the Liberal Democratic Party (LDP) to power, regularly challenged in court. In early 2013 the nation watched as numerous suits challenging that election wended their way through the lower courts to yet another resolution by the Supreme Court. Observers wonder whether this may be the time the Court declares elections invalid, perhaps resulting in major legislative redistricting and dissolution of the Diet to be followed by elections under a new system.

Standing

The Supreme Court grand bench issued another landmark decision in 2005, this time effectively overturning a rule declared by one of the Court's petty benches just six years before. The case concerned Japan's "standing" doctrine. Standing rules require plaintiffs to show they have a sufficiently important interest in a dispute to justify a court accepting their case. When a court decides plaintiffs have no standing, the case is dismissed. Japan's Supreme Court has overseen the development of a narrow standing doctrine, which has generally limited access to the courts to parties who can show they have an interest directly within the scope of the stated purposes of a statute.

In a decision rendered on December 7, 2005, the grand bench changed course, recognizing the standing of local residents to challenge construction proposed by Odakyu Railways, a major Tokyo commuter line (Supreme Court 2005c). In that case, Odakyu had obtained approvals to construct an above-ground railway intersection and a 6.4-kilometer rail extension in the Setagaya district of Tokyo. Local residents filed suit, seeking a court order to nullify the approval and block construction. They asserted that the project would cause unacceptable levels of vibration and noise pollution and would otherwise damage their neighborhoods. They proposed that Odakyu build its new intersection underground.

In a similar case decided by the first petty bench in 1999, the Court denied standing and dismissed. Relying on this precedent, in 2003 a Tokyo High Court panel also dismissed the Setgaya residents' claim, leading to their appeal to the Supreme Court.[5] By overturning the High Court and recognizing standing, the 2005 grand bench judgment opened courtroom doors to litigants in similar situations who would otherwise be left with no hope of a remedy. Decisions like these can have a major impact on the role of courts in society (Takii 2009).

Discrimination between siblings

Statutory discrimination between children deemed to be "legitimate" and those who are not has been repeatedly challenged in one important area unrelated to the citizenship issue raised in the children's case. Article 900 of Japan's Civil Code limits the inheritance of children born out of wedlock to one-half that of their "legitimate" siblings. This rule applies in cases where the deceased leaves no effective will, so inheritance must be decided by law. One year after the Supreme Court's landmark decision in the children's case, a petty bench of the Supreme Court inexplicably ruled to reject a challenge to this provision of the Civil Code.

A similar case appeared on the Supreme Court docket, however, and in early 2013 it was referred to the grand bench. It is widely expected that the Court will deliver a new result declaring Civil Code Article 900 in violation of Constitution Article 14, thus achieving consistency with its decision in the children's case. In the children's case, the overseas voters case, the Setagaya residents case and some others, Japan's Supreme Court broke new ground, leading to expectations for a Court more willing to exercise its authority, especially to impose limitations on other branches of government. If these expectations are fulfilled, long-dormant provisions of the Constitution might come alive.

The Supreme Court's deference to other branches of government

To answer the question whether the Court has changed, we must also ask, "changed from what?" We examine some recent judgments that suggest the answer below.

Equality?

During the six decades from the time the Constitution took effect until the 2008 decision in the children's case, litigants who brought claims of government discrimination to the courts found little success. An especially poignant example of government discrimination reached the courts in the mid-1990s and was decided by the Supreme Court grand bench in 2005.

The plaintiff, Chung Hyang Gyun, is a *Zainichi* Korean woman who was employed by the Tokyo metropolitan government as a public health nurse. Like hundreds of thousands of other *Zainichi* residents, she is the descendant of people who came to Japan or were brought there by force during Japan's colonial era (Nozaki *et al.* 2006). She was born and raised in Japan and speaks Japanese as her native language. Moreover, her mother is a Japanese citizen. For powerful reasons of history and culture, however, she has not obtained Japanese citizenship (see Chapter 16).

Ms Chung was hired as a nurse by the Tokyo government in 1988, two years after it abolished nationality as a condition to such employment. After six years on the job, she applied to take an examination to qualify for promotion to a managerial position. That year she would be 44 years old, with a long career ahead. The Tokyo government turned down her application to take the exam on the grounds that she lacked Japanese nationality. There would be no promotion for Ms Chung.

She filed suit, challenging this decision as an unconstitutional infringement of her right to equal treatment and was vindicated by a 1997 High Court decision in her favor. Rather than comply with this ruling, however, the Tokyo government appealed.

In a 13–2 decision issued on January 26, 2005, the Supreme Court grand bench overturned the High Court ruling (Supreme Court 2005a). The Supreme Court relied on Constitution Article 15 which has been interpreted to require citizenship as a condition to the exercise of "public authority." Although all parties agreed that the management position Ms Chung sought does not entail the exercise of such public authority, Tokyo officials had adopted an "integrated management appointment system" which employed the same examination for positions that involve the exercise of public authority and those that do not. Their decision to employ this system barred all non-citizens, including *Zainichi* Koreans, from taking this examination, whatever position they might seek.

The Supreme Court decided that the convenience of the administrators who adopted the discriminatory system outweighed the interests of people like Ms Chung whose careers would be limited to the lower rungs of the ladder. Two justices filed dissenting opinions and the Court's opinion has been severely criticized in commentary by constitutional scholars (Martin 2010, 2011).

Various forms of discrimination against minorities and women persist in Japan. Although international human rights bodies and domestic advocates have long called for Japan to adopt effective anti-discrimination laws, Japan's legislators have so far refused to act (Committee on the Elimination of Racial Discrimination 2010; Japan Federation of Bar Associations 2013).

Restricting individual rights

Freedom of speech

Constitution Article 21 declares that, "Freedom of assembly and association as well as speech, press and all other forms of expression are guaranteed." Although the Supreme Court may have changed its approach in cases that raise discrimination claims such as the children's case and other cases described above, so far there is no evidence that the Court has changed its attitude toward litigants who claim that the police or other government officers have violated Article 21 or other fundamental rights.

The Court's preference for government action over individual rights is most obvious in its consistent rejection of free speech claims. Many of these cases arise in criminal prosecutions, where police have arrested or otherwise interfered with individuals engaged in speech activities.

A series of such cases arose in the aftermath of Prime Minister Koizumi Jun'ichiro's order to deploy a small Self-Defense Force unit to Iraq in January 2004. This was the first deployment of Japanese military forces into an active war zone since 1945. It led to broad opposition and the birth of a new national movement to protect Article 9, the war-renouncing clause of the Constitution (Junkerman 2008). The most heavily reported case was launched by the February 2004 arrest of three antiwar activists charged with criminal trespass because they had slipped one-page flyers into mailboxes at apartment buildings in Tachikawa, an outlying area of Tokyo with a large military base. The three were each detained in police cells for 75 days.

In an opinion that declared free speech to be a "pillar of democracy" that enjoys a "preferred status" in constitutional litigation, a district court panel found the three defendants not guilty of the trespass charge in December 2004. The government appealed and successfully obtained a guilty verdict from the Tokyo High Court, leading to the defendants' Supreme Court appeal.

Figure 3.2 This man was arrested after distributing leaflets criticizing the deployment of Japanese troops to Iraq. He was detained in a police cell for 75 days.
Source: (Credit: Lawrence Repeta)

A petty bench upheld the guilty verdict in a decision issued on April 11, 2008 (Supreme Court 2008a). Although the Court recognized that the defendants' sole purpose was to deliver a political message, and it further declared that, "in a democratic society freedom of speech must be respected as an especially important right," the Court then said that the Constitution "does not provide absolutely unlimited protection for freedom of expression. It is subject to limitations necessary and reasonable to serve the public welfare." The Court justified its guilty verdict by deciding that the "tranquility of the personal lives" of the residents outweighed the defendants' free speech claims.

The Court chose not to address the actions of the police in singling out these defendants for arrest while overlooking the actions of others who regularly enter the property in a similar manner to distribute commercial flyers and other material. Nor did it consider the propriety of a 75-day detention on such a charge.

Japan's constitutional scholars inform us that the Supreme Court has never found a single case in which the actions of the police violated the free speech rights of anyone. In a long list of cases where the Supreme Court has upheld restrictions on speech, Shigenori Matsui includes complete bans on door-to-door canvassing during election campaigns, bans on posters on public facilities, trees and electricity poles on public streets, injunctions against publication of material alleged to be defamatory and criminal prosecutions of individuals accused of defamation (Matsui 2011).

Freedom of assembly

Anyone who observes a public demonstration in Japan can see how rigidly police control marchers. Tight police control of public demonstrations is a legacy of a series of Supreme Court decisions in cases that arose from sometimes violent clashes between large bodies of demonstrators and massed riot police during Japan's turbulent early post-war era. Scholars point to a 1960 Supreme Court decision that was especially significant in laying the groundwork for what we observe in Japan today (Supreme Court 1960).

That decision upheld the constitutionality of a Tokyo ordinance that requires marchers to obtain permits in advance from local government authorities and empowers authorities to impose restrictions regarding time, marching routes and other details. Prior to the 1960 decision, several lower courts had ruled that such limitations violated the freedom of assembly guaranteed by Constitution Article 21. The Supreme Court put an end to such decisions. Today, all public demonstrations are tightly regulated under local ordinances.

As indicated in Figure 3.3, in Tokyo this usually means that marchers are restricted to the width of one lane of traffic and must stop at traffic signals like the cars alongside them.

In the aftermath of the 2011 nuclear disaster, large masses of ordinary citizens took to the streets for the first time since the anti-war era of the 1970s. Some demonstrations have attracted more than 100,000 participants (see Chapter 4). So far, it appears that

Figure 3.3 Anti-nuclear demonstrators are hemmed in by police at a central Tokyo rally following the Fukushima disaster in 2011.

Source: (Credit: Lawrence Repeta)

the police have generally acted with restraint. This appears to be the product of extensive consultations between organizers and the police prior to major events and broad support for the anti-nuclear message among the general public.

There have been, however, some arrests and lengthy detentions of anti-nuclear demonstrators (Relief Liaison Center 2013). There have also been some obvious examples of abuse of police authority, for example in the December 2012 arrest and detention of individuals who protested the processing of waste from the Tohoku tsunami zone in Osaka facilities. Like the arrests in the Tachikawa case described above, the arrestees caused no injury to person or property and no public disturbance, the arrests took place long after the event, in this case nearly two months later, and demonstrators were subject to lengthy detentions (Morris-Suzuki 2013).

Freedom of conscience and belief

The idea that a change in the attitude of the Supreme Court will extend to claims to protection for political speech and political belief seems especially unlikely in light of the Court's rulings in a series of cases decided in 2011, three years *after* the ruling in the children's case.

The controversy arose when local governments, led by the Tokyo metropolitan government under the flamboyant ultranationalist Governor Ishihara Shintaro, began to issue orders requiring all teachers to face the *hinomaru* flag and sing the *kimigayo* anthem at school ceremonies. Hundreds of teachers refused on the grounds that the flag and anthem symbolize the divinity of the emperor and Japan's wartime history of military aggression, and that participation in these rituals caused them severe stress and emotional pain. The teachers asserted that Constitution Article 19, which declares that "Freedom of thought and conscience shall not be violated," protects them from compulsory homage to these symbols of Japan's wartime past.

Litigation commenced when teachers challenged penalties imposed on them by local governments. Several cases found their way to the Supreme Court. In a series of judgments rendered by all three petty benches of the Court over a two-week period in summer 2011, the Court resoundingly held that the teachers were bound to follow orders. The Court ruled that whatever might be the personal feelings or beliefs of individual teachers, their compulsory participation in the flag and anthem rituals does not violate their rights under Article 19. They can lawfully be compelled to stand and sing and penalized if they do not follow orders to do so.

The local government ordinances and 2011 Supreme Court decisions are precursors to the LDP's 2012 proposals for thorough constitutional revision, which include specific language mandating that all people (not only public school teachers) respect the national flag and anthem. The LDP proposals will be discussed briefly below.

Procedural protections for persons accused of crime

Perhaps the most important right in any system of law is freedom from arbitrary restraint through imprisonment or other government action. Several provisions of Japan's Constitution are intended to protect this freedom by guaranteeing the rights of persons apprehended by government authorities. As described below, however, Japan's courts have interpreted these provisions in a manner that eliminates all but the most minimal procedural protections for persons accused of crime.

In Japan, any criminal suspect can be detained on the most trivial charge for 23 days before a public court hearing. Throughout the detention period, more than 90% of suspects are held in police stations. (A report by Japan's national bar association provides this description: "usually there is no sunlight to be introduced into the cells, no window to the outside and exercising space is very limited area within the building and actually used as a smoking area.") Interrogations can take place at any time. Although suspects are allowed to consult with lawyers, lawyers are not allowed to be present during interrogation.

After the initial detention period of 23 days, suspects are for the first time allowed to file requests for release on bail, but these requests are nearly always denied when opposed by the prosecution. This happened in the case of the Tachikawa peace activists described above. In that case there was no injury of any kind and no contested issues of fact. Although the sole issue was a theoretical legal question concerning the balance between free speech rights and trespass to private property, the defendants were detained in police cells for 75 days. Prosecutors demanded continued detention, but after 75 days a judge finally ordered their release on bail.

Lengthy detentions like this amount to punishment before courts have judged guilt or innocence and deny the accused a fair opportunity to prepare a defense. In the infamous Muraki prosecution, a rare case that resulted in a not guilty verdict, the defendant was detained for 163 days (Kingston 2011). The wisdom on the street is that if a suspect wants to be released, he should confess to the charges against him. This is the source of Japan's false confession problem.

United Nations bodies charged with monitoring compliance with human rights treaties have repeatedly decried this state of affairs and demanded reform. For example, the 10-member UN Committee Against Torture summarized its 2007 review of this system as follows: " … insufficient procedural guarantees for the detention and interrogation of detainees, increases the possibilities of abuse of their rights, and may lead to de facto failure to respect the presumption of innocence, right to silence and right to defence" (Committee Against Torture 2007).

The responsibility for such a one-sided system must be placed squarely at the door of the Supreme Court. The power of judicial review bestowed on the Court by Constitution Article 81 entrusts the Court with oversight for all rights declared in the Constitution, including the guarantee of fair criminal procedures.

After nearly three decades of studying criminal procedure in Japan, Daniel Foote described the approach of Japan's judiciary as "centered on deference to prosecutors." In Foote's words, "the Japanese judiciary interpreted narrowly, granting broad authority to the prosecution and limiting rights and protections for suspects and defendants, often in the face of rather explicit language in the Constitution … " (Foote 2010: 1).

Japan is commonly viewed as one of the world's leading democracies. How can it be that the Supreme Court of such a country can so steadfastly reject the claims of individuals who seek to exercise protection for fundamental rights?

Supreme Court appointments

There are many reasons for the deferential attitude of Japan's Supreme Court, including traditions carried over from the pre-war era, the Court's very heavy caseload, the advanced ages of the justices, and others (Matsui 2011). The most direct approach to understanding the attitude of the Court is to examine the backgrounds of the individuals selected to serve as justices.

The Constitution unequivocally places the power to appoint Supreme Court justices with the Cabinet. There is no public review of candidates by the Diet or any other body. We must assume that Cabinets exercise their power in a manner that suits their political preferences. Throughout most of the Court's history, Cabinets have been controlled by the LDP, which is usually described as "conservative" and "nationalistic." LDP leaders have openly demanded thorough revision of the Constitution since the party was founded in 1955. A cardinal element of the LDP program is to negate the human rights philosophy behind the 1947 Constitution and replace it with a vision of a society in which the duty of citizens to the state takes priority over individual rights (Liberal Democratic Party 2012).

Many writers suggest that LDP leaders need not formally revise the Constitution at all; they have already realized their goals through the appointment of Supreme Court justices who share their political philosophy. This phenomenon is commonly called *kaishaku kaiken*, literally "constitutional revision by interpretation." As illustrated in cases described above, the Court has generally interpreted the Constitution in a manner that limits individual rights while recognizing broad government power.

Political leaders have exercised their control over Supreme Court appointments through several customs that are not written into law. The first is the total secrecy that surrounds the process. The Japanese people learn the identities of new justices only *after* they have been appointed. A second custom is the limitation of appointments to individuals of relatively advanced age. With few exceptions, appointees are at least 64 years old. Because the Courts Act requires that all justices retire at the age of 70, individual justices tend to have relatively short terms of service. This effectively limits the impact of any individual justice on the Court's jurisprudence. The third distinctive custom is the practice of allocating a nearly fixed number of seats to candidates from different segments of the legal community (Repeta 2011). Over the long decades of the post-war era, these customs have become so deeply entrenched that they are virtually unquestioned in Japan's legal community.

Under the third unwritten custom, 10 of the 15 Supreme Court seats are reserved for career public officials and only five seats are allocated to persons who have spent most of their careers outside government. Of the 10 career officials, six have ordinarily spent their entire careers as judges, two as prosecutors, and two as bureaucrats unrelated to the Ministry of Justice. Of the five non-officials, four are ordinarily private lawyers and one is an academic.[6] The 10:5 ratio ensures that career government officials control not only the grand bench, but each of the three petty benches as well.

This allocation custom goes all the way back to appointment of the first Supreme Court in 1947. It has been subject to one significant adjustment, conducted by the Sato and Tanaka Cabinets from 1969 through 1973. This restructuring of the Court followed the turbulent 1960s, an era in which Japan experienced massive political demonstrations featuring violent clashes between police and demonstrators. It was also an era when liberal judges who held an expansive view of constitutional rights had great influence. LDP leaders publicly criticized courts that sometimes ruled in favor of demonstrators. Then they reshaped the Supreme Court to back up the police by replacing retiring justices with individuals who could be trusted to uphold their version of law and order. In the course of this process the Sato and Tanaka Cabinets re-allocated two seats that had been held by a private lawyer and an academic to a prosecutor and a bureaucrat, resulting in the 10:5 ratio that has prevailed ever since (Repeta 2011).[7]

As long as this appointment pattern remains in place, it is hard to imagine the Court taking an aggressive stance on behalf of individuals in conflict with the state.

Final comments

The 1947 Constitution brought a revolutionary change to Japan's constitutional order. The new order of popular sovereignty and individual rights matched the global movement toward greater protection for these values. The original draft of the 1947 Constitution was prepared by a small team of Allied officials while Japan was under occupation. Although this draft was reviewed and revised by the Diet before taking effect, the final text retains a very strong American influence. It is unquestionably a legacy of Japan's defeat in war and many of Japan's political leaders have harbored a deep resentment ever since.

The continued survival of the present constitutional order is in doubt. The LDP released comprehensive proposals to amend the Constitution on April 28, 2012, a date selected to commemorate the end of the Occupation 60 years before. The revision proposals begin with a re-wording of the Preamble and extend throughout the document. They take direct aim at the concept of universal human rights. This attack is explained in an LDP pamphlet released in October 2012:

> Rights are gradually formulated through the history, tradition and culture of each community. Therefore, we believe that the provisions concerning human rights should reflect the history, culture and tradition of Japan. The current Constitution includes some provisions based on the Western theory of natural rights. We believe these provisions should be revised.
>
> (Liberal Democratic Party 2012)

According to the LDP, human rights are not universal. As revealed in the proposed revisions, their view of "the history, culture and tradition of Japan" rejects the primacy of individual rights and replaces it with citizen duties to the state. This theme plays out in several proposals that would subordinate freedom of speech and other rights to maintenance of "public order," and would create new "constitutional duties" such as the duty to respect the national flag and anthem.

The LDP won a landslide victory in the December 2012 elections under the leadership of Abe Shinzo, a man who has devoted his career to nationalistic causes and constitutional revision. After taking office he confirmed that revising the Constitution is a high priority. At this point, no one knows whether Mr Abe and the LDP will achieve their aims, but given the well-established pattern of Supreme Court deference on human rights issues and the outspoken hostility of LDP leaders, we cannot expect significant expansion of human rights protection in the foreseeable future.

Notes

1 In defense of the statute, government lawyers argued that marriage was reasonable evidence to show a connection between the father and the child and therefore a connection to Japanese society which justified recognition of citizenship.

2 All quotations from Japan's Constitution are taken from the English version published by the Japanese government at www.kantei.go.jp/foreign/constitution_and_government_of_japan/constitution_e.html. Experts sometimes dispute its accuracy in rendering various provisions of the Japanese original.

3 Professor Matsui (2011, 1398–99) points out that the Supreme Court has sometimes ruled to protect a fundamental right by narrowly interpreting a statute rather than declaring it unconstitutional.

4 Government lawyers argued on the basis of administrative convenience; it would be too difficult and time consuming for election officials to send a fair amount of information on each candidate to each voter. The Internet has effectively eliminated this argument.

5 Japan has a three-tiered court system similar to the US federal court system. There are 50 district courts, which have general jurisdiction and serve as courts of first instance for most cases. There are eight "high courts," intermediate appellate courts located in major cities around the country. The Supreme Court decides appeals from high court judgments and certain other cases.

6 Japan's legal profession is highly segmented, with most individuals spending their entire careers as judges, prosecutors or private attorneys. The one general exception to this rule is that retiring judges and prosecutors typically register as private attorneys after leaving government service. Regarding Supreme Court appointments, there are a few "hybrid" appointees, such as Sonobe Itsuo, who worked extended periods as both a judge and a full-time academic before his appointment to fill the academic seat on the Supreme Court in 1989.

7 All Cabinets since, including those that served during the brief interregna when the LDP was out of power, have followed this appointment pattern.

Bibliography

Committee Against Torture (2007) *Consideration of Reports Submitted by States Parties under Article 19 of the Convention*, Concluding Observations, Conclusions and Recommendations of the Committee against Torture, August 3, 2007.

Committee on the Elimination of Racial Discrimination (2010) *Consideration of Reports Submitted by States Parties under Article 9 of the Convention*, Concluding Observations, April 6, 2010.

Foote, Daniel H. (2010) "Policymaking by Japan's Supreme Court in the Criminal Justice Field," *Hoshakaigaku* 72: 1.

Japan Federation of Bar Associations (2013) *Report of JFBA Regarding the Third Periodic Report by the Government of Japan under Articles 16 and 17 of the International Covenant on Economic, Social and Cultural Rights*, January 18, 2013.

Junkerman, John (2008) "The Global Article 9 Conference: Toward the Abolition of War," *The Asia-Pacific Journal*, May 25.

Kingston, Jeff (2011) "Justice on Trial: Japanese Prosecutors Under Fire," *The Asia-Pacific Journal* 9(10:1), March 7.

Liberal Democratic Party (2012) *Nihonkoku Kempõ Kaisei Sõan—Q & A* (Draft reform to Japan's Constitution, Q & A), www.jimin.jp/activity/colum/116667.html.

Martin, Craig (2010) "Glimmers of Hope: The Recent Evolution of Equality Rights Doctrine in Japanese Courts, from a Comparative Perspective," 20(2) *Duke Journal of Comparative & International Law* 167.

——(2011) "The Japanese Constitution as Law and the Legitimacy of the Supreme Court's Constitutional Decisions: A Response to Matsui, 88(6) *Washington University Law Review* 1527.

Matsui, Shigenori (2011) "Why is the Japanese Supreme Court so Conservative?" 88(6) *Washington University Law Review* 1375.

Morris-Suzuki, Tessa (2013) "Freedom of Hate Speech: Abe Shinzo and Japan's Public Sphere," *The Asia-Pacific Journal* 11(8:1), February 25.

Nozaki, Yoshiko, Inokuchi, Hiromitsu, and Kim, Tae-young (2006) "Legal Categories, Demographic Change and Japan's Korean Residents in the Long Twentieth Century," *The Asia-Pacific Journal*, September 10.

Relief Liaison Center (Kyuen Renraku Center) (2013) *Dan'atsu no Doko* (Trends in repression), qc.sanpal.co.jp/tendency/.

Repeta, Lawrence (2011) "Reserved Seats on Japan's Supreme Court," 88(6) *Washington University Law Review* 1375.

Sato, Iwao *et al.* (2009) *Shō-Tokushū: Saikōsaibansho wa Kawattaka—Iken Shinsa to Seisaku Keisei wo Kangaeru* (Special feature: Has the Supreme Court changed? Thinking about judicial review and policy formation), 82(4) *Hōritsu Jiho* 46.

Supreme Court (1960) *Decision of the Supreme Court*, G.B., July 20, 14 Keishū 1243.

——(2005a) *Decision of the Supreme Court*, G.B., January 26, 59 Minshū No. 1: 128.

——(2005b) *Decision of the Supreme Court*, G.B., Sept. 14, 59 Minshū No. 7: 2087.

——(2005c) *Decision of the Supreme Court*, G.B., Dec. 7, 59 Minshū No. 10: 2645.

——(2008a) *Decision of the Supreme Court*, 2nd P.B., April 11, 62 Keishū No. 5: 1217.

——(2008b) *Decision of the Supreme Court*, G.B., June 3, Shūmin No. 228: 101.

Takemae, Eiji (2002) *The Allied Occupation of Japan*, New York: Continuum.

Takii, Shigeo (2009) *Saikōsaibansho wa Kawattaka—Ichi Saibankan no Jiko Kenshō* (Has the Supreme Court changed? The self-validation of one judge), Tokyo: Iwanami Shoten.

Yamaguchi, Susumu and Miyaji, Yū (2011) *Saikōsai no Antō—Shōsū Iken ga Jidai wo Kirihiraku* (Shadow fighting at the Supreme Court—minority opinions open the way to a new age), Tokyo: Asahi Shinsho.

4 Civil society

Past, present, and future

Akihiro Ogawa

Shimin shakai

Japan has developed a rich tradition of civil society in the post-World War II era. Civil society, which is translated as *shimin shakai*, can be defined as a public sphere that broadly refers to non-state institutions and associations that are critical to sustaining modern democratic participation. A variety of actors play active roles in Japanese associational life.

Among them, the neighborhood association, termed *chōnaikai* or *jichikai*, is probably the most conventional and longest-surviving Japanese civil-society organization. This type of association is a territory-based organization functioning as a basic unit of social and political engagement in Japanese daily life (Bestor 1989). Closely interacting with the local government, mostly at the municipal level, neighborhood associations collect garbage for recycling, organize seasonal festivals, take the national census, work to prevent juvenile delinquency, and deliver disaster relief in emergencies. All registered households are expected to maintain active membership in local neighborhood associations. Across the country, there are some 300,000 of these types of civil-society groups, according to the most recent figure available from the Ministry of Internal Affairs and Communications (MIAC 2008).

Public interest legal persons, or *kōeki hōjin*, are other conventional actors in Japanese civil society. Article 21 of the Japanese Constitution guarantees freedom of assembly and association. However, this guarantee does not mean any group can automatically obtain legal status. In fact, the Japanese government has traditionally intervened aggressively in the incorporation process followed by non-profit organizations. The Japanese Civil Code, which was written in 1896, strictly regulated the establishment of major third-sector organizations under Article 34. Originally, there were two types of public interest bodies legally institutionalized in Japanese society: incorporated foundations (*zaidan hōjin*) and incorporated associations (*shadan hōjin*). However, a reform of public interest corporations was undertaken in the 2000s, and as of 2008, people could set up a general incorporated foundation (*ippan zaidan hōjin*) or a general incorporated association (*ippan shadan hōjin*) simply through registration at the Legal Affairs Bureau (*hōmukyoku*). No approval or permission by central or local government is necessary. In order to obtain more favorable tax treatment, a foundation or an association can separately apply for status as a public interest incorporated foundation (*kōeki zaidan hōjin*) or a public interest incorporated association (*kōeki shadan hōjin*). For example, the popularly known PTA, or Parent-Teacher Association, is an incorporated association under Japanese law. As of February 2013, the PTA was applying for new status as a public interest incorporated association. Meanwhile, as subcategories in the non-profit sector, religious organizations, private schools, private hospitals, and local social welfare councils are also granted legal status as such.

Besides these two conventional actors, this chapter examines two further entities in Japanese civil society: non-profit organizations (or NPOs) and social movements more broadly. Both are currently active and prominent in the early 2010s. First, my focus is on characterizing the NPOs established under the NPO Law (formally the Law to Promote Specified Nonprofit Activities), enacted in December 1998. It is called *NPO hōjin* in Japanese, and is a subcategory of the public interest legal bodies I mentioned above. Within the NPO sector, I observe a bifurcation. One set of NPOs is classified as *GoNPO* (pronounced *gonpo* in Japanese), and groups of this type primarily function as providers of services, including social welfare and lifelong education, or as subcontractors of the local government (see Ogawa 2009 for an example of an NPO as a lifelong education service provider). Another contrasting set of NPOs may be termed social enterprises (*shakaiteki kigyō*), which often act in parallel to the government. Empowered social enterprise practitioners often see NPOs as a vehicle to realize social entrepreneurship within local communities. Social entrepreneurs take strong initiative to define problems and try to solve them in a very independent manner. In this chapter, I introduce two social enterprises: Florence and Entrepreneurial Training for Innovative Communities (ETIC), both Tokyo-based NPOs. These organizations are actively expanding their social businesses, flexibly responding to local demands, and directly delivering their services to the end users.

Second, I look at social movements, reflecting the active involvement of a diverse array of civil-society actors, such as labor unions, informal citizens' groups, and others. In giving a brief overview of the Japanese social movement landscape, I discuss the case of anti-nuclear rallies that have taken place across the country following the Fukushima nuclear disaster of March 2011. Demonstrations in the summer of 2012 attracted a total of nearly 1 million people in Kasumigaseki, the heart of national administration and politics located in central Tokyo (Ogawa 2013). An event of this scale is both significant and reminiscent of the anti-US-Japan security treaty (or *Anpo*) demonstrations in the 1960s. Thus, through the lens of civil society, this chapter argues how contemporary Japan is experiencing a pivotal moment, testing the dynamism of its citizens and their willingness to participate in social and political life.

NPOs

Japanese NPOs proliferated in the aftermath of a devastating earthquake in 1995 in Kobe, western Japan. Nearly 1.3 million volunteers participated in the rescue efforts to aid the victims. Efforts and contributions on such a massive scale highlighted the need for a national-level social structure that could support the voluntary third sector. As a result of this unprecedented volunteerism, the NPO Law was crafted in 1998. The creation of the NPO Law represented a considerable step toward liberalizing the nonprofit sector in Japan. This reform laid the foundation for more robust civil-society actors to meet the challenges generated by the so-called Lost Decade of the 1990s (Kingston 2004).

The administrative process for incorporation is quite simple. To establish an NPO, one fills out necessary forms contained in an NPO application packet, which is usually prepared by the prefectural government and can be downloaded from the Internet on each prefecture's website. The packet includes a cover page, articles of association, and budget forms. Then, the applicant is required to choose from among 20 activity areas set forth by the NPO Law: social welfare; social education; community development; sightseeing promotion; rural development; promotion of science, culture, the arts, or sports; environmental conservation; disaster relief; community safety; human rights protection or peace promotion; international cooperation; gender equality; sound nurturing of youth; information technology development; promotion of science and technology; promotion of economic activities; vocational training; consumer protection; NPO support; and activities related to the ordinances articulated by prefectural or designated municipal governments. An NPO can cross-register for several categories. Among the options, social welfare and social education (or lifelong learning) are the two most popular. Following registration, an application undergoes a relatively straightforward recognition process. The governor of the prefecture in which the NPO is located, or the Cabinet Office in the case of an NPO with offices in at least two prefectures, authenticates the establishment of the organization. By incorporating legally, the NPO can own or rent real estate, open a bank account, and subscribe to telephone and other services. Prior to the enactment of the NPO Law, these kinds of contracts were under individuals' names.

As of February 2013, nearly 50,000 NPOs have been formally established in Japan and many are gaining traction. However, the nascent NPO sector is not homogenous. As a result of my research on Japanese civil society, spanning over a decade, I can confirm that these nascent NPOs can be grouped into two distinct categories.

On the one hand, there are NPOs that act as providers of services or as subcontractors of the local government. The *Asahi Shimbun* (January 30, 2009), a major national daily, wrote a feature article on Japanese NPOs that dubbed this particular type "GoNPO." This moniker simply stands for "government-led NPOs." In fact, I have consistently observed that the government plays a key role in establishing and operating Japanese NPOs, and this breed of NPO can be classified as one of the most prevalent among NPOs in Japanese civil society.

A particular case with which I have been involved since 2001 showcases this category of NPO (Ogawa 2009). The case concerns an NPO, which in my research I called SLG (a pseudonym), located in eastern Tokyo, which focuses on community-oriented lifelong learning. SLG is one of the biggest lifelong learning NPOs in Japan, both in terms of membership and funding. About 130 local residents register as unpaid volunteers, and they plan courses on various subjects, administer courses in order to facilitate participants' learning, and also collect and provide information on learning opportunities to local residents via the Internet, local cable TV, and newsletters. SLG offers more than 100 courses a year, and 10,000 local residents in total take courses as part of their lifelong learning activities. The organizational mission of SLG is to promote learning for local residents taught by other local residents; in so doing, this NPO advances the agenda of local government officials who want a community-oriented lifelong learning program.

SLG illustrates an NPO taking on a role often associated with government. Originally, the municipal government was responsible for promoting lifelong learning in the 1990s, part of a national initiative aimed at addressing the needs of Japan's aging population. The government built and operated a public facility promoting lifelong learning activities in the local community. However, after the collapse of the asset-inflated bubble economy in the early 1990s, the government could no longer finance and operate the public facility, and thus, organized—or I would say, "invited"—local residents "voluntarily" to operate the public lifelong learning center. I noticed that such "invited" volunteers had much in common: educated, middle-class housewives and retired men. After the enactment of the NPO Law of 1998, the government instructed the group of volunteers to incorporate as an NPO, which I would describe as a government-led, top-down process of NPO-ization. In September 2000, SLG registered as an NPO and its subcontracting relationship continues while most of its funding comes from the municipal government.

Some NPOs like SLG were indeed established at the behest of local governments which sponsored NPOs as a more cost-efficient means to deliver services that the state could no longer afford to provide. This subcontracting enabled the government to provide the same social service at minimum cost through the mobilization of community volunteers. Although the government has succeeded in cutting costs by sponsoring social service delivery NPOs, they are to a significant degree co-opted by the state because they are dependent on state funding. This approach fails to contribute to social diversity or increased pluralism, and limits dynamic and critical social and political participation, all of which are key components of sustaining modern democratic life. Even though there are some 50,000 NPOs, clearly numbers alone do not necessarily signal a vibrancy in Japanese civil society and democracy.

On the other hand, I see another trend emerging in the Japanese NPO world. Another set of NPOs can be classified as *shakaiteki kigyō*, or social enterprises. A social enterprise is one of the most dynamic entities in the global third sector (Ridley-Duff and Bull 2011). While social enterprises are a global phenomenon today, the concept originated in Italy in the late 1980s. A few years later, it appeared in the United States, where philanthropy was a driving force in the non-profit sector, and the term then gained popular currency across Europe in the mid-1990s (cf. Kerlin 2010). While recognizing the conceptual diversity of social enterprises, I define social enterprises as not-for-profit private organizations that provide goods or services directly related to their explicit aim to benefit the community. In Japan, social enterprises are relatively new (Laratta *et al.* 2011). Social enterprises are nevertheless expected to be highly significant newcomers, according to their ability to generate local employment, to support and revitalize local communities, and to contribute to economic growth. According to the Japanese Ministry of Economy, Trade, and Industry (METI), about 8,000 people are engaged in social enterprises in Japan, with their businesses boasting an annual turnover of ¥240 billion, as of 2008 (METI 2008). Social enterprises in Japan tackle a variety of social issues, including childcare support, food safety, environmental protection, community development, and so on.

The Democratic Party of Japan (DPJ)-led national government (2009–12) contributed to a positive environment for establishing social enterprises in Japan. The New Public Commons (*atarashii kōkyō*) has been a policy buzzword in Japanese society since the late 2000s, particularly under DPJ Prime Ministers Hatoyama Yukio (2009–10) and Kan Naoto (2010–11). This term invokes socio-political imagery that attempts to redefine the boundaries of moral responsibility between the state and the individual, with greater emphasis on the virtues of public self-help. The policy rationale for the New Public Commons was enunciated in 2000 by the Commission on Japan's Goals in the 21st Century (*21 seiki nihon no kōsō kondankai*), under the auspices of Prime Minister Obuchi Keizo (1998–2000) of the Liberal Democratic Party (LDP). The commission emphasized the importance of empowering individuals and creating a new public sphere, *inter alia*, shifting responsibility from the state to civil society. Furthermore, this new concept of the public commons was directly reflected in the discussion surrounding the revision of the Fundamental Law of Education, Japan's educational charter, in the early 2000s. One of the discussion records documented: "We are stepping into a new era in which we are supporting a sense of values that we call the New Public Commons. That is, we try to independently solve the social problems we face, including the life improvement issues connected with the daily lives of the local community … " (Central Council for Education 2003, 5).

As one of the relevant examples related to the formation of the New Public Commons, the Tokyo-based NPO Florence is illustrative. The NPO principally provides day care services for sick children. The service was started to accommodate the simple but strong demand of working parents—in particular, working mothers—who cannot help but leave their sick children in childcare centers during the work week. Usually, regular childcare centers ban sick children, deeming their care the parents' responsibility, but all families have children who get sick and few parents can easily get time off work at a moment's notice. Komazaki Hiroki, founder of Florence, identified this problem and thought that it would inhibit creating a flexible society where all have access to childcare, opportunities to work, and possibilities for self-actualization (Komazaki 2007: 63–65). After graduating from college, Komazaki established an NPO in 2004 with the mission of resolving the "sick child care" problem discouraging parents from having a career and raising children at the same time. The NPO hired local experienced mothers, who would visit the homes of sick children, instead of running childcare facilities. In addition, the NPO developed a mutual aid system. A monthly membership plan covers seasonal variations, and ranges in price from ¥7,600–¥8,000 (as of February 2013), depending on the age of the child. This approach contrasts to the pay-as-you-go plans offered by private babysitting companies. Florence provides care for children from sixth months in age through the sixth grade, on weekdays from 08:30 to 20:00. In the past, the public expected that such social services were the responsibility of the local government. However, redefining the public's relationship with the government, ordinary individuals have started up socially relevant businesses actually to solve social problems efficiently and quickly. They have been successful, too. Florence has extended the business in the Tokyo metropolitan area to the neighboring prefectures of Chiba and Kanagawa. In fiscal year 2011, the NPO earned nearly ¥450 million, almost double earnings from the previous year.

Recently, the social enterprise type of NPOs has gained momentum following the March 11, 2011 disaster in the Tohoku region in northeastern Japan. Kawato *et al.* (2012) describe these NPOs, which maintain close working relationships with the local government as well as local businesses, cooperating in the current efforts toward reconstruction that demand coordinated action from all actors. The activities of the Entrepreneurial Training for Innovative Communities (ETIC), a Tokyo-based NPO, are an interesting example. The NPO was originally started as a student organization at Waseda University in 1993 and later gained NPO status in 2000. ETIC is interested in creating programs and training opportunities for young people to help develop social entrepreneurship and start-up venture businesses for the benefit of society—and ultimately, in contributing to social innovation. Shortly after March 11, this NPO started its Disaster Recovery Leadership Development Project, which dispatched young individuals in their twenties or thirties as full-time staff members on reconstruction projects developed by local citizens in the disaster-affected areas. The reconstruction projects spanned all fields: medical and welfare, education, community revitalization, industry revitalization, and so on. The dispatched youth, who would serve from three months to one year, were expected to play key roles in advancing the recovery efforts and addressing the real needs in the communities.

According to ETIC's annual report (ETIC 2012), 74 young people out of a total of 171 applicants were dispatched to 47 projects by the end of February 2012. The annual report actually presents some interesting cases. A 31-year-old woman who was previously working at a travel agency and fair trade company joined a social business. She has taken a leadership role in restarting the production and sale of an octopus charm—a symbol of the recovery of Minami-Sanriku, a small town devastated by the March 11 tsunami, but previously well known for its octopus fishing (ETIC 2012, 10). Meanwhile, a 25-year-old man who was working at a consultancy company jointly established a new business with the local people of Oshika during a leave of absence. His business makes accessories using local materials such as fishing nets and antlers. He is in charge of production management, sales promotion, accounting, generating local employment, and is aiming to establish a sustainable community business (ETIC 2012, 12). This ETIC-led project is operated with local partners in Tohoku, with the goal of nurturing social entrepreneurship. Many stakeholders see social enterprises as a pragmatic organizational means to rebuild communities and businesses destroyed by the 3/11 disaster. Social enterprises—as a new form of civil society—have embarked on various missions in the affected region, and a growing number of self-motivated Japanese youth with a entrepreneurial mindset and professional skills are actively participating in a social experiment to move Japan forward.

Social movements: a sketch of grassroots dynamism

Social movements, or *shakai undō*, have a rich history in modern Japan. Japanese people have highlighted social and political issues through demonstrations and collective organization. Briefly looking at the Japanese social movement landscape in the early post-World War II period, it is clear that anti-nuclear social movements led by peace activists within key umbrella organizations, such as *Gensuikin* (Japan Congress against A- and H-Bombs) and *Gensuikyō* (Japan Council against Atomic and Hydrogen Bombs), became particularly important due to Hiroshima and Nagasaki. The anti-nuclear sentiment was further enhanced after the Lucky Dragon No. 5 (*Daigo fukuryū maru*) incident of March 1, 1954, in which 23 Japanese fishermen were exposed to nuclear radiation from the American hydrogen bomb test at Bikini Atoll. In fact, Japan's anti-nuclear activism in the 1960s, amid the economic miracle, was perhaps some of the most vigorous in the world at that time. In 1960, Japan also witnessed the emergence of the anti-US-Japan security treaty movement, *Anpo*. Directly mobilized by political parties, mostly socialist and communist in orientation, young college students as well as labor unions fiercely clashed with the authorities. Later in the 1970s and 1980s, Japanese social movements then extended the protest "tradition" into environmental (or anti-pollution) activism and consumer movements mainly led by housewives.

Since the beginning of the 21st century, I have been conducting participant observation-based ethnographic fieldwork on Japan's civil society development. My fieldwork has included NPOs incorporated under the 1998 NPO Law, alluded to earlier, as well as several other social movement entities—key actors in Japanese civil society. One of them is a peace group called the Article 9 Association (*9 jō no kai*). As Japan pursued more conservative politics in the mid-2000s, led by hawkish Prime Ministers Koizumi Junichiro (2001–06) and Abe Shinzo (2006–07, 2012–) of the LDP, the Article 9 Association banded together to oppose the revision of Article 9 of the Japanese Constitution—the clause renouncing war and adhering to pacifism. This was initially prompted by Koizumi's decision to send troops to Iraq in January 2004, the first post-World War II deployment in a war zone. Japanese intellectuals, including Oe Kenzaburo (Nobel Prize literature laureate), Sawachi Hisae (author), Tsurumi Shunsuke (philosopher), and others have played vital roles in leading this civic movement, which they launched in June 2004. Local communities and occupation-based groups are the principal actors in the Article 9 Association. Each group sponsored a regular series of independent study groups to discuss and confirm the meaning of Article 9 (Ogawa 2011). The number of grassroots Article 9 Association groups in late 2007 reached a peak level of nearly 7,000. The organization accepts all people, regardless of gender or age. However, the majority of participants apparently belong to the generation that experienced the *Anpo* movement as college students in the 1960s. The return of Abe as prime minister at the end of 2012 poses a new challenge, as he seeks to remove constraints on the military and has stated that he wants to revise the war-renouncing Article 9.

On the other hand, since the late 2000s, I have observed younger citizens organizing a series of demonstrations in Koenji in Suginami Ward, a hub of youth culture in western Tokyo where the many music bars, funky restaurants, CD shops, and second-hand shops attract young people from all over. The demonstrations were the brainchild of Matsumoto Hajime, an owner of a second-hand shop. Cooperating with other owners of second-hand shops and bars, Matsumoto organized a movement called *Shirōto no ran*, or Amateur's Riot. The group has since demonstrated over the past five years against social phenomena such as the deterioration of the working environment and the falling income levels experienced by young people. Amateur's Riot criticizes income disparities in Japanese society, popularly called *kakusa*, and that young people such as themselves are regarded as losers, or *makegumi*. Matsumoto, born in 1974, was a former student activist and a *freeter*—young Japanese workers who are trapped in unstable, low-paying jobs—after graduating from college in Tokyo.[1] I saw one of the demonstrations in Koenji in 2009, and I was impressed with the street party atmosphere. Demonstrators wore whatever they wanted: I saw people dressed in animal costumes and as cosplay girls, kimono girls, and so on. They were dancing, singing, shouting, chatting with each other, eating, and drinking in the streets. The demonstration centered on truck stages from which DJ booths and musicians were blasting punk rock and hip-hop, popular styles of music that featured prominently in the nationwide anti-nuclear rallies following the Fukushima disaster.

The Fukushima nuclear disaster since March 2011 has galvanized anti-Establishment demonstrations. One of the first demonstrations against the Tokyo Electric Power Company (TEPCO), operator of the Fukushima nuclear reactors, happened on March 20, just nine days after the disaster. Sono Ryota, a 30-year-old member of the *precariat*—a newly emerging social class characterized by insecurity and uncertainty, the name of which draws from the adjective *precarious* and the noun *proletariat* (Ogawa 2013; cf. Sono 2011)—stood alone in front of the TEPCO headquarters, shouting, "*Genpatsu iranai*" (no more nuclear plants!). Sono's direct action against TEPCO, which symbolized a winner, or *kachigumi*, in Japanese *kakusa* society, was motivated by some of the same concerns aired at the Koenji demonstrations. In fact, Matsumoto's Koenji-based group organized an anti-nuclear rally on April 10, 2011, just one month after the great earthquake, and perhaps 15,000 people marched, mostly youth.

Consequently, this mobilization of the young was followed by several anti-nuclear demonstrations, including the Goodbye Nuclear Power Plants (*Sayonara genpatsu*) rallies organized by the Citizens' Committee for the 10 Million People's Petition to Say Goodbye to Nuclear Power Plants. Practically, the committee aimed, as its full name would suggest, to collect 10 million signatures against nuclear power plants. Over 8 million signatures were collected as of early March 2013. Ultimately, the group envisions a dynamic shift in Japan's nuclear energy policy toward a more sustainable, renewable energy emphasis. The committee was organized by leading Japanese intellectuals, including several core members from the Article 9 Association, including Oe Kenzaburo, Sawachi Hisae, and Tsurumi Shunsuke, in addition to Uchihashi Katsuto (author) and Ochiai Keiko (author). Actually, it would seem that the participant base of these two major social movements—namely, the anti-constitutional revision and anti-nuclear energy movements—are overlapping. Anti-nuclear sentiments were indeed revived easily nationwide, and the legacies of Hiroshima and Nagasaki were central to the committee's activism. In the document asking for signatures, for example, the committee clearly expresses the purpose of their petition, saying:

> With the issues faced by the survivors of the atomic bombing of Hiroshima and Nagasaki still unresolved, now we have also become victims of nuclear energy. At the same time, we have become perpetrators of damage. Furthermore, we fear that the current situation may result in immeasurable harm to children, including those who are not yet born. Human beings cannot coexist with nuclear power.
>
> (Excerpt from the Petition for the Realization of Denuclearization and a Society Focused on Natural Energy[2])

In fact, this movement convenes its secretariat at the headquarters of *Gensuikin*, which has been a leader in Japan's anti-nuclear movement since the early post-war era. The committee has regularly organized demonstrations against nuclear energy, including rallying 60,000 people in Meiji Park in September 2011, and 170,000 people in Yoyogi Park in July 2012, with vast crowds chanting, "*Genpatsu iranai*" (no more nuclear power!).

Until the recent nuclear crisis, honestly speaking, I observed that ordinary people in Japan, including myself, were not saying much about the country's nuclear energy policy. The issue of nuclear plants was classic not-in-my-backyard (NIMBY) politics. In fact, as Avenell (2012) argues, without victims to defend or the occurrence of high-profile incidents, anti-nuclear power activists enjoyed none of the popular energy that fueled the earlier anti-pollution activism that developed around the outbreak of Minamata disease. Further, for most people living in urban areas, nuclear plants are invisible, as they are located far away in remote areas. Aldrich (2008) makes an interesting point in noting that the locations of nuclear power plants are not selected randomly; Japanese policy makers have chosen locations based on the level of social capital. He further argues: "[B]y placing atomic reactors in rural, depopulating, often poverty-stricken areas where horizontal associations were waning, decision makers hoped to avoid controversy and strife" (Aldrich 2012, 136).

I would argue that young people played a significant role in reversing public apathy in this arena by igniting a kind of grassroots dynamism against the use of any nuclear power. In the spring and summer of 2012, every Friday night, Japanese people witnessed a series of anti-nuclear demonstrations in front of the prime minister's residence. The number of demonstration participants reached 150,000 on July 13, 2012 (although the police reported only 10,000). This series of protests was organized by another group going by the name of the Metropolitan Coalition Against Nukes (*Hangenren*). Thirteen Tokyo-based informal citizens' groups, all of which are active in energy and environmental issues, participated in this network. Since the coalition is a network, there is no one definitive leader. The organizers are in their forties, and Misao Redwolf, an illustrator and head of the informal group called No Nukes More Hearts, serves as a spokeswoman. They united over a single issue: to protest against bringing Japan's nuclear reactors back online after they had all been shut down by May 2011 for safety checks. The demonstrations gained momentum when Prime Minister Noda Yoshihiko decided in June 2012 to restart two reactors at the Oi nuclear plant in Fukui Prefecture. The restart was justified out of concern for an electricity shortage in the summer months, but in fact Japan had enough electricity that summer without the nuclear reactors' output. It appears that the government did not want to let it be seen that a "nuclear-free" Japan was possible and hoped to resume normal operations at the nation's other reactors.

"*Saikadō hantai, Oi wo tomero*" (say no to the nuclear reactors' restart, Stop the Oi operations!) were their rallying cries. One interesting aspect was the diversity of the participants. Among the crowd of demonstrators, in addition to youth, were women (especially mothers with their children), victims from Fukushima, and labor union members. All the demonstrators were venting their anger over the national crisis caused by the disaster at the Fukushima Daiichi nuclear power plant. They got information on when and where to demonstrate via social networking media like Twitter—a great tool for information dissemination and one that publicized demonstration activities. The coalition organized an action at the heart of political power on July 29, 2012 as thousands of demonstrators surrounded the Diet (national parliament) building in Tokyo's Kasumigaseki district, mounting a candlelight vigil. The organizers said the number of participants reached 200,000, although the police estimated the number at around 12,000. This may have been the first time in 40 years that protesters had occupied the National Diet square (Ogawa 2013). I was there.

Japan's civil society: looking to the future

Civil society originally was a product of Western culture, but it is adaptable to various cultural contexts because it is seen to be a powerful vehicle for realizing citizens' interests and promoting reform. In fact, each society and culture molds its own version of civil society. To date, Japanese civil society tends to be seen and portrayed as monolithic, belying the very real differences between types of civil society organizations ranging from NPOs that operate at the behest and in support of the state and social movements that challenge its agenda. Susan Pharr explains that Japan has an "activist state," meaning that through funding and tax treatment, the Japanese state has successfully institutionalized specific kinds of civil society groups to promote state ideology while marginalizing those that take critical or independent stands (Pharr 2003, 324).

Japanese NPOs were institutionalized in Japanese society as a direct response to the great earthquake that hit Kobe in 1995. The government bureaucracy's ineffective efforts to deal with the tragic situation paled in comparison to the impressive work of volunteers at the disaster site. The contribution of volunteers dramatized the need for a social structure that would bolster a voluntary third sector. The examples I raised in this chapter—neighborhood associations, public interest legal bodies, NPOs (both GoNPO and social enterprises)—are all supported by and operated under the "activist state." Further, I would argue that Japanese NPOs have been a key form of agency in the Japanese neoliberal state promoting a small government ideology, especially since Koizumi Junichiro's LDP administration in the early 2000s (Ogawa 2009). In this model, NPOs will continue to play their supporting role under the activist state.

On the other hand, I am struck by the dynamism of contemporary Japanese social movements, focusing on the antinuclear demonstrations following the Fukushima nuclear crisis. The Japanese antinuclear energy movement channels people's anger and uneasiness about the state's nuclear energy policy—embodying a general mistrust of the government—into a political voice. It is such grassroots social movements that can galvanize the Japanese public and propose alternative visions for Japan's future, but can an anti-Establishment social movement revamp Japanese energy policy making given the power of the "nuclear village" (*genshiryoku mura*)? It is has been sustained by institutional and individual pro-nuclear advocates, including electricity companies, government officials, media, and academia, over the past six decades and owns the corridors of power (Kingston 2012). These networks of power defending nuclear energy remain resilient.

Back in 2009, a powerful social movement involving an alliance of organizations put income disparities and the plight of the precariat on the national political agenda and helped propel the DPJ to an historic victory. The DPJ flailed about, however, and achieved very little in terms of promoting the interests of the precariat or addressing income disparities. In 2011, Prime Minister Kan (2010–11) positioned the party to reap reward from the political backlash against nuclear power by calling for a gradual phasing out of nuclear energy, a policy in tune with anti-nuclear public sentiments (70%–80%). Prime Minister Noda (2011–12), Kan's successor, squandered this advantage, however, by favoring nuclear power. A discredited DPJ was thrashed in the 2012 elections and the LDP, architect of labor market deregulation that widened disparities and the main backer of nuclear power, regained control. Thus, in these two cases the politics of the street has not translated into change in the arena of mainstream politics and policy outcomes.

So the question is not whether Japanese citizens are alienated and not if they can be mobilized in large-scale demonstrations, but whether all the sound and fury can be translated into significant policy shifts. Ignoring public opinion and the "summer of discontent" in 2012, Prime Minister Abe stands poised to derail plans to phase out nuclear energy by the 2030s, as promised by the DPJ government. The anti-nuclear movement thus faces a serious challenge with this policy reversal, and it is uncertain it can prevail over the nuclear village's machinations (see Chapter 8). A government determined to override public opinion on nuclear energy has drawn a line in the sand and it is uncertain how civil society can respond to this test of wills.

In giving social movements ample space for activism, but ignoring their policy objectives, it appears that the state is jury-rigging a pressure valve, allowing a venting of citizen anger while powerful institutions proceed with longstanding agendas undeterred. Pharr (2003) reminds us that the state seeks to dominate civil society and has succeeded with NPOs. Taming social movements, however, can't succeed by pulling the purse strings, but biding time while they lose momentum may be a viable subverting strategy.

Notes

1 Matsumoto's homepage is available at hajime.dotera.net (accessed February 12, 2013).
2 The petition document is available on the committee's website at: sayonara-nukes.org/shomei/. The document is available in Japanese, English, French, German, Italian, and Spanish.

Bibliography

Aldrich, Daniel P. (2008) *Site Fights: Divisive Facilities and Civil Society in Japan and the West*, Ithaca, NY: Cornell University Press.

——(2012) "Networks of Power: Institutions and Local Residents in Post-Tōhoku Japan," in Jeff Kingston (ed.) *Natural Disaster and Nuclear Crisis in Japan: Response and Recovery after Japan's 3/11*, London: Routledge, 127–39.

Asahi Shimbun (2009) "Kanmin kyōdō e shikō" (Trial to state-private collaboration), January 30.

Avenell, Simon A. (2010) *Making Japanese Citizens: Civil Society and the Mythology of the Shimin in Postwar Japan*, Berkeley, CA: University of California Press.

——(2012) "From Fearsome Pollution to Fukushima: Environmental Activism and the Nuclear Blind Spot in Contemporary Japan," *Environmental History* 17(2): 244–76.

Bestor, Theodore. C. (1989) *Neighborhood Tokyo*, Stanford, CA: Stanford University Press.

Central Council for Education (2003) *Atarashii jidai ni fusawashii kyōiku kihonhō to kyōiku shinkō kihon keikaku no arikata ni tsuite* (On the Fundamental Law on Education and a basic plan for education promotion in the new era), Tokyo: Central Council for Education, www.mext.go.jp/b_menu/shingi/chukyo/chukyo0/toushin/030301.htm (accessed February 6, 2013).

ETIC (2012) *Annual Report 2011–12*, Disaster Recovery Leadership Development Project, www.etic.or.jp/recoveryleaders/report/annua_report (accessed February 11, 2013).

Kawato, Yūko, Pekkanen, Robert and Tsujinaka, Yutaka (2012) "Civil Society and the Triple Disasters: Revealed Strengths and Weaknesses," in Jeff Kingston (ed.) *Natural Disaster and Nuclear Crisis in Japan: Response and Recovery after Japan's 3/11*, London: Routledge, 78–93.

Kerlin, Janelle A. (2010) "A Comparative Analysis of the Global Emergence of Social Enterprise," *Voluntas* 21(2): 162–79.

Kingston, Jeff (2004) *Japan's Quiet Transformation: Social Change and Civil Society in the 21st Century*, London and New York: Routledge.

——(2012) "Power Politics: Japan's Resilient Nuclear Village," *The Asia-Pacific Journal* 10(43:1), October 29.

Komazaki, Hiroki (2007) *Shakai wo kaeru wo shigoto ni suru* (Making social change a profession), Tokyo: Eiji shuppan.

Laratta, Rosario, Nakagawa, Sachiko and Sakurai, Masanari (2011) "Japanese Social Enterprises: Major Contemporary Issues and Key Challenges," *Social Enterprise Journal* 7(1): 50–68.

METI (Ministry of Economy, Trade and Industry) (2008) *Sōsharu bijinesu kenkyukai hōkokusho* (Report on social enterprises), Tokyo: METI.

MIAC (Ministry of Internal Affairs and Communications) (2008) *Chien ni yoru dantai no ninka jimu no jyōkyō ni kansuru chōsa kekka* (Results of a survey on administrations by territory-based organizations), Tokyo: MIAC.

Ogawa, Akihiro (2009) *The Failure of Civil Society? The Third Sector and the State in Contemporary Japan*, Albany, NY: SUNY Press.

——(2011) "Peace, a Contested Identity: Japan's Constitutional Revision and Grassroots Peace Movements," *Peace & Change: A Journal of Peace Research* 36(3): 373–99.

——(2013) "Demanding a Safer Tomorrow: Japan's Anti-Nuclear Rallies in the Summer of 2012," *Anthropology Today* 29(1): 21–24.

——(forthcoming, 2013) "Precariat at the Forefront: Anti-Nuclear Rallies in Post-Fukushima Japan," *Inter-Asia Cultural Studies* 14(2).

Pharr, Susan J. (2003) "Conclusion: Targeting by an Activist State: Japan as a Civil Society Model," in Frank. J. Schwartz and Susan. J. Pharr (eds) *The State of Civil Society in Japan*, Cambridge: Cambridge University Press, 316–36.

Ridley-Duff, Rory and Bull, Mike (2011) *Understanding Social Enterprises: Theory and Practice*, London: Sage.

Sono, Ryota (2011) *Boku ga tōden mae ni tatta wake* (The reason why I stood in front of Tokyo Electric Power Co. Headquarters), Tokyo: Sanichi shobō.

5 Japan's contemporary media

David McNeill

For a nation with a reputation for being buttoned up and homogenous, Japan has a strikingly colorful and diverse media. The world's third-largest economy boasts a mass-selling communist *and* religious daily newspaper and a readership in the hundreds of thousands for both scandalous tabloid weeklies and highbrow monthly magazines.[1] It is home to one of the planet's most powerful public service broadcasters, the ad-free, quasi-governmental Nippon Hōsō Kyōkai (NHK), which also produces a 24-hour English channel; and the world's most widely read newspapers, led by the *Yomiuri Shimbun*, which has a total combined (morning and evening) print circulation of about 10 million—over 14 times that of the venerable *New York Times*. It publishes millions of manga comics every week, some dealing with high-browed topics such as economic models, history and even Marxism (McNeill 2008). It has one of the world's liveliest and most eclectic Internet and blogging cultures.

Japan is rightly proud of its sophisticated system of media distribution, with almost 100% diffusion of terrestrial TV, one of the world's highest (80%) diffusion rates of the Internet, and (since 2012) full nationwide digital broadcasts. Over 90% of newspapers are delivered to homes and most families receive at least one of the main dailies. Unlike many Asian countries, all forms of freedom of expression are legally guaranteed in Japan, thanks to its 1946 Constitution, written under the US Occupation and reflecting the high ideals of its liberal-minded creators. Article 21 specifically notes: "No censorship shall be maintained." Not surprisingly, visitors to Japan encounter a relatively uninhibited range of information freely available on the airwaves, in bookstores and news kiosks, and in cyberspace.

Yet, that diversity and openness is deceptive. The news media in Japan is highly conservative and shackled by institutional constraints: an unusual and widely criticized system of information distribution that encourages journalists to collude with official sources, discourages independent lines of enquiry and institutionalizes self-censorship. Mainstream reporters shun critical stories about Japan's imperial family, war crimes, the death penalty, religion and other issues, striving to achieve a bland consensus that only rarely troubles the nation's political and economic elite. Critics say powerful talent agencies have turned television programming into inoffensive primetime mush, and an enormous advertising industry has narcotized the nation's critical faculties. Like most advanced nations, Japan's media is highly concentrated and is dominated by just six major companies that are very susceptible to political and economic pressure. If the media's ideal role is to be the nervous system of democracy, keeping it alert and helping citizens to make informed political decisions, Japan can hardly claim to be always served well.

Some of these problems are hinted at in the latest (2013) World Press Freedom survey, published by journalism watchdog Reporters Without Borders. Japan is ranked just 53rd, behind most advanced democracies and even Lithuania and Ghana (Reporters Without Borders 2013). The survey notes that Japan fell from 22nd place because of "censorship of nuclear industry coverage" and "failure to reform" its press club system. Indeed, the ongoing Fukushima nuclear disaster has exposed many of the faults in Japan's media landscape. Even before the triple meltdown at the Daiichi plant began in March 2011, critical coverage of nuclear power was muted at best. Seismologists such as Ishibashi Katsuhiko and leading nuclear heretics, most famously Koide Hiroaki, who accurately predicted disaster, long complained that they were shut out of the mainstream media (Moret 2004; Ishibashi 2007; Koide 2011). Many Japanese had never heard of the Hamaoka Nuclear Power Plant, dubbed one of the world's most dangerous, until then Prime Minister Kan Naoto shut it down in 2011. The media rarely covered it.

One important factor in the dearth of coverage about nuclear power and many other issues is advertising. The electricity industry is Japan's biggest commercial sponsor, collectively spending ¥88 billion (roughly US$1 billion) a year (Nikkei Advertising Research Institute 2012; Honma 2012). Tokyo Electric Power Company's (TEPCO) roughly ¥24 billion alone is roughly half what car giant Toyota spends in a year. This huge spending surely discourages critical scrutiny. The role of advertising in filtering media content is well documented elsewhere (Herman and Chomsky 1988; McChesney 1998), but Japan may be unusual because of the overwhelming dominance of two companies, Dentsu and Hakuhodo. Between them, they handle 70% of all advertising spending in the country, and Dentsu alone is responsible for nearly half. That financial clout allows them to control major chunks of newspaper space and TV airtime used exclusively for their clients. Reporting stories that upset those clients invites a catastrophic loss of revenue. "This is a terrifying prospect for the media," said Honma Ryu, a former advertising executive who wrote a book about the industry (Honma 2012).

Visitors to Japan are often struck by the trashy, irreverent and ribald primetime fare on offer on the nation's commercial television, but few would describe it as intellectually nutritious. Advertising agencies have filtered much of the primetime content, leaving little behind to disrupt the buying mood. Much of the thin entertainment gruel on display during what Japan calls its golden time is the product of talent agencies that provide a conveyor belt of young, handsome actors, lissome female singers, comedians and people simply known as "talent." The stars are groomed into commodities and used to fill out variety programs, dramas and commercials. The biggest of these agencies are Johnny and Associates, a supplier of male "talent," and Yoshimoto Kōgyō, which is famous for managing comedians. Like the studios of Hollywood's golden age, the agencies closely manage their talent and attempt to suppress scandals when they emerge. When Inagaki Goro, a member of the pop group SMAP, was arrested on traffic violation charges in 2001, for example, it was widely believed that his company leaned on the networks to soften their coverage (West 2007).

The dark side of this entertainment industry has been documented, though of course rarely, if ever, on TV. The burnout rate for talent is high and many quickly sink back into civilian life none the richer. One of Japan's most ubiquitous stars, Suzuki Ami, for example, was blacklisted by the industry in 2000 for suing her management company in a bid to end her contract (McClure 2002). For years she simply disappeared from the airwaves, much to the surprise of her fans. *Enka* singer Kobayashi Sachiko also fell afoul of media bosses after she broke with her management company. The talent agencies stay in business by enforcing strict discipline on stars in this way and staying on the right side of the broadcasting and advertising industries they serve. It is important to note, too, that Japan has no independent body to monitor broadcasting content along the lines of the British watchdog Ofcom or the Federal Communications Commission in the United States.

Calculating the exact influence of advertising on media content in Japan is impossible, partly because whistleblowers like Honma are rare. It is instructive, however, to compare domestic and foreign media coverage of Japan's most prestigious corporations when they run into problems. During major car recalls, for example, local coverage is often strikingly low-key. Until Toyota President Toyoda Akio was summoned to testify before the US Congress in February 2010, Japan's mass media gave relatively little coverage to the company's largest ever car recall. Magazines ran stories alleging a US plot to destroy Japan's car industry. We might bear in mind here Honma's view that the "criteria for reporting news in Japan is directly related to the amount of advertising revenue that the media receives."

Given Japan's clear constitutional prohibition on censorship, it is self-censorship, or *jishuku* (self-restraint) that often stops the media from divulging information that is in the public's interest. In the week after the Fukushima crisis erupted, for example, Japan's airwaves filled up with pro-nuclear scientists, including some directly involved in the stricken plant (McNeill 2011).[2] There was just a single notable appearance on TV by an academic critical of nuclear power, according to one careful study (Ito 2012). Fujita Yuko, a former professor of physics at Keio University, speculated on Fuji TV on the evening of March 11 that the Daiichi reactors were in a "state of meltdown." He was never asked back. Journalists covering the crisis quickly settled on the explanation that "partial" fuel-melt was suspected, a line maintained for two months until operator TEPCO confirmed the triple meltdown. As media critic Takeda Toru later wrote, the overwhelming goal throughout the crisis, by both the authorities and big media, seemed to be suppressing panic, not alerting citizens to the possible dangers (Takeda 2011). No evidence has emerged that the government attempted to control TV coverage—it is much more likely that broadcasters controlled themselves.

Jishuku was also evident when journalists from the nation's big media organizations went to report from inside the 20-kilometer contaminated zone around the Daiichi power plant. Or didn't report it: most of the big newspapers and TV companies pulled out of the zone after March 12, 2011, and did not return for weeks, ceding reporting of one of the world's most important and compelling stories to freelancers and foreign journalists. In Minami-soma, the nearest city to the Daiichi plant, reporters evacuated en masse without telling the mayor, earning his public wrath. When questioned afterwards, the journalists said it was "unsafe" in the zone, which is true, but this does not explain why they did not use their considerable resources to protect themselves, or why they did not try to out-scoop their rivals (Birmingham and McNeill 2012). For that, we have to look elsewhere.

Cartels and press clubs

Japanese reporters for the big media organizations have little to gain from breaking ranks during major news stories such as Fukushima because they form cartel-like arrangements to prevent rival scoops. In particularly dangerous situations, managers of

TV networks and newspapers will form agreements (known as "*hodo kyotei*") in effect collectively to keep their reporters out of harm's way. The volcanic eruption of Mt Unzen in 1991 and the 2003 invasion of Iraq, both of which led to fatalities among Japanese journalists, solidified these agreements—one reason why so few Japanese reporters could be seen during the Iraq War, or in conflict zones such as Burma (Myanmar), Thailand or Afghanistan. In these places, freelancers did much of the heavy lifting.

Full-time reporters for Japan's top newspapers and broadcasters are generally staffers with a strict line of command and lifetime employment. The emphasis at these companies is on a heavily descriptive, fact-based style; most careful studies of news gathering at Japanese news organizations estimate around 90% of information comes from official sources (Freeman 2000; Hall 1998; Legewie 2010; DeLange 1998). Not surprisingly, critics have long noted one glaring result: homogenized content (van Wolferen 1990). Investigative reporting is limited and most of the stories carried in Japanese newspapers are not bylined. In practice, this means that journalists have little incentive to get scoops, and freelancers do much of the investigative reporting.

No account of Japan's media landscape is complete without noting the main conduit for this information—its press clubs. Essentially newsgathering organizations attached to the nation's top government, bureaucratic and corporate bodies, press clubs have traditionally been elite closed shops, banned to all but journalists working for Japan's top media. Foreign reporters, freelancers, tabloid and magazine journalists were excluded for decades and have only recently started to gain entry. The Japanese Newspaper Publisher and Editors Association, the main industry to benefit from them, defends press clubs, commending them for their accuracy and calling them "voluntary institution[s]" of journalists "banding together" to "work in pursuit of freedom of speech and freedom of the press" (Nihon Shimbun Kyokai 2013). Critics retort that they are elite news management systems, channeling information directly from what Herman and Chomsky (1988) call the "bureaucracies of the powerful" to the public, locking Japan's most influential journalists into a symbiotic relationship with their sources. Journalists, according to this view, are little more than well-paid mouthpieces.

One of the system's harshest critics is Uesugi Takashi, a freelance Japanese journalist and author. He says rival reporters in Japan often share information and notes with politicians after press conferences or interviews (Uesugi 2010). "In the foreign media, sharing and exchanging information among different companies is considered plagiarism," he points out. In his experience, journalists in Japan must tell politicians beforehand exactly what they are going to ask before interviews, allowing them to prepare the answers. Declining these requests means risking being barred from asking questions. Journalists prevent nonmembers from breaking these rules or indeed any challenge to the system.

The internal workings of this system could be seen during a rare media tour of Japan's secretive gallows in September 2009. Bureaucrats at the Justice Ministry had reluctantly allowed the tour, possibly under pressure from abolitionist Justice Minister Chiba Keiko, who was trying to trigger debate on the death penalty. Hundreds of reporters applied. As chairman of the Foreign Press in Japan, I lobbied on behalf of foreign correspondents and was repeatedly told "nothing had been decided yet." Meanwhile, elite journalists in the Justice Ministry Press Club were being briefed to prepare for the morning of August 27, and to keep the date secret from "outsiders." Sanitized pictures, without the all-important hangman's noose, subsequently ran on

NHK and a handful of other media outlets, along with anodyne reports by trusted journalists. Not surprisingly, the death penalty debate never materialized. Support for hanging in Japan is at a record high (Feigenblatt and Global Integrity 2010). The press club journalists will undoubtedly say they got the best possible information to the public. However, it is possible to characterize this episode in a very different way: elite journalists collaborating with elite bureaucrats to stage-manage a difficult story about an uncomfortably controversial issue.

The other side of the story

Although newspapers are trusted for their accuracy and widely read in Japan, most ordinary people know they overwhelmingly represent the official view, so every week millions turn to magazines for an alternative. Circulation figures for most of the nation's magazines have been slipping for years but the largest weeklies, such as *Shukan Gendai*, *Shukan Bunshun* and *Shukan Shincho*, still sell 250,000–450,000 copies a week. Many of these publications emerged during the immediate post-war years, when they lured Japan's huge urban, mainly male readership with the promise of insights into stories skimmed over or ignored by the mainstream media. Over the years they have helped fill in some of the missing detail about Japan's corporate, political and business elite. In 2007, for example, *Bungei Shunju* carried excerpts from the diary of Ogura Kuraji, a former chamberlain to Emperor Hirohito, in which Japan's wartime monarch predicted that swaths of the South Pacific would fall under his rule. Prime Ministers Mori Yoshiro and Koizumi Junichiro were both wounded in the 2000s by stories in the weeklies alleging they were less than morally upright. The weeklies often perform the same function as, say, the British tabloids—airing a scandal and claiming a political scalp. In 1999, for example, Tokyo's Chief Prosecutor Norisada Mamoru was forced to quit after allegations surfaced in the scandal rag *Uwasa no Shinso* that he had enjoyed a publicly funded affair with a young hostess. The same year *Shukan Bunshun* went to war with one of Japan's most influential media Svengalis, Johnny Kitagawa, founder of Johnny & Associates, detailing a string of sexual assaults against minors. The story was of course ignored by the rest of the nation's media.

The investigative reputation of the weekly press partly rests on one of Japan's most famous modern political scandals. In 1974 Prime Minister Tanaka Kakuei was forced to quit less than two and a half years after taking office when it was revealed he had enriched himself through illegal land schemes. That story was broken not by the 100 or so highly paid and officially accredited journalists hanging on Tanaka's every word in the Prime Minister's Office press club, but by a freelancer named Tachibana Takashi working for *Bungei Shunju*. Magazine journalists in Japan are of course barred from the press clubs, so the best of them know all the tricks for digging around in the political dirt. Two years later, the Japanese public learned that Tanaka had also taken millions in bribes from the US aircraft maker Lockheed to help it sell its TriStar planes in Japan, but they learned it first from a probe by the US Security and Exchange Commission, not from their own media.

"We all knew that Prime Minister Tanaka was corrupt. We all knew it," Takeuchi Ken, one of the journalists in the press club later admitted (Gamble and Watanabe 2004, 51–52). "All the information that … Tachibana used in his *Bungei Shunju* scoop was public information. He just analyzed it and put it together in a way that we did not have to as members of the press club."

It is important, however, not to overstate the case for the weeklies. Many of the stories they carry are not the product of investigative journalism but of malicious bureaucratic or political infighting. Because they often rely heavily on anonymous sources the magazines often simply fabricate quotes, or even whole stories. Like the British gutter press, Japan's weeklies are riddled with racist, sexist and xenophobic content. Many journalism scholars believe their peak has long passed (Gamble and Watanabe 2004). Moreover, despite their reputation for giving a much wider spread of opinions and political perspectives than the mainstream media, it is possible to detect an increasing right-wing drift. *Bungei Shunju*, *Shukan Shincho*, *Shukan Bushun* and *Chuo Koron* are all essentially conservative publications. Several, notably *Seiron* and *Shokun*, would be classed as very right wing by European standards, consistently arguing, for example, against holding Japan to account for its war crimes. In the last few years, the magazines have run increasingly hysterical stories about Chinese intentions in Asia, adding to and greatly complicating the longstanding bilateral historical animosity while stoking domestic nationalism.

Case study 1: punished for a scoop—Abe Shigeo and the *Nikkei*

As a financial reporter for the *Nikkei*, Japan's leading business daily, journalist Abe Shigeo had one of the most prestigious jobs in Japanese journalism when he unearthed a major scoop in 1994. Abe and his team trawled financial statements to reveal that Yamaichi Securities, one of the world's largest brokerages, had buried millions of dollars in red ink off the books, setting up dummy companies to absorb the losses. Corporate extortionists, known as *sokaiya*, had discovered the ruse, so the company was paying them off, but before the story could run, Abe's bosses at the *Nikkei* spiked it.

Yamaichi staggered on for another three years before collapsing in 1997 under the weight of more than ¥300 billion in debt. Abe says publishing the story would have saved shareholders and taxpayers much of that money. Later he learned that the head of Yamaichi had called the president of the *Nikkei* and asked for the story to be buried. To get him out of the way, Abe says the newspaper sent him to its London office into a kind of five-star exile, likening it to *shimanagashi*, the feudal practice of dispatching political troublemakers away to live on remote islands. He eventually quit to work for a weekly magazine.

Abe is not the only journalist punished in Japan for an important scoop. In perhaps the most notorious case, *Mainichi* journalist Nishiyama Takichi found that the Japanese government had agreed to secretly absorb substantial costs of the reversion of Okinawa from the United States to Japanese rule in 1972, including US$4 million to restore farmland that was requisitioned for bases (Sekiguchi 2007; Nishiyama 2010; McNeill 2011b). The story resulted in Nishiyama's public and professional humiliation. He was convicted of handling state secrets after revealing his source, a married Foreign Ministry clerk with whom he was having an affair. The government and certain media outlets hounded both from their jobs. The secretary subsequently divorced; Nishiyama left journalism to work in his parents' business. The mainstream media largely shunned the story until 2000 and 2002, when declassified US diplomatic documents from the National Archives and Records Administration proved beyond all doubt that the secret pact existed. A senior Ministry of Foreign Affairs official later concurred. However, Nishiyama, now in his eighties, has never been officially cleared.

Abe, however, enjoyed a vindication of sorts. He went on to start the monthly investigative magazine *Facta*, relying on subscribers and private money from a rich donor to insulate it from corporate and advertising pressure. In 2011, the magazine revealed that Olympus, one of Japan's best-known corporate brands, was involved in the same illegal practice of burying financial losses. Again, the *Nikkei* initially declined to publish the year's biggest business scoop. It was not until the story made the front pages of the business press in Europe and America months later that the *Nikkei* and other leading vernacular newspapers began catching up. When Olympus' British Chief Executive Michael Woodford tired of waiting for the story to break in Japan, he called a foreign publication, *The Financial Times*. Woodford later noted that even then it still took the mainstream Japanese media a full week to pick up the story, trailing most of the world's major news outlets.

The Olympus story was the product of the same ferreting techniques Abe used when working on Yamaichi. "Our approach is to use the skills we've built up as financial experts over the years to follow irregularities. If you study corporate accounts long enough, something odd often pops up and you follow that trail till you find the reason" (McNeill 2012). He says another ex-*Nikkei* journalist was tipped off to the Olympus problems by a whistleblower. He doubts the journalist could have persuaded his editors at the *Nikkei* to run the story. "There are no real scoops in Japanese newspapers," he says. "They are almost always authorized leaks." The dearth of proper media scrutiny leaves more corporate malfeasance untouched and may be one reason why so many Japanese companies have declined since the 1990s, he adds.

These episodes, stretching over 40 years, point to several systemic issues, none of them unique to Japan: entrenched editorial hierarchies, susceptibility to corporate and political power and a reluctance to challenge officialdom. What's distinctive, perhaps, is how entrenched these hierarchies are among Japan's big media, and the strikingly homogenous responses across the media landscape. Even when the scandals were relatively well known, other media outlets were slow to dig into them, leaving both Abe and Nishiyama hanging out to dry. It is possible to imagine the men being fêted elsewhere as journalistic heroes. In Japan, their diminished professional status recalls a saying in the press club system: "No scoop is everybody's happiness" (Farley 1996, 137).

Case study 2: the lingering taboo—Japan's imperial family

A litmus test of media freedom in Japan is its coverage of the emperor. If journalists and public commentators accept that he is off limits to scrutiny, they will likely accept it elsewhere too. Unfortunately, the media record here is not good. Though officially stripped of his divinity by the 1947 constitutional reforms, the emperor has been treated with great circumspection in the media since. Emperor Hirohito (1901–89) largely escaped journalistic scrutiny about his controversial role in the war. The media tiptoed around anything that could be considered disrespectful, even the dementia suffered by his wife Empress Nagako until her death in 2000. The imperial taboo has lightened since Emperor Hirohito's death in 1989, when his reign was posthumously and without a hint of irony dubbed Showa, or "shining peace." However, the mainstream media still pulls its punches when it comes to the nation's first family.

It was not always so. In the 1950s, the media in Japan was arguably more openly critical of the emperor than it is now, until a famous incident created the template for subsequent coverage. In December 1960, the magazine *Chuo Koron* published a parody called *Furyu Mutan* in which the narrator has a dream that left-wing radicals take over the imperial palace and decapitate Crown Prince Akihito (now the emperor) and Princess Michiko in front of an enthusiastic crowd. In a debate that goes to the heart of Emperor Hirohito's wartime role, the narrator argues bitterly about who was responsible for ending the war. The satire provoked fury in the Imperial Household Agency (IHA), the bureaucracy that supervises the family, and among ultra-nationalists, who demonstrated daily outside *Chuo Koron*'s Tokyo offices. Finally, on February 1, 1961, a 17-year-old rightist broke into the home of *Chuo*'s President Shimanaka Hoji, killed a maid with a sword and severely wounded Shimanaka's wife.

The *Furyu Mutan* incident was a watershed with profound consequences for the freedom of the press. It was an "epoch-making thing, a turning point from fairly open debate about the emperor to implicit taboo about the emperor," says critic and philosopher Asada Akira. "It was much more common to question the existence of the emperor before then" (in McNeill 2005b). The author of the article Fukazawa Shichiro went into hiding, Shimanaka apologized repeatedly, *Chuo Koron* pulled in its horns and other publishers followed suit. The magazine *Bungei Shunju* baulked at publishing the follow-up to (subsequent Nobel Prize winner) Oe Kenzaburo's anti-rightist novel, *17*, and no mainstream publisher ever dared to publish such a satire again. Even today, in a much freer media environment, Japanese people in the public eye are always mindful of the threat of censure and ultra-right intimidation when they consider making pronouncements about the imperial family. Mainstream journalists seldom write anything not officially sanctioned by the IHA as illustrated by Mori Yohei, a former *Mainichi* newspaper correspondent who once covered the IHA. Now a university professor, he gathered material through the freedom of information law to write a book on how much the imperial family costs taxpayers (Mori 2004). He explains that he could not have written such a book as a correspondent, instead having to quit journalism before he could do his job.

The self-imposed reporting restrictions mean that over the years, the foreign media has repeatedly scooped Japanese journalists who failed to get such stories past their own editors. In 1975, Bernard Krisher, Tokyo bureau chief of *Newsweek* magazine, finally asked Emperor Hirohito about his wartime role. In 1992, the IHA successfully persuaded the massed ranks of the Japanese media to obey a six-month embargo on the engagement of Crown Prince Naruhito and diplomat Owada Masako. The story was an open secret among journalists in Tokyo until T.R. Reid of *The Washington Post* broke the embargo in 1993. When the new imperial couple struggled to produce an heir, Japanese journalists who suspected that the princess was receiving fertility treatment were warned off the story, which was later carried in foreign newspapers and magazines. In 2003, Japanese magazines carried anonymously sourced articles that suggested Princess Masako was depressed and wanted to abdicate and get a divorce, but officially accredited IHA journalists who had heard about her depression steered clear. In May 2004, when *The Times* (London) newspaper ran a story headlined "The Depression of a Princess," it was initially condemned, then accepted, by royal watchers in the Japanese media.

Post-Hirohito, Japan's weekly magazines have grown far less circumspect about carrying critical stories on the imperial family. In 2001 one of the most liberal publications, *Newsweek Japan*, carried a prominent feature on Emperor Akihito's admission of his family's mixed Korean origin. Unusually for imperial pronouncements, this one has been barely covered in Japan's newspapers and television, in contrast to South Korea, where it was front-page news. In 2005, *Newsweek* commissioned me to write a front-page story called "Does Japan Need its Imperial Family," though the strict directive was to steer clear of any discussion about abolishing the monarchy. Publication passed without incident. The following year, however, the magazine spiked a proposed front-page article on the imperial succession issue, in the week before Princess Kiko gave birth to the family's first male heir in 40 years. The article, tentatively titled "Wouldn't a Girl be Better for Japan," was judged "against the public mood" by editor Takeda Keigo (McNeill 2006).

Princess Masako, who has virtually retired from official duties for a decade, has been the target of a string of quietly vitriolic articles, often anonymously sourced, questioning her work ethic, dedication to her husband, even her patriotism. In 2006 I interviewed a journalist who penned an article for the woman's weekly *Josei Seven*, claiming that Masako was fleeing Japan for refugee status with her daughter Aiko. When I asked him for sources the journalist said he had made the story up, heedless, apparently, of any professional or personal retribution. Anything goes, apparently, when it comes to the former high-flying diplomat, cut down to size by the Imperial Household Agency. It is noteworthy, however, that as a commoner who married into the imperial family, like her mother-in-law Empress Michiko, she is not protected by the unspoken taboo against publicly criticizing members of the imperial bloodline (Gamble and Watanabe 2004, 23).

Balkanized net

Given the structural rigidities hardwired into the mainstream media, it is perhaps not surprising that Japanese have taken so enthusiastically to the Internet's relatively open frontiers. Over 40% of the population uses social networks and the country leads the world in blog engagement, with more people in Japan spending more time on blogs than any other place on earth (New Media Trend Watch 2012). Some online media companies have become increasingly powerful in recent years, notably the video sharing website NicoNicoDoga (www.nicovideo.jp), which built a reputation in the aftermath of March 11, 2011 for offering real-time news and full press conferences cut short by the main networks.

The dwindling ability of the big networks completely to control the news agenda became apparent in 2010 when leaked coastguard footage of a Chinese fishing trawler colliding with a Japanese patrol boat appeared on YouTube.com after at least one TV network snubbed the story. Japan's government initially refused to release the video, possibly out of concern that it would worsen already strained ties with Beijing. One of Japan's most powerful politicians, Ozawa Ichiro, a long-time critic of press clubs and a self-described victim of a witch hunt by big media and Japan's prosecutors, has turned to the Internet to get his unedited message out to voters (*Asahi Shimbun* 2011). Media critic Uesugi also relies heavily on cyberspace, as one of the founders of the Free Press Association of Japan (www.fpaj.jp), which offers an alternative to the "consensus" news delivered by the discredited press club system. It remains to be seen how much ground Japan's established media will cede to cyberspace in the coming years, or what impact the shift online will have on the problems cited in this chapter. One unedifying trend has been the growth of a distorting online echo effect. Popular discussion websites, most notoriously 2 Channel (www.2ch.net) are credibly accused of fuelling conspiracy theories, xenophobia, ultra-nationalism, and hate speech among young people who distrust the establishment media. As has been noted elsewhere, the Internet in Japan may be offering the promise of more freedom while actually encouraging people to retreat into conservative, Balkanized online communities. Few advanced countries can afford that less.

Conclusion

Paradoxically Japan's technologically rich media smorgasbord does a poor job of elucidating many of the key issues facing the nation, among them nuclear power, the US-military alliance, accountable government, the future of the imperial family and business corruption. Much of Japan's media output can only be considered a vast waste of human talent and resources; cosseted and coopted journalists act as paragons of conformity and seldom challenge power. Unfortunately, there are few signs that Japan's army of media workers is inclined to reform the journalistic status quo.

Acknowledgement

The author would like to thank Mark Austin, Kaori Hayashi and Jeff Kingston for their helpful suggestions and editing.

Notes

1 The *Seikyo Shimbun*, a newspaper run by religious group Soka Gakkai, claims a daily circulation of 5 million–6 million. *Shimbun Akahata*, the daily newspaper of the Japanese Communist Party has a claimed circulation of 1.6 million.

2 Sekimura Naoto, a consultant with the Ministry of Economy, Trade and Industry's (METI) Advisory Committee on Energy and Natural Resources, for example, was heavily featured on NHK. He had written reports verifying the structural soundness of the Fukushima plant.

Bibliography

Arita, E. (2012) "Keeping an Eye on TV News Coverage of the Nuke Crisis," *The Japan Times*, July 8, www.japantimes.co.jp/news/2012/07/08/national/keeping-an-eye-on-tv-news-coverage-of-the-nuke-crisis/ (accessed May 2, 2013).

Asahi Shimbun (2011) "Ozawa Turns to Internet Media to get his Message Out," October 21, ajw.asahi.com/article/behind_news/politics/AJ2011102115407 (accessed April 28, 2013).

Birmingham, L. and McNeill, D. (2012) *Strong in the Rain: Surviving Japan's Earthquake, Tsunami and Fukushima Nuclear Disaster*, New York: Palgrave Macmillan.

DeLange, W. (1998) *A History of Japanese Journalism: Japan's Press Club As the Last Obstacle to a Mature Press*, Richmond, UK: Routledge.

Farley, M. (1996) "Japan's Press and the Politics of Scandal," in S.J. Pharr and E.S. Krauss (eds) *Media and Politics in Japan*, Honolulu: University of Hawaii Press.

Feigenblatt, Hazel and Global Integrity (eds) (2010) *The Corruption Notebooks. vol. VI*, Washington: Global Integrity.

Freeman, L.A. (1996) "Japan's Press Clubs as Information Cartels," Japan Policy Research Institute, Working Paper No.18, April, www.jpri.org/publications/workingpapers/wp18.html (accessed October 6, 2011).

——(2000) *Closing the Shop: Information Cartels and Japan's Mass Media*, Princeton; Princeton University Press.

Gamble, A. and Watanabe, T. (2004) *A Public Betrayed: An Inside Look at Japanese Media Atrocities and their Warnings to the West*, Washington: Regnery.

Hall, I. (1998) *Cartels of the Mind: Japan's Intellectual Closed Shop*, New York: W.W. Norton.

Herman, E. and Chomsky, N. (1988) *Manufacturing Consent: The Political Economy of the Media*, New York: Pantheon Books.

Honma, R. (2012) *Dentsu to Genpatsu no Hodo* (Dentsu and the Nuclear Coverage), Tokyo: Akishobo.

Ishibashi, K. (2007) "Why Worry: Japan's Nuclear Plants at Grave Risk from Quake Damage," *The Asia-Pacific Journal Japan Focus*, August 11, www.japanfocus.org/-Ishibashi-Katsuhiko/2495 (accessed April 5, 2013).

Ito, M. (2012) *Terebi Wa Genpatsu Jiko Dou Tsutaetenoka?* (How did television cover the nuclear accident?), Tokyo: Heibonsha.

Koide, H. (2011) *Genpatsu no Uso* (The Lies of Nuclear Power), Tokyo: Fusosha.

Legewie, Jochen (2010) *Japan's Media: Inside and Outside Powerbrokers*, Tokyo: Communications and Network Consulting Japan.

McChesney, R. (1998) "Making Media Democratic," *Boston Review*, Summer, www.bostonreview.net/BR23.3/mcchesney.html (accessed April 7, 2013).

McClure, S. (2002) "If At First You Don't Succeed," *The Japan Times*, January 16, www.japantimes.co.jp/culture/2002/01/16/culture/if-at-first-you-dont-succeed/ (accessed April 22, 2013).

McNeill, D. (2005a) "Does Japan Need its Imperial Family?", *Newsweek Japan*, December 7.

——(2005b) "What Role Japan's Imperial Family," *The Asia-Pacific Journal Japan Focus*, December 16, www.japanfocus.org/site/view/2164 (accessed April 21, 2013).

——(2006) "Still Taboo After All These Years: Japan's New Imperial Heir and the Media," *The Asia-Pacific Journal Japan Focus*, October 15, www.japanfocus.org/site/view/2247 (accessed April 20, 2013).

——(2008) "A Revolutionary Working for Marx's 'Capital'," *The Independent*, November 20, www.independent.co.uk/news/world/asia/a-revolutionary-reworking-for-marxs-kapital-1026331.html (accessed April 4, 2013).

——(2011a) "Nuclear Scientists Accused of Singing Industry's Tune," *The Chronicle of Higher Education*, July 4.

——(2011b) "Implausible Denial: Japanese Court Rules on Secret US-Japan Pact Over the Return of Okinawa," *The Asia-Pacific Journal Japan Focus* 9(41:2), October 10, www.japanfocus.org/-David-McNeill/3613 (accessed April 12, 2013).

——(2012) "Power Without Responsibility," *No1. Shimbun*, November, no1.fccj.ne.jp/index.php?option=com_content&view=article&id=756 (accessed April 13, 2013).

Moret, L. (2004) "Japan's Deadly Game of Nuclear Roulette," *The Japan Times*, May 23, www.newmediatrendwatch.com/markets-by-country/11-long-haul/54-japan (accessed April 27, 2013).

Mori, Y (2004) *Tennoka no Saifu* (The Imperial Family's Purse), Tokyo: Shinchosha.

New Media Trend Watch (2012) "Japan," www.newmediatrendwatch.com/markets-by-country/11-long-haul/54-japan (accessed April 27, 2013).

Nihon Shimbun Kyokai (2013) "Kisha Club Guidelines," www.pressnet.or.jp/english/about/guideline/ (accessed April 30, 2013).

Nikkei Advertising Research Institute (2012) phone interview, July.

Nishiyama, T. (2010) *Kimitsu o Kaijiseyo Sabakareru Okinawa Mitsuyaku* (Disclose the secret Okinawa agreement), Tokyo: Iwanami Shoten.

Reporters Without Borders (2013) *World Press Freedom*, en.rsf.org/press-freedom-index-2013,1054.html (accessed April 5, 2013).

Sekiguchi, T. (2007) "Okinawa-Gate: The Unknown Scandal," *Time Magazine*, May 1, www.time.com/time/world/article/0,8599,1616328,00.html (accessed April 9, 2013).

Takeda, Tōru (2011) *Genpatsu Hōdō to Media* (Media and reporting on nuclear power), Tokyo: Kōdansha Gendai Shinsho.

Uesugi, T. (2010) "Japanese Journalism is Collapsing," in *No1 Shimbun*, March, www.fccj.or.jp/node/5491 (accessed April 20, 2013).

van Wolferen, Karel (1990) *The Enigma of Japanese Power: People and Politics in a Stateless Nation*, New York: Vintage Books.

West, M.D. (2007) *Secrets, Sex and Spectacle: The Rules of Scandal in Japan and the United States*, Chicago: University of Chicago Press.

Part II

Nuclear and renewable energy

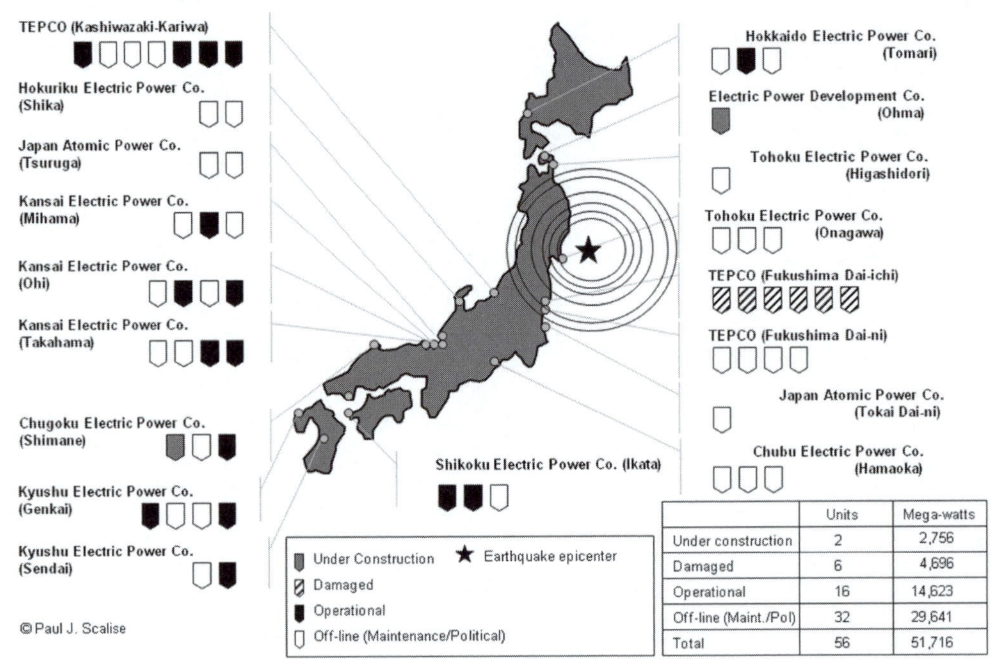

	Units	Mega-watts
Under construction	2	2,756
Damaged	6	4,696
Operational	16	14,623
Off-line (Maint./Pol)	32	29,641
Total	56	51,716

Map 2 Nuclear Power Plant operational Status Map, July 2011
Source: (© Paul J. Scalise)

6 Revisiting the limits of flexible and adaptive institutions

The Japanese government's role in nuclear power plant siting over the post-war period

Daniel P. Aldrich[1]

This chapter systematically examines the Japanese government's deliberate creation of institutions and strategies designed to alter citizen preferences and reduce resistance to often controversial facilities. I show that the Japanese government has not only created such strategies in an attempt to smooth the siting of nuclear power plants and other large-scale facilities, but has continually upgraded and refined these tools as it has learned from its experiences. These results support previous work, which found that bureaucratic and political leaders in democracies are extremely resistant to being swayed by public opinion and, instead, find confluence with public opinion by employing various measures to influence it. This study demonstrates that the Japanese government simultaneously delegates authority for bargaining to private utilities while intensively utilizing a variety of policy tools to structure citizen preferences before any actual citizen-utility bargaining over specific sites. Despite the innovation and flexibility shown by the Japanese central government in pursuing its siting goals through flexible, adaptive institutions, Japanese citizens have stalled or ended many siting projects in the past decade. The compound disaster of earthquake, tsunami, and nuclear meltdowns at the Fukushima Dai-ichi site on March 11, 2011 (3/11), has only slightly slowed the state's attempt to further its nuclear energy goals (see Chapters 7 and 8).

How Japan has been so successful at siting controversial facilities

Observers have been struck by a seeming incongruity: Japan, the only nation in the world against which atomic weaponry has been used, has been able to develop one of the most advanced civilian nuclear energy programs in the world, complete with plans for fast breeder reactors, mixed-oxide (MOX) fuel use, and nuclear fuel recycling, while other advanced industrial democracies have abandoned these goals (Pickett 2002; Aldrich 2010). Even before the 3/11 disaster, utilities in the United States ceased ordering new nuclear plants in the mid-1970s, Germany had set up a moratorium on new plants, and France had cancelled its ambitious plans for a fast breeder reactor. Following 3/11, Germany moved to abandon nuclear power (which provides roughly a quarter of its power), as did Italy, Switzerland, and Belgium (Aldrich 2011). Despite protests that began against the very first attempt at siting reactors in Japan (*Asahi Shimbun*, September 3, 1957) and continued against almost every consecutive attempt (*Hangenpatsu Shimbun*, 1997; *Nikkei Shimbun*, August 6, 1988), along with repeated talk amongst Japanese scholars of a *kaku arerugi* (nuclear allergy), Japanese communities continue to volunteer to host such facilities. Some have even volunteered to host interim and medium-term radioactive waste storage facilities (interviews with Diet (national parliament) members, winter 2002; site visit and interviews at Rokkasho, spring 2012). Even following the hydrogen explosions, full fuel meltdowns, and radioactive contamination caused by the Fukushima crisis, surveys of local communities across Japan show continued support in early 2013, with 54% of 135 host communities approving nuclear restarts (*Yomiuri Shimbun*, January 7, 2013).

In terms of other large-scale public works facilities, such as dams and airports, the Japanese state has also pushed ahead of other advanced democracies. Japan's ministries continue to pursue myriad costly construction projects despite protests from local communities and data showing that initial estimates of long-term demand that triggered project planning were often inflated (McCormack 1996; Kerr 2001). Japan has more than 3,000 dams, eight international airports, and 54 reactors (of which only two are currently operational)—and the current Liberal Democratic Party (LDP) government under Prime Minister Shinzo Abe plans on building more of each. How has the Japanese state been so successful in its planning and siting of nuclear power plants, dams, and airports? Cultural and procedural explanations provide two often heard answers to this question.

Many researchers have argued that cultural factors have been the primary issues in citizen-state relations. Doi (1974), Lebra (1976), Nakane (1978), and Pye (1985), among others, have argued that Japan's political culture involves vertical hierarchy, tradition, social consensus, repression of the self for the sake of the group, and compromise. These culturalist theories share the belief that citizens will often refrain from speaking or acting out against a policy due to peer pressure and socialization. Comparative studies of Japan's political culture have labeled it one of low political efficacy—that is, a society in which citizens do not believe that their input makes a difference in the outcome of political processes (Nakamura 1975). More importantly, Japanese citizens' lack of belief in their efficacy itself acts as a barrier to participation—believing their involvement to be a waste of time, many opt for exit, not voice (Hirschman 1970; see LeBlanc 1999 for an analysis of how women in Japan often remove themselves from the world of mainstream politics). Following Fukushima, however, hundreds of thousands of Japanese residents marched against nuclear power, and a number of citizens have taken on new forms of contentious politics in their protests against nuclear policy (Aldrich 2013a).

Others have posited that procedural and constitutional structures, not cultural factors, deeply affect state-citizen interactions. Cohen, McCubbins, and Rosenbluth have argued that Japan's program lacks access points—that is, channels through which common people can speak directly to decision makers. As a result, citizens and nongovernmental organizations (NGOs) opposed to the program have had little success at slowing down or stopping the construction of new plants as was done in North America (Cohen *et al.* 1995). Similarly, Pekkanen has argued that political factors, specifically the regulations and procedures relating to formal recognition as a nonprofit group in Japan, have created many ineffective local citizen groups and few powerful national ones (Pekkanen 2002a, 2002b). Vosse has similarly shown how nonprofit status has been an elusive goal for the majority of NGOs which remained unrecognized by the central government and unable to incorporate, access cheaper mail rates, receive tax-deductible contributions, and sign contracts (Vosse 2000; see also Nakamura 2002). Groups that sought nonprofit status could only do so with the sponsorship of a government ministry or agency, which would place a retired bureaucrat on its board of directors (Broadbent 2002: 22). Although the number of NGOs has surged after alterations to the NPO law, "[i]n terms of actual policy outcome, their influence has been largely limited" (Kamimura 2001, 13). These analysts have focused on passive structures that may discourage citizens from mobilizing around political and social issues (see Avenell 2010 for a description of the Japanese government's interaction with civil society).

An active and innovative central government

No doubt both Japan's political culture and existing procedures have dampened citizen resistance to government policies. However, this chapter elucidates the extent to which the post-war Japanese central government has created, and then improved, institutions designed to penetrate society to alter preferences and suppress resistance. Earlier studies of Japan's nuclear power field focused on the reciprocal consent between the government and power utilities, arguing that the state maintains jurisdiction over nuclear power but delegates negotiation for specific plants to energy companies such as the Tokyo Electric Power Company (TEPCO) (Samuels 1987). Similarly, Lesbirel (1998) understood that the state had delegated negotiations to the private sector and investigated bargaining power between local communities and private utilities.

This study builds on these earlier works to illuminate how the state simultaneously delegates the task of siting nuclear power plants to private companies but nevertheless seeks to influence civil society through a variety of policy tools. I join with other scholars such as Garon (1997) and Nakamura (2002) in emphasizing the active and creative responses of the state in handling, avoiding, and co-opting citizen resistance. McAvoy (1999) and Jacobs and Shapiro (2000) have underscored the importance of the ways in which public opinion does not sway bureaucratic and political leaders; instead, they attempt to sway it.

This chapter focuses on the ways in which the central Japanese government has attempted to further its national energy, infrastructure, and transportation goals, often over the objections of local citizens. In order to construct the airports, dams, nuclear power plants, and other facilities thought necessary for advanced industrial societies but unwanted by their neighbors, the Japanese state has developed a wide range of methods to further the national interest. This chapter will focus on the siting of nuclear power facilities as that struggle has led to the development of the broadest range of Japanese policy instruments. Although in Japan private utility companies like TEPCO carry out the siting and management of nuclear power plants like private firms in North America, the government in Japan plays a fundamental role in the process. Like other democracies that have promoted energy plans built on nuclear energy, Japan has faced increasing resistance to atomic reactors over time (Rosa and Dunlap 1994). The Japanese state has identified the possible obstacles to its energy plans, primarily fishing cooperatives, local government leaders, youth, and women, and targeted them with programs designed to make them less likely to oppose the technology. Although these strategies have been less successful in recent years, and the Fukushima accident has to some degree cast a cloud over Japan's future nuclear energy plans, the presence of these policy instruments has been under-studied and the Japanese government's role in siting them under-theorized.

Classifying state tools

This chapter builds on the work of Schneider and Ingram (1990) by classifying state tools into five main categories: authority, incentive, capacity, symbolic/hortatory, and learning. Authority tools, "grant permission, prohibit, or require action under designated circumstances" (ibid., 514) and include land expropriation measures. Incentive tools rely on "tangible payoffs, positive or negative, to induce compliance or encourage utilization" (ibid., 515) and, among other mechanisms, involve redistribution to host communities. Capacity tools, "provide information, training, education, and resources to enable individuals, groups, or agencies to make decisions or carry out activities" (ibid., 517). Symbolic and hortatory tools, "bring into decision situations and cultural notions of right, wrong, justice, individualism, equality, obligations, and so forth" (ibid., 519). In Japan, yearly awards ceremonies to "helpful" local politicians, personal visits by bureaucrats to targeted communities, the creation of Nuclear Power Day to celebrate atomic energy, and targeted public relations campaigns on television and in the media comprise some of the hortatory tools that the Ministry of International Trade and Industry (MITI, now Ministry of Economy, Trade, and Industry—METI) has developed. Learning tools are those used by the state to learn from past experience and draw lessons through evaluation. I will argue that METI's Agency for Natural Resources and Energy (ANRE) has constantly monitored citizen responses better to update its tactics and strategies. It has conducted, among other learning tools, environmental assessment and public hearings to learn what issues concern citizens as well as a ministerial council to coordinate analysis of siting problems.

Authority tools: eminent domain

Japan's protection of individual property rights has a long history, but the post-World War II Constitution provided a mechanism for the government to override citizens in certain cases. Called the *Tochi shūyō hō* in Japanese, the law of eminent domain allows government officials at the prefectural and central levels to approve the forced removal of land from citizens for *kōkyō jigyō* (public industries and facilities) projects, which provide not just private goods but semi-public and public ones as well. Railroad tracks, subway stations, power transmission lines, dams, airports, and power generation facilities fall under this designation. Even though private companies often carry out the planning and construction of these facilities, project planners, if a prefectural level committee approves, can expropriate land as necessary (Adachi 1991).

Land expropriation has been used most infamously by the central government during the construction of the New International Airport at Narita in Chiba Prefecture in the mid-1960s and the early 1970s. At that time, activists and farmers in the Sanrizuka Shibayama Union to Oppose the Airport movement refused to sell, and the government, once permission was received to expropriate, sent in thousands of police officers to evict the tenants forcibly. In the resulting battles student radicals and farmers dug into towers and trenches raining metal missiles, Molotov cocktails, and rocks on riots police equipped with water cannon, shields, and staves. Four police officers were killed along with two citizens (Bowen 1975; Apter and Sawa 1984).

The Ministry of Construction (now the Ministry of Land, Infrastructure, Transport, and Tourism—MLIT) regularly uses the Land Expropriation Law to force an end to struggles with local landowners over the construction of dams which would destroy their homes and villages (interviews with MLIT officials February 2003). For example, several hundred citizens had to be relocated because a reservoir created by a recently completed dam in Kanagawa Prefecture would soon submerge their homes (interview, February 2003). Even with the understanding that their resistance could result in receiving less than market value for their property, some refused to sell. The expropriation of land in the Shimouke and Matsubara Dam cases in Oita Prefecture along with the removal of the Ainu minority group in the Nibutani Dam case in Hokkaido provided ammunition to anti-dam opponents who claim that the government relies too heavily on coercive methods.

Japanese authorities have discussed using the expropriation law in the field of nuclear power plant siting, but have never done so. The desire to use expropriation was especially strong during the Maki-machi wrangle, when after many years of the siting process for a nuclear power plant in Niigata Prefecture local citizens successfully brought about a citizen's referendum (*jūmin tōhyō*) that prevented the sale of land to the utility. Internal memos from MITI bureaucrats to their colleagues indicate that they all agreed that the nuclear facility would fit under the legal definition of a "public enterprise," but that the possible negative reaction combined with difficulties in convincing the legal authorities that the plant could not have been located in an alternative location prevent them from using the power. In interviews METI officials stated that they felt if they had used expropriation in the Maki-machi case, future mayors who might have supported the facility would be disinclined to do so (interviews, fall 2002).

Hortatory tools

MITI officials decided that their presence, often lacking in the affairs of communities far from Tokyo, would smooth the siting process of often unwanted facilities, so they began to visit targeted communities to explain the energy needs of the nation and warn about coming shortages if nuclear power plants were not constructed (OECD 1984). For example, in the case of Kaminoseki in Yamaguchi Prefecture, as negotiations between land owners, fishermen, and the utility dragged on for more than two decades, MITI officials visited the local citizens and began a series of talks about the need for the plants in the overall energy scheme (interviews with utility officials, 5 November 2002). MITI and the Science and Technology Agency (STA) also began establishing branch offices and "atomic energy centers" in 1972 in potential host localities to show the seriousness of government intent and to provide bureaucrats with direct access to their constituents. These centers allowed citizens to speak directly with representatives from the central government, a rare event for many of them.

When anti-nuclear groups protested against the Kashiwazaki-Kariwa complex in Niigata Prefecture, the STA sent in the former science and technology minister to give a "pep talk" (*happa wo kake*) to the people emphasizing the importance of building such plants quickly for solving the national "energy crisis" (Kamata 1991, 230). METI officials from local branch offices, such as those in Hiroshima, often travel to or invite local government bureaucrats from local towns targeted for nuclear power to discuss implementing the project. Beginning in 2001, METI and ANRE officials began traveling to the prefectures of Fukui, Fukushima, and Niigata—the prefectures with the highest concentration of nuclear power plants—to carry out public relations activities on a permanent basis in three- or four-person teams (interview with METI officials, 28 August 2002).

Along with "coming to the people" to encourage them to accept nuclear power plants, MITI officials created a series of yearly awards ceremonies to praise officials who assisted in the siting process and "bringing the people to them." Beginning in the early 1980s, MITI and the Prime Minister's Office began a program to celebrate and reward local government officials who had contributed to the successful siting of nuclear power plants and other facilities. This program, called the *Dengen ricchi sokushin kōrōsha hyōshō*, or Citation Ceremony for Electric Power Sources Siting Promoters, occurs annually in July (METI ANRE 2001). At the event, the winners travel to Tokyo to meet with the prime minister at his residence and receive their plaques and certificates directly from him in front of national media outlets (*Asahi Shimbun*, July 28, 2000; July 27, 1989; July 28, 1988; July 28, 1987; July 31, 1986). METI created this hortatory program to encourage mayors from towns targeted for reactors to do all they could (in the face of potential recall elections) to assist the nation (*Denki Shimbun*, July 28, 2000).

Government planners, responding to years of opinion polls that showed that young women and mothers had the greatest antipathy to nuclear facilities, began to focus their efforts on that demographic subset. Newspaper articles have stressed that women sit at the heart of many anti-nuclear power plant campaigns (*Asahi Shimbun*, July 5, 1988). In interviews, METI officials confirmed that women were "important opinion holders" and that they believed swaying their opinion was important (interviews with METI officials, 21 January 2003). The advertisements on Nuclear Power Day—October 26—were often images of women, accompanied by children, with messages of safety, security, and energy needs. Along with focusing on women, Japanese government officials recognized the power held by local fishing cooperatives, *gyogyō rōdō kumiai*. Because Japanese utility companies use water drawn from the ocean for cooling their reactors, the cooperation of fishing cooperatives is crucial to the success of nuclear plants. Japanese law requires companies that impinge on the fishing areas of cooperatives to purchase the rights to those areas in perpetuity, with the fishing cooperative needing a two-thirds majority vote to approve compensation plans for the purchase. Cooperatives have a number of reasons to resist, and concerns about the loss of livelihood along with fears about potential radioactive contamination (JAIF 1966, 10(2)). Reluctant fishing cooperatives unwilling to negotiate with power utilities have stalled and canceled a number of planned projects. In Kaminoseki in Yamaguchi Prefecture, the fishing cooperative at Iwaishima has refused to speak with government or business negotiators, forcing an indefinite delay of the project (interview with local residents in Kaminoseki, 4 November 2002). In Ashihama, Maki, and elsewhere, activist fishermen derailed plans for nuclear plants (Lesbirel 1998); because of these delays, reports have surfaced that utilities have offered as much as ¥15 billion in compensation.

Further, the Prime Minister's Office ordered a number of studies to be carried out to reassure fishermen that the effects of both temperature increases and potential radioactivity would be negligible. The government has also sponsored fish farms that are heated by the discharged water itself along with studies and lectures published in magazines read by fishermen. These studies, published in regular columns in journals such as *Suisankai* (Fishing World) assure readers that they should not be concerned about radioactivity or fishing catch size (*Suisankai* 2000, 2002). In many cases METI contracted the fish farming projects to organizations such as the Japan Fishery Resources Conservation Association, with budgets ranging from ¥40 million for each fish farm. Thus, METI has tried to ensure the cooperation of fishing associations through both reassurance about safety and providing jobs in farm fishing projects.

Incentive tools

METI has created several systems for rewarding communities that host electricity producing facilities, whether hydroelectric, thermal, or nuclear. In the language of political economy, the central government provides side payments to host communities through an invisible redistributive system. The central government created the most well known of such compensation systems called the *Dengen Sanpō* in the early 1970s by institutionalizing previously ad hoc compensation measures. It began as a series of incentives for communities called the Atomic Energy Zoning Plan in Tokaimura district—the first area to receive a nuclear reactor—which provided funds for roads, ports, and bridge construction in the late 1960s. Until 1971, Tokai was the only area to receive this funding from the Atomic Energy Commission. However, after several years of pleas from other localities demanding similar incentives, MITI proposed a Diet bill that would "facilitate the development of local areas near power plants through roads, ports, industrial infrastructure, and radiation monitoring" (JAIF 1978, 17(2), 30). If local governments with nuclear, fossil fuel, or hydroelectric plants wanted a new school, road system, or similar infrastructure project, the government would help pay for a large percentage of it (*Asahi Shimbun*, July 1, 1974).

When first established, the Three Power Source Development Laws had ceilings on the amount of money the government would provide along with a five-year limit (the shorter of the following: the period from start to finish for the plant construction work or five years after its start) (see Yoshioka 1999, 144–45; and JAIF 1974, 19(9), 19). While money was available to all power plant communities, the largest amount went to nuclear hosting communities (Lesbirel 1998, 36). By 2002, out of 20 subcategories of grants and subsidies, all 20 were available only to nuclear power plant communities, with 10 available to thermal plants and 11 to hydroelectric plants (METI 2002, 7). The Dengen Sanpō system fits well with Japan's well known pork barrel system in which the long-ruling LDP distributes money to construction and other firms in conservative rural areas traditionally supportive of the LDP (see Johnson 1982; Woodall 1996). One reporter told me that, "construction firms are huge fans of nuclear power plants, and support mayors who in turn push for additional subsidies and funds that can be used in construction" (*Asahi Shimbun* staff writer, August 28, 2002).

Although officially established in 1974, MITI began to alter the framework for these redistributive channels within two years (*Asahi Shimbun*, July 6, 1976). By 1979, the government provided localities with subsidies of up to 70% of the cost of facilities. The tax rate base for providing them increased from the initial rate of ¥85 per 1,000 kWh in the 1970s to ¥445 per 1,000 kWh by 2000 (Ohkawara and Baba 1998, 7). Further, at the beginning of the program, the money was used for subsidies only for "hard" infrastructural project such as roads, bridges, and ports, but over time METI has allowed localities to spend the money on parking lots, industrial parks and commercial developments (JAIF 1978, (22)). Citizens soon wearied of the *hakomono*, or empty box, approach, where local governments with depopulating, graying communities would build beautiful but unused structures like concert halls, soccer stadiums, and gyms (interview, summer 2002). Because of feedback from communities, MITI soon allowed money to be spent on "soft" items such as job training, publicity, invitations for firms to move to the area, and maintenance for existing facilities. Since then the list of acceptable projects has expanded to cover a range of projects deemed beneficial to the local economy, including interest payments on project loans (Ohkawara and Baba 1998, 8). In 2002, the duration of eligibility for subsidies and grants was increased four-fold to more than 20 years (METI 2002). METI also allows Dengen Sanpō funds to be spent not only on localities that actually have a plant planned or under construction, but even those that are merely considering it (interviews, August 8, 2002). Figure 6.1 details the amount of money available through the Dengen Sanpō since its inception.

Capacity tools

Beginning in the 1970s, MITI came to the realization that citizens had at least two distinct fears about nuclear power facilities. The first involved a generalized concern about health and lifestyle over the possibility of an accident or radiation leakage. The second concern focused on livelihoods, especially for farmers and fishermen, who believed if their community were to host a nuclear power plant, customers would cease to purchase their goods out of a fear of radioactive contamination. MITI responded with a program in which citizens in areas targeted for nuclear power plants would be taken via bus or airplane to other localities to view working power plants and speak with neighbors there. By being exposed to a situation in which the power plant was already accepted, citizens were taught the normalcy of life near plants and shown how farmers, fishermen, and women coexisted successfully with these projects (*Asahi Shimbun Yamaguchi Shikyoku* 2001). One resident told me that the government had flown local residents from their coastal village all the way up to Rokkasho in Aomori at the tip of the mainland of Honshu to see the facilities there (interview with local resident, winter 2002). Utility company employees supported this story and added that the government had also funded trips to the nearer sites of Shimane and Genkai to

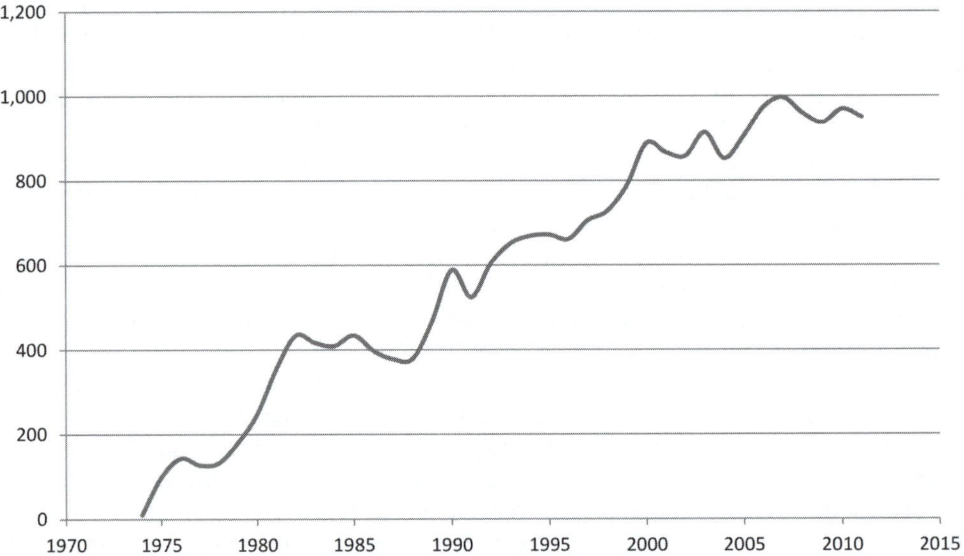

Figure 6.1 Dengen Sanpō from its inception (in hundreds of millions of yen)
Source: (Calculated from data available through METI's Dengen ricchi chiiki taisaku kofukin data, www.meti.go.jp/information_2/publicoffer/review.html)

build "consensus" among local citizens (interview with electricity utility officials, November 5, 2002).

The Japan Atomic Energy Relations Organization (JAERO) began offering 300 or so free classes and seminars a year in the early 1970s to local communities and schools that could vouch for the presence of five or more attendees. Given three weeks' notice, JAERO would send its trained cadre of teachers to schools, houses, hospitals, and public facilities to provide a one- or two-hour seminar on the safety and necessity of nuclear power (JAERO brochure, 2002). Additionally, METI, both directly and through JAERO, provides a number of programs for middle and high school students ranging from educational materials (with a syllabus on nuclear power) to field trips to visit functioning nuclear power plants. To teach children, JAERO provides primers that use events from the history of Japan's nuclear program along with weekly comics often reprinted or serialized in national newspapers and comic books (manga). JAERO records in 2001 showed that educators provided classes and seminars to more than 4,500 people across Japan, ranging from Hokkaido in the north to Yamaguchi Prefecture in the south.

Along with focusing on citizens who live (or could live) near nuclear power plants, MITI began programs to educate and train local government officials and leaders to convince their citizens of the importance of their role in the larger energy program. In the 1980s, the central government began to invite local government officials from areas suitable for nuclear power plants. In these three-day seminars, organizations like JAERO provide information to local politicians and town council members detailing the funding that will be made available to the community and laying out arguments for the plant along with ways to handle negative reactions. MITI set up a "Junior Leaders Conference" where information on nuclear plants was passed along to town politicians and bureaucrats along with bringing in leaders from "failed" siting attempts to explain what went wrong (interview with bureaucrats, winter 2002).

Learning tools

Over time, as citizen resistance has increased, the government decided that a more coordinated approach to siting, involving not only the prime agency of MITI/METI but also agencies like MOC (now MLIT) which issues relevant permits, the Ministry of Finance which approves the budget, and the Environment Agency, which theoretically could suspend the siting process on environmental grounds, would further assist the siting process. In December 1976 the government established the Ministerial Council for Promoting a Comprehensive Energy Policy (Sōgō Enerugi Taisaku Suishin Kakuryō Kaigi) under the chairmanship of the prime minister. It had two main strategies for furthering siting: first, setting up a liaison meeting for the construction of power plants; and second, designation by the council of a power plant as an Important Electric Power Resource Requiring Special Measures (Yō Taisaku Juyō Dengen). Being designated as such allows localities to receive additional levels of subsidies, up to double the normal levels.

Further, because of increasing responsibilities, MITI moved in 1970 to discharge its public relations activities to JAERO which receives all of its funding from the government. Then, to handle the enormous amount of material directed at encouraging localities to take on nuclear power plants, MITI bureaucrats spun off the Japan Industrial Location Center in 1978. This organization then created the Center for the

Development of Power Supply Regions in 1990. The Industrial Location Center handled not only nuclear power plant siting, but also unwanted facilities like petroleum storage facilities along with overall public acceptance issues until 1990. Then, it tightened its focus to assist with large-scale factories, *kombinato* (chemical plants), and the like, and the Center for the Development of Power Supply Regions became the sole organization handling public relations campaigns for nuclear, thermal, oil, and electricity generating facilities. It handles the execution of the Dengen Sanpō and acts as a clearinghouse for information on the benefits of hosting nuclear power plants. The Center publishes monthly bulletins and updates communities on the economic and administrative programs available to them as hosts. The Center is also responsible for the annual Electricity Home Town Fair at the Makuhari Mese Convention Center outside Tokyo in Chiba. Confronting fears that the presence of a nuclear power plant would drive away customers, the fair is a prominent branding event that heightens public awareness of local products from these hosting communities and has actually increased sales (interview, November 20, 2002).

Conclusions: continuity, not change, post-disaster

The 3/11 compounded disaster took the lives of roughly 16,000 coastal residents in the Tohoku region, damaged thousands of homes and businesses along with transportation infrastructure, and altered the broader perspective of the "nuclear renaissance" of the time while puncturing the "safety myth" promoted by advocates of the atomic energy program from the outset. A number of advanced industrial democracies, including Germany, Belgium, Italy, and Switzerland, moved away from nuclear power despite the economic costs. In the wake of the Fukushima meltdowns, Prime Minister Naoto Kan expressed a desire to end Japan's dependence on nuclear power and his policy of subjecting reactors to stress tests led to the shut-down of all of Japan's 50 reactors by May 2012. Opinion polls showed a sea change in the public's perception of nuclear energy—until March 2011 the majority of Japanese citizens supported the continuation of Japan's nuclear policy and the creation of new nuclear plants. Following the disaster, which has made tens of thousands perhaps permanently homeless because of radioactive contamination in their hometowns, more than 70% of the population wished to replace nuclear power with other sources. Nonetheless, in June 2012 Prime Minister Yoshihiko Noda approved the restart of two reactors and adopted a more positive stance on nuclear power. Since the election of the LDP in the Lower House elections in December 2012, decision makers reverted to supporting the pre-Fukushima national goals of relying on nuclear energy and building new plants. This policy shift is welcomed by utilities because they have invested heavily in nuclear capacity at the government's behest while many hosting communities support reactor restarts so that the flow of financial rewards will resume.

Overall, the period after the 3/11 reactor meltdowns can be seen as one involving more continuity than change. While communities near existing nuclear power plants that do not receive inducements are opposed to restarting reactors because they face the same risks without the benefits of hosting communities, a majority of hosting communities support restarts despite all the negative publicity (Aldrich 2013b). Because the tremendous subsidies from the Dengen Sanpō have created a "cycle of addiction" (Hasegawa 2004) and a "culture of dependence" (Fackler and Onishi 2011), many Japanese localities continue to envision nuclear power plants not as a hazard but instead an economic benefit. That said, a number of current host communities, as mentioned previously, have indicated that they do not support restarts. Whether this is a negotiating ploy to gain additional subsidies or a reflection of new anxiety remains to be seen. The Japanese institutions that have sought to influence energy discourse remain in place and active. While the new Nuclear Regulation Agency (NRA) seems to be taking its job of formulating stricter safety standards seriously, whether it can show independence from the state in the medium and long term remains uncertain.

This chapter has shown how the development of the world's most advanced commercial nuclear program (in terms of the closed fuel cycle, the use of MOX fuel, and the creation of recycling facilities) was not an organic, bottom-up process, but rather a top-down one involving a variety of specialized policy instruments. Rather than envisioning the views of the public as the base on which to build energy policies, the Japanese government's Agency for Natural Resources and Energy along with a variety of related quasi-governmental organizations have sought to lead the public. Through financial incentives, wooing of local elites, public awards ceremonies, educational programs for women and children, targeted jobs for fishermen, and the creation of annual "hometown fairs," the state has hoped to bring civil society on board as an ally, or at least divide it, in the promotion of this controversial technology.

The 3/11 disaster, while causing many Japanese citizens to doubt the use of nuclear energy, has not generated major changes in political institutions governing and promoting the field (although the NRA may serve as a counterbalance), nor has it altered the financial realties for local host communities. The LDP and Prime Minister Abe have "reset" the government's approach to pre-Fukushima days. Since the 1950s, the Japanese government's innovative and adaptive approach to nuclear power has focused on convincing the public and those local communities that bear the bulk of the negative externalities that nuclear power is safe and necessary. Given how devastating the nuclear disaster has been to the hosting towns in Fukushima, and the belated October 2012 admission by TEPCO that it was negligent in not adopting appropriate safety measures, including evacuation drills in the event of an accident, the time seems ripe for the state to embrace democratic, transparent, and participatory decision-making processes and treat citizens as partners, and not targets for persuasion.

Note

1 An earlier version of this chapter appeared as "The Limits of Flexible and Adaptive Institutions: The Japanese Government's Role in Nuclear Power Plant Siting over the Post War Period," in S. Hayden Lesbirel and Daigee Shaw (eds) *Managing Conflict in Facility Siting: An International Comparison*, Cheltenham, UK and Northampton, MA: Edward Elgar Publishing Ltd, 2005, 109–34. With permission from Edward Elgar publishers, I have updated and revised the chapter for inclusion in this edited volume. Thank you to Ruth Atherton of Edward Elgar for clearing permission, Jeff Kingston for his suggestions, the Japan–US Educational Commission (JUSEC) under Dr Satterwhite for the Fulbright fellowship which provided support while this chapter was revised, and Ken Hartman for advice and editing.

Bibliography

Adachi, Tadao (1991) *Tochi shūyō Seido no Mondaiten* (Some problems with the land expropriation system), Tokyo: Nihon Hyoron Sha.

Aldrich, Daniel P. (2010) *Site Fights: Controversial Facilities and Civil Society in Japan and the West*, Ithaca: Cornell University Press.

——(2011) "Nuclear Power's Future in Japan and Abroad: The Fukushima Accident in Social and Political Perspectives," *ParisTech Review*, August 25.

——(2013a) "Rethinking Civil Society-State Relations in Japan after 3/11," *Polity* 45(2).

——(2013b) "A Normal Accident or a Sea-Change? Japanese Communities Respond to the 3/11 Disaster," *Japanese Journal of Political Science.*

Apter, David and Sawa, Nagayo (1984) *Against the State: Politics and Social Protest in Japan*, Cambridge, MA: Harvard University Press.

Asahi Shimbun Yamaguchi Shikyoku (2001) *Kokusaku no yukue: Kaminoseki genpatsu Keikaku no Nijū nen* (The direction of national policy: 20 years of planning for a nuclear power station at Kaminoseki), Kagoshima: Nanbo Shinsha.

Avenell, Simon (2010) *Making Japanese Citizens: Civil Society and the Mythology of the Shimin in Postwar Japan*, Berkeley: University of California Press.

Bowen, Roger (1975) "The Narita Conflict," *Asian Survey* 15(7): 598–615.

Broadbent, Jeffrey (2002) "Japan's Environmental Regime: The Political Dynamics of Change," in Uday Desai (ed.) *Environmental Politics and Policies in the Industrialized Countries*, Cambridge, MA: MIT Press.

Center for the Development of Power Supply Regions (1997) *Outline of Operations Booklet.*

Cohen, Linda, McCubbins, Matthew and Rosenbluth, Frances (1995) "The Politics of Nuclear Power in Japan and the United States," in Peter Cowhey and Matthew McCubbins (eds) *Structure and Policy in Japan and the United States*, Cambridge: Cambridge University Press, 177–202.

Doi, Takeo (1974) *Amae no Kōzō* (The structure of dependence), Tokyo: Kobundo.

Fackler, Martin and Onishi, Norimitsu (2011) "Utility Reform Eluding Japan after Nuclear Plant Disaster," *The New York Times*, May 31.

Garon, Sheldon (1997) *Molding Japanese Minds*, Princeton, NJ: Princeton University Press.

Hangenpatsu Shimbun (Anti Nuclear Newspaper) (1978–98) *Issues 1–240*, Tokyo: Hangenpatsu Undō Zenkoku Renraku Kai.

Hasegawa, Koichi (2004) *Constructing Civil Society in Japan: Voices of Environmental Movements*, Melbourne: TransPacific Press.

Hirschman, Albert (1970) *Exit, Voice, and Loyalty*, Cambridge, MA: Harvard University Press.

Jacobs, Lawrence and Shapiro, Robert (2000) *Politicians Don't Pander*, Chicago: University of Chicago Press.

JAERO (Japan Atomic Energy Relations Organization) (Zaidan Hōjin Nihon Genshiryoku) (2002) *Activities Report.*

JAIF (Japan Atomic Industrial Forum) (n.d., various years) *Atoms in Japan Industry Notes.*

Johnson, Chalmers (1982) *MITI and the Japanese Miracle*, Stanford: Stanford University Press.

Kamata, Satoshi (1991) *Kamata Satosho no Kiroku 3: Shōsūha no Koe* (The third diary of Kamata Satoshi: the voices of small groups), Tokyo: Iwanami Shoten.

Kamimura, Naoki (2001) *Japanese Civil Society, Local Government, and US-Japan Security Relations in the 1990s: A Preliminary Survey*, Japan Center for Area Studies Occasional Paper 11.

Kerr, Alex (2001) *Dogs and Demons: The Fall of Modern Japan*, London: Penguin Books.

LeBlanc, Robin (1999) *Bicycle Citizens*, Berkeley: University of California Press.

Lebra, Takie (1976) *Japanese Patterns of Behavior*, Honolulu, HI: University of Hawaii Press.

Lesbirel, S. Hayden (1998), *NIMBY Politics in Japan*, Ithaca: Cornell University Press.

McAvoy, Gregory (1999) *Controlling Technocracy: Citizen Rationality and the NIMBY Syndrome*, Washington, DC: Georgetown University Press.

McCormack, Gavan (1996) *The Emptiness of Japanese Affluence*, New York: M.E. Sharpe.

METI (Ministry of Economy, Trade, and Industry) (2002) *Dengen ricchi no Gaiyō* (A summary of power supply siting).

METI ANRE (Agency for Natural Resources and Energy) (2001) *Heisei 13 nendo Dengen ricchi sokushin kōrōsha hyōshō ni tuite* (About the 2001 citation ceremony for electric power sources siting promoters).

MITI (Ministry of International Trade and Industry) (n.d.) *Dengen sanpō katsuyō jireishū* (Listing of actual uses of the three laws relating to electricity production), Tokyo.

Nakamura, Karen (2002) "Resistance and Co-optation: The Japanese Federation of the Deaf and its Relations with State Power," *Social Science Japan Journal* 5(1): 17–35.

Nakamura, Kikuo (ed.) (1975) *Gendai Nihon no Seiji Bunka* (Modern Japanese political culture), Kyoto: Mineruba Publishers.

Nakane, Chie (1978) *Tateshakai no rikigaku* (The workings of vertical society), Tokyo: Kodansha.

OECD (Organisation for Economic Co-operation and Development) (1984) *Nuclear Power and Public Opinion*, Paris: OECD.

Ohkawara, Toru and Baba, Kenshi (1998) *Nuclear Power Plant Siting Issues in Japan*, Central Research Institute of the Electric Power Industry, Report EY97003.

Pekkanen, Robert (2002a) "Japan's New Politics? The Case of the NPO Law," *Journal of Japanese Studies* 26(1), winter.

——(2002b) "Hō, kokka, shimin shakai" (Law, the state, and civil society), *Leviathan* 27.

Pickett, Susan (2002) "Japan's Nuclear Energy Policy," *Energy Policy* 30: 1337–55.

Pye, Lucian (1985) *Asian Power and Politics*, Cambridge, MA: Harvard University Press.

Rosa, Eugene and Dunlap, Riley (1994) "Poll Trends: Nuclear Power: Three Decades of Opinions," *Public Opinion Quarterly* 58: 295–324.

Samuels, Richard (1987) *The Business of the Japanese State*, Ithaca: Cornell University Press.

Schneider, Anne and Ingram, Helen (1990) "Behavioral Assumptions of Policy Tools," *The Journal of Politics* 52: 510–29.

Suisankai (Fishing World) (2000) *Genpatsu to Gyogō no Kyōsan wa Kanō ka* (Can fishing cooperatives and nuclear plants live together?), 2: 64–67.

Vosse, Wilhelm (2000) *The Domestic Environmental Movement in Contemporary Japan*, unpublished PhD dissertation, University of Hanover, Germany.

Woodall, Brian (1996) *Japan Under Construction*, Berkeley: University of California Press.

Yoshioka, Hitoshi (1999) *Genshiryoku no Shakaishi* (The social history of nuclear power), Tokyo: Asahi Shimbun Sha.

7 Who controls whom?

Constraints, challenges and rival policy images in Japan's post-war energy restructuring

Paul J. Scalise[1]

Introduction

In the early days of the new millennium, representatives from the Federation of Electric Power Companies of Japan (FEPC) approached Liberal Democratic Party (LDP) members behind the scenes. They requested a hearing on a Ministry of Economy, Trade and Industry (METI)-sponsored bill that would force power companies to develop renewable energy sources for on-grid consumption at a time when rising electricity prices, difficulties in securing supply, and scandalous examples of failed liberalization attempts abroad were already dimming prospects of further reforms at home. The FEPC had the support of numerous groups, both within the business community and among consumers. These supporters were by no means resource poor, and their diversity seemed to assure that they would have legitimacy in the public eye, too. The LDP members were receptive, and the initiative to block the renewable energy bill began in earnest.

Sometimes a political battle seems to tick all the right theoretical boxes for success, yet still fails to win. The fight to block the renewable energy bill was just such an issue. Electric power companies and their allies disliked most renewable energy sources because they were well known to be costly, unreliable, and lacking in density and scale, meaning that many new generating sites would have to be found. Opponents of the bill were well connected, gave campaign contributions to both the government and the opposition, had the vocal support of energy-intensive corporations wanting lower prices and higher security, and had key support of well-established politicians and other allies within the ministries. Their issue was consistent with the public's wish for higher disposable income, and had minimal organized opposition in Japan. In contrast, proponents of renewable energy in Japan, which was part of a global "green" movement of advocacy journalists, activist scholars, and alternative energy firms, began in the late 1980s as a fledgling technology but attracted only limited and vague support. Nevertheless, on June 7, 2002, despite organized resistance from the electric power industry, the Act on Special Measures Concerning the Use of New Energy by Operators of Electric Utilities (Act No. 62) passed.

Ten years later, another opportunity to sideline a renewable energy initiative arose, this time a bill forcing the electric power companies to purchase renewable energies at pre-determined rates known as the feed-in-tariff (FIT) for fixed periods of time in order to entice suppliers into the Japanese market. The costs to the utilities would then be passed along to ratepayers, thus raising what were already some of the highest electricity prices in the industrial world and further decreasing consumer welfare. Once again, the electric power companies and their allies in business and the ministries objected—this time, publicly and vociferously. Nevertheless, on August 30, 2011, despite organized resistance by a range of incumbent political actors, another renewable energy bill passed into law. Why?

Much has been written about political resource endowments and their influence (or lack thereof) in political decision-making theory. In a sense, it is fairly well accepted that political resources manage to induce the support of economically depressed and fragmented local host communities for the siting, licensing, and construction of essential facilities such as hydroelectric dams, nuclear power plants, and high-transmission electric power towers (Lesbirel 1998; Aldrich 2008; also see Chapter 6). Unlike the execution of *existing* policies designed to induce top-down local compliance, however, the issue of who controls whom at the national policy-making level—the classic "who governs" debate surrounding all of Japanese political economy—is a much more complicated process. Previous scholarly attempts to identify exactly *who* governs the electric power and energy sectors—the politicians, the bureaucracy, or the private sector—have led some scholars to conclude that no one actor clearly dominates the others (c.f. Johnson 1978; Samuels 1987; Scalise 2009; Hymans 2011). The question therefore seems not to be *who controls whom*, since that varies over time, but *how* and perhaps *when* structural reform takes place.

In this chapter, we discuss the history and drivers of change in Japanese post-war energy market restructuring on both an economic and political level. The analysis reveals that many of the untested assumptions regarding alleged profit-maximizing, goal-oriented economic behavior of well-organized actors utilizing political resources to capture beneficial policies (rent seeking) in the decision-making process fail to explain puzzling market transformations adequately. Japan's electric power sector has been plagued by rising electricity prices, declining operating profits, and mounting institutional and systemic obstacles in turning the tide for decades. Rather than ignoring these counter-intuitive market developments, the chapter builds upon the work of Goldstein and Keohane (1993), Jones (2001), Woll (2008), and other scholars suggesting that objective or material self-interest is subordinate to ideational roadmaps—sometimes called "policy images"—guiding actor preferences, decisions, and perceptions of fairness. We begin by analyzing one of the most salient casualties of these conflicting policy images: consumer welfare.

High prices, negative images, and declining profits

Observers often note a distinct feature of the Japanese electric power market. Despite having some of the lowest electricity losses to the transmission and distribution grid in the industrialized world, few blackouts, and relatively high technical, allocative and scale efficiencies compared to American and other foreign utilities, Japanese retail prices for electricity remain among the highest in the world (Goto and Tsutsui 1998; Hattori 2002; Tone and Tsutsui 2007; Scalise 2012). Before the tragic events of the triple earthquake-tsunami-nuclear disaster of March 11, 2011 (3/11), residential rates converted for purchasing power parities averaged US$182.8 per megawatt-hour (MWh) in 2010, while the Organisation for Economic Co-operation and Development (OECD) average was 20% lower. What was true for households was even more noticeable for industry. Japanese industrial customers paid the second highest electricity prices in the OECD (US$154.3/MWh) compared to the average of US$110.8 (OECD and IEA

2012, 132). In addition, they would have saved US$27 billion had they paid OECD average prices which were some 30% lower.[2] What caused these high electricity prices?

Most analyses begin with Japan's market structure. Created in 1951 out of the remnants of the country's semi-nationalized mega-utility and regional distribution companies, or *hassoden*, nine vertically integrated, privately owned electric power companies emerged. These companies, known as general electric power utilities, or *ippan denki jigyōsha*, were the product of "natural monopoly" theory—the globally accepted economic idea that one firm literally "monopolizing" the high upfront costs associated with construction and maintenance of a high-power transmission grid not only avoided wasteful duplication of network assets by new entrants into the market, but also allowed for economies of scale and a reasonable return on investment (Joskow 1997, 2000). These nine de facto exclusive franchises directly controlled roughly 80% of their respective regions' electricity power needs on a kilowatt-hour (kWh) basis via a densely packed and complex network of generation, transmission, and distribution assets. Because of an historical accident in which foreign technologies were imported from two different countries, however, Japan literally became a nation divided. Eastern Japan, or the 50Hz region, occupied 43% of the network spanning from Tokyo to Hokkaido. Western Japan, or the 60Hz region, occupied the remaining 57% of the network. Because electrical output must be maintained at a fixed setting, Japan requires frequency converters to transfer electricity from the 50Hz region to the 60Hz region. However, the capacity of these converters is limited in scope, creating bottlenecks at key cross-border areas between prefectures and service regions (Scalise 2012).

In the early post-war period, these transmission constraints barely mattered. Japan's electricity prices were not only comparable to the rest of the industrial world, but the low transmission losses over long distances suggested that the economic theory of natural monopoly worked. In 1961, Japanese consumers paid on average 10%, 12%, and 54% less than consumers in the United States, UK, and West Germany, respectively (Sangyō kōzō chōsakai 1964). This price equilibrium shifted suddenly and dramatically in the aftermath of the 1973 Arab–Israeli War (see Figure 7.1a). When Arab states placed an embargo on oil exports to the West, including Japan, oil prices increased four-fold, thus putting upward pressure on electric utility fuel costs and expenditures. The share of imported fuel costs in Japan's average electricity price rose from 20% to over 40%. Perhaps not surprisingly, an electricity market relying on three-quarters of its generation to come from what was once believed to be an inexpensive imported fossil fuel experienced a major shock. Calls for *gaman*, or patience, initially proved credible, as power companies reassured the public that Japan's import vulnerability and lack of self-sufficiency were unavoidable facts of life.

Nevertheless, these arguments became difficult to justify over time as oil prices readjusted downwards, but electricity prices remained conspicuously high. The coming years saw the Japanese-language media, Diet (national parliament) standing committees, and *shingikai* (ministerial advisory councils) act as strategic policy venues for opposing groups interested in creating rival narratives to identify villains, explain high prices, and promote policy agendas.

The Japan Communist Party (JCP), longtime vocal critics of the electric power industry, first suggested in the 1980s that electricity prices would be lower if executive compensation and personnel costs were reduced substantially (*Asahi Shimbun*, February 18, 1986). Yet personnel costs, while certainly higher than wages in the average manufacturing sector, never exceeded 27% of the average electricity price in the 1950s and steadily declined thereafter, indicating that personnel costs were not driving high electricity prices (Figure 7.1a). Taxes, too, were held up to close scrutiny by lobbyists and interest groups seeking either relief or to downplay the comparative generation cost advantage of nuclear power. To be sure, Japanese electricity prices incorporated five separate taxes into the pricing structure: corporate tax (*hōjin zei*), enterprise tax (*jigyō zei*), electric power development tax (*dengen kaihatsu zei*), fixed asset tax (*kotei shisan zei*), and miscellaneous taxes (*zatsu zei*). Yet, unlike European countries like Denmark, Austria, and the Netherlands where taxes would constitute anywhere between 25% and 50% of the retail electricity price (Jacobs 1999), Japan's electricity-related taxes never exceeded 7% of the consumer's burden. Nor were interest payments on debt a driver of high electricity prices, despite high corporate leveraging and calls by institutional investors for greater returns on shareholders' equity. Interest rates remained artificially low while debt service expenditures fell year-on-year after 1986.

The principal driver behind Japan's chronically high post-oil shock retail prices was the conflicting nature of supply and demand in a geographically constrained and densely populated industrial economy. Once thought to be mere conditions of high worldwide oil prices in the wake of the 1973–74 oil shock—circumstances that could not be fixed easily—Japan's persistently high electricity prices after oil prices (and by extension fuel costs) readjusted downwards in 1985 stemmed from two increasingly incompatible preferences of the general electorate: a desire by consumers for abundant, stable, relatively inexpensive, and environmentally friendly electric power versus a growing intolerance of risk by those living near the facilities.

On the supply side of the equation, the law required electric power companies to provide "universal service." Article 18(2) of Section 2 of the Electric Power Industry Law, METI, stated that an electric power company could "not refuse to supply electricity to meet general demand in its service area … without justifiable grounds." Failure to comply would incur huge financial penalties (Lesbirel 1990, 270). Since electricity cannot be stored in large quantities, utilities were forced to build generating facilities capable of meeting peak demand from any and all consumers. On the demand side of the equation, however, rising power consumption coupled with emerging "not-in-my-backyard" activism, or NIMBYism, led to protracted negotiations with farmers, fishermen, and other civil-society actors leading to cost overruns and delays (Fischel 2001; Aldrich 2008). As foreign and domestic news of nuclear criticality accidents, hydroelectric dam failures, and other negative images exacerbated Japan's already delicate siting problems, civil society's uneasiness about such essential facilities grew in the 1980s. Consequently, electric power reserve margins—the extra capacity above what was needed—gradually declined compared to other industrial electricity markets as demand slowly outpaced supply (Newbery and Green 1996; Scalise 2009, 99).

Despite facing local siting challenges to essential facilities, the pressure to build and maintain stability within a technically efficient grid system translated into three interrelated costs passed onto electricity consumers in 1986–97: maintenance, depreciation, and "other" (Figure 7.1b). Each cost—maintenance (187% increase), depreciation (333% increase), other (385% increase)—was a reflection of the mounting hurdles to ensuring energy security, environmental friendliness, and supporting economic growth.[3] Each was a reflection of the rising construction and operating costs associated with siting delays and increased regulations for all large-scale generation sources to assuage public safety concerns. Each was an attempt to address unpopular images (discussed below) and the perceived risks associated with each imperfect power source. Indeed, passing these expenditures onto ratepayers faced increasing opposition from consumers who continued to expect minimal increases matched by supply stability.

As electricity prices sluggishly tried to keep pace with rising expenditures, the operating profit margins of incumbent suppliers—the proportion of revenue that remains after deducting costs—gradually fell from 13% in 1986 to low single digits by 2011. The "cost of the NIMBY"—high electricity prices, decreasing consumer welfare, and declining supplier profitability in the face of mounting obstacles—has plagued the Japanese electric power market since the mid-1980s.

Restructuring: revisiting cause and effect

Starting with George Stigler (1971) and later repeating in various guises with Ramseyer and Rosenbluth (1993), Katz (1998), and George Mulgan (2002), among many others, the general economic theory of regulation assumes that well organized, politically adept industries will seek regulatory change, effectively "buying" it with resources and electoral support, only when such policy change serves their economic self-interest. There is little doubt that Japan's high retail electricity prices and burgeoning costs (discussed above) have created both welfare losses and growing financial risks for consumers and suppliers alike. What needs explanation is why decision makers not only tolerated this lose-lose situation for so long, but also why structural reforms neither corrected the problem nor later favored the interests of well-organized and resource-rich incumbent interests as some theorists assumed.

As the puzzling political defeats introduced at the beginning of this chapter suggest, narrowly focusing on the resource endowments of interest groups to explain policy outcomes generates more questions than answers, and sometimes leads to incorrect predictions. Although limited space prevents us from providing an in-depth analysis here, we can expand briefly on the question of political influence. Critics of Japan's electric power companies suggest that organized cash contributions to political parties by executives, media advertising budgets, and apparent linkages to bureaucrats and politicians somehow suppress criticism and help explain policy outcomes favoring nuclear power (Dewitt *et al.* 2012; Kingston 2012; Kōno 2011). Defenders dismiss these charges by noting that the companies have not contributed to political parties since 1974, that their advertising budgets are focused exclusively on promoting *ōru denka jūtaku*, or the complete electrification of the Japanese household, and that the former bureaucrats who are employed by power companies (in a practice known as *amakudari* or "descent from heaven") are best viewed as pointless sinecures with little policy benefit to the electric power companies (interview with Federation of Electric Power Companies of Japan, 2012).

These claims and counter-claims often degenerate into heated indignation, with both sides tending to overstate their cases. Electric power companies refuse to be drawn into public debates about the legitimacy of energy policy, choosing to respond to their critics only when information is factually incorrect (interview with Federation of Electric Power Companies of Japan, 2012). While the companies' stated reason for avoiding official public debates (i.e. the unwillingness to be perceived as self-interested actors) is probably true, we can be fairly certain that providing a vital necessity (electricity) for the sake of fueling economic growth does not extend to increased unemployment resulting from restructuring. Presumably, no division of an incumbent electric power

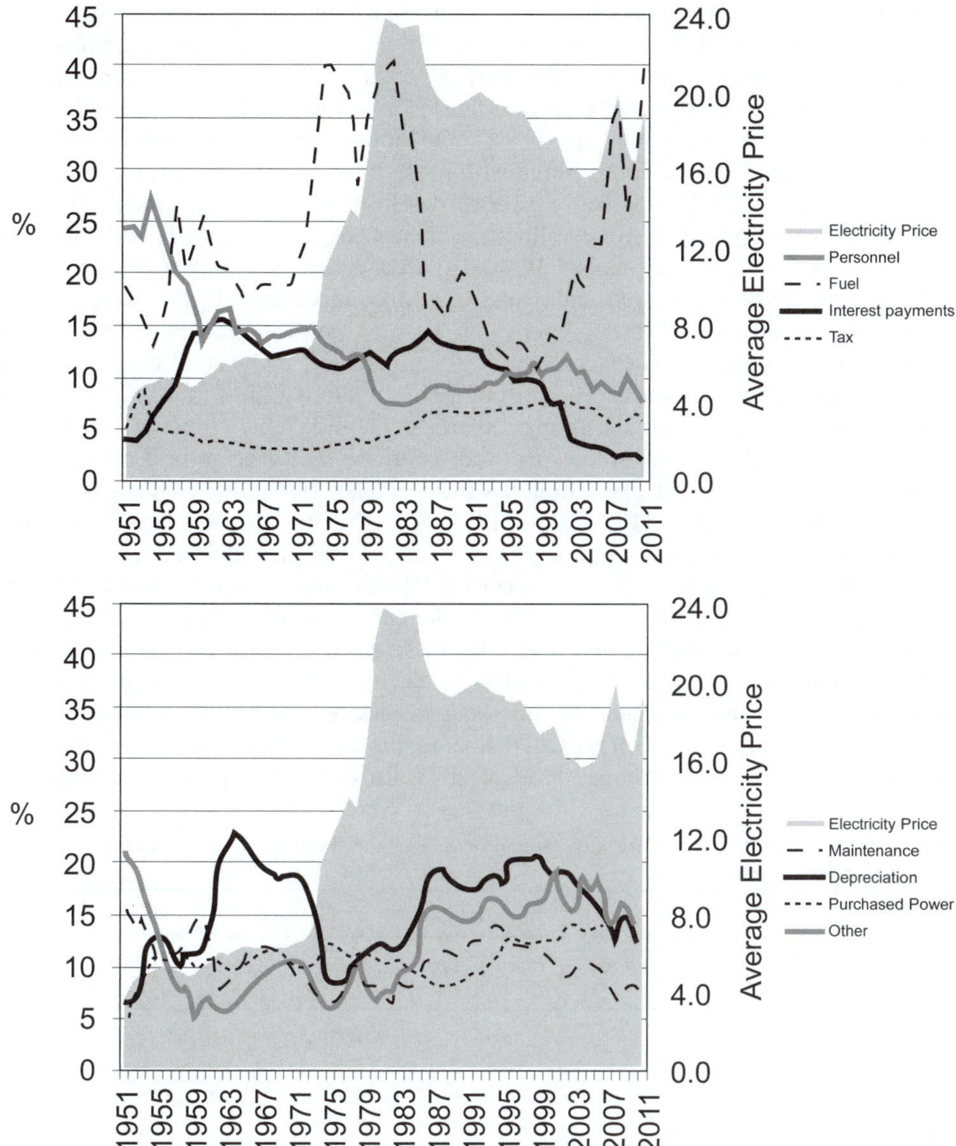

Figure 7.1 Average electricity prices and component expenditure trends (1951–2011)
Source: (For electricity tariffs and their component expenditures per kWh, 1951–2000, see Kantō no denki jigyō to tōkyō denryoku (Electric power industry and TEPCO Kanto region), CD-ROM (2000), Tokyo: Tōkyō denryoku; for tariff and expenditure data per kWh, 2001–11, see Yūka shōken hōkokusho (Annual report, various years), Tokyo: Tokyo Electric Power Corporation)

supplier prefers to see its budget reduced or its employees downsized because of competition.

Critics of electric power companies, on the other hand, incorrectly confuse the coincidence of political resource endowments with cause. Are electric power labor unions "buying" Democratic Party of Japan (DPJ) votes with their cash contributions to the party, or is the practice a long-held tradition of supporting political parties that are *already* predisposed to the interests of labor unions? Are power companies that buy advertising space in major media outlets seeking to suppress unfavorable news coverage, or is the practice the logical extension of targeting high-circulation media outlets for specific commercial purposes? Do utility companies seek out former bureaucrats to gain needed connections within the bureaucracy, or do retired bureaucrats seek out utility companies for purely selfish reasons? In short: do votes, news coverage and political access follow the money, or does money follow the votes, news coverage, and political access? Western and Japanese journalists alike routinely publicize the political resource endowments and connections of the electric power companies, suggesting conflict of interest at best or political malfeasance at worst. However, the existence of cash contributions, advertising budgets, and sinecures for retired bureaucrats in the electric power companies tells us little to nothing about the agenda-setting and decision-making process in the Japanese energy sector.

Sophisticated and rigorous studies in other countries and sectors find that political resource endowments often exert limited to no impact on policy outputs (Chappell 1982; Welch 1982; Grenzke 1989; Mayer 1991; Sorauf 1992; Baumgartner *et al.* 2009). What can be said of Japan's electric power market is equally illuminating. Table 7.1 provides us with a snapshot of one aspect of Japan's structural reform over time by examining the votes of political parties in the Upper and Lower House standing committees in the National Diet that oversee Japanese electric power legislation. Between 1995 and 2007, Japan moved to liberalize its electric power market. Phase 1 (1995) introduced a bill to the National Diet allowing wholesale bidding competition. Phase 2 (1999) expanded the legislation to begin liberalizing approximately 30% of the retail market at the "extra-high voltage" level of 20kV for contract supplies of 2,000kW or

Table 7.1 Diet committee voting on amendments to the Electric Power Industry Law by political party

Party	*1995*				*1999*				*2003*				*2007*			
	For		*Against*		*For*		*Against*		*For*		*Against*		*For*		*Against*	
	L	*U*	*L*	*U*	*L*	*U*	*L*	*U*	*L*	*U*	*L*	*U*	*L*	*U*	*L*	*U*
LDP	✓	✓			✓	✓			✓	✓						
JSP[1]	✓	✓			✓	✓					✓	✓				
JCP	✓	✓					✓	✓			✓	✓				
DPJ[2]					✓	✓			✓	✓						
NFP	✓															
Liberal			None		✓					✓	✓			Cancelled		
Meikai					✓											
CGP									✓	✓						
Heisei		✓														
Shinroku		✓														
Taiyō	✓															
Other																

Source: (House of Representatives and House of Councilors (various years); design by author)
Notes: L=Lower House, U=Upper House, NFP=New Frontier Party (*shinshintō*). Each year represents the Diet session in which the MITI minister presented draft revisions of the Electric Power Utility Law to both standing committees for their consideration.
[1] The JSP was renamed the Social Democratic Party of Japan, or SDPJ, in 1996.
[2] The DPJ was formed in April 1998.

more. Phase 3 expanded to the remaining industrial and commercial customers covering approximately 60% of the retail market. Phase 4 was intended to liberalize the market for the remaining residential customers, but ultimately came to naught.

What started with unanimous acceptance of reform in 1995 among ruling and opposition parties alike in both houses of the National Diet eventually collapsed by 2007, only to resurface again in 2011 in the wake of the nuclear crisis. What drove these developments? It is tempting to conclude that political parties—from the far left to the far right of the spectrum—were effectively "bought" by powerful forces within the establishment; that what started with votes against further liberalization of the electric power sector by the JCP in 1999 and spread to other political parties was the result of outside persuasion, not independent political thought. As demonstrated below, however, these assumptions are tenuous.

Table 7.2 matches the years in which electricity restructuring was placed on the national agenda with the cash contributions of proponents of restructuring (energy-intensive sectors and new entrants) versus opponents (incumbent power suppliers). Contributions from companies, subsidiaries, affiliates and executives are totaled to present a full picture of each sector's potential influence with the LDP (the party dominating the cabinet). Electric power companies discontinued corporate donations to the LDP in 1974, but their executives and subsidiaries contributed between 0.1% and 0.5% of total LDP revenues, compared to a range of 0.4% to 3.0% by energy-intensive industries and 0.0% to 0.2% by new entrants. It is certainly true that resources tend to be concentrated more in the hands of large energy-intensive industries such as steel, chemicals and autos than in the hands of incumbent power suppliers or new entrants, but less troubling if those resources never increased the groups' chances of political success.

The JCP, relying predominantly on revenues from its lucrative newspaper *Akahata*, and nothing from political action committees (PACs) and corporations cannot be accused of having its votes "bought" by special interests when it turned against restructuring in 1999. Nor can the Japan Socialist Party (JSP) be accused of being bought when roughly 80% of its revenues come from publications and other sources such as campaign matching funds, and virtually none from PACs let alone incumbent power suppliers or electric power labor. Perhaps the most thought-provoking cases are

Table 7.2 Total cash contributions to LDP (executives, subsidiaries, corporate) (in yen)

	1995	*1999*	*2003*	*2007*	*2012*
Electric power	20,189,975	100,509,994	107,022,015	131,524,035	74,665,053
(% LDP rev.)	0.1	0.3	0.4	0.5	0.4
Steel	451,862,000	179,520,000	145,240,000	151,510,000	79,920,000
(% LDP rev.)	3.0	0.5	0.5	0.6	0.5
Autos	174,212,000	145,818,000	227,622,000	237,324,000	193,639,000
(% LDP rev.)	1.2	0.4	0.9	0.9	1.1
Chemicals	70,883,000	47,700,000	23,400,000	75,830,000	29,600,000
(% LDP rev.)	0.5	0.1	0.1	0.3	0.2
New entrants	–	30,900,000	6,140,000	24,540,000	38,620,000
(% LDP rev.)	0.0	0.1	0.0	0.1	0.2

Source: (*Kanpō* (Cabinet Gazette), various years; cash contribution data collated by author)

the ruling LDP and its largest opposition party, the DPJ. Both parties receive cash contributions from proponents *and* opponents of reform. If political resources matter, how should we interpret the voting patterns of the LDP and DPJ, which voted consistently for further liberalization despite the repeated objections, and criticisms of incumbent suppliers and labor on the electric power industry advisory council (*denki jigyō shingikai*) between 1999 and 2003? With the further liberalization of residential customers and vertical unbundling[4] of incumbent power suppliers back on the national agenda in 2013 (*The Nikkei Weekly*, February 11, 2013), the assumption that incumbent power suppliers (¥74.6 million) should have more political influence than new entrants (¥38.6 million) because of their slightly higher campaign contribution levels to the ruling LDP seems even *less* compelling than ever.

Policy images, issue frames and technical realities

Why does much of the conventional (journalistic) wisdom assume that large economic actors "buy" public policy favorable to their narrow interests when so many scholars have difficulty demonstrating a consistent and independent effect? One compelling explanation lies in the power of perception—how issues are defined by some actors and understood by others. In his chapter, Daniel Aldrich discusses the tools by which government molds preferences, thus suggesting that political perception—like political behavior itself—is fundamentally malleable. If true, the underlying assumption of the economic theory of regulation that economic actors have fixed, clear and goal-oriented preferences in pursuing their interests becomes far less certain in explaining the past and predicting the future.

To be sure, post-war electric power companies—rightly or wrongly—presented their investment decisions as the rational result of cost-benefit analyses in the midst of changing techno-economic environments. The selection of electric power sources was arguably a function of resource availability, application technology, the useful life expectancy of a generation asset, utilization rates (i.e. the ratio of demand to potential output), and political will. Cheap and plentiful hydroelectric power in the 1950s subsequently shifted to domestic coal once most available dams and rivers were captured. Diminishing supplies of domestic coal gave way to inexpensive oil following import liberalization in 1961. A diversified energy portfolio consisting of liquefied natural gas (LNG), nuclear power, and coal gained prominence once the 1973 and 1979 oil shocks exposed the dangers of overreliance on oil, followed by the rise of nuclear power in an age of rising fossil fuel prices and increasing environmental concerns over greenhouse gas emissions.[5]

While the shift in post-war power sources from one to another is a publicly verifiable fact, the puzzle remains: if incumbent suppliers were both politically powerful and economically self-interested as the theory assumes, why were they unable to block regulatory and legal changes in electric power market (liberalization) and basic energy policy (renewable energy) from the 1990s onwards that ironically introduced further techno-economic risks to their self-interests despite repeated objections?

Part of the answer stems from the deliberate creation of narratives to capture the public imagination in the midst of perceived national priorities. Japan's underlying economic realities discussed in this chapter require a careful balance between supply and demand—a balance aided by (but not always successful in controlling) what political scientists commonly describe as "problem representation," "affect priming," "salami tactics," "feature extraction," or "issue framing" of perceived losses and gains (Kahneman and Tversky 1979; Levy 1997; Quattrone and Tversky 1988). Yet what applies to the electorate equally applies to governments. Because Japanese decision makers, like other people, have limited attention spans that are institutionally constrained by time, energy, resources, and expertise (Jones and Baumgartner 2005; Noble 2007; Scalise and Stewart 2009), the ability to highlight certain factors over others as relevant in the decision-making process allows policy entrepreneurs and activists an opportunity to control the "image" of Japan's energy policy. Crises, disasters, personal experience and symbols, or what John Kingdon (1984) calls "windows of opportunity," can effectively re-define the *perceived* problems, and consequently, perceptions about what can be done to address them.

Japan's "lost decades" and the events surrounding the nuclear meltdown at Fukushima Dai-ichi Nuclear Power Plant, owned and operated by the Tokyo Electric Power Corporation (TEPCO), turned a once technical subject relegated to a select few market participants into a broader political discussion involving suppliers, consumers, new entrants, politicians, bureaucrats, and academics. In *shingikai* (ministerial advisory councils), standing parliament committees, and mass media outlets policy entrepreneurs and activists waged policy image campaigns in attempting to capture the upper hand. In the case of electric power restructuring, the battle over the politics of economic/regulatory ideas in justifying the status quo or leading the country towards a competitive generation of market-led actors to scrutinize foreign regulatory blueprints and outputs in the hope of achieving consensus (Scalise 2009). Likewise, in the case of energy policy, the battle over rival narratives to identify villains and trot out old solutions to newly prioritized problems attempted to repeat the process (Samuels 2013). Each side emphasized its strengths and either ignored or downplayed the inconveniences, thus highlighting the importance of selective framing and incomplete perception in politics.

For the incumbents, the objective was (and is) a return to the *status quo ante.* They frame energy policy in terms of Japan's import vulnerabilities, its lack of natural resources, the need to maintain security of supply, and protection against blackout risk. A large-scale, centralized, vertically integrated power network emphasizing an increasing role for nuclear power (set to rise from approximately 30% of total electric power generation in 2010 to 50% by 2030, according to the 2010 Basic Energy Plan) provided what power companies and their allies advocated: relatively cheap, stable, high-density, large-scale, baseload power sources with minimal greenhouse gas emissions and air pollution, and importing fuel (e.g. uranium) from a wide array of stable democracies. For the opposition, the objective was reversed: to re-frame any narrative of energy policy to promote a distributed, community-based renewable energy economy that places decision making into the hands of local municipal governments and away from an allegedly collusive and profit-maximizing "nuclear village" and its allies (see Chapter 9). Proponents of change selectively emphasize secondary costs and risks of some power sources while failing to apply the same scrutiny or even skepticism to others: "back-end" costs such as nuclear waste disposal, compensation costs of displaced families from (real and perceived) nuclear crises, the perceived health risks from radiation exposure,[6] safety concerns regarding irradiation of the food supply, terrorism, and sometimes security issues surrounding the development of nuclear weapons. Proponents of reform claim that the FIT will eventually contribute to lower generation prices for renewable energy sources and increased creation of "green" jobs, while opponents of reform point to rising electricity prices from higher rates and the ambiguity of net job creation in the energy sector.

Both sides downplay the consequences of NIMBY activism in Japan. For defenders of the *status quo ante*, little mention is made of rising construction costs brought about by delays related to protracted negotiations with local communities fearing radiation exposure (nuclear), air pollution (coal/oil), damage to the ecosystem (large hydro/geothermal), or private property rights (all). For proponents of change, little mention is made of limited siting options for large-scale solar and wind projects with low power densities, and how these limitations stir concerns about low-frequency noise pollution (wind), aesthetic degradation (solar), rising compensation costs for land-use approval (wind/solar/biomass), and potential wildlife displacement (all). Nor are proponents of reform quick to acknowledge how limited scale issues lend to rising carbon dioxide emissions and further greenhouse gas emissions in the absence of nuclear power and large hydroelectric dams. Thus, the nature of issue framing requires ownership of a policy image in the hope of limiting negative feedback and capturing the imagination of the electorate.

Conclusions

Despite (or perhaps in part because of) the restructuring of energy and electric power in 2000–11, electricity prices have risen steadily in many industrial democracies. In Denmark, Spain, and Germany, where both restructuring and increased market share of new renewables via the feed-in tariff system, taxes, and various inducement mechanisms have been implemented, electricity prices for residential customers adjusted for purchasing power parity have risen by 48%, 72% and 134%, respectively. For industrial customers, the price increases have been even more pronounced: 99%, 249%, and 287%, respectively (OECD/IEA 2012, 55–56). In Japan, by contrast, despite strong increases in the price of imported fossil fuels in 2000–11 leading to a corresponding increase in fuel costs per kWh (Figure 7.1a), electricity prices for the average residential and industrial customers have risen only sluggishly at 30% and 25%, respectively, thanks to a political inability to increase retail electricity prices greatly, partial cost-cutting by incumbent suppliers slowing the rate of profitability decline and cash flow erosion, and a more diversified fuel mix offsetting increased electricity demand since the 1970s. That sharp rises in European electricity prices have experienced little political backlash despite sizeable consumer welfare losses underscores the importance of policy "image" and issue framing in energy policy. How long the German government and renewable energy proponents can maintain the current policies for renewables without consumers turning against them is an open question (*Spiegel Online*, August 29, 2012).

As discussed in this chapter, no actor in Japan controls the policy agenda completely, consistently, and unquestionably. Since evaluations of the trade-offs between a menu of imperfect power sources and their distribution capacities seldom lead to unambiguous conclusions, any piece of information regarding power sources and electric power distribution is subject to interpretation and to uncertainty. Mathematical probabilities by knowledgeable individuals help to provide decision makers with a probability calculus to weigh various choices against their correlate risks. However, when operating within a framework of unlimited demands by the general public on the one side, and limited resources, energy, and time to supply answers by decision makers on the other, policy makers, like other people, often rely on what Bryan D. Jones and Frank R. Baumgartner (2005) call "disproportionate information-processing"—filtering through the information "noise" in order to arrive at a basket of indicators that either reinforce or refute the status quo using pre-conceived paradigms for the sake of protecting and promoting the public interest.

The rise and fall of neoliberalism in the electric power market, the passing of renewable energy laws, and the ultimate uncertainty surrounding nuclear power's role in the generation mix are all connected to Japan's decision-making process in the same way: change in the economic regulatory structure did not depend on the demands of regulated industries or other well-organized groups as the economic theory hypothesizes, but rather change depends on well-accepted regulatory ideas on market structure and technological use imported from abroad and diffusely filtered into Japan's decision-making process during periods of perceived institutional crisis.

Japan's attention to energy policy gradually shifted to include new priorities involving China and the domestic economy after the traumatic events of 3/11. The 2011 groundswell of anti-nuclear public protests in 2011 and 2012 driven by fear and radiation concerns, the anti-nuclear conversion of DPJ Prime Minister Kan Naoto, and media attention culminating in 18,641 nuclear-related articles in the *Asahi Shimbun* in 2011 (75% negative) shifted considerably by the end of 2012. Anti-nuclear protests no longer drew large numbers in front of the prime minister's residence. Kan's successor Noda Yoshihiko favored a cautious reduction in nuclear power by 2030, and presided over the restart of two nuclear reactors in the summer 2012. By December 2012 election, the LDP was re-elected despite its desire to return Japan to the nuclear energy *status quo ante*. In an election that was expected to be a referendum on nuclear power, the central concerns of voters shifted to the economy and the security threat of China. Whatever issues the anti-nuclear and reformist lobby brought to the national agenda in the aftermath of the Fukushima nuclear meltdown were sidelined in early 2013. The electorate came to view supporting economic growth and social security reform as far more important than energy policy (*Nikkei-R*, 2012). Nuclear safety inspection checks were implemented, talks of resumed nuclear construction and restarts provoked little media reaction, while public concerns about the negative economic impact due to the stoppage of nuclear reactors rose to 72% of those polled among the Japanese electorate (*Yomiuri Shimbun*, March 5, 2013). Under PM Abe Shinzo, anti-nuclear activists that had served on energy policy decision-making committees were removed.

Indeed, with no definitive regulatory blueprints (or consensus) for the roles of nuclear power, renewable energy, or an increasingly liberalized electric power market appearing on the horizon, the almost immediate "about face" in public opinion is difficult to explain without considering the "images" available to the general public (Baumgartner and Jones 1993). These "images" could slowly revert to their pre-Fukushima norms without a strong consensus supported by imported foreign roadmaps providing regulatory certainty and certain economic outcomes. In 2012, the *Asahi Shimbun* reduced its coverage of nuclear-related issues by 30% while the actual tone of that coverage has increasingly focused on "practical" and "financial" concerns related to the economy. As of the time of writing this chapter, the coverage continued to fall in 2013.

Governments, like individuals, have limited attention spans. By focusing on one issue, they necessarily ignore others. The only way to resolve the competing demands on public policy is to decrease attention on all policy issues simultaneously in an attempt to address whatever the public seems to prioritize via polling and media attention. The result is a fleeting hip-hop from one fashionable policy exercise to another. As Baumgartner *et al.* (2009, 49) remind us, "Control the definition of the terms in the debate, and you control the direction of public policy." Japan's energy policy remains in a state of flux, but undoubtedly competing positive and negative issues will exert a major influence on its evolution.

Notes

1 This chapter was made possible by funding from the Japan Society for the Promotion of Science (JSPS). The author would like to thank Daniel P. Aldrich, Scott T. Hards, Llewelyn Hughes, Jeff Kingston, Alex Luta, and Gregory Noble for their useful suggestions and comments. Special thanks to Julie Battail, the author's intern, who over a four-month period worked with him at the National Diet Library and at the University of Tokyo collating and analyzing financial and statistical data related to this project.

2 There are over 55 listed electricity prices per kWh in Japan varying by supply circuit capacity and voltage. This chapter uses the average overall electricity price of the sector for simplicity in order to illustrate changes in price and expenditure.

3 Depreciation (*genka shōkyakuhi*) is a non-cash cost associated with tangible fixed assets. These tangible fixed assets include power plants, equipment, vessels, vehicles, buildings, structures, and other fixed assets. As these assets lose their value over time due to wear and tear, age, or obsolescence, Japanese electric power companies—like all companies—must write off these asset devaluations in their profit-and-loss statements in order to prepare for the asset's eventual replacement.

4 A technical term in economics used to describe the separation of a single electric power company's generation, transmission, and distribution assets into separate legal or corporate entities.

5 Parties to the United Nations Framework Convention on Climate Change (UNFCCC) adopted the Kyoto Protocol in 1997, and entered it into force in 2005. Japan was a signatory. In 1998–2013, five additional nuclear reactors went into operation: Onagawa No. 3 (2001), Hamaoka No. 5 (2004), Higashidori No. 1 (2005), Shika No. 2 (2005), and Tomari No. 3 (2009). As of 2013, Shimane No. 3 and Ohma No. 1 were under construction. For a useful overview of government activism in Japan's energy sector given the rising impetus of climate change, see Hughes (2012).

6 Although no direct fatalities were attributed to radiation exposure from the nuclear crisis at Fukushima Dai-ichi Nuclear Power Plant, estimates for future cancer development tend to vary by political framing. Official estimates from the World Health Organization (WHO 2013) and other established medical experts conclude that the overall risk to increased cancers to be "small," while anti-nuclear proponents such as Arnie Gundersen predict that Fukushima will 'lead to one million extra deaths from cancer' (McNeill 2012).

Bibliography

Aldrich, Daniel P. (2008) *Site Fights: Divisive Facilities and Civil Society in Japan and the West*, Ithaca: Cornell University Press.

Baumgartner, Frank R., Berry, Jeffrey M., Hojnacki, Marie, Kimball, David C. and Leech, Beth L. (2009) *Lobbying and Policy Change: Who Wins, Who Loses, and Why*, Chicago, IL and London: University of Chicago Press.

Baumgartner, Frank R. and Jones, Bryan D. (1993) *Agendas and Instability in American Politics*, American Politics and Political Economy Series, Chicago, IL: University of Chicago Press.

Chappell, Henry W. (1982) "Campaign Contributions and Congressional Voting: A Simultaneous Probit-Tobit Model," *Review of Economics and Statistics* 64(1): 77–83.

DeWit, Andrew, Iida, Tetsunari and Kaneko, Masaru (2012) "Fukushima and the Political Economy of Power Policy in Japan," in Jeff Kingston (ed.) *Natural Disaster and Nuclear Crisis in Japan: Response and Recovery after Japan's 3/11*, London and New York: Routledge, 156–71.

Fischel, William A. (2001) "Why are there NIMBYs?" *Land Economics* 77(1): 144–52.

George Mulgan, Aurelia (2002) *Japan's Failed Revolution: Koizumi and the Politics of Economic Reform*, Canberra: Asia-Pacific Press, Asia-Pacific School of Economics and Management.

Goldstein, Judith and Keohane, Robert (1993) *Ideas and Foreign Policy: Beliefs, Institutions and Political Change*, Ithaca, NY: Cornell University Press.

Goto, Mika and Tsutsui, Miki (1998) "Comparison of Productive and Cost Efficiencies among Japanese and US Electric Utilities," *Omega* 26(2): 177–94.

Grenzke, Janet M. (1989) "PACs and the Congressional Supermarket: The Currency is Complex," *American Journal of Political Science* 33(1): 1–24.

Hattori, Toru (2002) "Relative Performance of US and Japanese Electricity Distribution: An Application of Stochastic Frontier Analysis," *Journal of Productivity Analysis* 18(3): 269–84.

Hughes, Llewleyn (2012) "Climate Converts: Institutional Redeployment and Public Investment in Energy in Japan," *Journal of East Asian Studies* 12(1): 89–118.

Hymans, Jacques E.C. (2011) "Veto Players, Nuclear Energy, and Nonproliferation: Domestic Institutional Barriers to a Japanese Bomb," *International Security* 36(2): 154–89.

Jacobs, Scott H. (1999) "Regulatory Reform in Japan," in Joanna R. Shelton (ed.) *OECD Reviews of Regulatory Reform*, Paris: Organisation for Economic Co-operation and Development.

Johnson, Chalmers (1978) *Japan's Public Policy Companies, Aei-Hoover Policy Studies*, Washington: American Enterprise Institute for Public Policy Research.

Jones, Bryan D. (2001) *Politics and the Architecture of Choice: Bounded Rationality and Governance*, Chicago, IL: University of Chicago Press.

Jones, Bryan D. and Baumgartner, Frank R. (2005) *The Politics of Attention: How Government Prioritizes Problems*, Chicago, IL: University of Chicago Press.

Joskow, Paul L. (1997) "Restructuring, Competition and Regulatory Reform in the U.S. Electricity Sector," *The Journal of Economic Perspectives* 11(3): 119–38.

——(2000) *Economic Regulation, Critical Ideas in Economics*, Cheltenham, UK and Northampton, MA: Edward Elgar.

Kahneman, Daniel and Tversky, Amos (1979) "Political Implications of Loss Aversion," *Econometrica* 47: 263–91.

Katz, Richard (1998) *Japan, the System that Soured: The Rise and Fall of the Japanese Economic Miracle*, Armonk, NY: M.E. Sharpe.

Kingdon, John W. (1984) *Agendas, Alternatives, and Public Policies*, Boston: Little, Brown.

Kingston, Jeff (2012) "The Politics of Disaster, Nuclear Crisis and Recovery," in Jeff Kingston (ed.) *Natural Disaster and Nuclear Crisis in Japan: Response and Recovery after Japan's 3/11*, London and New York: Routledge, 188–206.

Kōno, Taro (2011) *Genpatsu to nihon ha ko naru: minami ni mukau beki ka, soko ni sumitsuzukeru beki ka*, Tokyo: Kodansha.

Lesbirel, S. Hayden (1990) "Implementing Nuclear Energy Policy in Japan: Top-Down and Bottom-up Perspectives," *Energy Policy* 18(3): 267–82.

——(1998) *NIMBY Politics in Japan: Energy Siting and the Management of Environmental Conflict*, Ithaca: Cornell University Press.

Levy, Jack S. (1997) "Prospect Theory, Rational Theory, and International Relations," *International Studies Quarterly* 41: 87–112.

Mayer, Kenneth R. (1991) *The Political Economy of Defense Contracting*, New Haven: Yale University Press.

McNeill, David (2012) "The Government Could Still Save Lives: Nuclear Expert Witness Arnie Gundersen Discusses Fukushima's Radioactive Fallout," *The Japan Times*, September 16.

Newbery, David M. and Green, Richard (1996) "Regulation, Public Ownership and Privatisation of the English Electricity Industry," in Richard J. Gilbert and Edward P. Kahn (eds) *International Comparisons of Electricity Regulation*, Cambridge: Cambridge University Press.

Noble, Gregory W. (2007) "Stealth Populism: Administrative Reform in Japan," in Gerald E. Caiden and Tsai-Tsu Su (eds) *The Repositioning of Public Governance: Global Experience and Challenges*, Taipei, Taiwan: Taiwan Public Affairs Center, 199–232.

OECD and IEA (2012) "Electricity Information: 2012 with 2011 Data," ed. International Energy Agency, Paris: International Energy Agency.

Quattrone, George A. and Tversky, Amos (1988) "Contrasting Rational and Psychological Analyses of Political Choice," *American Political Science Review* 82: 719–36.

Ramseyer, J. Mark and Rosenbluth, Frances McCall (1993) *Japan's Political Marketplace*, Cambridge, MA: Harvard University Press.

Samuels, Richard J. (2013) *3.11: Disaster and Change in Japan*, Ithaca: Cornell University Press.

——(1987) *The Business of the Japanese State: Energy Markets in Comparative and Historical Perspective, Cornell Studies in Political Economy*, Ithaca: Cornell University Press.

Sangyō kōzō chōsakai (1964) *Nihon no sangyō kōzō* (Industrial structure in Japan), Vol. 3, Tokyo: Tsūshō Sangyō Kenkyūsho.

Scalise, Paul J. (2009) "The Politics of Restructuring: Agendas and Uncertainty in Japan's Electricity Deregulation," doctoral dissertation, University of Oxford.

——(2012) "Japan's Distribution Challenge: Lessons from Abroad," in *Powering Ahead: Perspectives on Japan's Energy Future*, London: The Economist Intelligence Unit, 24–28.

Scalise, Paul J. and Stewart, Devin (2009) "Think Again: Japan's Revolutionary Election," *Foreign Policy*, October 1.

Sorauf, Frank J. (1992) *Inside Campaign Finance: Myths and Realities*, New Haven: Yale University Press.

Stigler, George J. (1971) "The Theory of Economic Regulation," *Bell Journal of Economics and Management Science* 2(1): 3–21.

Tone, Kaoru and Tsutsui, Miki (2007) "Decomposition of Cost Efficiency and its Application to Japanese-US Electric Utility Comparisons," *Socio-economic Planning Sciences* 41(2): 91–106.

Welch, William P. (1982) "Campaign Contributions and Legislative Voting: Milk Money and Dairy Price Supports," *Western Political Quarterly* 35(4): 478–95.

WHO (2013) "Health Risk Assessment from the Nuclear Accident After the 2011 Great East Japan Earthquake Tsunami Based on a Preliminary Dose Estimation," Geneva: World Health Organization.

Woll, Cornelia (2008) *Firm Interests: How Governments Shape Business Lobbying on Global Trade*, Ithaca, NY: Cornell University Press.

8 Japan's nuclear village

Power and resilience

Jeff Kingston

The March 2011 Fukushima nuclear accident spurred expectations in the Japanese public and around the world that Japan would pull the plug on nuclear energy.[1] Indeed, in July 2011 Prime Minister Naoto Kan announced that he no longer believed that nuclear reactors could be operated safely in Japan because it is so prone to devastating earthquakes and tsunami; by May 2012 all of Japan's 50 viable reactors were shut down for safety inspections. Plans to boost nuclear energy to 50% of Japan's electricity generating capacity were scrapped and the government enacted subsidies to boost renewable energy. Controversially, however, in June 2012 Prime Minister Yoshihiko Noda (2011–12) approved the restart of two nuclear reactors, sparking mass protests that continued throughout Japan's summer of discontent, the largest since the turbulent 1960s.

Three major investigations into the Fukushima accident were released in 2012, detailing the absence of a culture of safety in the nuclear industry and the cozy and collusive relations between regulators and the utilities that compromised safety (Funabashi Report 2012; Hatamura Report 2012; National Diet Report 2012). All three investigations assert that the meltdowns were preventable, and refuted Tokyo Electric Power Company's (TEPCO) claim that the massive tsunami was an inconceivable event that caused the three meltdowns and hydrogen explosions (Lukner and Sakaki 2013).

Finally, in October 2012, TEPCO confessed that it had erred in not adopting stricter safety measures and could have prevented the nuclear crisis had it done so (*Asahi*, October 13, 2012). TEPCO's in-house investigation report issued in mid-2012 flatly denied responsibility or shortchanging safety (TEPCO 2012), but a subsequent TEPCO reform panel including international experts came to completely different conclusions. TEPCO finally acknowledged what had been extensively reported about its downplaying of tsunami risk and resistance to adopting international safety standards. It also admitted that employees were not properly trained to operate emergency equipment and lacked crisis management skills. The utility concedes that it did not manage risk properly because it feared that any measures to improve safety at the Fukushima plant would stoke the anti-nuclear movement, interfere with operations, raise costs, and create legal and political problems. This mea culpa is an extraordinary development, one that highlights the shortcomings and wrongdoing of the nuclear village.

These damning revelations about the absence of a culture of safety undermine public faith in regulators and the utilities and seemed to suggest that Japan might gradually phase out nuclear power. The government solicited public opinion in the summer of 2012 and found that 81% of respondents favored eliminating nuclear energy by 2030 (Kingston 2012c). Despite overwhelming anti-nuclear public sentiments, however, the Noda cabinet did not officially endorse the nuclear-free option, and left the energy policy door open to further deliberation while allowing construction of new reactors to resume. Moreover, the new Nuclear Regulation Authority (NRA) is headed by a prominent pro-nuclear expert, and is mostly staffed by former members of the discredited Nuclear and Industrial Safety Agency (NISA) and the Nuclear Safety Commission (NSC) which were blamed for regulating in favor of the regulated and lax monitoring of nuclear reactor operators. New safety guidelines issued by the NRA indicate that it is serious about improving safety at Japan's reactors, requiring costly upgrades, strict monitoring, and delays in restarts, but Prime Minister Abe Shinzo (2012–) is a determined proponent of nuclear energy.

Why has Fukushima not been a game-changing event? This paper examines the institutional actors in nuclear energy and their resilience in the face of public anger and anxieties. These institutions enjoy considerable advantages in terms of energy policy making and have enormous investments at stake.

Nuclear village

The "nuclear village" is the term commonly used in Japan to refer to the institutional and individual pro-nuclear advocates in the utilities, the nuclear industry, the bureaucracy, the Diet (Japan's parliament), business federations, the media, and academia. This is a village without boundaries or residence cards, an imagined collective bound by solidarity over promoting nuclear energy. There is considerable overlap with the so-called "Iron Triangle" of big business, the bureaucracy and the Liberal Democratic Party (LDP) that has called the shots in Japan from the mid-1950s and the evocative moniker "Japan, Inc.," a reference to cooperative ties between the government and private sector.

On the eve of March 11, 2011 Japan had 54 nuclear reactors generating nearly one-third of its total electricity supply, evidence of just how influential this interest group has been in promoting its agenda. Over the decades, as Japan's nuclear sector grew, so did the nuclear village's power and influence (Hymans 2011). There has been a proliferation of vested interests in nuclear power that benefit from its expansion. The nuclear village is not monolithic on policy, and there are disagreements between members over various issues that are bitterly contested, but these are the squabbles of a gated community where cooperation and reciprocity prevail. The village shares a common mentality and sensibilities about nuclear energy, and that means ostracizing naysayers and critics and denying them the access and benefits that "members" enjoy. This modern version of the traditional rural practice of *murahachibu* (village ostracism) has been the stick, while access to vast resources and corridors of power is the carrot. Researchers who do not support the village consensus on the need, safety, reliability and economic logic of nuclear power do not get grants and are denied promotions. Journalists who criticize the nuclear village are denied access and other perks while politicians seeking contributions, and media companies eager for a slice of the utilities' massive advertising budgets, trim their sails accordingly.

This carrot-stick strategy was evident in the muzzling of mainstream media as soon as the Fukushima accident began to unfold (see Chapter 5). According to Honma Ryu, advertising powerhouse Dentsu quashed negative coverage of the nuclear industry following the Fukushima disaster (Honma 2012). Lucy Birmingham and David McNeill also report that the mass media (including non-commercial broadcaster Nippon Hōsō Kyōkai—NHK) was overly deferential to the nuclear village in initially downplaying the severity of the nuclear accident at Fukushima (Birmingham and McNeill 2012). Although the international media reported the mid-March 2011 meltdowns early on in the crisis, the Japanese media never mentioned them for over two months and relied extensively on experts with pro-nuclear views. Japan's *kisha* system of press clubs rendered the mainstream media captive to government and utility sources (Freeman 2000). Just as crossing the nuclear village carried consequences, support conferred benefits; while Fukushima's reactors were in meltdown, the chairman of TEPCO was in China treating favored members of some of Japan's largest media organizations to an expense account junket.

The nationalization of TEPCO in 2012 is another good example of just how powerful the nuclear village is (Kingston 2012c). The government injected funds equivalent to 75% of TEPCO's market value, but after prolonged wrangling the government only secured 51% voting rights while TEPCO retains considerable autonomy in reorganizing and revamping operations. As of May 2012, TEPCO received injections, loans and guarantees totaling some US$45 billion (*Wall Street Journal*, May 12, 2012), but the mounting costs of compensation and the problem-plagued decommissioning have boosted the bill to an estimated US$100 billion as of mid-2013 (DeWit 2013). An *Asahi* editorial criticizes the quasi-nationalization because it revamps little at great cost while preventing a much needed restructuring of Japan's power supply system (*Asahi*, June 28, 2012). The costs of the fiasco at Fukushima, and now TEPCO's ongoing risks, have simply been passed on to taxpayers. Legally insulated by nationalization, TEPCO finally admitted it had been deceiving the public for 19 months, acknowledging that the disaster could have been prevented had it acted responsibly and prioritized safety (*Asahi*, December 14, 2012).

A nuclear-free Japan by 2030, an option overwhelmingly backed by the public as of 2013, is unlikely. The power network promoting nuclear energy is not planning to go out of business at home or overseas. Indeed, the LDP's landslide victory in the December 2012 Diet elections for the Lower House and in the July 2013 Upper House elections bolstered the industry as the party is openly pro-nuclear and supports restarting the nation's reactors. Furthermore, promotion of reactor exports continues; in 2012 Toshiba increased its stake to 87% in Westinghouse, while Hitachi and Mitsubishi have tie-ups with GE and Areva, putting Japan at the nexus of the global nuclear industrial comples. In 2013 Turkey awarded a $22 billion reactor contract to a Japanese-led consortium while contracts with Vietnam, the United Arab Emirates and others are pending.

The nuclear village's remarkable ability to evade accountability, secure nationalization on advantageous terms, avoid a government decision on phasing out of nuclear energy and resume exports demonstrates its resilience and power. It has openly lobbied the government and actively promoted its case in the media while also working the corridors of power and backrooms where energy policy is decided. Here it enjoys tremendous advantages that explain why it has prevailed over public opinion concerning national energy policy. Its relatively successful damage control is an object lesson in power politics.

Regulatory capture versus culture of safety

Regulatory capture refers to the situation where regulators charged with promoting the public interest defer to the wishes and advance the agenda of the industry or sector they are supposed to regulate. Those with a vested interest in specific policy or regulatory outcomes lobby regulators and influence their choices and actions. Frank von Hippel, a nuclear physicist and expert on nuclear policy at Princeton University, argues that in the United States, "[n]uclear power is a textbook example of the problem of 'regulatory capture'—in which an industry gains control of an agency meant to regulate it" (von Hippel 2011). In Japan, nuclear regulators have also long been regulating in the interests of the regulated (Ramseyer 2012). The Nuclear and Industrial Safety Agency was the nuclear regulatory authority operating from within the Ministry of Economy, Trade, and Industry (METI), which has long promoted nuclear energy. METI and NISA were solicitous of TEPCO's concerns as well as those of the Federation of Electric Power Companies, meaning that policies and regulatory implementation favored utility interests. Japan's Diet investigated the Fukushima disaster and concluded that regulatory capture was at the heart of the nuclear accident and the absence of a culture of safety (National Diet Report 2012). There has been an institutionalized culture of complacency and deceit in NISA and TEPCO that explains why Fukushima in particular and the nuclear industry in general settled for inadequate safeguards and emergency procedures (Kingston 2012b). Regulatory capture explains why the risks of operating nuclear reactors were systematically downplayed and mismanaged in ways that compromised operational safety.

In the context of Japan's Iron Triangle, the cooperative ties between the utilities and nuclear regulators have been standard operating procedure since the 1960s. MITI (the Ministry of International Trade and Industry, now METI) believed that nuclear energy was critical to Japan's economy and acted accordingly in promoting it, similar to the policies it carried out to promote industrialization in many other sectors of the economy (Johnson 1982). MITI played a key role in promoting nuclear energy, deploying vast government resources and subsidies that sent a clear signal to business that nuclear energy was a national priority. This green light encouraged utilities to ramp up nuclear power and Japanese companies to enter the nuclear energy business via tie-ups with overseas vendors, notably Toshiba-Westinghouse, Hitachi-GE and Mitsubishi-Areva, while reassuring investors and lenders.

The close ties among political, business, bureaucratic and scientific circles—as well as the mass media—regarding Japan's nuclear power policy is typical in this global industry, as qualified experts are drawn from a "limited pool of fish" (Bloomberg, December 12, 2007). This network nurtures solidarity and a group-think that marginalizes dissenting opinions. Government agencies and the utilities depend extensively on the technical expertise of private-sector specialists employed by the major vendors. Under the circumstances, it is not surprising that oversight was lax and regulators deferred to industry demands while rubber stamping requests and averting eyes from safety lapses.

In the United States, a "revolving door" between business and government is shorthand for the collusive relations that lie at the heart of regulatory capture. In Japan, regulatory capture is embodied in the system known as *amakudari* (descent from heaven), the practice in which senior government officials secure post-retirement, well-paid sinecures at firms or industries they once supervised (Colignon and Usui 2003). These firms hire ex-officials because of the bureaucracy's extensive regulatory and discretionary powers and the consequent need to maintain good relations and channels of communication with the government over critical matters. The conflict of interest implicit in *amakudari* generates considerable controversy, but the practice persists despite frequent efforts to eradicate it. In Japan, these collusive ties have compromised nuclear safety (National Diet Report 2012; *The New York Times*, April 26, 2011).

Outing the village

Madarame Haruki, as chairman of the Nuclear Safety Commission (2010–12), gave testimony in the Diet in February 2012 that pulled back the curtain on the nuclear village. Madarame was a prominent advocate of nuclear energy and one of the nuclear village headmen, so his testimony revealing that the nuclear industry relentlessly opposed adopting stricter international safety standards was credible and damaging (Bloomberg, February 16, 2012). Over the preceding years, Madarame actively participated in promoting the myth of safety and supporting industry efforts to cut corners (Repeta 2011). Testifying for a utility in 2007, Madarame rejected the plaintiff's contention that two backup generators might fail simultaneously. Speaking volumes about the nuclear village's culture of safety, Madarame asserted that worrying about such possibilities would "make it impossible to ever build anything" (*The New York Times*, May 16, 2011). However, as the Hatamura Report (2012) asserts, worrying about such possibilities and worst-case scenarios is obligatory for nuclear reactor operators and assuming them away is an inexcusable dereliction of duty. The increased costs of meeting tougher safety standards pose a threat to the nuclear industry, explaining why *The Economist* concludes that building and operating nuclear reactors is economically unviable (*The Economist* 2012). This is precisely why the nuclear village has fought to contain such costs at the expense of operational safety.

In his testimony before the Diet in February 2012, Madarame spoke of officials ignoring nuclear risks and admitted, "We ended up wasting our time looking for excuses that these measures are not needed in Japan" (AP, February 15, 2012). Madarame drew attention to NISA specifically warning utilities in 1993 about the risk of a station blackout causing the cessation of cooling systems—precisely what happened at Fukushima (*Asahi*, June 6, 2012). At that time NISA urged utilities to develop a defense in depth in terms of power sources to maintain cooling systems in the event of a catastrophic event, but the utilities downplayed the dangers and argued that existing backup systems were sufficient. NISA backed down and their sensible suggestions to adopt appropriate countermeasures and improve operating safety were ignored, leaving Japan's nuclear reactors vulnerable to station blackout. Madarame also asserted that he and his colleagues had " … succumbed to a blind belief in the country's technical prowess and failed to thoroughly assess the risks of building nuclear reactors in an earthquake-prone country" (*The New York Times*, February 15, 2012). He said that regulators and the utilities missed many opportunities to improve operating safety, that safety regulations were minimally enforced and fundamentally flawed, and that regulators were toothless and overly solicitous of utility interests. In a sector where a culture of safety should have been a priority, the nuclear safety czar revealed a culture of complacency.

Before Madarame's high-profile outing of the nuclear village, its manipulation of nuclear policy had not gone unchallenged, but 14 lawsuits by local citizens challenging operating licenses on grounds of overlooked seismic dangers and faulty siting have not been successful. There are only two instances where the courts ruled in favor of the plaintiffs, and these were overturned on appeal (*The New York Times*, May 16, 2011). In one of these cases, the court ruled in 2005 that there was no scientific evidence supporting the plaintiff's contention that the Kashiwazaki nuclear plant in Niigata was sited adjacent to an active fault line. In 2007, a 6.8 magnitude earthquake shut Kashiwazaki down and later TEPCO admitted that in 2003 it had "discovered" this fault line, but apparently failed to inform authorities. Automated emergency systems at Kashiwazaki worked as planned, but the command center was inaccessible because the single entrance door was jammed owing to land subsidence, meaning that plant operators were fortunate that systems and equipment were not damaged by a quake that exceeded design specifications (Kingston 2010).

Seismic experts in Japan have drawn attention to a number of other nuclear plants located on or near active fault lines. For example, the Hamaoka plant located closer to Tokyo than Fukushima, was shut down by Chubu Electric at the instigation of PM Kan in May 2011 because experts believe there is a very high probability of a large quake and tsunami in the area. In mid-2012, the government ordered new seismic inspections, but as the *Asahi* notes, "[e]ven when experts pointed out the possibility of the existence of active faults, utilities kept denying that the faults posed safety threats without publishing sufficient materials and information to support their arguments. We are tempted to suspect that the government and utilities were also concerned that making active responses to the danger of active faults would jeopardize the operations of the nuclear power plants" (*Asahi*, July 20, 2012). The power companies' track record of concealing or withholding inconvenient facts, and boldly dissembling, undermines public confidence. Kono Taro, a senior LDP Diet member, captured the prevailing attitude towards utilities when he bluntly suggested that TEPCO officials, " ... don't tell the truth ... It's in their DNA" (Reuters, March 20, 2011).

PM Noda Yoshihiko faced strong opposition to his plans to hasten the restart of reactors in the summer of 2012 due to widespread doubts about whether the safety tests, conducted by the utilities under the supervision of the discredited NISA, are reliable. Madarame Haruki stoked these doubts when he announced in March 2012 that the stress tests were not sufficient to ensure the operational safety of reactors. PM Noda's cabinet then hastily cobbled together a provisional set of 30 safety guidelines that would be used to determine whether to restart a reactor (*Japan Times*, April 6, 2012). As it turned out, the two Oi reactors met only 20 out of the new 30 safety criteria, including the most important and expensive safety measures such as a larger seawall and a remote command center, but were restarted on the utility's promise that it would complete safety upgrades over the next few years. This means that the reactors were reactivated based on the hope that some critical countermeasures would prove unnecessary; Fukushima demonstrates the folly of such wishing risk away.

TEPCO withheld 2008 in-house research from NISA until March 7, 2011, four days before the disaster, indicating that it knew Fukushima was vulnerable to a massive tsunami but had nonetheless decided against building a higher seawall because it was deemed too expensive. Tsunami risk should have come as no surprise as the Tohoku coastline was struck by major tsunami in 1611, 1677, 1793, 1896 and 1933, and in the decade prior to 3/11 numerous reports warned of contemporary tsunami risk in Fukushima. The 3/11 tsunami was no black swan, once-in-a-thousand years event (AP, March 27, 2011). Tsunami are a known risk in Tohoku, and happen with alarming regularity. There are tsunami stones dotting the coastline warning future generations to heed the perils. Why did TEPCO and the government ignore the risks and site so many reactors in a tsunami zone? This collaboration in risky site selection is emblematic of the nuclear village's shortchanging of safety. There are other good reasons for public skepticism towards utilities.

Back in 2000, a whistleblower informed METI that TEPCO's nuclear plant repair and maintenance records had been systematically falsified since the 1980s (Kingston 2010). METI then called TEPCO and told executives that they had a problem: there was a whistleblower. METI's inclination was to put a lid on the story, but when the media reported TEPCO's duplicity, it had no choice but to shut down all of TEPCO's reactors in 2002 and order inspections. In 2007, the government reported that seven of Japan's 12 utilities admitted they had falsified safety records for 30 years (Bloomberg, December 12, 2007). Despite such warning signs about insouciance regarding operational safety and cost cutting on repairs and maintenance, at the end of February 2011, shortly before the meltdowns, NISA extended the operating license of the 40-year-old Fukushima Daiichi #1 reactor. NISA did so even as they expressed reservations about a dubious maintenance record and stress cracks in the backup diesel generators that left them vulnerable to tsunami; these generators were inundated and failed to keep reactor cooling systems working on March 11, 2011, one of the factors in the meltdowns.

While the public is anxious about the risks of restarting reactors before new safety countermeasures are in place, Ramseyer (2012) explains the legal and financial calculations that make this attractive to the utilities. Limited liability means the utilities can shift the risks so that in the event of a catastrophic accident, the government and taxpayers have to cover the losses. Thus the potential downside of restarting before safety countermeasures are taken is financially much more attractive than the certain downside of keeping the reactors idled, while bringing a reactor online confers considerable benefits on the utilities and its shareholders and lenders. In short, the nuclear village captures the benefits while externalizing the most catastrophic risks. Hosting communities also stand to reap benefits, but evacuees from near the Fukushima plant know all too well about TEPCO's empty promises; 150,000 residents remain displaced as of 2013. A decades-long pattern of relying on the utilities to monitor their own compliance with safety standards, giving them the benefit of the doubt and letting them shape regulations and policies affecting their business, has come at a high cost to public safety.

Buying cooperation

Inducements were liberally distributed to the communities that agreed to host nuclear reactors (*The New York Times*, May 30, 2011; *Japan Times*, July 14, 2011; *Mainichi Daily News*, July 5, 2011). Remote coastal towns suffering from depopulation and grim economic prospects suddenly were given a lifeline (Aldrich 2008). Hosting reactors was a lucrative option for these towns and a risk worth taking given the downward-spiraling alternative (Dusinberre 2012). Spigots were opened and subsidies lavished on hosting towns where suddenly there were well-paid jobs attracting an influx of residents and generating tax revenues. Town coffers were brimming with the benefits of hosting, enabling them to build and maintain an expanded infrastructure and attractive amenities such as sports facilities, parks, community centers and museums, all made possible by the village's largesse. The economic bubble propped up by these village outlays created a subsidy addiction in hosting towns, a reliance that made them pliant (Onitsuka 2012).

When Prime Minister Kan declared in July 2011 that all reactors be subject to two-stage stress tests to ensure operational safety, he was slashing revenues for hosting towns. By May 2012, the new stress tests shut down all of Japan's nuclear energy capacity and for the first time in 40 years the nation was not generating a single kWh from nuclear energy. While many Japanese applauded this development as a sensible response to the debacle at Fukushima, hosting towns felt the pinch. However, there were no blackouts, and even if the two reactors in Oi had not been restarted, Japan in the sweltering summers of 2012 and 2013 faced no power shortages. Conservation has become the new commonsense norm for households and industry while new solar projects came online equivalent to two nuclear reactors electricity generating capacity in 2012–13 alone, exceeding even the most optimistic expectations (see Chapter 9).

Public opinion

> Right now, we know that we can live without nuclear energy. It's only because the government does not want to put the nuclear industrial complex out of business that they don't contemplate the other solutions.
>
> (Norimichi Hattori, a spokesman for the network of groups opposed to nuclear energy in Japan known as Metropolitan Coalition Against Nukes, *Japan Today*, August 27, 2012)

Best-selling manga author Kobayashi Yoshinori conveys the angry zeitgeist of the post-Fukushima anti-nuclear movement (Kobayashi 2012). This conservative pundit has long promoted a glorifying and exonerating version of Japan's shared history with Asia in a series of very popular manga. As such he has been a darling of the conservative Establishment. So it is astonishing that in 2012 Kobayashi turned on this Establishment, penning a withering and powerful indictment of the nuclear village and its insidious influence. In his typical no-holds-barred style, he points out that fellow conservatives are supporting the nuclear village for financial benefit, and how researchers who support nuclear power are showered with grants while opponents go unfunded and are excluded from energy advisory groups. He compares TEPCO to Aum Shinrikyo, the religious cult that released sarin gas in Tokyo's subways in 1995. The *Sankei* and *Yomiuri* newspapers are blasted for supporting nuclear power, as he presents detailed information on why nuclear power is not necessary and accuses pro-nuclear advocates of manipulating electricity supply and demand statistics to scare the public into submitting to the dictates of the imperious nuclear village. In the same style as his previous manga, his demagogic alter ego relentlessly hammers his opponents while leaving the reader in no doubt that this is a battle against evil (the nuclear village) which must be won to safeguard Japan's future.

While public opinion favors phasing out nuclear power, the Abe government favors it to boost the economy. Who gets to decide? As Aldrich explains, "Japanese leaders and civil servants envision public opinion as malleable; in this approach, the people's perspective should be changed to match the perspective of the administration rather than elevated as a guidestar which should be followed" (Aldrich 2012, 131). Official reluctance to allow the public to have a say in national energy strategy post-Fukushima is evident in the derailing of all efforts to hold a national or local referendum on nuclear energy. The government is unwilling to risk the "Italy syndrome" whereby voters pulled the plug on nuclear energy in June 2011. It has also taken a proactive approach to public opinion. In June 2011, less than three months after the Fukushima catastrophe, METI was attempting to fast-track reactor restarts, issuing public reassurances that operational safety had been confirmed and sponsoring a town hall Internet meeting in Kyushu to solicit public opinion about bringing local nuclear reactors back online. This public relations (PR) campaign imploded as the media reported that the local power company had orchestrated participation in a bid to fabricate public support for the reactor restart. It subsequently emerged that this sham was standard operating procedure at a series of similar events staged by regional utilities; NISA and METI officials were fully involved in these efforts to orchestrate favorable public opinion towards nuclear power (NHK News, July 29, 2011; Kingston 2012a).

While over 70% of the Japanese public favored phasing out or significantly reducing nuclear energy as of February 2013, the nuclear village was fighting back. Keidanren and other large business organizations have lobbied vigorously to block efforts to downsize nuclear power, citing growing trade deficits due to energy imports and increased business flight overseas because of Japan's high and rising costs of electricity. Pro-nuclear advocates also raised the issue of global warming, pointing out that in the absence of nuclear power Japan could not meet its CO_2 emission-reduction pledges; that remains uncertain, but the business-friendly LDP has never been enthusiastic about the 25% reduction by 2020 pledged by PM Hatoyama Yukio in 2009. In addition, the utility lobby disingenuously portrays renewable energy as unreliable and too costly while overlooking the massive subsidies that nurtured nuclear energy in Japan and the mounting tab for Fukushima (see Chapter 9).

Despite an aggressive PR campaign promoting nuclear power, the public remains leery; 80% nationwide do not trust the government's nuclear safety measures (*Asahi*, March 13, 2012). In the largest demonstrations in Tokyo since the 1960s, tens of thousands of Japanese took to the streets in 2012 on multiple occasions to pressure the government to abandon nuclear power and not proceed with plans to restart any nuclear reactors (see Chapter 4; Arita 2012). As of mid-2013, public anxieties remain strong due to ongoing problems with decontamination efforts at Fukushima, involving leakages of contaminated water, repeated power cuts to critically important cooling systems, and concerns about disposal of radioactive debris and storage of spent fuel rods. This abysmal situation provoked strong criticism from the normally docile and pro-nuclear International Atomic Energy Agency about persistent safety lapses and botched decontamination efforts.

Prime Minister Noda Yoshihiko's cabinet backtracked from initial pronouncements in September 2012 that it would seek to eliminate nuclear energy by the 2030s under severe pressure from the Japanese business lobby, demonstrating that it was more willing to risk public ire than defy the nuclear village (Kingston 2012d). This wavering is one of the factors behind the implosion of Noda's Democratic Party of Japan (DPJ) in the national elections in December 2012, but these elections were not the expected referendum on nuclear power and instead focused on the rising security threat from China and the DPJ's maladroit management of the economy (*Asahi*, December 17, 2012). Prime Minister Abe is counting on public prioritizing of economic concerns to support his nuclear advocacy; the devaluation of the yen caused by "Abenomics" is boosting the trade deficit as imported fuels cost more.

While the large demonstrations and signs of a more robust civil society in 2012 stoked a degree of euphoria about the prospects of a green revolution, the election of the pro-nuclear LDP is a reminder about prevailing realties. The key is that the nuclear village retains veto power over national energy policy and therefore citizens will not get to decide the outcome. In Jacque Hymans's view, nuclear institutions are "extremely well insulated from democratic processes" and not subject to the passions of public opinion. He writes: "Opinion swings are certainly worth tracking, but it is also necessary to recognize that in countries with large numbers of nuclear veto players, whichever direction the political winds end up blowing, abrupt, radical nuclear policy reorientations are very difficult to achieve and are therefore rare" (Hymans 2011, 160). Hymans also reminds us that Japanese corporate links with GE, Westinghouse and Areva mean that "Japan now sits at the epicenter of the global nuclear energy industry. Given the economic stakes involved, the government simply cannot ignore the manufacturers' nuclear policy preferences" (Hymans 2011, 181).

The financial stakes are high, and if Japan terminates nuclear power, the pain would extend beyond the utilities and vendors; lenders and investors, including Japan's major banks and insurance firms, will also face huge losses. Pulling the plug on nuclear power might drive four of Japan's 10 utilities into insolvency (*The New York Times*, August 30, 2012). In addition, there have been strident voices from the political right calling for the retention of nuclear energy because it leaves available the nuclear weapons option (Hymans 2011). Moreover, Washington warned Tokyo that phasing out nuclear energy would harm bilateral relations because it would raise concerns about Japan's large stockpiles of plutonium and uncomfortable questions about the consistency of US nuclear non-proliferation efforts targeting Iran and North Korea. This is another reason to assume that Fukushima will not lead to an overhaul of national energy strategy.

Regulatory revamp?

The Nuclear Regulation Authority (NRA) established in September 2012 has conducted on-site inspections indicating that some reactors are sited on active fault lines, but as of mid-2013 has not made a decision about shutting them down. Utilities threaten legal challenges to NRA assessments that cast a cloud over nuclear safety. In a December 2012 meeting with regulators from the United States, UK and France, NRA Chairman Tanaka Shuichi blasted lax safety precautions in the nuclear industry, but it remains to be seen if his tough words are matched by action (*Asahi*, December 15, 2012). He pushed through strict new safety regulations, but the key as always is in implementation and monitoring of compliance. For example, there are only nine inspectors overseeing the 3,000 workers engaged in the troubled decontamination and decommissioning efforts at Fukushima, a bungled operation that has been left to the discretion of TEPCO which decided against bringing in outside experts. The utility failed to anticipate the problem of what to do with massive volumes of highly radioactive wastewater that are accumulating at the plant and leaking into the ocean as improvised responses have proven inadequate. Apparently, nobody questioned the advisability of the planned dumping of the toxic wastewater into the ocean. *The New York Times* reporter Martin Fackler concludes that TEPCO, "is lurching from one problem to the next without a coherent strategy … a cautionary tale about the continued dangers of leaving decisions about nuclear safety to industry insiders" (*The New York Times*, April 29, 2013). Despite this and many other red flags on nuclear safety, with the pro-nuclear LDP back in power, the political pressures on the NRA to compromise on safety and resume business as usual are intense. In July 2013 four utilities applied to restart ten reactors based on the new safety guidelines, but the ongoing crisis at Fukushima complicates the prospects.

In August 2013 Prime Minister Abe announced that the government was taking over the Fukushima decommissioning because TEPCO's incompetence and a cascade of revelations about radiation spewing into the ocean threatened Tokyo's bid for the 2020 Olympics and also plans to restart reactors. While Prime Minister Abe reassured the International Olympic Committee that the situation is under control, the media suggested that his remarks were misleading and a top TEPCO executive publicly differed with this rosy assessment. It is apparent that TEPCO cut corners on dealing with radiation contaminated water to save money in ways that compromised safety. (Asahi September 18, 2013) Abe now "owns" the problem, but the government believes it can not do worse than TEPCO and his personal reassurances were a decisive factor in Tokyo winning the 2020 Olympics and creating more favorable circumstances for reactor restarts. In addition, Abe has become an active pitchman for nuclear plant exports, so phasing out nuclear energy might lead potential customers to opt for other providers. And, Washington has been pressuring Japan not to terminate nuclear energy because it is concerned about Japan's large stockpiles of plutonium. If these are not going to be used as fuel for reactors, what is their purpose? Nuclear weapons non-proliferation concerns have global implications, especially since the ruling LDP's Secretary General Ishiba Shigeru has stated Japan needs to maintain nuclear energy to show other nations that it retains the nuclear bomb option.

Conclusion

The Diet found the nuclear village guilty and responsible for not taking measures to prevent Fukushima and for inadequate emergency responses. However, it is unlikely that there will be a significant shift in Japan's nuclear energy policy anytime soon despite the Diet's verdict and public opinion favoring a phasing out of nuclear energy. Hymans's historical institutionalist angle on veto players and the policy rigidity they sustain suggests that public preferences about nuclear energy will not prevail. The nuclear village is able to block "radical Japanese nuclear policy change in any direction, even in the face of the most serious disaster Japan has faced since World War II. After all, even in crises, veto players tend to stand up for their perceived interests" (Hymans 2011, 188).

The Abe cabinet's strong support for restarting idled reactors is a stunning vindication of Hymans's analysis. With the LDP back in charge, barring a serious nuclear accident, it seems clear that the veto players will prevail and Japan will not phase out nuclear power. The summer of discontent in 2012 marked the high point of the anti-nuclear movement, prompting the village's most significant intervention when it appeared that PM Noda's cabinet had officially sanctioned phasing out nuclear energy in September 2012; major business lobbies publically protested and persuaded the Noda cabinet to reverse course (Kingston 2012d). So the apparent policy drift in 2012 bought time and as of 2013 national energy strategy, and reliance on nuclear power, is settling back into established policy ruts. The village worked to reframe public discourse by shifting attention away from the safety lapses, meltdowns and lingering dangers to more prosaic assessments based on electricity supply and demand, trade imbalances, and economic recovery. Policies are made in the back rooms and corridors of power, not on the streets, exactly where the village controls the commanding heights.

Institutions are not destiny, but in Japan's nuclear sector they are proving quite sturdy and resourceful. It was never going to be easy to reset the national energy strategy or take on the nuclear village even if it seemed that Fukushima was a game-changing event that would open the way for sweeping policy reform. It was likely that public outrage would dissipate and that policy inertia would prevail, thereby minimizing reform. Given the cascade of tawdry revelations stemming from the Fukushima disaster, it has been tricky for the village to spin the saga. Yet it engaged in surprisingly effective damage control, spreading blame, obfuscating responsibility, and otherwise shaping public discourse while tapping its networks of power to reinstate nuclear energy into the energy mix. It has also forestalled efforts to restructure the power sector and separation of energy generation from transmission that are vital to Japan's renewable energy expansion (see Chapter 9). While the policy-making process may appear obscure, and policy makers unable to prioritize an array of demands and options (see Chapter 7), this positive outcome for nuclear advocates overcame the steep odds of three meltdowns and vast public opposition, one that attests to the power and resilience of the nuclear village to realize its agenda. However, restarting Japan's fleet of nuclear reactors, especially those near active fault lines, and looming "not-in-my-back-yard" (NIMBY) battles over nuclear waste disposal, will spark further battles contesting this agenda.

Note

1 This chapter draws on Kingston 2012a, 2012b, 2012c, 2012d.

Bibliography

Aldrich, Daniel (2008) *Site Fights*, Ithaca, NY: Cornell University Press.

——(2012) "Networks of Power," in Jeff Kingston (ed.) *Natural Disaster and Nuclear Crisis in Japan*, Abingdon: Routledge, 127–39.

Arita, Eriko (2012) "Citizen's Groups Propel Rising Wave of Antinuclear Activism," *Japan Times*, August 9.

Birmingham, Lucy and McNeill, David (2012) *Strong in the Rain*, New York: Palgrave Macmillan.

Colignon, Richard and Chikako Usui (2003) *Amakudari: The Hidden Fabric of Japan's Economy*, Ithaca, NY: Cornell University Press.

DeWit, Andrew (2012a) "Japan's Remarkable Renewable Energy Drive-After Fukushima," *The Asia-Pacific Journal* 10(11:10), March 11.

——(2012b) "Japan's Energy Policy at a Crossroads: A Renewable Energy Future?" *The Asia-Pacific Journal* 10(38:4), September 17.

——(2013) "Water, Water Everywhere: Incentives and Options at Fukushima Daiichi and Beyond" *The Asia-Pacific Journal* 11(32:6), August 12.

DeWit, Andrew, Iida Tesunari and Kaneko Masaru (2011) "Fukushima and the Political Economy of Power Policy in Japan," Jeff Kingston (ed.) *Natural Disaster and Nuclear Crisis in Japan: Response and Recovery after Japan's 3/11*, Routledge, 156–71.

Dusinberre, Martin (2012) *Hard Times in the Hometown*, Honolulu: University of Hawaii Press.

The Economist (2012) *Special Report on Nuclear Energy*, March 10.

Freeman, Laurie (2000) *Closing the Shop: Information Cartels and Japan's Mass Media*, Princeton: Princeton University Press.

Funabashi Report (2012) *Rebuild Japan Initiative Foundation, The Independent Investigation Commission on the Fukushima Nuclear Accident*, February, rebuildjpn.org/en/fukushima/report.

Hatamura Report (2012) *Investigation Committee on the Accident at the Fukushima Nuclear Power Stations of TEPCO*, July, icanps.go.jp/eng/.

Honma, Ryu (2012) *Dentsu to Genpatsu Hodo* (Dentsu and Media Coverage of the Nuclear Crisis), Tokyo: Akishobo.

Hymans, Jacques (2011) "Veto Players, Nuclear Energy and Nonproliferation," *International Security* 36(2), Fall: 154–89.

Johnson, Chalmers (1982) *MITI and the Japanese Miracle*, Palo Alto: Stanford University Press.

Kingston, Jeff (2010) *Contemporary Japan*, London: Wiley-Blackwell.

——(2012a) "The Politics of Disaster, Nuclear Crisis and Recovery," in Jeff Kingston (ed.) *Natural Disaster and Nuclear Crisis in Japan: Response and Recovery after Japan's 3/11*, Abingdon: Routledge, 188–206.

——(2012b) "Mismanaging Risk and the Fukushima Nuclear Crisis," *The Asia-Pacific Journal* 10(12:4), March 19.

——(2012c) "Japan's Nuclear Village," *The Asia-Pacific Journal* 10(37:1), September 10.

——(2012d) "Power Politics: Japan's Resilient Nuclear Village," *The Asia-Pacific Journal* 10(43:1), October 29.

Kobayashi, Yoshinori (2012) *Datsu Genpatsu-ron* (Exiting Nuclear Power), Tokyo: Kodansha.

Lukner, Kerstin and Sakaki, Alexandra (2013) "Lessons from Fukushima: A Comparison of the Investigation Reports on the Nuclear Disaster," *The Asia-Pacific Journal* 11(19:1), May 13.

National Diet Report (2012) *The Fukushima Nuclear Accident Independent Investigation Commission, Official Report*, July 5, naiic.go.jp/en/.

Onitsuka, Hiroshi (2012) "Hooked on Nuclear Power: Japanese State-Local Relations and the Vicious Cycle of Nuclear Dependence," *The Asia-Pacific Journal* 10(3:1), January 16.

Perrow, Charles (2011) "Fukushima and the Inevitability of Accidents," *Bulletin of the Atomic Scientists* 67(6): 44–52.

Ramseyer, J. Mark (2012) "Why Power Companies Build Nuclear Reactors on Fault Lines: The Case of Japan," *Theoretical Inquiries in Law* 13(2), January: 457–85.

Repeta, Lawrence (2011) "Could the Meltdown Have Been Avoided?" in Jeff Kingston (ed.) *Tsunami: Japan's Post-Fukushima Future*, Washington, DC: Foreign Policy, 183–94.

TEPCO (2012) *Fukushima Nuclear Accident Analysis Report (Summary)*, June 20, www.tepco.co.jp/en/press/corp-com/release/betu12_e/images/120620e0102.pdf.

von Hippel, Frank (2011) "It Could Happen Here Too," March 23, *The New York Times*.

9 Japan's renewable power prospects

Andrew DeWit

Galvanized in particular through international embarrassment at Fukushima Daiichi's repeated releases of radiation-laced water into the sea, Japan has ramped up its renewable energy and efficiency initiatives. On September 8, 2013, in the wake of the International Olympic Commission's vote to award the 2020 Summer Olympics to Tokyo, Japanese Prime Minister Abe Shinzo committed his cabinet to "make every effort to accelerate the spread of renewable energy sources and promote energy conservation" (Asahi Shimbun, September 14, 2013). The majority of Japan's local governments, central agencies and private sector had already been making progress on various sustainability projects. This chapter argues that national politics impedes Japan from taking the lead in the swiftly evolving global transition towards building resilient green communities (Orr 2012). Japan's monopolized electricity utilities are at the core of vested interests impeding reforms that are key to this transition. These interests dominate the central government's policy-making councils and national politicians' calculus of what is viable (see Chapters 7 and 8). The central government thus plays an ambivalent role despite the need for more aggressive and coordinated commitments to renewable energy and efficiency.

The core of the ongoing paradigm shift is smart and distributed renewable power, "one of the greatest technological challenges industrialized societies have undertaken" (Resnick Institute 2012). Deploying distributed power is essential to mitigating and adapting to climate change's mounting toll on energy and transport infrastructure, agriculture, and much of what we take for granted in contemporary society. Globally, civilian and military projects are realizing a green resilience the magnitude of which already reaches into the trillions of dollars (Nikkei BP 2010; PEW Research Center 2013; SBI Energy 2012).

Post-Fukushima Japan also has ample reasons to reconsider its energy mix due to concerns over nuclear safety and its high cost. It has the capacity to undertake vanguard renewable and energy efficiency initiatives through its still-potent economic strengths, coupled with innovative capital, leading-edge technologies and activist city-regions. These factors have the potential to pull Japan into the front ranks of building resilience, diffusing sustainable growth among cities and depressed regions alike (Mizobata 2013). America's military-centered energy industrial policy regime, focused on renewables and efficiency, is clear evidence that decisive and even disruptive state intervention is essential (DeWit 2013b), but rapid progress in Japan depends, most of all, on overcoming vested interests' capacity to obstruct change.

Distributed energy

First, what is distributed power and how does it differ from centralized power? Aside from conventional hydropower, most electricity is generated by burning billions of tons of coal and other fossil fuels, or by reacting radioactive fuels, to boil water and then use the steam to drive turbines that generate electrical current. These finite substances possess great energy density per unit volume, but their use exacts unsustainable environmental costs. By contrast, distributed renewable power generation harvests the dispersed but far greater energy in sunlight, wind, wave action and other recurrent processes.

The technological and political economy differences between centralized and distributed power systems are yet unfolding, but already resemble the gulf between telecommunications' old and emergent paradigms. The static model of the monopoly phone company and landline telephones went into eclipse in the 1990s. In its place is a still swiftly evolving and expanding market of multiple providers and ubiquitous mobile devices, the ancillary functions of which—as cameras, credit cards, music players, and the like—continue to proliferate, disrupting markets far beyond telephony. Distributed power features a similarly rapid evolution of hardware and software as well as diffusion of opportunity. It also shrinks material consumption and markedly reduces environmental damage. This is because renewable power does not require the continuous mining, refining, transport and incineration of billions of tons of fuel as well as disposal of its toxic waste in the biosphere, to the detriment of present and future generations.

Transitions between paradigms always see the new grow within the old. Power economies are not replaced overnight, though newly developing countries and regions can leapfrog into the new paradigm just as many have done in telecommunications. In most countries, distributed and renewable generation is encountering varying levels of political friction from incumbent interests within legacy systems dominated by large-scale, conventional forms of power generation. Renewables will require backup by conventional sources for some time, with hybrid pairings of renewables and distributed natural gas often viewed as the most economically and environmentally appealing (Channell *et al.* 2012). However, the conventional wisdom that renewable, distributed power is decades away is at odds with the empirical reality of rapid deployment and cost reductions (Pernick *et al.* 2013).

Japan's highly centralized power paradigm differs considerably from other nations' power markets. Japan's ¥17 trillion (US$180 billion) power economy is probably the most centralized of the Organisation for Economic Co-operation and Development (OECD) countries. Japan's fleet of 50 nuclear reactors—all shutdown as of September 2013—and large-scale thermal (mostly coal and natural gas) power—are largely owned by 10 monopolized regional utilities that also own the country's Balkanized transmission grid. By contrast, America's $360 billion power market possesses—like most OECD countries—a potentially advantageous diversity through 3,200 utilities and separate management of the transmission network by the North American Reliability Council (EIA 2012). Institutional diversity helps open up the political space for deploying distributed power and building the business models that are likely to become global standards.

In early April of 2013, the Japanese Cabinet announced that it would embark on reforming power markets and separating control over generation and transmission. Yet the power industry's vested interests gutted explicit commitments to implementing this reform, meaning that the government's announcement may turn out to be an empty promise. The monopolies worry that unbundling ownership and control of the grid might shrink their scale and undermine their business model by offering consumers more options and lower prices. This might further impair the utilities' post-Fukushima capacity to attract investment and secure cheap financing. Moreover, such a structural reform would probably make financial institutions more cautious about lending to utilities that own nuclear facilities (*Sankei Shimbun*, April 6, 2013).

Yet without unbundling generation and transmission, the monopolies will continue to impede the rise of competitors by charging onerous rates for access to the grid. This is precisely what they did in the wake of deregulation of large-lot power markets from 1995. Hence 60% of Japan's power economy is de jure deregulated already, but the monopolies have used their control of the grid to keep competition to only 4% of the market. Preserving the power of the monopolies in this way stifles the potential of innovation and competition, saddling Japan with a high cost and vulnerable electricity sector.

Paradigm shift

The Fukushima nuclear debacle in mid-March of 2011 revealed centralized power's vulnerability to cascading failures. Fukushima's protracted problems are proving enormously costly while undermining the Japan brand and confidence at home and abroad. The blackout caused by Hurricane Sandy in New York at the end of 2012 also underscored centralized power's weaknesses in the face of natural disasters supercharged by climate change (*Financial Times*, March 1, 2013). In addition, centralized power is dangerously fragile in the face of cyber threats, geomagnetic disturbances, and other acts or events. These hazards have motivated the US military, in concert with that country's most advanced clusters of innovation, to become a front-runner in deploying distributed power to "island" its bases from the conventional grid (DeWit 2013b).

Another profound challenge to the dominant paradigm is the collision between water scarcity and surging energy demand. Thermal power depends heavily on water for fuel extraction, refining, and especially for cooling, but escalating climate change, the depletion of aquifers, and other factors are imposing physical limits that at the very least will require expensive new technology. For example, the 2003 European heat wave that killed over 70,000 people saw a forced shut-down of French nuclear reactors, the cooling of which relied on river water. Even as demand for power spiked, the rivers' declining volumes and rising temperatures made it impossible to cool these costly, centralized power assets. This phenomenon is becoming ever more common. In 2012, seawater became too warm to cool the US state of Connecticut's Millstone reactor on the Atlantic Coast, forcing a 12-day shutdown. A comprehensive analysis of China's massive 500 gigawatts of thermal generation warns that 85% of it is concentrated in increasingly water-scarce regions (BNEF 2013).

By contrast, renewables and other distributed-power technologies have minimal demand for water, making them crucial for sustainability (Nelder 2012).

Opening up opportunity

Much like the old paradigm of telecommunications, centralized power is also being hollowed out by the intersection of technological change and public demand.

Increasing numbers of consumers are simultaneously becoming producers of power, or "prosumers," predominantly by installing solar panels on their roofs and selling some of it back to the grid. For example, Australia's national average of owner-occupied household solar reached 20% as of 2013, with projections of 50% to 75% by 2017 (Parkinson 2013). Power markets are thus evolving towards distributed power through technological change, public policy, and popular demand.

The equity aspect—so important in our era of destabilizing inequalities—is also starkly different in the centralized and distributed models. Daniel Aldrich's chapter in this volume illustrates very well how Japanese local communities benefit from hosting large-scale conventional power plants, but the monopoly utilities and their investors receive the bulk of the benefits. Distributed power's solar, wind, and other renewable resources are so widely dispersed that it perforce spreads the pecuniary and other returns much more broadly, among far more local communities as well as their households, farmers, small businesses, and other interests. In 2010, 51% of Germany's renewable generating capacity was operated by private individuals and a further 11% by farmers, with the big utilities far behind at 4% (Morris 2013). Public policy and popular action is accelerating that diffusion of opportunity in a host of countries.

The global context for Japan's post-Fukushima policy choices is thus a reality wherein distributed power is already being deployed in the world's largest civilian and military economies. The chairperson of the American Federal Energy Regulatory Commission (FERC), Jon Wellinghof, made the shift to distributed power explicit in late 2012 (Clarke 2012). California and Hawaii have already lifted regulatory barriers that capped distributed power to 15% of power generation (Gallucci 2011), and other US states are following suit (Stanfield 2013). The FERC is accelerating this with regulatory changes at the federal level (Marcacci 2013). The FERC's "Energy Infrastructure Update" for 2012 reveals that renewable power accounted for just about half of all new power installation in America (Massey 2013).

In short, there are multiple drivers for the deployment of distributed power and smart infrastructure. Smart and distributed power reduces greenhouse gas emissions and material consumption, accelerates technological development, and stimulates the growth of entire new industries. It is effectively taking the baton from the telecommunications revolution, and thus melding energy, IT and biotechnology. These fusing sectors constitute roughly 20% of the average industrialized economy, a solid basis for a sustainable economic and environmental growth model.

Expanding market scale

As to current market assessments, Figure 9.1 is from a 2010 Nikkei BP (Nikkei BP 2010) survey to determine the distributed and smart power market's cumulative value over the two decades to 2030. The ¥3100 trillion ($32 trillion) figure, six times Japan's 2012 gross domestic product (GDP) of ¥520 trillion ($5.5 trillion), was derived from an examination of 100 of 300–400 smart city projects, which deploy distributed power and other advanced sustainable infrastructure, then underway around the world. Shortly thereafter, however, smart city projects more than doubled in China alone, from roughly 165 in late 2011 (*Nikkei Shimbun*, November 21, 2011) to over 400 by the end of 2012 (Takesue 2012). The Nikkei BP assessment is thus a significant underestimate, but remains very instructive because it illustrates the overall scale of the market as well as the speed of its expansion.

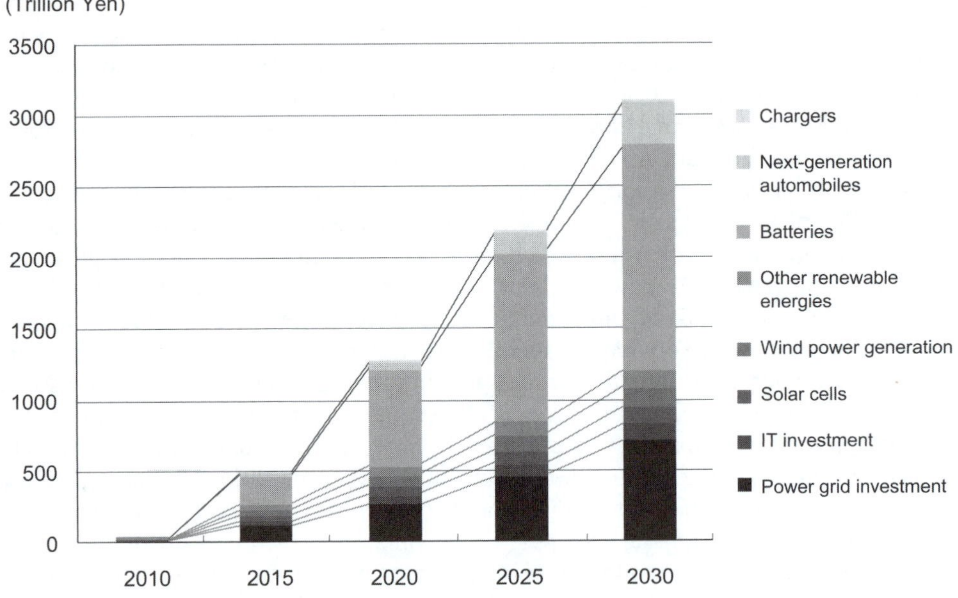

Figure 9.1 Global Smart City Market, 2010–2030
Source: (Figures from Nikkei BP 2010 survey)

More recently, Fuji Keizai projects that smart city markets in Japan alone grew from ¥1.1 trillion ($11.7 billion) in 2011 to ¥1.47 trillion ($15.6 billion) in 2012, and projects an increase to ¥3.80 trillion ($40.5 billion) by 2020 (a 340% expansion from 2011). Fuji Keizai also predicts that annual global investment in smart projects will increase from ¥16.332 trillion ($174 billion) in 2011 to ¥40.555 trillion ($432 billion) by 2020 (Fuji Keizai 2012).

Japan's policy initiatives

Since 2008, the central government has sponsored "eco-model cities." These are separated into four categories, including large urban (Yokohama), mid-sized urban (Toyota City), smaller regional (Iida City) and rural communities (Shimokawa-cho). These eco-model projects emphasized carbon reductions, recycling and some deployment of renewable energy, but also stressed enhanced livability through improvements in elderly care, access, and other amenities suitable for a rapidly aging society.

In January 2012, after the Fukushima meltdowns, Japan's most advanced eco-model cities, such as Kitakyushu and Yokohama, were selected for a new program promoting 11 "environmental future city" initiatives. The new initiative targets several of the Tohoku communities (such as Sendai), to disseminate lessons from the eco-model city program in the ongoing rebuild of Tohoku. The ambition is to rebuild Tohoku communities with a focus on renewable energy, increasing the communities' resilience, generating economic opportunities and showcasing Japan's eco-technologies to the world (Cabinet Secretariat 2012).

However, more aggressive initiatives are underway that are independent from the central government's flagship programs. For example, the Tokyo Metropolitan

Government (TMG) that runs a city of 13 million residents and millions more daily commuters is installing a predominantly natural gas-fired distributed power generation and grid network while also working towards a renewable energy target of 20% by 2020. The power project was initially aimed at maintaining essential transport and other functions in the event of large-scale blackouts like in 2011, but between fiscal years (FY) 2012 and 2013, TMG dramatically increased its budget for "realizing a smart energy city" from ¥40 million ($425,000) to ¥10.3 billion ($109.3 million). TMG projects its new spending on distributed power and related items to stimulate roughly nine times that much in private-sector economic activity in addition to 5,000 jobs. In 2013, TMG created a new "Energy Division" in its Bureau of the Environment to coordinate its efforts to support distributed power while liberalizing power markets and enhancing efficiency (*Tokyo Shimbun*, March 27, 2013). It also skillfully used existing power law to revise its libraries' and other facilities' power contracts with Tokyo Electric Power Company (TEPCO), saving 10% on power costs by purchasing power from independent providers. TMG's initiatives deliberately threaten TEPCO's centralized and monopolized power generation and distribution model (Toshikawa 2012).

Also working to undermine centralized generation are TMG's 23 wards, which are comparable to cities in their size and power. Setagaya Ward's (population 840,000) policies include aggressively pursuing renewable energy and efficiency while cancelling contracts with TEPCO wherever possible. Setagaya manages 601 public facilities, 217 of which are in the large-voltage market wherein current power law allows consumer choice. Setagaya put roughly half of these large-lot power contracts out to tender for 2012. TEPCO thereby lost power contracts with 111 ward facilities, and the shift to independent power suppliers resulted in a saving of ¥29.4 million ($312,000). In 2013, Setagaya plans to expand the program to 163 facilities and projects that will roughly double its savings (Hosaka 2013; Setagaya 2013).

TMG is acting within a larger bloc of regional authorities, including the surrounding prefectures of Chiba, Saitama and Kanagawa as well as the conurbations of Kawasaki, Yokohama, and Saitama. Due south of TMG, for example, Kanagawa Prefecture (population 9.05 million) is increasing its renewable power self-sufficiency to 6% by 2014 and targets 16% by 2020, with a goal of 45% distributed generation by 2030 (Kanagawa Prefecture 2013, Kankyo Bijinesu, September 9, 2013). The prefecture also determined that in 2013 fully 90% of its facilities would abandon TEPCO for independent power suppliers, saving roughly ¥150 million ($1.6 million) in power costs (*Nikkei Shimbun*, February 1, 2013).

Moreover, the Kanagawa capital of Yokohama City (population 3.7 million) is slated to set up its own power company in 2014 (a first for post-war Japan), and is also planning to boost renewable energy sources to 20% of its power needs by 2030 (*Nikkei Shimbun*, March 22, 2013). The city of Saitama also adopted an "Energy Smart Action Vision" in 2013, which commits it to quadrupling its renewable energy supply and reducing its power demand 10% by 2020 (*Nikkei Shimbun*, March 21, 2013). Osaka Prefecture and Osaka City are doing likewise (*Sankei Shimbun*, April 5, 2013). Most other prefectures, urban centers and towns are taking similar steps, including termination of contracts with the regional monopoly. What seemed unlikely, indeed impossible, in Japan, is swiftly becoming the new norm.

The private sector is involved in all of these distributed energy and smart city projects and some firms are taking their own initiative. For example, Panasonic is showcasing its technology in a ¥60 billion ($637 million) "Fujisawa Smart Town," due to open in the spring of 2014 with a population of 3,000. The project aims at 30% renewable energy as well as sufficient backup storage for a full three days in the event of natural disaster (Kanellos 2012). In 2013, Panasonic launched a joint venture with such other blue chip firms as Mitsui, Tokyo Gas, NTT, and Sumitomo Mitsui Trust Bank, "to manage and provide the sustainable and smart services throughout the entire town." These firms are collaborating to gain experience useful to land contracts in overseas smart city and smart town projects (Panasonic 2013).

The Fukushima disaster made clear the need to improve disaster resilience. Local governments and the central government agencies that work with them thus increased their spending on renewable energy, efficiency, energy storage capacity and conservation. For FY 2012, expenditures in these areas totaled ¥202 billion ($2.14 billion) for central agencies and ¥88.7 billion ($942 million) for the prefectures and designated cities,[1] and the trend for such investments is onward and upward.

Local governments also administer special finance packages (with central government support), targeting expansion of renewable energy and energy efficiency at small and medium-size enterprises (SMEs), and among farmers and households. These low-interest loans encourage gains in energy efficiency through the diffusion of such equipment as LEDs (light-emitting diodes) and Business Energy Management Systems. The local and central governments also offer related tax exemptions and other special measures.

The feed-in tariff

Japan's distributed power initiatives were greatly amplified by the July 1, 2012 introduction of the "feed-in tariff," or FIT, the most effective and efficient policy for diffusing renewable energy (IEA-RETD 2012). Figure 9.2 shows that the FIT is a mechanism whereby the extra cost of producing renewable power is passed on to the utilities' customer base. The FIT guarantees stable markets and prices for renewable energy in order to attract private-sector investment. The public sector sets a premium price for renewable power depending on the generation type, assumed costs, and other factors. The utilities are obliged to purchase this renewable power from authorized producers, such as households, and then authorized to cover the extra costs by boosting consumers' electricity rates. Accelerated diffusion of distributed power in tandem with deliberate cuts in FIT rates drive down costs. Since renewable energy in Japan is at present more expensive than conventional energy, without the price and market guarantee of the FIT most households and businesses would not invest in renewables. However, renewables' declining costs have seen, for example, wind become competitive with gas in the United States (Channell *et al.* 2012), and renewable costs continue to fall through diffusion and technological advance while the costs of conventional power generation are increasing (REN21 2013).

Prior to Fukushima, Japan's FIT was limited to solar power. The Japanese power community and their bureaucratic allies had sought to use the FIT to reduce reliance on fossil fuels. They aimed at a limited (20% by 2030) expansion of renewables while targeting a 50% reliance on nuclear power by 2030. This compromise was worked out in the pre-Fukushima energy policy-making circles that were clustered in the capital and dominated by the so-called "nuclear village" of pro-nuclear advocates in the utilities, bureaucracy, politics, media and academia.

Japan's post-Fukushima energy policy

After Fukushima, Japan's FIT was redefined in the political debate. It went from being a technocratic tool to reduce reliance on fossil fuels to a more populist instrument aimed at phasing out nuclear power. This FIT reset owes much to the efforts of former Prime Minister Kan Naoto and Softbank's CEO Son Masayoshi. Kan got the FIT passed by the Diet (national parliament) in August 2011 while both were key actors in diffusing awareness of the FIT as well as altering its purpose (DeWit *et al.* 2012). For example, Softbank CEO Son launched his Natural Energy Councils in May of 2011. The prefectural council includes 36 of 47 Japan's prefectures, while the council for designated cities (cities with over 500,000 inhabitants) has attracted 17 of 20. As of early 2013 the councils' membership includes over 200 firms, among them such corporate giants as Kyocera.

This organizational effort to diffuse renewable energy is being replicated throughout the country. A host of new councils, agencies, and study groups focus on promoting various types of renewables. Centralized energy also confronts a growing challenge from local communities that are using 3/11 as a catalyst to increase their disaster preparedness and reliance on sustainable energy (Samuels 2013).

As of 2013, Japan has some of the highest FIT tariffs in the world. For example, the ¥42 per kilowatt-hour (kWh) premium for large-scale (over 10kW) solar set in 2012 is roughly triple the prevailing rate in Germany. These initial prices applied to projects contracted within FY 2012 ranging from 20 years for megasolar, wind and small hydro, to 10–15 years for household solar and geothermal. The FIT rate for large-scale solar was cut by 10% in early 2013, to ¥37 per kWh for new contracts, but cuts in the FITs foster innovation and price reduction, and Japan's reduced rate is still deemed sufficient to attract investments given rapidly declining system costs (*Japan Times*, March 13, 2013).

As of mid-March 2013, Japan's revamped FIT had led to 1.178 gigawatts of new renewable capacity, slightly more than the capacity of one large nuclear reactor. Fully 1.119 gigawatts of this new capacity was solar power, a substantial addition to Japan's cumulative 4.8 gigawatts of solar from the preceding decades (Watanabe 2013). IMS Research and Bloomberg New Energy Finance both project that Japan will become the world's second largest solar market (behind China) with well over 5 gigawatts of new capacity coming online in 2013 (IMS 2013). Japanese banks also forecast the domestic solar market to be worth ¥1.8 trillion ($19 billion) over the three years from 2013, or about eight times the ¥223 billion ($2.3 billion) total of solar investments in 2012 (Watanabe *et al.* 2013).

The monopolized utilities and their allies in the business community argue that the FIT is unreasonably burdensome, but as in Germany, power-intensive businesses get a break on the FIT. Japan's Agency for Natural Resources calculates the current additional costs for a typical household to rise from a moderate ¥87 per month to ¥120 per month, the price of a soda at the station kiosk. Moreover, even in notoriously high-cost Japan, solar's (over 10kW) average system costs dropped in 2012 from ¥325,000 ($3,400) per kWh to ¥280,000 ($2,950). Further sharp declines are anticipated, boding well for Japan's global competitiveness (*Nikkei Shimbun*, March 12, 2013).

Like many of its counterparts in the industrialized world, Japan would appear to be on the cusp of a distributed power revolution. The prospect of a paradigm shift and the financial attractions of policy supports like the FIT are bonding innovative capital with

SMEs, farmers, households, finance and other sectors. This emerging paradigm offers a robust and sustainable growth option to a country desperate for an economic growth strategy.

The power of efficiency

Even with this projected boom, renewable power generation will not soon supplant post-Fukushima Japan's over 90% reliance on expensive fossil fuels. However, it is not necessary to replace all the lost nuclear generation capacity. One reason is that distributed power generation and transmission reduces power demand. In Japan, roughly 60% of the energy produced in centralized plants is wasted as heat, with a further 5% lost in power transmission. By contrast, even distributed natural gas-fired power generation (in so-called "co-generation") wastes only 11% of the energy as heat (Ozawa 2012, 167), and with renewables like wind and solar, there is no heat loss. There is often minimal or no transmission loss as well, especially when the solar panel is on the house, factory, hotel or retail outlet's roof. Moreover, the deployment of interactive smart grids and demand-management technologies further enhances efficiencies.

Studies by the International Energy Agency (IEA) demonstrate that even more radical energy efficiency improvements are possible with current technology. IEA member countries' current policies are slated to increase energy efficiency by an average of 1.8% per year through 2035 versus 0.5% per year over the previous decade. Yet the IEA's chart reproduced in Figure 9.2 shows us that the "unrealized energy efficiency potential" is about 80% in buildings and power generation and about 60% in transport and industry. These are astounding figures and underscore just how much is at stake and what is possible.

Rising energy costs and awareness of climate change are enhancing the business interest in energy efficiency. In early 2013, SBI Energy estimated that the global energy efficiency market will expand from $595.4 billion in 2012 to $3.3 trillion by 2023 (SBI Energy 2012). This expansion seems likely to accelerate with the ongoing emergence of business models that link dispersed efficiency opportunities with big finance (NRDC 2013).

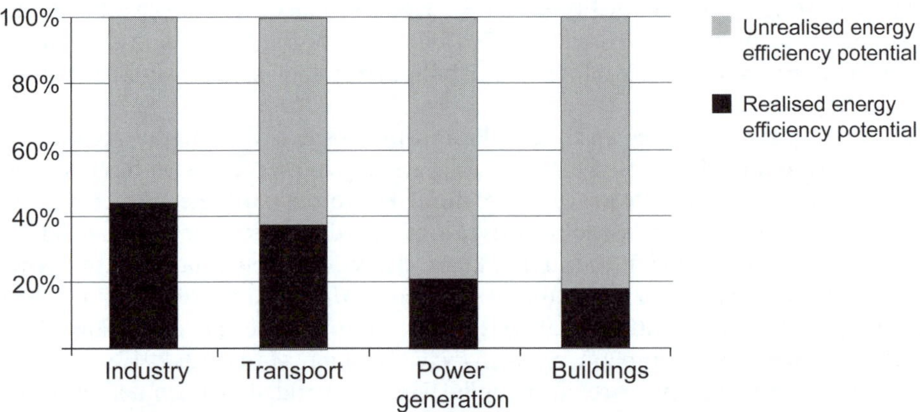

Figure 9.2 Energy efficiency potential used by sector in the New Policies Scenario
Source: (World Energy Outlook 2012; © OECD/IEA 2012, fig. 9.9, p. 291)

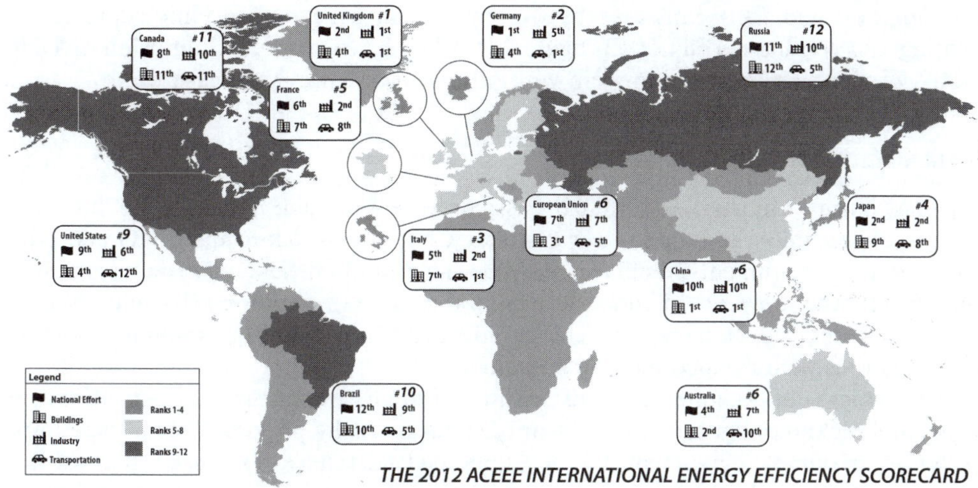

Figure 9.3 The 2012 ACEEE international energy efficiency scorecard
Source: (aceee.org/files/image/topics/international-scorecard-map.jpg)

Japan is, of course, widely believed to be the world's most energy-efficient economy, but according to the American Council on an Energy-Efficient Economy (ACEEE), Japan ranks only fourth out of 12 countries/regions, such as China, the European Union, Germany, and the United States (ACEEE 2012). The 12 economies represent 78% of global GDP, 63% of global energy consumption, and 62% of global CO_2 emissions.

Japan could significantly boost energy efficiency by adopting more robust standards for electric motors, buildings, and a variety of other areas (DeWit 2013a). Let us take just one salient example: Japan has a surprisingly poor deployment of district heating and cooling (DHC) systems. DHC infrastructure centralizes the energy for heating and cooling provision in one district plant and then distributes it via pipes to office buildings, residences, and other network customers. DHC can greatly reduce the inefficiencies of having heat and cooling generation capacity in each of a given district's buildings and residences. DHC has high infrastructure costs that pay off through very low operation and maintenance costs (EGEC 2007). Manhattan's district steam heating system (which can also be used for cooling) was installed in 1882 and features low emissions and fuel efficiency, although a dozen steam explosions since 1987 underscore the importance of regular maintenance. Yet the Japanese Ministry of Economy, Trade, and Industry (METI) energy white paper of 2012 reveals that Japan's deployment of DHC totals a meager 736 kilometers of piping (with 22,997 terajoules (TJ) of energy heat delivered annually), whereas the United States has 3,206 kilometers (and 365,818 TJ), while Sweden's total is 21,100 kilometers (181,612 TJ).

DHC systems are also in the midst of a revolution encompassing the three aspects of energy input, energy throughput, and energy output. The input aspect sees the use of waste heat, renewable energy, and burned refuse rather than fossil fuels. The throughput revolution aspect includes new materials and more efficient means of producing and laying pipe. The output aspect involves the use of IT and sensors that allow more efficient targeting of heating and cooling.

Moreover, Japan has excellent technical capacity in DHC. The Skytree tower facility in Tokyo, opened in May of 2012, includes a DHC network that cuts energy consumption and CO_2 emissions by over 40% compared to conventional means of heating and cooling (METI 2012, figure 223-3-1). Hence, expanded diffusion of DHC would seem a wise choice in tandem with other robust efficiency measures.

"Abenomics": low tech, high waste

Japanese Prime Minister Abe Shinzo has gained considerable attention for his eponymous "Abenomics" economic revival strategy, but in contrast to the TMG and other sub-national governments' emphasis on renewables and efficiency, Abenomics is light on both. Indeed, only ¥200 billion ($2.1 billion) of the ¥10.3 trillion ($103 billion) fiscal stimulus is directed at increasing energy efficiency, and even that minimal spending lacks rigorous performance standards (Ohmae 2013).

Abenomics is so weighted towards traditional public works that the central government itself acknowledges it cannot identify enough worthy projects. While some infrastructure requires maintenance and upgraded disaster resilience, the Liberal Democratic Party (LDP) has long squandered vast sums on white elephant projects that have helped pushed the public debt-to-GDP ratio to over 230%, the highest in the OECD by far. Abenomics promises more waste and more debt (Nikkei Construction 2013).

Nuclear bias

Japan also seems significantly handicapped by the weight of vested interests in the critical area of energy research. As we see from Figure 9.4, the most recent comparative data indicate fully 55% of Japan's 2010 energy research, development and demonstration (RD&D) budget is allocated to centralized and large-scale nuclear power. This focus on nuclear energy is very high compared to 33% in France, 31% in Germany, 19% in the United States, and 17% in Brazil.

Nuclear energy represents a significant opportunity cost as research on other energy options is underfunded, and nuclear power is much more expensive than advocates acknowledge. Indeed, Kobayashi Tatsuo of the Japan Center for Economic Research has argued that the full cost of nuclear power is at least double the government's

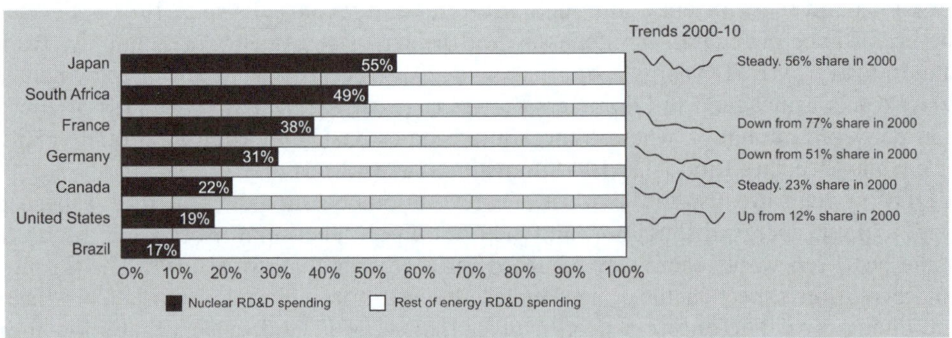

Figure 9.4 Share of nuclear in government energy RD&D spending, 2010
Source: (Copyright OECD/IEA, Energy Technology Perspectives 2012: Pathways to a Clean Energy System, 2012: fig. 2.8, 70)

official figure of ¥10 per kWh (*Financial Times*, December 3, 2012). These costs may rise if financial institutions start charging a lending premium for accident risk (*Sankei Shimbun*, April 3, 2013).

Even so, Japan's central government remains focused on nuclear at the expense of other options. The Abe government still appears more determined to restart nuclear reactors that have been shut down post-Fukushima rather than promote distributed power and efficiency. Japan's longstanding emphasis on nuclear power is one reason it has so little renewable power installed (about 3% of total electricity capacity as compared to Germany's 26%), even though it was once a renewable leader and has no significant endowments of conventional energy resources. The fallout from Fukushima includes disruption of the "nuclear renaissance," but even before that there was growing awareness that its real costs have rendered it commercially unviable (*The Economist* 2012). New-build nuclear now confronts stiff competition from cheaper and less vulnerable distributed renewable and gas-fired power (Channell *et al.* 2012). Proponents of nuclear exports insist that the developing world is on the cusp of a nuclear boom, but nearly half of planned global nuclear energy expansion is concentrated in China, and especially given frayed relations, Japan will not play a significant role in that business.

Japan's energy policy is far too crucial for sustainable growth to have the central and sub-national governments working at cross-purposes. To the extent that Japanese central government support and policy coordination focuses on reviving nuclear power, it will shortchange renewable energy, efficiency and smart grid initiatives. The country will thus risk losing yet more ground in boosting its own energy security, disaster resilience and in tapping the potential of global markets.

Conclusion

This chapter has examined centralized versus distributed power paradigms, as well as the ongoing efficiency revolution, and how they relate to post-Fukushima Japan's economic opportunities. Japan has a fair amount of distributed, renewable power investment underway, accelerated by the feed-in tariff, but the Abe Cabinet is ambivalent about promoting renewable energy and energy efficiency and is thus ceding ground to global competitors. Abenomics therefore appears to be favoring conventional public works to stimulate growth at the expense of a high-tech growth strategy with enormous potential.

Centralized, large-scale power generation, especially nuclear, appears to have peaked as a paradigm, due to technological and market developments and the ineluctable water problem. In Japan, it is also undermined by the need to boost disaster resilience in a country subject to powerful seismic events. Yet Japan's monopolized utilities and its big power-unit makers, including Hitachi and Toshiba, seek to maintain the status quo, and are relying on continued central government support to do so. By contrast, most local governments, innovative businesses, and the public appear to want paradigm change. The power of this pressure from below is crucial to bolstering Japan's green growth potential and international competitiveness.

Note

1 Figures compiled by author, from local and national budgets.

Bibliography

ACEEE (American Council on an Energy Efficient Economy) (2012) "The 2012 ACEEE International Energy Efficiency Scorecard," www.aceee.org/portal/national-policy/international-scorecard.

BNEF (Bloomberg New Energy Finance) (2013) "China's Power Utilities Exposed to Water Disruption," March 25.

Cabinet Secretariat (Government of Japan) (2012) "Future City Initiative," futurecity.rro.go.jp/pdf/reference/Pamphlet_H24futurecity_en.pdf.

Channell, Jason, Lam, Timothy and Pourreza, Shariar (2012) "Shale and Renewables: A Symbiotic Relationship," *Citi Research*, September 12.

Clarke, Chris (2012) "Federal Energy Expert Backing Distributed Generation," *Rewire*, September 6.

DeWit, Andrew (2013a) "Abenomics and Energy Efficiency in Japan," *Asia-Pacific Journal* 11(6:2), February 11.

——(2013b) "The US Military, Green Energy, and the Spiders at Pearly Harbor," *Asia-Pacific Journal* 11(9:5), March 4.

DeWit, Andrew, Iida Tetsunari and Kaneko Masaru (2012) "Fukushima and the Political Economy of Power Policy in Japan," in Jeff Kingston (ed.) *Natural Disaster and Nuclear Crisis in Japan: Response and Recovery After Japan's 3/11*, Routledge.

The Economist (2012) "Nuclear Power: The Dream that Failed," *The Economist*, March 10.

EGEC (European Geothermal Energy Council) (2007) "Geothermal District Heating," September.

EIA (Energy Information Administration) (2012) "What is the Electric Power Grid, and What are some Challenges it Faces?" April 27.

Fuji Keizai (2012) "A Survey of Smart Community-Related Markets," November 22 (in Japanese).

Gallucci, Maria (2011) "Hawaii, California Removing Barrier Limiting Rooftop Solar Projects," *Mother Nature Network*, December 27.

Hosaka Nobuto (2013) "Saving YEN 60 million by Dumping Tokyo Electric Power Company," *Asahi Shimbun Digital*, March 5 (in Japanese).

IEA (International Energy Agency) (2012) *World Energy Outlook 2012*, Paris: IEA.

IEA-RETD (IEA Implementing Agreement for Renewable Energy Technology Deployment) (2012) *Renewable Energy Action on Deployment: READy Policies for Accelerated Deployment of Renewable Energy*, Amsterdam: Elsevier.

IMS (2013) "Japan to Install More than 5 Gigawatts of PV Systems in 2013—Overtaking Germany and the US," press release, March 18.

Kanagawa Prefecture (2013) "Pursuing Kanagawa's Smart-Energy Plan," March 19 (in Japanese).

Kanellos, Michael (2012) "Panasonic's Next Product: A Small Green Town," *Forbes*, October 9.

Marcacci, Silvio (2013) "FERC Regulatory Change Could Boost Distributed Solar in the US," *CleanTechnica*, January 18.

Massey, Nathanael (2013) "Renewable Surged in 2012, According to FERC Report," *Governors' Wind Energy Coalition News*, January 24.

METI (Ministry of Economy Trade and Industry) (2012) *Energy White Paper 2012*, www.enecho.meti.go.jp/topics/hakusho/2012energyhtml/2-2-3.html.

Mizobata Mikio (2013) "A Consideration of Factors Depressing Local Development," Daiwa Institute of Research Column, March 6 (in Japanese).

Morris, Craig (2013) "German Energy Freedom: Moving Beyond Energy Independence to Energy Democracy," Heinrich Boll Stiftung, February.

Nelder, Chris (2012) "The Energy-water Nexus, 2012 Edition," *The Energy Futurist*, August 22.

Nikkei BP (2010) "The Smart City Market will be Worth a Cumulative Total of 3,100 trillion Yen for 2011–30—Nikkei BP Cleantech Estimates Based on its Research on 100 Smart Cities Worldwide," September 27.

Nikkei Construction (2013) "The Return of Public Works via the Re-Regime Change of the Government," *Nikkei Construction*, February 25: 32–35 (in Japanese).

NRDC (Natural Resources Defense Council) (2013) "On-Bill Financing Programs: Overview and Key Considerations for Program Design," August 8, www.nrdc.org/energy/on-bill-financing-programs/default.asp.

Ohmae Ken'nichi (2013) "The Abe Cabinet's Emergency Economic Measures are Election Measures Made by the Authorities," *ZakZak*, January 20 (in Japanese).

Orr, David (2012) "Can we Avoid the Perfect Storm?" *Solutions* 3(3), June.

Ozawa Shoji (2012) *Power-Cut Society: An Energy Revolution Starting from the Community*, Tokyo: Kodansha (in Japanese).

Panasonic (2013) "Panasonic Establishes Fujisawa SST Management Company," news release, March 7.

Parkinson, Giles (2013) "Australia May Have Up To 10 GW of Solar PV by 2017," *Reneweconomy*, March 12.

Pernick, Ron, Wilder, Clint and Winnie, Trevor (2013) *Clean Energy Trends 2013*, Clean Edge Report, March.

PEW Research Center (2013) "Innovate, Manufacture, Compete: A Clean Energy Action Plan," January 17.

REN21 (2013) "Renewable Global Futures Report 2013," Renewable Energy Network 21 Report, January.

Resnick Institute (2012) "Grid 2020: Towards a Policy of Renewable and Distributed Energy Resources," Resnick Institute Report, September.

Samuels, Richard (2013) *3–11: Disaster and Change in Japan*, Ithaca: Cornell University Press.

SBI Energy (2012) "Energy Efficiency Global Products and Services Markets," December 3.

Setagaya (2013) "Press Conference with the Ward Chief (March 1, 2013)," Setagaya Ward transcript, March 8 (In Japanese).

Stanfield, Sky (2013) "Improving Risk-Based Review to Enable Developers to 'Fly' Through Interconnection Hurdles," *Renewable Energy World*, March 18.

Takesue Teruyoshi (2012) "In Order to Participate in China's Smart City Market," Nomura Research Institute, November (in Japanese).

Toshikawa Takeo (2012) "Tokyo's Power Generation Plan is Aimed at 'Blowing a Hole' in TEPCO," *ZakZak*, July 3 (in Japanese).

Watanabe Chisaki (2013) "Japan Adds 1,178 Megawatts of Mostly Solar Energy in Nine Months," Bloomberg News, March 15.

Watanabe Chisaki, Sato Shigeru and Kawamoto Shingo (2013) "Japan Banks Follow Goldman to $19 billion Solar Market," Bloomberg News, February 7.

Part III

International dynamics

10 Bad war or good war?

History and politics in post-war Japan

Sven Saaler

War apologies and the "beautification" of war in contemporary Japan

When Abe Shinzô became prime minister of Japan for the second time in late December 2012, the international press paid close attention to his views on Japan's history during the 20th century. Concern was expressed not only in Chinese, Korean and German newspapers and journals,[1] which are generally highly sensitive to exculpatory views of Japan's wartime history, but also in the international media over Abe's attempts to "revise" the accepted view that the Asia-Pacific War (1931–45)[2] was a war of aggression (*shinryaku sensô*) on the part of Japan. In an editorial titled "Back to the Future," the UK *Economist* warned that Abe's "scarily right-wing cabinet bodes ill for the region" (*The Economist*, January 5, 2013). *The New York Times* criticized Abe's renewed "attempt to deny Japan's history" as a "shameful impulse," which could "inflame tensions with South Korea and make cooperation [with Japan's neighbors] harder … Any attempt to deny the [war] crimes and dilute the apologies [for the war and Japanese war crimes] will outrage South Korea, as well as China and the Philippines, which suffered under Japan's brutal wartime rule" (*The New York Times*, January 2, 2013). A report from the conservative Heritage Foundation had already warned before the elections that "Abe's revisionist historical statements on Japan's wartime actions are indeed troubling and would needlessly exacerbate regional tensions" (Klingner 2012, 6). The author advised that it would be helpful to "privately counsel Abe not to push his revisionist history agenda. Retracting previous Japanese government statements on Japanese wartime actions, as Abe has recommended, would needlessly inflame long-simmering regional animosity. Instead, Japan should revise its statements of atonement and apology in ways that will satisfy Korean sensitivities" (ibid., 8).

Do these Western media statements constitute Japan-bashing? Hardly. As this chapter will show, the international outrage over Abe's views of Japan's wartime history masks a wide gulf between the views of the political elite and the historical awareness of the Japanese population as a whole. Most Japanese do not share Abe's obsession with presenting Japan's wartime history in a more favorable light (cf. Saaler 2005, chapter 3; Yoshida 2011, chapter 5, section 1); on the contrary, they wish to continue the discussion on war responsibility[3] and want to avoid a further deterioration in relations with Korea, China and other countries. By promoting a more favorable (in their view) interpretation of the war, the historical revisionists surrounding Abe have started a "war over memories" (Richter 2008, 52) and polarized the nation. During his election campaign in December 2012, Abe used tactics such as encouraging online "followers" to attack those who did not share his views and "silencing opponents" through Internet bullying (Morris-Suzuki 2013).

In his most recent move, Abe has suggested that the Murayama Statement (*Murayama danwa*)—a major public apology for the war and a symbol of Japan's successful reconciliation policies during the 1990s (cf. Berger 2012)—be replaced with a new and "forward-looking statement" (interview with Abe in *Sankei Shimbun*, December 30, 2012). In August 1995, on the 50th anniversary of the end of the war, Prime Minister Murayama stated:

> During a certain period in the not too distant past, Japan, following a mistaken national policy, advanced along the road to war, only to ensnare the Japanese people in a fateful crisis, and, through its colonial rule and aggression, caused tremendous damage and suffering to the people of many countries, particularly to those of Asian nations. In the hope that no such mistake be made in the future, I regard, in a spirit of humility, these irrefutable facts of history, and express here once again my feelings of deep remorse and state my heartfelt apology.[4]

Since its promulgation, the Murayama Statement has been reconfirmed by every Japanese prime minister, including Abe himself during his first tenure in 2006–07, as the official position of the Japanese government on the Asia-Pacific War (1931–45). With its references to a mistaken national policy and "colonial rule," and its characterization of the Asia-Pacific War as a "war of aggression," it has become widely recognized as a genuine statement of apology. Despite this, some observers have emphasized that the Murayama Statement is vaguely worded and fails to address adequately the question of "war responsibility" and that a more forthright and concrete statement of apology is needed. These critics also argue that a move in the opposite direction—a "downgrading" of the Murayama Statement in some way—would deliver a heavy a blow to Japan's international reputation.

The debate over the Murayama Statement is not an isolated phenomenon. It is a part of broader discussions in post-war Japanese society about how the history of the Asia-Pacific war should be presented in both a domestic and international context, about appropriate ways of commemorating the war dead, and about history education in Japanese schools. In this chapter, I examine issues of history and historical memory in post-war Japan and explain their significance in contemporary debates involving Japanese society and politics as well as in an international context.

Good war or bad war? The shaping of historical consciousness

On September 2, 1945, representatives of the Japanese government and the victorious Allied forces signed the instrument of surrender on board the American battleship *Missouri* in Tokyo Bay. This act ended World War II, which had begun on September 1, 1939 with Germany's invasion of Poland, but it also brought an end to the Asia-Pacific War, which had started in 1931 with Japan's invasion of Manchuria, China's northeast. While some Japanese were shocked to hear the emperor announcing the nation's surrender on August 15, 1945, most were relieved that the war was over.

> The wartime generation was soon to see defeat as an opportunity to make a fresh historical start. After years of traveling through a "dark valley," it was time to

> rebuild at home, not pursue the senseless folly of overseas conquest … Unconditional surrender was humiliating, … but the end of the fighting also meant a return to some semblance of normal life—no more blackouts, no more bombing, no more nights spent in the air raid shelters. The majority of the civilian population, especially the women and children, were relieved that the long ordeal was finally at an end.
>
> (Duus 1998, 254)

Given the mood of Japanese society expressed in this characterization, the war itself and the military establishment that had pushed Japan into war were seen in a highly critical light. In late August 1945 future Prime Minister Yoshida Shigeru spoke of Japan's defeat as a liberation from military rule. He argued that given the enormous tasks that lay ahead, such as "the surgical removal from politics of the cancer called the army, an enlightening of politics and an uplifting of the morals of the people, a renewal of foreign policy and a promotion of science, the reconstruction of finances and the economy … , this defeat (*haisen*) was not necessarily bad" (cited in Yoshida 2005, 91). In this somber post-war environment, an historical interpretation took shape that put the blame for Japan's path to war on a "small cabal of irresponsible militaristic leaders" (Dower 1999, 480) who, at one point, had got out of control (*gunbu dokusô*). This historical interpretation was, first of all, produced by academic historians, many of whom were strongly influenced by Marxism (Conrad 2010), and disseminated by history teachers, many of whom were organized in the—also Marxist—teachers' union Nikkyôso (cf. Aspinall 2001). Gradually, the view of the war as a war of aggression was accepted by the majority of the population and is, at present, deeply rooted in Japanese society, as opinion polls show (cf. Saaler 2005, chapter 3; Yoshida 2011).

As a byproduct of the thesis that the Japanese people were merely misled by a small group of militarists, a "victimization" narrative has developed (cf. Orr 2001; Yoshida 2011). To be sure, a large number of Japanese suffered tremendously during the war, including the victims of the atomic bombings of Hiroshima and Nagasaki, and the people of Tokyo, where 100,000 civilians were killed in a single air raid in March 1945 (Katsumoto 2011). While some claim that this "victim consciousness" has given rise to an historical amnesia regarding Japan's acts as a perpetrator, others have pointed out that it has also produced feelings of solidarity with the victims of Japan's wartime aggression, in particular the Koreans and Chinese who suffered under Japanese colonial and military rule or during the Sino–Japanese War (1937–45) (cf. Orr 2001).

The historical view of the Asia-Pacific War as a war of aggression, instigated by a small clique of militarists, could not have penetrated the Japanese psyche so thoroughly without being popularized in the mass media. As academic historians and educators have noted, aspects of popular literature have contributed strongly to the shaping of the historical consciousness of the Japanese (Nakamura 1998, 26). Of outstanding importance in this context are the historical novels (*rekishi shôsetsu*) of the popular writer Shiba Ryôtarô (1923–96).[5] Many of Shiba's works deal with the "bright Meiji period," the time in the late 19th and early 20th centuries when Japan was undergoing modernization. However, in his essayistic writings Shiba characterized the war years of the 1930s and early 1940s as a "dark valley" in Japanese history, a period in which Japan "lost its way" and embarked on a "mistaken national policy." According to Shiba, "the term 'Greater East Asian Co-Prosperity Sphere' was of course a mere glorification in order to justify Japanese colonial rule in Asia" (Shiba 1997, 235). He describes the war that was started by Japan in 1931 unambiguously as "a war of aggression" (ibid., 240). It is partly due to the influence of the "Shiba view of history" (*Shiba shikan*) that exculpatory narratives of the Asia-Pacific War have made few inroads into Japanese society at the grassroots level.

However, the popular media also contains countervailing narratives that emphasize that the war was forced on Japan and that Japan fought a war of self-defense, or even a war with the objective of liberating Asia from the colonial yoke of the West (see Saaler 2007; and Seaton 2007). While the mainstream narrative puts responsibility for the nation's "bad war" on the military cliques, thus absolving the great mass of Japanese, this revisionist narrative emphasizes that if the war was as evil as its critics claim, it would mean that the soldiers who fought the war were also tainted, possibly even criminals. Since this is inconceivable for the revisionists, they insist that the war was not a "bad war" in the first place.

A good example of this approach is the work of cartoonist Kobayashi Yoshinori. In the monthly (biweekly until late 2012) journal *SAPIO*, to which he has been a frequent contributor, Kobayashi began a new series, entitled "On Greater East Asia" ("*Daitôa-ron*"), in the issue of October 10, 2012 (pp. 59–74). This number carried a provocative cover title, "Advocating a 'Vision of Asian Prosperity': 'New Greater Asian Co-Prosperity Sphere'—without China, and Korea is Disliked by Asians Anyway."[6] Kobayashi is notorious for his provocative cartoons that have challenged self-critical views of the war since the 1990s. Together with a number of intellectuals he has been promoting an "anti-American etiquette" (the title of one of his books; Kobayashi and Nishibe 2002), claiming that the manipulation of post-war Japanese history education by the Americans, in alliance with Japan's Marxist-inspired historians and educators, has led to a distorted view of history being taught to Japanese youngsters today. In his view, Japan must break free of this "mind control" and the people need to rid themselves of the "masochistic" interpretations of history (*jigyaku shikan*) to which they are still subjected. "On Greater East Asia" offers an ersatz narrative of a Japan ruled by the ideology of Pan-Asianism,[7] fighting wars unselfishly with the noble objective of liberating Asia from colonial rule. This view of Japan's wars is in accord with that of Abe Shinzô, who frequently appears in Kobayashi's cartoons, but also with those who promote one of Japan's major sites for the commemoration of the war dead, the Yasukuni Shrine, to which I will return later.

History education

In addition to aspects of popular culture, history education has been the major factor in sustaining a deeply rooted understanding of the Asia-Pacific War as a war of aggression in Japanese society. Under the "guidance" of the occupation forces, Japanese history textbooks were rewritten in the late 1940s and early 1950s. They were stripped of pre-war propaganda and rewritten with the aim of contributing to democratization—a major objective of the Allied occupations of both Germany and Japan. However, until the 1980s, Japanese textbooks did not go into the details of Japan's wartime history. It was only when international outrage erupted over a reported attempt in 1982 by the Ministry of Education to force textbook publishers to replace the term "aggression" in relation to the war in China in the 1930s with the term "advance" that the contents of history textbooks started to change. Based on the Neighboring Nations' Clause (NNC) introduced in response to this incident (see Saaler 2005, 135), by the

1990s textbooks included more-or-less detailed descriptions of many wartime events and war-related issues, including the questions of war responsibility and war crimes.

These changes, in turn, triggered the emergence of a strong movement—as some researchers have termed it (Tawara 2001, 46; Richter 2001)—opposing what its supporters see as a harmful trend towards the "masochistic" education of Japanese youngsters. Even before the 1990s, there was opposition to the new way of teaching history introduced during the occupation period—sometimes from the Japanese government itself. Through a process of approval, the Ministry of Education (Monbushô) regularly prevented textbooks with an "exaggerated emphasis" on Japan's wartime past from joining the number of officially approved texts. The historian Ienaga Saburô (1913–2002), whose own textbook was denied approval for use in high schools, opposed what he considered to be a system of censorship through the Japanese courts for more than three decades (Nozaki 2008). Although his lawsuits had only limited success, they did create a general awareness among Japanese of the sensitivities around history education.

However, it was the "movement for historical revisionism" in the 1990s that took the debate over history and memory in Japan to a new level, particularly as a result of the strong involvement of politicians in the issue (cf. Saaler 2005, chapter 1). A committee established by the Liberal Democratic Party (LDP) must be considered the starting point for historical revisionism as an organized movement. In reaction to comments by Prime Minister Hosokawa Morihiro, who had declared that he considered the Asia-Pacific War to have been a "war of aggression," conservative LDP members established the "History Examination Committee" (Rekishi Kentô Iinkai, hereafter HEC) in 1993. Hosokawa was the first Japanese prime minister to make such a statement; his admission was particularly noteworthy because he was the grandson of Konoe Fumimaro—the prime minister at the time of the outbreak of full-fledged war between Japan and China in 1937. Already in 1993, Abe Shinzô was at the center of the revisionist movement as a member of the HEC. After hearing submissions and lectures, the committee summarized its opposition to Hosokawa's views in a publication with the title *Summary of the Greater East Asian War* (Rekishi Kentô Iinkai 1995). Individual politicians-turned-historians, such as Justice Minister Nagano Shigeto, further undermined Hosokawa's position when he declared in 1994:

> I still think the interpretation of [the Greater East Asian War] as a war of aggression is wrong … Japan stood at the brink of extinction, stood up and fought for its existence. At the same time, Japan seriously thought about liberating [Western] colonies and establishing the East Asian Co-Prosperity Sphere … Its war objectives as such were, at the time, basically within justifiable limits.
>
> (cited in Wakamiya 1995, 10)

Also in 1994, a number of groups wishing to promote the Asia-Pacific War as a "bright war" posted a full-page advertisement in the daily *Sankei Shimbun* (after being turned down by the conservative *Yomiuri Shimbun* several times) with the provocative headline "Japan is not an aggressor nation! The 'heroic souls' [i.e. the dead soldiers] were not perpetrators in an aggressive war" (cited in Yoshida 2011, 232). The organizations behind this advertisement included the Association to Answer to the Heroic Souls (Eirei ni kotaeru kai), the Association of Shinto Shrines (Jinja Honchô), the Japan Bereaved Families Association, the Kaikôsha (an organization of former members of the Imperial Army), the National League of Veterans Organizations and the Japan Association of Disabled Veterans.

While these conservative groups failed to prevent Prime Minister Murayama issuing his statement introduced above, they succeeded in preventing an unambiguous apology being issued by the Japanese Diet (national parliament) (cf. Saaler 2005, 72–78; Mukae 1996). Further, the historical revisionists in the LDP's HEC continued their lobbying in a number of new groups, particularly the Society for the Creation of New History Textbooks (Atarashii Rekishi Kyôkasho o Tsukuru-kai, or Tsukuru-kai for short), founded in 1996 (Tawara 2001, 139–40). Although most of these former politicians are not trained historians, they have continued to make strong claims about Japanese history education to the present day. In 2001, they published a *New History Textbook* for use in Japanese middle schools, which received harsh criticism both internationally and domestically and eventually failed to win a significant share of the market (cf. Saaler 2005). As time went on, the Tsukuru-kai lost momentum, membership declined, and the society broke up in 2007 when the more radical members founded two offshoot organizations—the Society for the Improvement of Textbooks (Kyôkasho kaizen no kai) and the Japan Education Revival Association (Nippon Kyôiku Saisei Kikô). However, as the election of Abe as prime minister demonstrates, the views advocated by these groups are still a force to be reckoned with in Japanese political life.

The increased intensity of the debates about history and history education has also had positive results: since the 1990s, there have been a growing number of international initiatives aimed at writing a common history of East Asia. The establishment of committees at the government level as well as private initiatives by universities, non-governmental organizations (NGOs) and historians' groups have resulted in dozens of bilateral and multilateral symposia, in addition to a number of publications ranging from conference proceedings to the first supplementary textbooks on East Asian history to be published by a multinational group of authors (Nicchûkan 3koku kyôtsû rekishi kyôzai iinkai 2005; Rekishi kyôiku kenkyûkai and Rekishi kyôkasho kenkyûkai 2007; Shin and Sneider 2011; and many more). In addition, excerpts from Japanese middle school textbooks were made available in English translation on a website supported by the Japanese Ministry of Foreign Affairs (JE-Kaleidoscope). However, as the result of the withdrawal of financial support, the website went offline in 2012 and the translations, which were heavily subsidized by the Japanese taxpayer, are no longer publicly accessible.

In Japan, these various multinational initiatives have reinforced the move to teach history with the aim of contributing to reconciliation with Japan's neighbors, a trend going back to the introduction of the NNC in 1982 discussed above. While current Prime Minister Abe and some of his cabinet ministers have expressed opposition to the NNC on several occasions, rescinding it would be very provocative and send a very negative message to China and Korea in particular.

Commemoration

While almost 3 million Japanese died during the Asia-Pacific War (1932–45), there has been no central national memorial for the war dead in Japan (cf. Saaler 2005, chapter 2). The major reason for this situation reflects the issues lying at the heart of the debates about history education—a lack of a consensus regarding the character of

World War II, particularly among the elite groups, which, in any society, are the leading actors in the shaping of commemorative and memorial institutions.

A drive in the 1950s to build a "national memorial," comparable to the "Tomb of the Unknown Soldier" found in many countries, resulted in the creation of the Chidorigafuchi National Cemetery. This facility holds the remains of more than 350,000 unidentified war dead. The ongoing activities to recover the remains of servicemen (*ikotsu shûshû*) from former battlefields in Southeast Asia and the Pacific result in new names being added every year. Although the Chidorigafuchi memorial was created in the 1950s amid heated controversy (cf. Saaler 2005: chapter 2; Akazawa 2005, chapter 3), it is not widely known inside or outside Japan, notwithstanding its authoritative name. For Japanese, the name "Chidorigafuchi" is associated with cherry blossom—this scenic spot near the Imperial Palace sets the standard for the official opening of the "cherry blossom season" every year in late March. The National Cemetery situated there, however, hardly comes to mind. It is also generally ignored in research and news coverage of war-related matters. This is not the case with the Yasukuni Shrine located a short walk away.

Founded in the 1860s, the Yasukuni Shrine developed into a major site of commemoration for the war dead in pre-war Japan. While Yasukuni was originally founded with the objective to worship the victors in Japan's civil wars of the 1850s and 1860s, it developed into the Japanese version of a national memorial, commemorating a growing number of fallen soldiers in the escalating series of wars in which the nation found itself embroiled. The Yasukuni Shrine played a similar role to the national memorials founded in European countries in the 19th century, and, with even greater significance, since World War I (Mosse 1990; cf. also Akazawa 2005, chapter 1; Takahashi 2005). Since Yasukuni also occupied a central place in the development of State Shinto (cf. Shimazono 2010), it has to be considered an institutionalization of the "sacred" character of the Japanese nation. Through the "cult of the fallen," it "provides the nation with martyrs and ... with a shrine of national worship" (Mosse 1990, 35). In Yasukuni, the "Myth of the War Experience" is constructed and maintained, which looks

> back upon the war as a meaningful and even sacred event ... The memory of the war was refashioned into a sacred experience which provided the nation with a new depth of religious feeling, putting at its disposal ever-present saints and martyrs, places of worship, and a heritage to emulate ... The cult of the fallen soldier became a centerpiece of the religion of nationalism.
>
> (Mosse 1990, 7)

Barely escaping destruction during the post-war period, when the American occupation authorities enforced the de-militarization of Japanese society and the abolition of State Shinto (Hardacre 1989, chapter 7; Mullins 2010; Akazawa 2005, chapter 2), the shrine was transformed into a "private religious body" (*dokuritsu shûkyô hôjin*), as which it continues to operate today. Over the years, however, the Yasukuni Shrine has reaffirmed its role as the central site of commemoration of Japan's war dead. Supported by a coalition of conservative politicians, veterans organizations and the Bereaved Families Association, the shrine has successfully continued to obstruct the creation of a "new institution" for the non-religious commemoration of all the nation's war dead. In Yasukuni, the victims of Japan's aggression are ignored, and Japanese civilian casualties and soldiers whose remains cannot be identified do not have a place. While Chidorigafuchi was planned as an all-encompassing commemorative site, the Yasukuni Shrine eventually succeeded in limiting the dead commemorated in Chidorigafuchi to those excluded from Yasukuni.

One of the issues at stake in considering the "Yasukuni problem" is the separation of religion and the state, which is stipulated in Art. 20 of the Constitution. It is questionable whether official visits by representatives of the state to the Yasukuni Shrine are in accord with the Constitution, and politicians who have insisted on visiting the shrine have been challenged in a number of lawsuits, although court rulings have proven inconclusive. Attempts to resolve the issue by re-nationalizing the shrine—gazetting it as a national memorial—have failed, due to opposition from various groups and political parties (Hardacre 1989, 145–49; Akazawa 2005, chapter 4). However, scholars such as Shimazono Susumu have pointed out that Shinto has never really ceased to be the "official religion" of Japan, as can be seen in the close relationship between the Imperial House and Shinto shrines (Shimazono 2010).

In Japan today, the issue of the separation of politics and religion resurfaces each time politicians make official visits to the Yasukuni Shrine (cf. Akazawa 2005, chapter 5). After almost two decades of self-restraint on the part of politicians, it was Koizumi Jun'ichirô who during his term as prime minister (2000–06) paid annual visits to the shrine, ostensibly to gain support for his cabinet, which, in terms of intra-party coalitions, lacked a strong base. Like his predecessors, Koizumi reaffirmed the Murayama Statement as the official position of his cabinet with regard to Japan's wartime past, but by persisting with his visits to the shrine he simultaneously sanctioned the historical interpretation advocated by Yasukuni and its supporters.

While the constitutional issue is, above all, a domestic matter, the historical interpretation advocated by the Yasukuni Shrine has become a part of the international discussions around the politics of history in contemporary Japan. The history of 19th- and 20th-century Japan embodied in the shrine finds a particular expression in an historical museum (originally founded as a "war museum") located in the shrine's precincts—the Yûshûkan (cf. Saaler 2005, chapter 2). The interpretation of history presented here reflects the revisionist positions discussed above, and is in stark contradiction to the Murayama Statement, which explains why some scholars refer to the "Yûshûkan problem" rather than the "Yasukuni problem" (ibid.). While the Murayama Statement speaks of a war of aggression and uses the term "Asia-Pacific War," the Yûshûkan situates the Asian theatre of World War II in the framework of a "100-year war" of Japan against the West, with the noble objective of liberating other Asian peoples from European and American colonialism. Imbued with this ideology, and freely using wartime terminology such as the "Greater East Asian War," it is hardly surprising that the exhibitions in the Yûshûkan omit mention of the effects of colonial rule and Japanese war crimes. The "Nanjing Massacre" of 1937, for example, is presented as a mere "incident," in which no civilians were killed and which involved the Chinese side violating international rules of warfare while Japanese troops restored "peace" to the Chinese capital. While some scholars seek to explain the narrative set forth in the Yûshûkan as somehow standing outside history—"a distinct type of patriotic narrative about the past" which is "not subject to the norms of historical inquiry" (O'Dwyer 2010, 156)—the museum's claim to ownership of the *truth* (*shinjutsu*), as expressed in its pamphlets and publications, cannot be ignored by academic historians.[8]

Another controversial issue, related to the shrine's interpretation of history, is the fact that the "deities" enshrined there include 14 of Japan's wartime leaders—men who did not, like the majority of the "Gods of Yasukuni," die on the battlefield, but were executed as war criminals following the Tokyo War Crime Trials or died in prison. Visiting the Yasukuni Shrine and showing reverence to those venerated there also involves paying one's respects to convicted war criminals. Thus, it is little wonder that official visits by Japanese politicians to the shrine arouse concerns in China and Korea about their real attitude to Japan's wartime past. Moreover, this honoring of war criminals could be seen as contrary to the Peace Treaty of San Francisco signed by Japan and 48 other countries in 1951. Article 11 of the treaty states that Japan accepts the rulings of the International Military Tribunal for the Far East (IMTFE), the Tokyo trials. However, the minister of education in the current Abe cabinet, Shimomura Hakubun, has openly challenged article 11 (Shimomura and Motoya 2010). A Japanese commentator recently poured scorn on this move:

> If Abe and Shimomura want to "review" the "Tokyo War Tribunal view of history," the logical requirement would be that the Japanese government would formally disavow the Tribunal's conclusions and notify all the forty-eight countries that signed the Treaty of Peace with Japan accordingly. It appears that Abe and his far-rightist ilk do not understand how unrealistic and ridiculous such a move would be regarded.
>
> (Narusawa 2013)

Doing so would openly challenge the very foundations of post-war Japan—the Peace Treaty of San Francisco and Article 11 of the Constitution—in ways that would isolate Japan from the international community and alienate neighbors.

In addition to Chidorigafuchi and the controversial Yasukuni Shrine, there are many war memorials and sites of commemoration in Japan. Such memorials have also been erected throughout East Asia and the Pacific region—not to mention the large number of Chinese, Korean and other "sites of memory" relating to the war. A total of 579 "memorials for the consolation of the souls of the war dead" (*ireihi*) built by Japanese veterans' organizations are spread throughout Southeast Asia and the Pacific (Yoshida 2011, 223). While these memorials constitute quiet expressions of remembrance far away from home, a large number of peace memorials and peace museums in Japan (cf. Yamane 2006), such as the Hiroshima Peace Museum and the Okinawa Prefectural Peace Museum, have been disseminating strong pacifist messages based on the historical experience of these regions—the atomic bombing of Hiroshima and the Battle of Okinawa that cost the lives of one third of the island's population. Today, Hiroshima and Okinawa stand at the forefront of Japan's post-war pacifist movement and oppose revisionist claims of a "bright war." For Hiroshima, this stance is linked to the global movement against nuclear weapons; in the case of Okinawa, to the ongoing opposition to American military bases on the islands (see Yoneyama 1999, 2000). The United Nations Educational, Scientific and Cultural Organization (UNESCO) World Heritage Site at the A-bomb dome in Hiroshima has become a universal symbol of peace, and the Okinawan Cornerstone of Peace (Heiwa no ishiji) is a shining example of the commemoration of war dead in a spirit of reconciliation, at least in Japan. It is composed of rows of granite blocks on which are inscribed the names of those who died in the Battle of Okinawa—not only Japanese casualties, but also members of the invasion forces.

The major gap in the Japanese memorial landscape is still the lack of a memorial for the victims of Japanese aggression and colonial rule. While there are several memorials for forced laborers, who were brought to Japan following the announcement of "national mobilization" in 1938, a site to commemorate the victims of Japanese aggression has never been seriously discussed. As long as Japan continues to deflect attention from its own actions during the Asia-Pacific War, but focuses on Japanese victimhood in the past and perceptions of a "China threat" in the present, the debates over its failure to "come to terms with its past" will continue to haunt the nation and harm Japan's reputation in the international arena.

Conclusion

In terms of making apologies and paying reparations for past wars, in the educational sphere and in memorials and monuments, history is, sometimes literally, set in stone. An historical narrative engraved in stone and displayed in public space has, by virtue of its very solidity and apparent public sanction, a strong claim to authenticity and truth. Thus, these authoritative narratives are perceived as *history* and cannot evade the scrutiny of "historical inquiry," as some observers suggest. The creators and supporters of such memorials and narratives need to take historical facts into account and have to deal with criticism based on "historical inquiry" if they make irrational claims. This is particularly true when a narrative claims validity beyond the boundaries of the group that created it, e.g. in case of wars, which are always a matter of at least two parties. If a narrative is criticized or rejected by a majority of the group or by a larger number of individuals concerned—including those outside of the group—then polarization and estrangement are unavoidable. Since war memories are shared by all sides involved, provocative views such as those espoused by historical revisionists lie at the very core of Japan's contemporary "history problem."

In the long run, questions of how to teach history or how best to commemorate the war dead come down to a simple choice: should public memory exist to fuel chauvinistic narratives legitimizing war and the mobilization of military force, or should such narratives be advanced with the aim of bringing about reconciliation, dialogue and peace? In the case of Japan's historical revisionists, the latter purpose is clearly not a priority.

Notes

1 See, for example, the article "Atavistic Abe" in the German weekly *Der Spiegel*, m.spiegel.de/international/world/a-877691.html.

2 In this article, I use the term Asia-Pacific War for the series of wars that took place in East Asia between 1931–45. For a discussion of the terminology relating to Japan's wars in East Asia, see Narita *et al.* 2005 and the eight-volume series *Iwanami kôza Ajia-Taiheiyô sensô*.

3 In a 2006 opinion poll by the *Asahi Shimbun*'s research institute (Asahi Sôken), only 18% of respondents agreed that the reasons for the Asia-Pacific War had been well explained, while 69% believed that efforts to clarify war responsibility were insufficient (*Asahi Sôken Repôto* no. 193, 2006, 190). A similar poll by *Yomiuri Shimbun* produced similar results; cf. YSSSKI 2006.

4 Accessible in full at www.mofa.go.jp/announce/press/pm/murayama/9508.html; on the significance of the Murayama Statement cf. also Togo 2012.

5 On Shiba Ryôtarô and the impact of his historical novels on the historical consciousness of the Japanese, see Saaler 2005, chapter 3; Nakamura 1998. Not only were Shiba's novels bestsellers, but they have been recycled in movies, TV dramas, computer games and

multimedia CD-ROMs. Some of his works have been translated into English, Korean, Chinese and other languages.

6 See www.shogakukan.co.jp/magazines/detail/_sbook_2300210112 for the cover slogan.

7 On the ideology of Pan-Asianism, see Saaler and Koschmann 2007; and Saaler and Szpilman 2011.

8 Cf., for example, the pamphlet *Yasukuni Jinja Yûshûkan* (undated, distributed in 2005). While this claim does not appear in the museum's recent publications, a video shown in one of the "visual rooms" at the museum claims to "recover the historical truth from the distortions of the Tokyo Trials" (*Tôkyô saiban de yugamerareta rekishi no shinjitsu ni semaru*): www.yasukuni.jp/~yusyukan/movie/movie.php.

Bibliography

Akazawa Shirô (2005) *Yasukuni Jinja. Semegiau "senbotsusha tsuitô" no yukue*, Iwanami Shoten.

Aspinall, Robert W. (2001) *Teachers' Unions and the Politics of Education in Japan*, State University of New York Press.

Berger, Thomas (2012) *War, Guilt, and World Politics after World War II*, Cambridge University Press.

Conrad, Sebastian (2010) *The Quest for the Lost Nation: Writing History in Germany and Japan in the American Century*, University of California Press.

Dower, John W. (1999) *Embracing Defeat*, Norton.

Duus, Peter (1998) *Modern Japan*, Boston: Houghton Mifflin.

Hardacre, Helen (1989) *Shintô and the State, 1868–1988*, Princeton University Press.

Katsumoto, Saotome (2011) "Reconciliation and Peace through Remembering History: Preserving the Memory of the Great Tokyo Air Raid," *The Asia-Pacific Journal* 9(3:4), japanfocus.org/-Saotome-Katsumoto/3472.

Klingner, Bruce (2012) "U.S. Should Use Japanese Political Change to Advance the Alliance," *Backgrounder* 2743, November 14.

Kobayashi Yoshinori and Nishibe Susumu (2002) *Hanbei to iu sahô* (An etiquette called anti-Americanism), Shôgakkan.

Morris-Suzuki, Tessa (2013) "Freedom of Hate Speech. Abe Shinzo and Japan's Public Sphere," *The Asia-Pacific Journal* 11(8:1), February 25, japanfocus.org/-Tessa-Morris_Suzuki/3902.

Mosse, George L. (1990) *Fallen Soldiers: Reshaping the Memory of the World Wars*, Oxford University Press.

Mukae, Ryuji (1996) "Japan's Diet Resolution on World War Two. Keeping History at Bay," *Asian Survey* XXXVI: 1011–30.

Mullins, Mark (2010) "How Yasukuni Shrine Survived the Occupation," *Monumenta Nipponica* 65(1): 89–136.

Nakamura Masanori (1998) "The History Textbook Controversy and Nationalism," *Bulletin of Concerned Asian Scholars* 30(2): 24–29.

Narita Ryûichi *et al.* (eds) (2005) *Naze, ima Ajia Taiheiyô sensô ka* (Iwanami kôza Ajia-Taiheiyô sensô, vol. 1), Iwanami Shoten.

Narusawa Muneo (2013) "Abe Shinzo, a Far-Right Denier of History," *The Asia-Pacific Journal* 11(1:1), January 14, www.japanfocus.org/-Narusawa-Muneo/3879.

Nicchûkan 3koku kyôtsû rekishi kyôzai iinkai (ed.) (2005) *Mirai o hiraku rekishi* (A history that opens the future), Kôbunken.

Nozaki Yoshiko (2008) *War Memory, Nationalism, and Education in Postwar Japan, 1945–2007: The Japanese History Textbook Controversy and Ienaga Saburo's Court Challenges*, London: Routledge.

O'Dwyer, Shawn (2010) "The Yasukuni Shrine and the Competing Patriotic Pasts of East Asia," *History & Memory* 22: 2147–77.

Orr, James (2001) *The Victim as Hero: Ideologies of Peace and National Identity in Postwar Japan*, University of Hawai'i Press.

Rekishi Kentô Iinkai (History Examination Committee) (ed.) (1995) *Daitôa Sensô no Sôkatsu* (Summary of the greater East Asian war), Tentensha.

Rekishi kyôiku kenkyûkai and Rekishi kyôkasho kenkyûkai (eds) (2007) *Nikkan kôryû no rekishi* (The history of Japanese-Korean exchange), Akashi Shoten.

Richter, Steffi (2001) "Nicht nur ein Sturm im Wasserglas: Japans jüngster Schulbuchstreit," *Internationale Schulbuchforschung* 23: 277–300.

——(ed.) (2008) *Contested Views of a Common Past*, Campus.

Saaler, Sven (2005) *Politics, Memory and Public Opinion: The History Textbook Controversy and Japanese Society*, Munich: Iudicium.

Saaler, Sven and Koschmann, J. Victor (eds) (2007) *Pan-Asianism in Modern Japanese History: Colonialism, Regionalism and Borders*, London and New York: Routledge.

Saaler, Sven and Szpilman, Christopher W.A. (eds) (2011) *Pan-Asianism: A Documentary History, Volume 1 & 2*, Lanham: Rowman & Littlefield.

Seaton, Philip (2007) *Japan's Contested War Memories: The "Memory Rifts" in Historical Consciousness of World War II*, London and New York: Routledge.

Shiba Ryôtarô (1997) *Kono Kuni no Katachi 4* (The shape of this country, vol. 4), Bungei Shunjû.

Shimazono Susumu (2010) *Kokka Shintô to Nihonjin* (State Shinto and the Japanese), Iwanami Shoten.

Shimomura Hakubun and Motoya Toshio (2010) "Japan Must Take Another Look at All Facets of its Modern History, Including the Kono Statement, Murayama Statement, and Tokyo Trials Historical Viewpoint," *Bigtalk* 257, www.apa.co.jp/appletown/bigtalk/bt1212/english_index.html.

Shin, Gi-Wook and Sneider, Daniel C. (2011) *History Textbooks and the Wars in Asia. Divided Memories*, New York and London: Routledge.

Takahashi Tetsuya (2005) *Yasukuni mondai* (The Yasukuni problem), Chikuma Shobô.

Tawara Yoshifumi (2001) *Abunai Kyôkasho. 'Sensô Dekiru Kuni' o Mezasu 'Tsukuru-kai' no Jittai* (The dangerous textbook: the truth about the "Tsukuru-kai" and the "war-capable nation" it aims to create), Gakushû no tomo-sha.

Togo, Kazuhiko (2012) *Japan and Reconciliation in Post-War Asia. The Murayama Statement and its Implications*, Basingstoke.

Wakamiya Yoshibumi (1995) *Sengo Hoshu no Ajia-kan* (Views of Asia held by post-war conservatives), Asahi Shimbunsha.

Yamamoto Jôhô (ed.) (2010) *Kokka to tsuitô* (State and commemoration), Shakai Hyôronsha.

Yamane, Kazuyo (2006) "Japanese Peace Museums: Education and Reconciliation," in Alan Hunter (ed.) *Peace Studies in the Chinese Century*, Ashgate.

Yoneyama, Lisa (1999) *Hiroshima Traces: Time, Space, and the Dialectics of Memory*, University of California Press.

——(2000) "On the Battlefield of Mabuni: Struggles over Peace and the Past in Contemporary Okinawa," *East Asian History* 20: 145–68.

Yoshida Yutaka (2005) "Sensô sekinin-ron no genzai" (Contemporary debates on war responsibility), in Narita Ryûichi *et al.* (eds) *Naze, ima Ajia Taiheiyô sensô ka* (Iwanami kôza Ajia-Taiheiyô sensô, vol. 1), Iwanami Shoten, 87–124.

——(2011) *Heishitachi no sengoshi* (The soldiers: a post-war history), Iwanami Shoten.

YSSSKI (Yomiuri Shimbun Sensô Sekinin Kenshô Iinkai) (2006) *Kenshô. Sensô Sekinin* (Analyzing war responsibility), Chûô Kôronsha.

11 Territorial disputes with Korea and China

Small islets, enduring conflicts[1]

Mark Selden

In the 1970s a major geopolitical shift opened the way for the emergence of a vibrant East Asian regional economy linking the United States, People's Republic of China (PRC), Japan and the Republic of Korea (ROK—South Korea), Taiwan (Republic of China, or ROC), Hong Kong and Singapore. The establishment of interlocking and increasingly dynamic regional relations, boosted by a tacit United States–China entente directed against the Soviet Union, together with US defeat in the US–Indochina Wars, paved the way for fundamental realignment signaling the end of the post-war divisions in East Asia. The end of the Cold War in 1989, coinciding with the democratization of ROK, promised further dividends and closer economic and diplomatic integration.

However, Japan's relations with other regional powers remain enmeshed in two types of intertwined disputes that evoke earlier hostilities. Saaler in Chapter 10 covers disputes centering on controversies over historical memories of colonialism and war. Here we consider the historical roots and contemporary trajectory of territorial conflicts involving China, Japan and Korea over islands so small as to seem insignificant. Yet they are capable of rousing nationalist passions and fueling an arms race in all three nations in an era in which China's rise and the relative decline of Japanese and American power create new tensions.[2] These are long-standing sovereignty disputes and legacies of the US failure to specify precisely the terms of territorial settlement in the San Francisco Treaty of 1951. They imbricate with larger issues of energy and fisheries rights and have flared up repeatedly in recent years, triggering diplomatic brinksmanship and saber rattling.

The Korea–Japan clash over Dokdo/Takeshima

Dokdo/Takeshima (Korean and Japanese names, respectively, hereafter Dokdo) remains a sharp thorn in the side of contemporary Japan–ROK relations. The contentiousness of the issues is emblematic of unresolved political and territorial legacies of two centuries of colonialism in East Asia as well as of the post-war territorial disposition of the San Francisco Treaty and the global conflict that it mirrored and defined. The story has frequently been told in terms of Japan–ROK conflict. We explore its historical and contemporary ramifications here in a triangular century-long framework involving Japan, Korea and the United States.

From many angles the problem should be among the simplest to resolve of several outstanding conflicts that divide Japan and Korea. The two islets and some 35 rocks that comprise Dokdo are minuscule (totaling 46 acres), largely uninhabited (save for a Korean octopus fisherman and his wife, a poet, and a rotating team of approximately

Figure 11.1 Dokdo/Takeshima
Source: (Wikimedia, Author: 머찐만두 at Naver, commons.wikimedia.org/wiki/File:Dokdo_20080628-panorama.jpg (accessed May 8, 2013)

35 Korean coast guard/light house staff), and of scant direct economic value, though the fishing grounds in the area are rich and the environs may contain natural gas and mineral deposits.[3]

However, the combination of Korean anger over colonial legacies, territorial conflicts and multiple unresolved bilateral and regional issues, many of them legacies of Cold War/other war conflicts, ensures that the matter will continue to be contentious.

Since 1953 Dokdo has been under South Korean jurisdiction. Although the issue surfaced at various times including the 1965 negotiations over Japan–ROK normalization, it was not until 2005 that Japanese claims led to a public standoff over the islets. So, while tensions have repeatedly roiled the waters between Japan and South Korea since 1945, such as Korean anger over Japanese failure to make suitable apology and reparations to Korean comfort women and forced laborers, Dokdo was not prominent as a source of conflict. Although Dokdo is emotionally important to Koreans, there is no significant Japanese national constituency for whom the islets loom large.

Dokdo in long-term perspective

As Alexis Dudden (2008, 19) observed in *Troubled Apologies: Among Japan, Korea and the United States*, the competing historical claims by Japan and Korea provide no definitive basis for resolving the Dokdo controversy. However, the history of the long 20th century does offer some compelling context to examine these claims. While many analyses of the problem center on the post-colonial and post-San Francisco Treaty (1951) disposition of Dokdo, what is critical for understanding and assessing competing claims in the new millennium is that Japanese forces seized Dokdo in January 1905, the year in which Japan compelled Korea at gunpoint to accept a treaty that made it a protectorate (Totsuka 2011).[4] Control of Dokdo and nearby Ulleungdo Island played a role in Japan's decisive defeat of the Russian navy in the Russo–Japanese War. The 1905 Korea–Japan Treaty brought to an end a long epoch during which Korea's international relations were primarily governed by its tributary relationship with China and in which Chinese political and cultural influence was predominant.

Emboldened by military victories over China and Russia in 1895 and 1905, and bolstered by British and American support, Japanese forces disbanded the Korean army between 1907 and 1909 in a crackdown that took more than 15,000 Korean lives. In 1907, the Japanese compelled King Kojong, who opposed the protectorate, to retire in favor of his mentally retarded son Sunjong, en route to the annexation and subordination of Korea to colonial rule in 1910 (Lone and McCormack 1993, 41–47). In other words, for Koreans, the seizure of Dokdo is inseparable from the subjugation and humiliation of the nation at the hands of Japan, a trauma that remains vivid to this day. As Bruce Cumings (2005, 140) puts it, "Japanese imperialism stuck a knife in old Korea and twisted it, and that wound has gnawed at the Korean national identity ever since." For Japanese, by contrast, Dokdo was a matter of little moment. Certainly, it was among the least significant of the numerous territorial conquests over the coming decades.

Already in 1905, however, this was not simply a Japan–Korea, or even a Japan–Korea–China story. The Taft–Katsura Agreement, which formalized Japan's seizure of Dokdo, was a quid pro quo in which Japan endorsed US colonization of the Philippines in exchange for US recognition of its annexation of Korea. The 1895–1905 decade clearly displays the imperial ambitions of the two rising colonial powers in Asia, Japan and the United States. In this instance, their shared interests were at the expense of subjugated people in Korea and the Philippines. The United States would again play a critical role nearly half a century later in sowing the seeds for subsequent Japan–Korea conflict over Dokdo in the wake of the Asia-Pacific War.

The San Francisco Treaty, United States–Japan–Korea relations, and American wars in Asia

Kimie Hara (2007) has traced the post-war framing of the Dokdo and other territorial issues through successive US and US–UK drafts of the San Francisco Treaty in the context of the evolution of the US–Soviet/Chinese conflict—which she terms the Cold War system in the Asia-Pacific.

The critical point about the San Francisco Treaty is the fact that by leaving vague or unresolved the disposition and specific boundaries not only of North–South Korea and Taiwan–China, but also of Dokdo and a plethora of other contested insular territories in the South China Sea, the United States sowed the seeds of current conflicts. Hara (2007, 9) shows that these conflicts "all share the important common foundation of the San Francisco System, instituted by the Peace Treaty with Japan in 1951" (see also Calder 2004; and Iriye 1974). The parties to this legacy of territorial conflict, many of them excluded from the treaty itself by the United States, include Japan, the Republic of Korea, the Democratic People's Republic of Korea (North Korea), Taiwan, the PRC, the Soviet Union (Russia), and many Southeast Asian nations. In short, the United States crafted the decisive treaty shaping the post-war Asia-Pacific region in concert with its European allies while excluding all major countries of the Asia-Pacific, both allies and foes. The disputed territories in addition to Dokdo, all with multiple Asian claimants, include the Senkaku/Diaoyutai as well as Taiwan, the Southern Kuriles/Northern Islands, and the Spratly (Nansha) and Paracel (Xisha) Islands. Calder (2004, 135–39) highlights the US role in forging this "Arc of Crisis."

Through successive treaty drafts, US policies shifted in tune with geopolitical considerations in the context of the US–Korean War and US–Soviet/China conflict. This led in most instances to a more favorable disposition of territorial issues with respect to Japan, and in the case of Dokdo, at the expense of Korea. This coincided with the shift in the US position from initial sympathy toward anti-colonial movements, including those in China, Korea and Vietnam, to a Cold War preoccupation with the threat of communism. The logic of conflict with the Soviet Union and PRC led Washington to prioritize development of an empire of bases and territories in the Pacific involving US military occupation or colonization of Japan, Okinawa, South Korea, the Philippines, and Micronesia.

Early drafts of the San Francisco Treaty, which was to end the allied occupation of Japan and serve as a peace treaty between Japan and its former enemies, envisaged the return of Dokdo to Korea. From 1949, however, as US tensions with the Soviet Union and China intensified, drafts shifted towards recognizing Dokdo as Japanese territory. By the time the treaty was signed in September 1951, vague formulations about disputed territories left their precise disposition unresolved and opened the way for potential discord between Japan and its neighbors. Indeed, the treaty was silent on the question of Dokdo. Hara (2007, 44–45) suggests that deliberate vagueness in this and other territorial issues—failing to allocate islands to a specific nation and/or to pinpoint the latitude and longitude of territories—was John Foster Dulles's strategy to maximize US leverage.

Seokwoo Lee and Jon van Dyke (2010, 741–62) point out that a succession of early drafts vacillated on the issue of whether Dokdo was Japanese or Korean territory, suggesting there was awareness about the importance of clarifying sovereignty. However, the final text made no mention of Dokdo. Why? Where Hara suggests a Machiavellian explanation, Lee and van Dyke hold that the United States and its allies simply chose to complete the treaty quickly, leaving certain issues unresolved. They go on, however, to note that under Dulles's stewardship, and with the US–Korean War raging, a premium was placed on Japan's supporting role. Rather than grant Dokdo to Korea and risk both Japan's support and losing the territory in the event of a North Korean victory, the framers purposefully left the issue unresolved.

Whatever the logic driving the decision, Hara's explanation is consistent with the outcomes of the last six decades: not only Dokdo, but also the Northern Islands, Diaoyutai/Senkaku, the Paracels and others became minefields of conflict, allowing the United States to play a critical role in shaping the outcomes. Equally certain is the shared conclusion of Hara, Lee and van Dyke that the decision on Dokdo had little to do with assessing the historical claims and everything to do with US and allied geopolitical considerations. While the treaty drafters debated, Dokdo was not merely sitting idle; between 1947 and 1952, the United States turned the islets into a bombing range for Japan-based US pilots.

Shortly after the signing of the San Francisco Treaty, on January 18, 1952, Syngman Rhee proclaimed the so-called Rhee line defining the border dividing Japan and Korea, and including Dokdo on the Korean side. Although Japan protested and never recognized the ROK claim to Dokdo, the following year a small number of ROK forces occupied the island. In 1954 the ROK erected a lighthouse, and it has controlled the islets to the present. The ROK brushed aside repeated Japanese attempts to raise the question of Dokdo in the form of 24 notes between 1952 and 1960 (Lee and van Dyke 2010). In the wake of the 1953 Korean War armistice, neither Japan nor the United States publicly challenged this outcome and the issue of Dokdo disappeared as an international flashpoint. Or so it appeared.

Re-establishing Japan–ROK relations in a divided Asia

It took two decades after Japan's wartime defeat to normalize Japan–ROK diplomatic relations and the Rhee line and Dokdo were among the divisive issues. During negotiations leading to the 1965 Treaty on Basic Relations between Japan and the Republic of Korea, Japan repeatedly raised the Dokdo question but was rebuffed by Korean diplomats despite US efforts to broker a compromise involving a jointly administered lighthouse. In the end, as in the San Francisco Treaty, Dokdo is nowhere mentioned in the normalization treaty and the ROK retained de facto control of the islets.

The 1,200 pages of diplomatic documents on the 1965 Treaty that the ROK government released in 2005 reveal important elements of the settlement of claims pertaining to the colonial era. In the end, the ROK abandoned demands for compensation and accepted Japan's offer of US$800 million in grants and soft loans for development purposes. Although it had accepted $364 million in compensation for 1.03 million Koreans conscripted as laborers or soldiers in exchange for waiving all future claims, the ROK government paid victim families only modest sums of 300,000 won (approximately $1,200) for each death, using the lion's share of Japanese redress for industrialization and infrastructure projects. Despite the importance of normalizing diplomatic relations, the treaty provided no substantial basis for overcoming the contentious colonial past or paving the way for reconciliation.

In the decades following the 1965 Treaty, despite important developments including the end of military dictatorship and democratization at the end of the 1980s, Japan-ROK relations remained fraught. Indeed, historical conflicts surfaced repeatedly in the 1990s and since. Major issues long suppressed by the dictatorship and/or by US policy imperatives suddenly emerged, carrying important implications for Japan–ROK relations. From a South Korean perspective, the historical issues—notably the comfort women, forced laborers, and Japanese textbook treatments of colonialism and war—required unqualified Japanese recognition of wrongdoing, acceptance of responsibility, and compensation for Korean victims. These hopes were unfulfilled.

Against this background, other developments affected the question of Dokdo and many other "orphaned" islands the affiliation and boundaries of which were left vague in the San Francisco Treaty. The importance of the islets increased with the 1982 United Nations Convention on Law of the Sea (UNCLOS). In establishing the right to claim extension of territorial waters to 12 nautical miles from the coast, and Exclusive Economic Zones (EEZ) to 200 nautical miles from the baseline of territorial waters, these and many other islands attained enhanced significance (Drifte 2009). The prospect that natural gas and seabed minerals may be found in the area increased the value of the islands to both Japan and Korea.

Dokdo in regional perspective

The Dokdo question has repeatedly resurfaced since 1994, frequently in the wake of Japanese claims to the islets. When UNCLOS came into effect in that year, both the ROK and Japan laid claim to competing 200-mile EEZs (Kim 2005, 14; Lee and van Dyke 2010). In 1996 Japan's Foreign Minister Ikeda Yukihiko asserted Japan's sovereignty over Dokdo, the first of many such claims.

While the impasse continues, there are also signs of accommodation. In January 1999, the ROK and Japan established a provisional fishing zone in the East Sea (Sea of Japan), including Dokdo, suggesting a possible resolution of the territorial issue within a broader bilateral framework. However, given popular opposition to the agreement, and continued tensions over both territorial and historical issues, South

Korea declined to implement the joint regulatory measures (Kim 2005; van Dyke 2002, 397, 405).

Indeed, winds of accommodation quickly dissipated. On February 26, 2005, local officials in Shimane prefecture inaugurated "Takeshima Day," enshrining Japanese claims to Dokdo in a high-profile challenge to Korean control. In 2008 newly published Japanese textbooks also asserted claims to the islets while on February 22, 2011, officials from the then ruling Democratic Party for the first time attended a Shimane event claiming Takeshima for Japan (Koh 2011). In 2011, all 12 new middle school history and social studies texts approved by Japan's Ministry of Education claimed that Dokdo (Takeshima) belongs to Japan, and four described South Korea's sovereignty of the islands as an "illegal occupation" (*Japan News Today*, April 15, 2011; KBS World News, April 1, 2011). Japanese textbook claims to Dokdo came on the heels of the announcement that South Koreans had contributed 23 billion won ($20.9 million), a record sum, for relief efforts in the wake of the March 11, 2011 tsunami that struck Japan's Northeast coast.

The Dokdo issue is a microcosm of broader disputes over the nations' troubled past. The Japanese government has generally ignored or rejected repeated claims by victims and activists, including Korean comfort women and forced laborers, for unequivocal apologies and compensation for wartime atrocities. In the decades following the 1964 Japan–Korea Treaty, despite extensive documentation of the crimes committed against Koreans, Japanese courts have repeatedly denied all claims to compensation on grounds that the statute of limitations had expired (Underwood 2009; Lee 2010; Kang 2009). Thus, like other historical issues, the Dokdo issue remains a festering wound in bilateral relations. Suggestions about international mediation are met with Seoul's steadfast denials that there even is a dispute, a position that provokes Tokyo's official ire while leaving most Japanese indifferent; Takeshima Day has not caught on. President Lee Myung-bak, considered relatively pro-Japanese, upped the ante in 2012 when he became the first Korean leader to set foot on Dokdo, sparking a mini-crisis in bilateral relations. He did so partly to divert attention from a family financial scandal, but also to protest Japan's intransigence over the comfort women issue.

The China–Japan clash over the Senkaku/Diaoyutai islands

The Senkaku/Diaoyutai (hereafter Senkaku) conflict, like that of Dokdo, involves both Japan's rise as a colonial power in Asia and the post-1945 US-imposed Cold War East Asian order and its legal expression, the San Francisco Treaty of 1951. In contrast with Dokdo, which has been in Republic of Korea hands since 1953, the Japanese have had administrative control over the Senkakus since the reversion of Okinawa in 1972.

The issues are made more volatile by the fact that Japan's claims are challenged not only by the People's Republic of China, but also by Taiwan (McCormack and Norimatsu 2012, chapter 11; Hara 2007, chapter 7; Yabuki 2013; Lee and Fang 2012; Manyin 2013; Fatton 2013). Documents from the Ming dynasty show the islands to have been way stations in China's tributary trade with the Ryukyu kingdom, while fisherman and traders from Taiwan and Okinawa had long traveled to the Senkaku. From 1884, a Japanese businessman gathered albatross feathers and tortoise shells on the largest of the islands. In January 1895, during the first Sino–Japanese War, Japan laid claim to the Senkaku asserting that the islands were *terra nullius* (land without an owner). Because the April 1895 Treaty of Shimonoseki makes no mention of the

Figure 11.2 Map shows area of Senkaku (Diaoyu) Islands contested by China and Japan.
Source: (Wikipedia, Author: Jackopoid, en.wikipedia.org/wiki/File:Senkaku_Diaoyu_Tiaoyu_Islands.png (accessed May 8, 2013)

Senkaku, Japan has long maintained that their seizure had nothing to do with the war and thus is not subject to the 1943 Cairo Declaration calling for the return of all territory seized as war booty. From the perspective of PRC and Taiwan leaders, however, the issue of the Senkakus has everything to do with the war in which Japan's richest prize was Taiwan. As McCormack and Norimatsu (2012, 215) observe, Japanese insistence that the islands are "integral parts of Japan's territory," and there is no territorial dispute, run up against the fact that the islands were "unknown in Japan till the late nineteenth century (when they were first identified from British naval references), not declared Japanese until 1895, not named until 1900, and that name not revealed publicly until 1950."

In accepting the Potsdam Declaration in its 1945 surrender, Japan agreed to give up all its conquered territories taken from 1895 forward, most importantly Taiwan, Korea and Manchuria as well as the Micronesia Trust Territory. Following Japan's defeat in the Asia-Pacific War, the United States impounded Okinawa as its military colony, making it the core asset in its strategic domination of the Western Pacific. When it returned administrative authority over the islands to Japan in 1972, the bargain rested not only on the US–Japan Security Treaty that firmly bound Japan in a subordinate position to American power, but on preserving intact the huge US military presence that made Okinawa a fortress in the Pacific.

With the 1972 reversion of Okinawa to Japan, the Senkakus were also placed under Japanese administration. China (PRC) and Taiwan officially asserted "territorial sovereignty" over the islands for the first time in 1971 in the form of foreign ministry statements in June (Taiwan) and December (PRC) (Ministry of Foreign Affairs 2013). As in the case of Dokdo, the United States utilized several of the islets for bombing practice. In 1972, during the Tanaka Kakuei-Zhou Enlai meeting in Beijing to normalize diplomatic relations between the two countries, the question of the Senkakus was discussed, as it was again between Foreign Minister Sunoda Sunao and Deng Xiaoping in 1978. In both cases, the parties agreed to shelve the question of ownership for future resolution, leaving the islands under Japanese administration.[5]

The issues had remained latent while the United States occupied Okinawa and the Senkakus, but the claims became the subject of direct Sino–Japanese discussions at the highest levels, resulting in agreements in 1972 and 1978 at a time when important regional developments would increase their importance. These included reports of seabed hydrocarbon deposits in the adjacent waters followed by Chinese and Japanese claims to the resource rights. The 1982 UNCLOS expanded greatly the value of the Senkakus as it did for Dokdo by establishing a basis for resource claims in territorial waters. Subsequently, there were periodic discussions of joint resource development, including a short-lived 2008 agreement for joint development outside the contested zone.

In 2010 a clash occurred when Japanese coastguard ships prevented Chinese fishing boats from entering coastal waters in the vicinity of the Senkakus. The resulting collision, followed by the arrest and detention of the Chinese captain, provoked angry charges and countercharges and made world headlines. However when Tokyo's Governor Ishihara Shintaro announced in April 2012 plans to purchase the islands from their Japanese private owner, the issue went viral, stirring nationalist passions in China, Taiwan and Japan. Not to be politically outflanked, Prime Minister Noda stepped in to "thwart" the governor's mischief—in fact achieving Ishihara's aim of nationalization—by purchasing the islands at a higher price. At a single stroke, Japan obliterated the China–Japan compromise forged in the 1970s that had preserved peace, facilitated rapid two-way growth in trade and investment, and for four decades kept the Senkakus under Japanese administration (without prejudicing rival claims to sovereignty). The Japanese move infuriated Chinese nationalists on both the mainland and Taiwan. More, however, was involved than a Sino–Japanese clash. In response to a request by Japan's foreign minister, US Secretary of State Hillary Clinton affirmed that in the event of conflict, the United States would support Japan under provisions of Article V of the US–Japan Mutual Security Treaty, and a November 30, 2012 amendment to the National Defense Authorization Act for fiscal 2013 reaffirmed the point.

Given Japanese insistence that there is no territorial dispute over the ownership of the Senkakus, mirroring with unintended irony Korean assertions about Dokdo, what is the position of the United States, which returned not only Okinawa, but also the Senkakus to Japan in 1972? In his letter of October 20, 1971, Acting Assistant Legal Advisor Robert Starr stated:

> The governments of the Republic of China and Japan are in disagreement as to sovereignty over the Senkaku Islands. You should know as well that the People's Republic of China has also claimed sovereignty over the islands. The United States believes that a return of administrative rights over those islands to Japan, from which the rights were received, can in no way prejudice any underlying claims.
>
> (Manyin 2013)

Numerous subsequent statements have confirmed the US distinction between administrative rights and sovereignty. Yet, in the context of an Asian "pivot" by the Obama Administration, that is, a geopolitics that prioritizes the China threat, coupled with the staging of joint US–Japan military exercises directly targeting an island conflict, the US position is ambiguous. Yabuki Susumu, a leading China specialist in Japan, however, concludes that, "the US will not and cannot fight"—that is, it will not and cannot side with Japan over the Senkakus in the event of Sino–Japanese armed conflict. He cites the "mutually complementary and dependent structure" of the US and Chinese economies featuring trade 2.5 times that of China–Japan. In addition, China is the leading purchaser of US Treasuries. In short, he emphasizes, the United States–China economic and financial relationship now far outweighs that of United States–Japan.

Yabuki is surely correct that the US–China relationship, now far outweighs the US–Japan relationship in the eyes of American policy makers. Yet that weight has contradictory implications ranging from mutually beneficial interdependence to unwelcome dependence. Yabuki's formulation, however, ignores the growing recognition in Washington that China represents a threat to an American-dominated status quo in Asia. This strategic rivalry may well trump the dictates of economic ties and place a premium on bilateral relations with Japan and increased security burden sharing. Clearly, the Abe cabinet seeks both a stronger alliance with the United States and a higher military profile, one freed from constitutional constraints.

All the more important, then, that saner heads prevail in finding a means to resolve or temporarily shelve the Senkaku issue and prioritize the joint economic and financial interests of Japan and China, and indeed of the United States with both parties. The Japanese government's purchase and nationalization of the islands, however, is a provocation that makes such an outcome more than difficult.

Conclusion

Is it possible to bring together the two types of issues—territorial and historical injustices—within a broader framework of common understanding and a shared future that is cognizant of economic, cultural and perhaps geopolitical bonds that link the three great East Asian powers at the core of a regional accommodation? Such an approach would have to transcend the aggressive nationalisms that dominate not only Japanese official thinking, but also Korean and Chinese official and popular thought and policy as illuminated by territorial issues in order to focus on the important shared interests among East Asian nations. The issues are made yet more complex by the large geopolitical and economic presence of the United States and its deep relations with all three nations. The alternative—failure to take advantage of opportunities to create regional community—will surely impose a heavy price on all parties at a time when the benefits of accommodation are compelling.

The case for ROK sovereignty over Dokdo is strong (Lee and van Dyke 2010). That claim is reinforced by the historical circumstances of Japan's 1905 seizure of Dokdo and colonization of Korea, a claim enshrined in the Potsdam Declaration, and given added weight in light of Japan's failure to provide effective state apology and compensation for the victims of colonial-era atrocities such as forced laborers and the comfort women. While a strong case can be made for continued Korean control of Dokdo, there are also strong reasons for the Republic of Korea to be flexible in accommodating Japanese interests in the vicinity. The issue can best be resolved between the two nations within the framework of an agreement like the 1996 accord on fishing rights that established shared rights in the area. (The ROK government did not implement the agreement when historical issues inflamed ROK–Japan relations.) Such an agreement could extend to oil, gas and mineral development and other areas of mutual interest. It need not be limited to Dokdo, moreover, but could extend to other islands in the strait such as Tsushima. In this way, it could serve as a foundation for the two nations' cooperation. As we have noted, however, Koreans' deep resentment and an identity politics rooted in anti-Japanese nationalism, represent a significant barrier to accommodation. The fact that most Japanese care little about Dokdo, however, is currently outweighed by the conservative political elite's fear that any signs of reasonableness by Tokyo will be taken as a sign of weakness. Yet, there is much to be gained diplomatically by Japan unilaterally renouncing its territorial claims as a magnanimous gesture towards reconciliation.

The conflict over the Senkakus is more volatile and dangerous at the present time, in part because the geopolitics of the region is in flux as a result of the expansion of Chinese power, the relative decline of the United States, and the recent emergence of multiple territorial conflicts involving China across the Western Pacific. Under these circumstances, the Japanese government will be unable to maintain the fiction that there is no territorial conflict. If the claimants—including the PRC, Taiwan and Japan—are wise, they will negotiate forms of accommodation and cooperation that defuse the issue of sovereignty over the Senkakus through various joint arrangements that could include fishing rights and resource development so as to strengthen their mutual economic interests including trade, investment, fishing, and resource development. As in the case of Dokdo, however, there are multiple barriers to such arrangements, barriers far greater than in the Dokdo case given the geopolitical stakes.

One of these barriers is the fact that official and popular discourse in China (PRC and Taiwan) and Japan is driven by nationalistic impulses that tend to marginalize proponents of strategic compromise. A striking and important exception is the Japanese writer Murakami Haruki, who warned that self-righteous and provocative posturing over Dokdo and the Senkaku is:

> … like getting drunk on cheap sake. Drinking just a small cup of this cheap sake sends blood rushing to the head. People's voices get louder and those actions become violent. But after making a noisy fuss about it, when the dawn breaks all that will be left is a bad headache.
>
> (*Asahi Shimbun*, September 28, 2012)

Murakami, whose novel *The Wind-Up Bird Chronicle* tells of a Soviet–Japanese military clash, subsequently visited remote Nomonhan, site of the deadly historic clash of 1939, and wrote (Koh 2012): "As I stood in the middle of that barren wasteland, with cartridges and other wartime artifacts still scattered about, I helplessly felt 'why was so much life senselessly lost over this piece of empty land?'"

The clashes since 2010 between Japan and the ROK over Dokdo, and those between China and Japan over the Senkaku Islands, and the waves of nationalist sentiment and saber rattling provoked in each instance, make plain the volatility of territorial sea issues that are rooted in claims that frequently originate in the 19th century but have been exacerbated in the wars of the long 20th century (Drifte 2009). The alternatives to accommodation are catastrophic.

Notes

1 I am indebted to Reinhard Drifte, Kimie Hara, Jeff Kingston, Heonik Kwon and Gavan McCormack for insights and sources.

2 We put aside two major territorial challenges to regional harmony: the unresolved legacy of the US–Korean War and a divided Korea, and Soviet–Japanese territorial conflict over the Northern Islands (Sakhalin) discussed by Burrett in Chapter 12.

3 In addition to the residents, 613 households totaling 2,051 Koreans had formally established permanent residence on Dokdo as of 2007 in response to Japanese claims to the islets. In

2005, the first 26 Japanese residents established domicile; by February 2011, they numbered 69 and a total of 520 Japanese had established residence in areas contested by neighbors such as the Kuriles, Senkakus/Diaoyu, and Okinotorishima (Yoshida 2005). It should be noted that North Korea also claims Dokdo as Korean territory.

4 Totsuka argues that Japanese coercion, and the fact that the Korean king signed neither the 1905 nor the 1910 treaty renders them illegal and null and void from the outset. The issue has spawned an immensely contentious Korean and Japanese literature. Yet one wonders whether fruitful discussion might be directed toward interrogating the entire structure of international law that legitimated colonial rule.

5 Drawing on a memoir by Zhang Xiangshan, who had access to the minutes of the meeting, Yabuki has charged that Japan's Ministry of Foreign Affairs altered the discussion of the Senkakus in the 1972 minutes and destroyed those of the 1978 meeting to bolster its claim that there was and is no territorial issue. Tabata, who also had access to the Zhang memoir, merely notes that Tanaka's response is unclear. "Ryoyuken mondai o meguru rekishiteki jijitsu," *Sekai*, December 2012: 104–13. Thanks to Gavan McCormack for drawing the Tabata source to my attention.

Bibliography

Calder, Kent (2004) "Securing Security through Prosperity: The San Francisco System in Comparative Perspective," *Pacific Review* 17, March.

Cumings, Bruce (2005) *Korea's Place in the Sun: A Modern History*, New York: W.W. Norton, updated edition.

Drifte, Reinhard (2009) "Territorial Conflicts in the East China Sea—From Missed Opportunities to Negotiation Stalemate," *The Asia-Pacific Journal*, June 1, japanfocus.org/-Reinhard-Drifte/3156.

Dudden, Alexis (2008) *Troubled Apologies: Among Japan, Korea, and the United States*, New York: Columbia University Press.

Fatton, Lionel (2013) "The Pandora's Box of Sovereignty Conflicts: Far-reaching Regional Consequences of Japan's Nationalization of the Senkakus," *The Asia-Pacific Journal*, February 4, japanfocus.org/-Lionel-Fatton/3893.

Geocities (n.d.) *Territorial Dispute Over Dokdo*, dokdo-research.com/page4.html.

Hara, Kimie (2007) *Cold War Frontiers in the Asia-Pacific: Divided Territories in the San Francisco System*, London: Routledge.

Iriye, Akira (1974) *The Cold War in Asia: A Historical Introduction*, Englewood Cliffs, NJ: Prentice Hall.

Japan News Today (2011) "Japan has Approved New Textbooks Listing Disputed Islands Takeshima/Dokdo as Japanese Territory," April 15, www.japannewstoday.com/?p=2323.

Kang, Jian (with an introduction by William Underwood) (2009) *Assessing the Nishimatsu Corporate Approach to Redressing Chinese Forced Labor in Wartime Japan*, November 23, japanfocus.org/-Arimitsu-Ken/3256.

KBS World News (2011) "Japan's Unlawful Territorial Claim Over the Dokdo Islets," April 1, rki.kbs.co.kr/english/news/news_commentary_detail.htm?No = 21291.

Kim Young-koo (2005) "What is the Controversy Over Dokdo All About?" *Koreana* 19(3), autumn.

Koh, Yoree (2011) "DPJ Attends 'Takeshima Day' for the First Time," *Wall Street Journal*, February 24.

——(2012) "Novelist Murakami Weighs in on Japan," *The Wall Street Journal*, September 28, blogs.wsj.com/japanrealtime/2012/09/28/novelist-murakami-weighs-in-on-japan-territorial-rows/tab/print/; *Asahi Shimbun*, September 28, 2012.

Lee, Ivy (with an introduction by William Underwood) (2010) *Toward Reconciliation: The Nishimatsu Settlements for Chinese Forced Labor in World War Two*, August 9, japanfocus.org/-Ivy-Lee/3400.

Lee, Ivy and Fang Ming (2012) "Deconstructing Japan's Claim of Sovereignty over the Diaoyu/Senkaku Islands," December 31, www.japanfocus.org/-Fang-Ming/3877.

Lee, Seokwoo and van Dyke, John M. (2010) "The 1951 San Francisco Peace Treaty and its Relevance to the Sovereignty over Dokdo," *Chinese Journal of International Law* 9(4): 741–62.

Liancourt Rocks Bombing Range (1947–52) Beginning with SCAPIN 1778 in 1947, www.geocities.com/mlovmo/temp.html.

Lone, Stewart and McCormack, Gavan (1993) *Korea Since 1850*, New York: St Martin's.

Manyin, Mark (2013) "Senkaku (Diaoyu/Diaoyutai) Islands Dispute: U.S. Treaty Obligations," *Congressional Research Service*, January 23, www.fas.org/sgp/crs/row/R42761.pdf.

McCormack, Gavan and Satoko Oka Norimatsu (2012) *Resistant Islands: Okinawa Confronts Japan and the United States*, Lanham: Rowman & Littlefield (Japanese edition 2013).

Ministry of Foreign Affairs (2013) "The Senkaku Islands," March, www.mofa.go.jp/region/asia-paci/senkaku/pdfs/senkaku_en.pdf.

Totsuka, Etsuro (2011) "Japan's Colonization of Korea in Light of International Law," *The Asia-Pacific Journal*, February 28, japanfocus.org/-Totsuka-Etsuro/3493.

Underwood, William (2009) "Aso POWs, Lafarge, and the DPJ on WWII redress," NBR Japan Forum post, June 13, nbrforums.nbr.org/foraui/message.aspx?LID=5&pg=1&mid=35028.

van Dyke, Jon (2002) "North-East Asian Seas—Conflicts, Accomplishments and the Role of the United States," *The International Journal of Marine and Coastal Law* 17.

Yabuki Susumu (interviewed by Mark Selden) (2013) "China-Japan Territorial Conflicts and the US-Japan-China Relations in Historical and Contemporary Perspective," March 4, japanfocus.org/-Yabuki-Susumu/3906.

Yoshida, Reiji (2005) "26 Japanese Register Takeshima 'Domicile'," *Japan Times*, May 18.

12 An inconvenient truce

Domestic politics and the Russo–Japanese Northern Territories dispute

Tina Burrett

Since 1945, Russo–Japanese relations have been marred by conflict over the sovereignty of a group of four islands that Japan calls the Northern Territories and that Russia refers to as the Southern Kurils. Situated between the Japanese island of Hokkaido and the Russian Kamchatka Peninsula, the four islands were seized from Japan by Stalin during the last days of World War II. Since then, unyielding attitudes on both sides have stalled progress towards resolution of the dispute, and prevented the signing of a formal post-World War II peace treaty between Russia and Japan. The ongoing dispute has hampered bilateral relations and constrained cooperation in pursuit of common geopolitical and economic interests.

In the security sphere, Russia and Japan face the common challenges of rising Chinese economic and military power and of North Korea's nuclear program. Japanese and Russian policy makers harbor similar concerns regarding Chinese territorial ambitions. Yet neither Moscow's fear of Chinese territorial aggrandizement in the Russian Far East nor Beijing's increasingly aggressive territorial claims against Tokyo have encouraged Russian–Japanese reconciliation. In the economic sphere, the energy sector is an obvious area for Russian–Japanese cooperation. The Far East region of Russia possesses large reserves of oil and natural gas, while Japan depends on energy imports. Japan's thirst for foreign energy resources following the Fukushima nuclear accident in 2011, provides Tokyo with more incentive than ever for deepening bilateral energy ties. On the Russian side, much needed Japanese investment and technology would allow Moscow to exploit fully its energy reserves and help develop Russia's impoverished Far East. In short, there are good economic, security and foreign policy reasons for Japan and Russia to improve bilateral relations. Yet if anything, Russian–Japanese tensions over the Northern Territories have escalated in recent years, illustrated by Dmitry Medvedev's visit to the disputed islands in November 2010, the first such visit by a serving Russian or Soviet head of state.

In this chapter I argue that domestic political considerations within Russia and Japan better explain the intractability of the Northern Territories dispute than economic or systemic factors. Japanese and Russian politicians have long used nationalist rhetoric to represent the disputed islands as an indivisible part of their respective nations. Japanese citizens have been primed to consider the Northern Territories as part of their nation and national identity since they were invaded by Stalin on August 18, 1945, three days after Japan's surrender to the Allies. Russians are similarly primed to see the territorial issue in nationalist terms. For Russians, possession of the islands is connected with the legacy of World War II—an event that continues to exert significant influence on Russia's national psyche. Although since 1991 Russia has made territorial concessions in resolving border disputes with China (2005 and 2008), Norway (2010) and Ukraine (2012), none of these disputes arose as a result of World War II. Since the breakup of Russia's Soviet empire in 1991, defending territorial integrity has been a concern for all Russian leaders. Any settlement on the Northern Territories dispute would inevitably require Russia to make territorial concessions and Japan to drop part of its territorial claims. A compromise would therefore contradict decades of nationalist framing of the dispute and could damage leaders' reputation as defenders of the national interest.

Furthermore, the islands dispute has long provided Russian and Japanese politicians with a patriotic drum with which to muffle voices of criticism and discontent. I argue that leaders have failed to resolve the islands dispute in part because the dispute itself is more immediately politically expedient than improved bilateral relations. Resolution will only occur when the benefits to national interests clearly outweigh the loss of a politically useful nationalistic cause. Currently, a lack of settlement is not preventing either state from furthering their national economic goals. Economic ties between Russia and Japan have strengthened since the mid-2000s, despite worsening political relations from 2010. Growing bilateral trade and investment removes a possible incentive for Moscow to offer territorial concessions and renders a settlement unlikely in the short term. In the long term, changing geopolitical dynamics in Northeast Asia—in particular a common interest in counterbalancing the influence of China—may offer a more promising route to resolution of the dispute.

In the chapter that follows, I first provide a brief history of the dispute and of attempts to reach a settlement. I then examine economic, security and foreign policy explanations for the lack of settlement. My analysis will show that these factors are insufficient in explaining intransigence over the dispute. Finally, I explain why domestic factors are a key obstacle to overcoming the current impasse. I conclude by assessing recent developments in bilateral relations and the likelihood of a settlement in the near future.

The history of the Northern Territories dispute

Despite incentives to resolve the dispute and improve bilateral relations on both sides, Tokyo has demanded the return of all four disputed islands—Kunashiri, Etorofu, Habomai and Shikotan[1]—while Moscow has refused to negotiate until after the signing of a formal peace treaty. The Japanese argue that the Soviet declaration of war against Japan in 1945 was a violation of the five-year Neutrality Pact signed in 1941. The Japanese further argue that the Northern Territories have always been under Japanese sovereignty, and therefore are not subject to the terms of the 1943 Cairo Declaration, which stipulated that Japan would "be expelled from all territories which she had taken by violence and greed" (Nester 1993, 721).

The Russian claim is based on agreements reached in Cairo, Yalta and Potsdam, as well as the 1951 San Francisco Peace Treaty. In the 1951 Peace Treaty, Japan renounced all claims to the Kurils, the Japanese definition of which *excludes* the four disputed islands (Mack and O'Hare 1990, 338). As a result of this exclusion, the Soviets refused to sign the Peace Treaty. The Russians—like the Soviets before them—consider the four islands part of the Kurils and argue that the San Francisco Treaty makes no distinction between the northern and southern islands.

The first negotiations aimed at concluding a peace treaty began in 1955, and resulted in a Joint Declaration in 1956. The Soviets offered Japan sovereignty of the Habomai

Islets and Shikotan—representing just 7% of the disputed territory—in exchange for a peace treaty. Only after a treaty was signed would Moscow discuss control of the larger two islands. Although initially willing to accept Soviet terms, Japan subsequently reverted to its original four islands position under pressure from the fiercely anti-communist US Secretary of State John Foster Dulles (Nester 1993, 722; Clark 2005). As a result, although diplomatic relations between the two states were "normalized" by the 1956 Declaration, a peace treaty never materialized and the islands dispute remains unresolved.

The appointment of Mikhail Gorbachev as general secretary in 1985 began the next serious round of diplomatic discussions on the Northern Territories. Gorbachev's need for foreign investment provided Japan with potential leverage to extract concessions. Despite economic inducements, Gorbachev was unable to agree on a settlement with Tokyo. Gorbachev's domestic reforms had unintentionally triggered secessionist demands from the USSR's non-Russian republics. In this climate, Gorbachev could not risk ceding territory to Japan. Shock at the collapse of the USSR in 1991 intensified nationalistic feeling in Russia, restraining Gorbachev's post-Soviet successor Boris Yeltsin. As president, Yeltsin faced the same quandary as Gorbachev. In the early 1990s, Russia was in desperate need of economic partners, creating a renewed sense of optimism for a settlement in Japan. However, facing opposition from nationalist and communist legislators, the military, and the public at large, Yeltsin also was unable to cut a deal with Tokyo. The best Yeltsin could offer was a commitment to speed up efforts to conclude a peace treaty, a commitment codified by both states in the 1993 Tokyo Declaration.

Russia entered the new millennium with a stronger economy and a new president, Vladimir Putin. Instinctively more patriotic than Yeltsin, as well as more dependent on nationalistic voters, in his first summit with Japanese Prime Minister Mori Yoshiro in March 2001, Putin proposed a compromise based on the 1956 Declaration. However, while for the Russians the 1956 Declaration meant returning only Shikotan and Habomai, for some Japanese it meant the return of all four islands (Blanchard 2010, 697). The vague wording of the Declaration encouraged both sides to interpret its meaning to suit their own interests. Over the next six years, divisions between Moscow and Tokyo widened as Mori's successors, Prime Ministers Koizumi Junichiro and Abe Shinzo, insisted on the return of all the Territories as a prerequisite to signing a peace treaty.

Economic factors

The intractability of the Russian and Japanese positions on the Northern Territories cannot easily be explained by economics. The Northern Territories have little material value beyond access to fisheries, with no confirmed petroleum potential, and a terrain that makes it difficult to extract the tin, zinc and other metal deposits. Economics is not the prime motive driving the Northern Territories dispute and economic solutions alone will not lead to a compromise.

Deepening economic ties between Russia and Japan have not translated into progress on the islands dispute. From 2005 until the global financial crisis of 2008, bilateral trade grew rapidly, peaking at an all-time high of US$29 billion in 2008, up from $20 billion in 2007 and $10 billion in 2006 (Blagov 2008). Japanese investment in Russia has also expanded since 2005, growing from $567 million in 2006 to over $8 billion in

2009 (Weitz 2011, 147). In recognition of Russia's economic resurgence, in 2003 the Japanese government abandoned its strategy of limiting economic ties with Russia in an attempt to gain leverage in negotiations with Moscow and secure concessions on the Northern Territories. As a result, since 2007, Japanese car manufacturers Toyota, Nissan and Suzuki have all opened new plants in Russia. Furthermore, in May 2009 Russia and Japan concluded a nuclear fuel and technology agreement potentially worth billions of dollars to Japanese companies. As part of the agreement, Japanese corporations Mitsui and Marubeni were invited to mine uranium in the Russian Far East (Medetsky 2009). This deal on nuclear industry cooperation was originally scheduled for completion in 2007, but was delayed for two years owing to Japanese fears that its technology would be used to further the Russian defense industry. This delay represents the costs of mistrust and suspicion.

Although to date growing bilateral trade and investment have failed to translate into progress on the Northern Territories dispute, the potential for even greater economic rewards in the future may yet encourage a resolution. Despite deepening economic ties, Russia accounts for less than 2% of Japanese exports (JETRO 2013). Clearly, the ongoing Northern Territories dispute constrains bilateral trade and investment, leaving considerable untapped possibilities.

In 2005, Tokyo's reluctance to commit funds to a Russian pipeline pumping Siberian crude directly to a Pacific terminal prompted Moscow to reverse its earlier decision in favor of Japan, and reroute the first phase of the pipeline through China. Cool relations between Moscow and Tokyo have thus marred Japanese investment in Russia's lucrative energy sector, resulting not only in lost profits for Japanese companies, but also Japan's continued dependence on fossil fuels imported from the volatile Middle East (see Table 12.1).

Oil is Japan's most important energy source (Figure 12.1). In January 2013, 82.8% of Japan's oil imports came from the Middle East and 6.4% from Russia (Table 12.1).

Russo–Japanese ties in the energy sector have deepened in response to Japan's increasing reliance on fossil fuel imports since the March 2011 Tohoku earthquake and resulting disaster at the Fukushima Dai-ichi nuclear plant. Between 2011 and 2012, Japan's imports of crude oil rose by 2.7%—the largest rise in nine years—while its imports of liquefied natural gas (LNG) jumped by 12.2% to compensate for the

Table 12.1 Japan's oil imports, January 2013 (%)

Middle East 82.8%	Saudi Arabia	31.4
	UAE	21.1
	Qatar	12.5
	Kuwait	7.3
	Iran	5.9
	Oman	2.3
	Other	2.3
Other countries 17.2%	Russia	6.4
	South East Asia	6.0
	Africa	3.3
	Other	1.5

Source: (Japan Ministry of Economy, Trade and Industry, www.meti.go.jp (accessed March 9, 2013))

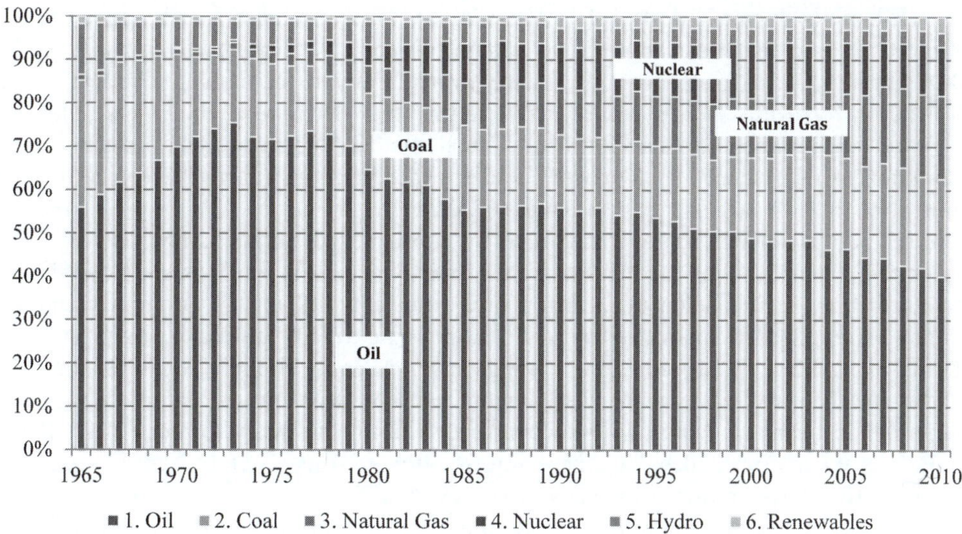

Figure 12.1 Japan's energy subdivision 1965–2010 (%)

temporary closure of the country's nuclear reactors that had been generating 29% of total electricity supply prior to Fukushima. As one of Japan's closest neighbors, it is logical that Russia should provide a large portion of these additional energy resources. In the immediate aftermath of the Tohoku earthquake, Russia donated 150,000 tonnes of LNG to Japan, as well as increasing its supply of coal (RT 2011b). Russia's exports of LNG to Japan rose from 6.29 million tonnes in 2010 to 8.3 million tonnes in 2012, making Japan Russia's leading market for LNG (International Gas Union 2011). Japan's need for hydrocarbons and Russia's position as a leading exporter of oil and gas make further collaboration in the energy sector a logical move for both states. In September 2012, Russian energy giant Gazprom and a consortium of Japanese companies agreed to construct a LNG plant in Russia's Far Eastern port of Vladivostok (Owen 2012). As a consequence of growing energy ties, 2011 became the first year in which bilateral trade exceeded $30 billion (MOFA 2012). Despite the extension of collaboration in the energy and other economic sectors, relations over the Northern Territories remain at an impasse, suggesting that economic factors are not facilitating or barring resolution. Yet, the potential mutual benefits are an attractive inducement, as the respective governments weigh their options.

Security factors

The Northern Territories are strategically located at the southern gateway to the Sea of Okhotsk, providing Russian nuclear submarines based at Kamchatka with a secure route in and out of the Pacific.

Although Russia's defense deployments in the Pacific region have decreased significantly since the end of the Cold War in 1989, Russian military forces are recently increasingly active near Japan. In September 2011, 24 Russian naval vessels, including a Slava-class guided missile cruiser passed through the Soya Strait that divides Sakhalin and Hokkaido (Japan Ministry of Defense 2012). This was the first time since the end of the Cold War that Russian naval vessels on this scale have passed through the strait. On February 7, 2013—the day of Japan's annual rally to demand the return of the Northern Territories—with impeccable timing two Russian fighter jets allegedly intruded on Japanese airspace, the first such incident in five years. Russia is also modernizing its defenses on Kunashiri and Etorofu, demonstrating its resolve to keep control of the two larger disputed islands (RT 2011a).

Yet Japan is not Russia's primary security concern in East Asia. The rise of China poses a geopolitical challenge to Russia that partly accounts for Moscow's decision to modernize its Pacific defenses. North Korea's nuclear and missile programs and US plans to strengthen its missile defenses also contribute to Russia's increasing presence in the region. Although Moscow and Beijing currently enjoy friendly relations, for most of the 20th century bilateral ties were encumbered by deep mutual enmity, a fact well remembered by many Moscow policy makers. Among the many former KGB officers in Putin's inner circle, illegal Chinese immigration in Russia's Far East is seen as a potential threat to territorial integrity (Kosyrev 2005).

Suspicion of Beijing within the Kremlin presents an opportunity for Japan. A settlement on the Northern Territories serves Russia's interests if it improves security links with Japan. An alliance counterbalancing the influence of China is also in Japan's interest. Dmitry Medvedev's visit to Kunashiri in November 2010 came amidst Japan's latest spat with Beijing over sovereignty of the Senkaku/Diaoyu Islands—rocky islets in the East China Sea controlled by Japan, but claimed by China and Taiwan. The timing of Medvedev's visit, less than two months after the arrest of a Chinese fishing boat captain for ramming a Japanese coastguard vessel, suggests that Moscow sought to take advantage of Tokyo's preoccupation with the territorial dispute. Similarly, in February 2013, Russia's violation of Japanese airspace occurred in the same week that China's military allegedly locked weapons-firing radar on Japanese naval forces near the Senkaku Islands. Facing territorial disputes on multiple fronts—including with Korea over Takeshima/Dokdo—inevitably weakens Japan's overall negotiating position. Resolving its territorial dispute with Moscow would enable Tokyo to concentrate its diplomacy on disputes with China and Korea that have perhaps more significant economic and strategic implications.

Foreign policy factors

During Putin's first presidency, from 2000–08, bolstered by rapid economic growth from rising energy prices, Moscow regained its assertiveness in international affairs. Putin's self-confidence and independence from the West led to tensions with the Administration of US President George W. Bush. In 2009, the Obama Administration came to office offering a "reset" in relations with Moscow. Although remaining at odds on a number of important geopolitical issues—most notably Syria and Iran—during Obama's first term Moscow and Washington worked together on a number of initiatives, including to reduce their nuclear stockpiles and to combat nuclear proliferation in other states.

In contrast, during the tenure of the Democratic Party of Japan (DPJ), which took office in August 2009, Tokyo's relations with Washington were tested by differences over the relocation of a US military base on Okinawa. Discord between the United States and Japan may have encouraged President Medvedev's visit to

Kunashiri, as friction with Washington left Japan looking vulnerable. Confirming Japan's isolation, two days after Medvedev's visit to Kunashiri, the US State Department announced that while Washington supports Japan's claims to the Northern Territories, the islands are not subject to the United States–Japan Security Alliance (Jiji Press 2010).

Since the end of the Cold War, pressure from Washington on Japan to maintain its claim to all four islands is no longer an impediment to resolving the Northern Territories dispute. Nor is Japan's security alliance with the United States an insurmountable obstacle to a settlement. Even after the United States and Japan announced plans to deploy a joint missile shield in northern Honshu—provoking condemnation from Moscow—Russia and Japan continued to engage in joint military exercises until the North Atlantic Treaty Organization (NATO) and its allies ended all joint exercises in response to Russia's war with Georgia in August 2008 (Weitz 2011, 143).

Domestic political factors

Economic, security and foreign policy issues relevant to the Northern Territories dispute do not constitute an insurmountable obstacle to resolution and in fact provide various incentives for a settlement. Domestic factors in Russia and Japan provide the missing piece of the puzzle in explaining the prolonged impasse. Leaders in Russia and Japan use strong nationalist rhetoric to mobilize public support for their policies on the islands. Decades of nationalist framing of the dispute make it difficult for leaders to agree to a settlement that would contradict their own rhetoric. Settlement would require both sides to moderate their territorial claims, potentially undermining the credibility of politicians who have framed the dispute in terms of justice and national pride. Damage to credibility could result in voter retribution—ranging from a decline in public support to defeat in an election. On several occasions since 1956, leaders in both countries have rejected settlement deals at the last minute in order to avoid alienating critical constituencies (Table 12.2).

Since the 1950s, the Japanese government has employed numerous initiatives to build and maintain public support for its "four islands at once" policy. From a young age, the Japanese are primed to see the islands as inherently part of Japan. In 2008, Japan's Education Ministry issued new textbooks depicting the four islands as Japanese territory (RT 2008). In Education Ministry guidelines issued in 2009, teachers were instructed to refer to the Northern Territories as "indigenous Japanese territory," in Japanese "*wagakoku koyuu no ryodo de aru*" (MEXT 2008, 49). The islands are also shown as belonging to Japan on maps and stamps.

In 1981, the Japanese government designated February 7 as "Northern Territories Day," an annual holiday to keep the islands dispute on the public agenda. The date was chosen to commemorate the anniversary of an 1855 treaty with Russia that solidified Japanese sovereignty over the islands. On Northern Territories Day in 2011, the Japanese Cabinet Office spent approximately ¥2 million on over 70 full-page advertisements in major newspapers to "promote nationwide momentum for the Northern Territories return" (*The Economist* 2011). The advert shows a young girl with a Japanese flag on one cheek, and a map of Hokkaido on the other—complete with the four disputed islands.

To draw national attention to the territorial dispute, in September 2004, Koizumi Junichiro became the first Japanese prime minister to view the islands by boat. Koizumi's

Table 12.2 Rejected offers of territorial concessions, 1945–2013

Date	*Offer*	*Outcome*
October 1956	Soviet Union willing to return Habomai and Shikotan, but will not recognize Japanese claims to Etorofu and Kunashiri	Joint Declaration
October 1991	Japanese government willing to be flexible about date and process of return of four islands in exchange for Soviet recognition of Japanese sovereignty	Soviet Union collapses before resolution of negotiations
March 1992	Kunadze Proposal: Russia willing to return Habomai and Shikotan (agreed in 1956 Joint Declaration) and to continue negotiations over Etorofu and Kunashiri	Japanese government rejects the proposal
April 1998	Kawana Proposal: Japan willing to accept return of sovereignty over the four islands without an agreed date for the return of administrative control to Japan	President Yeltsin rejects proposal by Prime Minister Hashimoto
November 1998	Moscow Proposal: Russia proposes putting the islands under dual management	Prime Minister Obuchi rejects the proposal by Yeltsin
March 2001	President Putin reaffirms offer to return Habomai and Shikotan first made in 1956 Joint Declaration as the starting point to concluding a peace treaty	Irkutsk Statement on continuing negotiations on a Peace Treaty. Negotiations collapse after Prime Minister Mori is replaced by Prime Minister Koizumi

Figure 12.2 Japanese stamps featuring the Northern Territories
Source: (www.ne.jp/asahi/cccp/camera/HoppouRyoudo/Stamp/hoppouryoudokitte.htm (accessed May 13, 2012))

sightseeing tour has since been repeated by both Liberal Democratic Party (LDP) and DPJ politicians, including in December 2010 by DPJ Foreign Minister Maehara Seiji, who viewed the islands from a plane (*Japan Times* 2010). Koizumi's boat trip followed shortly after LDP election losses, suggests that the prime minister was attempting to use the Northern Territories issue to mollify disgruntled voters. In July 2012, a second visit to Kunashiri was similarly deployed by Dmitry Medvedev to combat his increasing political insignificance after returning the Russian presidency to Vladimir Putin two months earlier.

For the Japanese government, keeping its territorial claim in the public consciousness is as important as the islands themselves. In pledging to gain the return of all four islands, Japanese politicians court favor with the 84% of voters who support a no-compromise approach to the dispute (*Yomiuri Shimbun* 2006). Examples of Japanese politicians inciting nationalist discourse in reference to the dispute are too numerous to list. Most infamously, speaking at the 2011 annual Northern Territories Day rally in Tokyo, Prime Minister Kan Naoto termed Dmitry Medvedev's visit to Kunashiri the previous November as an "unforgiveable outrage" (*Asahi Shimbun* 2011). Kan's uncharacteristic patriotic posturing suggests he was trying to burnish his nationalist credentials and stem a steady slide in his support ratings.

Predictably, Kan comments provoked condemnation in Russia, with Russian Foreign Minister Sergey Lavrov calling the speech "unacceptable" (Frolov 2011). A Kremlin spokesman forcefully stated that the president needed no one's permission to visit any part of the Russian Federation and that the sovereignty of the Kurils was not open to revision (ITAR TASS 2011). Russia's assertive language was likely driven by domestic considerations. According to a 2009 VTsIOM poll, 89% of Russians are against handing over the Kurils to Japan. Only 4% are ready to return the islands. Furthermore, Russian opposition to a handover is hardening. In 1994 only 76% of Russians were against it (RT 2009). Medvedev's visit to Kunashiri in November 2010 was also largely motivated by domestic politics. In November 2010 it was not yet clear whether Medvedev or Putin would represent their party in the 2012 presidential election. In the eyes of many voters, Putin's background in the security services and efforts to restore Russia's international standing make him a greater patriot than his protégé, who has been a civilian his entire career. It is possible that Medvedev's trip to Kunashiri was part of a campaign to steal Putin's reputation as patriot-in-chief. Even the date of Medvedev's visit was chosen to maximize his patriotic appeal. Medvedev landed on Kunashiri just three days before National Unity Day, a public holiday commemorating the liberation of Moscow from Polish invaders in 1612.

Within Russia, Medvedev is often negatively perceived as a pro-Western liberal. With elections approaching, Medvedev may have sought to use his visit to Kunashiri to demonstrate he was Putin's equal in defending national interests. Jeopardizing Russia's relations with the United States or China was too risky (Weitz 2011, 154), but Japan—a close US ally—was an easier target, as Russia has no strong political relations with Tokyo to endanger. Escalating tensions with Tokyo contradicts Moscow's strategy of attracting foreign investment to modernize Russia's economy, further suggesting that Medvedev's trip was aimed at a domestic audience.

Medvedev's Kunashiri visit was exhaustively reported by the Russian media, especially on government-controlled state television. Reporters from state-controlled Channel One followed Medvedev as he toured the island and met local residents. Medvedev's Kunashiri visit was followed by a tour of the islands by First Deputy Prime

Minister Igor Shuvalov in December 2010 and by Regional Development Minister Viktor Basargin and Deputy Defense Minister Dmitry Bulgakov in January 2011. More worrying for Tokyo, Russian Defense Minister Anatoly Serdyukov visited Etorofu and Kunashiri in February 2011 to inspect troops stationed on the islands. Responding to Serdyukov's visit, Japanese Foreign Minister Maehara Seiji likened the Russian defense minister's actions to "pouring a bucket of cold water" on Russian–Japanese relations (RIA Novosti 2011). The frequency of ministerial tours of the disputed island and the attention they received in the Russian media suggests that Moscow was being disingenuous in portraying these visits as routine.

Soon after Serdyukov's inspection of the Kurils' defenses, in mid-February 2011 Russia announced it would strengthen its forces on the islands, deploying artillery rockets and helicopter gunships. Research suggests that citizens respond emotionally to security threats, leading to enthusiastic public support for deployment of defenses to vulnerable regions (Wiegand 2005, 360). When territory is perceived to be threatened, it is easy for national leaders to mobilize public support using nationalist rhetoric. The defense of the Kurils thus presented the Russian government with the perfect cause with which to boost its popularity ahead of parliamentary elections.

The economic chaos and loss of international prestige Russia endured following the breakup of the Soviet Union guaranteed a place for nationalist groups in post-Soviet Russian politics. Left-wing nationalist parties—a category that includes the Russian Communist Party—have been the main rivals of all three post-Soviet Russian presidents. Vladimir Putin's appropriation of nationalist causes partly explains his enduring popularity with many Russian voters. Putin first won the presidency in 2000 with promises to restore Russian national pride, but since the 2008 global financial crisis—which hit Russia's hydrocarbon-dependent economy harder than most—support for Russia's extra-parliamentary nationalist groups is growing.

In response to the rising popularity of nationalist groups, Putin has intensified his own use of patriotic and militaristic themes. Ahead of the March 2012 presidential election, Putin penned a lengthy article on nationalism, calling for a clampdown on secessionist movements and for a greater emphasis on patriotic education in Russian schools (Weir 2012). Contradicting Putin's rhetoric of a "united Russia," anti-government protests sparked by rigged elections in December 2011 show exactly how polarized and fragmented the nation has become. Putin has lost the confidence of young, middle-class urban voters. It is the relatively well-to-do who shout "Russia without Putin" at anti-government rallies. Putin has thus been forced to turn to provincial Russia for support: a Russia where nationalist sentiments are bound up with fears of demographic crisis and territorial disintegration (Krastev and Holmes 2012). Dependence on such defensively nationalistic voters will inevitably restrict Putin's ability to negotiate a territorial compromise with Japan.

The use of the Northern Territories dispute for party-political advantage in Japan is well known. Now as in the past, Japanese politicians try to outdo each other as the champions of former island residents and their descendants. Hokkaido—the closest part of Japan to the territories—was an important battleground in the 2009 general election. Ahead of voting, both LDP and DPJ politicians were keen to show their commitment to gaining the return of all four islands—a position supported by 73% of Hokkaido residents (Williams 2010, 226). In late 2008, representatives from both main parties created a parliamentary group with the stated goal of compelling the government urgently to seek the return of all four islands. The group included then DJP leader Hatoyama Yukio, who represented Hokkaido's No. 9 district. Demonstrating toughness in defending Japan's territorial claims was essential if the DPJ—partly descended from the pacifist-orientated Japan Socialist Party—was to win office.

On becoming Japan's first DPJ prime minister in August 2009, Hatoyama took a more conciliatory position on the Northern Territories, suggesting his pre-election rhetoric was partly a domestic political ploy. Russian diplomats were hopeful that Hatoyama would follow in the footsteps of his grandfather Hatoyama Ichiro, who as prime minister signed the 1956 Joint Declaration that restored relations between Russia and Japan after World War II. However, the younger Hatoyama's open-minded approach to the islands dispute was not shared by his cabinet, or by officials in the Ministry of Foreign Affairs (MOFA) (interview with former MOFA official, November 2011). In November 2009, one week after Hatoyama's return from a successful meeting with President Medvedev, his government endorsed a document calling Russia's presence on the Northern Territories "illegal" (Togo 2010). This endorsement ended any chance of settlement negotiations restarting while Hatoyama remained prime minister.

In the context of domestic Japanese politics, the Hatoyama government's condemnation of Russia's presence on the islands was far from irrational. In Japan, leaders who do not take a strong stance on Japanese sovereignty over the Northern Territories come under intense attack from right-wing groups and their supporters in the Japanese media. Supporting anything other than the return of all four disputed islands *en bloc* has long been a political taboo. When Foreign Minister Aso Taro flirted with the idea of a 50/50 division of island territory in 2006, he was quickly forced to retreat due to criticism in the press (*Nikkei Shimbun* 2006).

Suggestions of a compromise are dismissed by MOFA officials and hardcore conservatives as undermining Japan's sovereignty (Bukh 2012, 503). MOFA remains committed to Japan's four-island policy for two important reasons. First, two ministry officials—Sato Masaru and Togo Kazuhiko—who publically voiced support for a gradualist two islands first solution—were forced out of MOFA by pressure from powerful right-wing groups. Particularly noteworthy in this regard is the Council on National Security Problems (*Anzen Hoshou Mondai Kenkyuukai*, or Anpoken) a right-wing think tank focusing on Japan's territorial issues established in 1968. Anpoken's influence derives from the close ties of its founder Suetsugu Ichiro with the LDP and MOFA (Williams 2006, 271). Second, MOFA believes that the current Russian administration—and Vladimir Putin in particular—are immovable on the Northern Territories issue. Therefore, they conclude, there is no point in Japan pursuing negotiations while Putin remains the dominant force in Russian foreign policy making. Worse still, ministry insiders worry that if negotiations started and failed, MOFA could get the blame (interview with former MOFA official, November 2011).

MOFA's inertia in seeking a resolution to the dispute is highlighted by its failure to act on an offer to start fresh negotiations made by Vladimir Putin in an interview with foreign journalists just prior to his re-election as president in March 2012. Using a term employed by judo referees to begin a match, Putin announced that if he became president, "we would give the order '*Hajime*'" on negotiations. Contradicting the nationalist sentiments of his earlier campaign speeches, Putin stated, "We don't need victory, but rather we need to reach an acceptable compromise, something like a tie" (*Asahi Shimbun* 2012). Putin's comments were not generally covered by the Russian media. One reason for this silence could be that Putin made his statement in an interview with foreign journalists. The more likely explanation, however, is that the Kremlin applied pressure on journalists not to report on a story that could damage Putin's public standing mere days before the presidential election.

In contrast, Putin's statement was widely reported in Japan. Newspapers commented on the potentially negative impact of a territorial compromise on former residents of the islands and their descendents (*Yomiuri Shimbun* 2012). The Japanese media's lukewarm greeting to Putin's proposition restrained MOFA's response. When Putin met Prime Minister Noda Yoshihiko in Mexico four months after making his initial offer to negotiate, he was surprised to hear that MOFA had made no preparations for beginning talks (interview with former MOFA official, July 2012). A month later, Dmitry Medvedev made his second visit to Kunashiri, indicating that Russia's leaders had grown tired of waiting for their Japanese counterparts to seize the initiative on negotiations.

Recent developments in bilateral relations and prospects for a territorial settlement

Evidence suggests that leaders in Japan and Russia are primarily influenced by domestic political factors when deciding policy on the Northern Territories. Politicians in both states seek to avoid the damage to their position that could result from agreeing to a territorial compromise. Leaders who have flirted with the idea of a compromise have quickly retreated in response to domestic opposition. Furthermore, the territorial dispute remains a convenient tool in domestic political competitions and to distract public attention from policy failures in other areas. As leaders in both states benefit politically from the existence of the dispute, they would require strong incentives to reach a settlement.

A territorial compromise would also require leaders to contradict their nationalist framing of the dispute, calling into question their reputation and credibility. In Japan, citizens have been primed by their government to see the islands' return as a step towards overcoming the national shame of defeat in World War II. The timing of the Russian invasion, which came after the atomic bombings of Hiroshima and Nagasaki, and Japan's surrender, adds an emotional element to the dispute. Before Japanese leaders can agree to a settlement they must first change their framing of the dispute. A discourse emphasizing the economic and security benefits of a settlement would be the most logical frames through which to refocus public opinion. Although a change in discourse would not deter the protests of a loud minority of nationalist activists, if mainstream Japanese opinion shifted in favor of a territorial compromise with Russia, MOFA might be tempted to abandon its risk-averse strategy.

There is some evidence that a shift in framing has already begun to occur. During Sergey Lavrov's visit to Tokyo in January 2012—the first visit by a Russian foreign minister in three years—the two countries agreed to visa liberalizations that would allow Japanese citizens to visit Russia for 90 days without a letter of invitation (MOFA 2012). Following Lavrov's successful visit, in March 2012, the Japanese government dropped the term "illegal occupation" regarding Russia's control of the Northern Territories, replacing it with "occupied without any legislative mandate" (Voice of Russia 2012). Compared to his predecessor, Prime Minister Noda toned down nationalist rhetoric on the dispute. Japan's annual Northern Territories Day came just days after Lavrov's visit. Unlike in previous years, the Japanese prime minister took an appeasing tone when addressing the annual rally in Tokyo, stressing his commitment to continuing negotiations. Even after Medvedev's second trip to Kunashiri in July 2012, there was no repeat of the angry exchanges that followed his visit in 2010. At the Asia-Pacific Economic Cooperation (APEC) Summit in Vladivostok in September 2012, Putin and Noda agreed to begin territorial discussions at the ministerial level in October, and set a date in December for Noda to visit Moscow (*Japan Times* 2012).

The DPJ's defeat in the December 16, 2012 general election put an end to Noda's plans to visit Moscow. Noda's successor, LDP leader Abe Shinzo, is a conservative with a nationalist reputation. Abe's victory has not necessarily torpedoed the prospects of a settlement on the Northern Territories. Should Abe choose to push ahead with negotiations, his nationalist credentials would assist him in convincing the Japanese people that a territorial compromise is in the national interest. Despite his nationalist views, as prime minister in 2006–07 Abe pushed to repair relations with China and South Korea after his predecessor, Koizumi Junichiro, had poisoned them with visits to the Yasukuni Shrine. In his second term, Abe has demonstrated a similar conciliatory attitude towards Moscow. The prime minister did not use Northern Territories Day in 2013 to berate Russia, even when two Russian fighter jets apparently violated Japanese airspace that very afternoon. Abe's decision not to allow this incident to derail relations with Russia suggests his preoccupation with other more pressing international issues—namely, the escalating militarization of the Senkaku/Diaoyu dispute and a new nuclear test by North Korea. Tokyo's ongoing tensions with Beijing over the Senkaku Islands may drive Abe to put aside concerns about a domestic political backlash and consider a territorial settlement with Moscow to facilitate improved bilateral relations and thus counterbalance Beijing's growing regional power.

In May 2012, the DPJ government asked former LDP Prime Minister Mori Yoshiro to serve as a special envoy to Russia. At Irkutsk in 2001, Mori had come close to agreeing a two-track territorial deal with Putin (see Table 12.2). The first track would include the return of the two smaller disputed islands to Japan, as set out in the 1956 Declaration. The second track would continue discussions on the future status of the two larger islands. On returning to office in December 2012, Abe retained Mori as the Japanese government's envoy to Russia, perhaps indicating his willingness to accept a compromise settlement similar to that discussed at Irkutsk. Mori was dispatched to Moscow as Abe's representative in February 2013 despite a controversial TV appearance the previous month in which Mori indicated his willingness to settle for the return of only three islands (*Japan Times* 2013).

If Tokyo were to approach territorial negotiations in a spirit of compromise would Moscow respond in kind? With Russia in a confident mood thanks to enhanced international prestige, it seems unlikely the current administration will concede anything more than the terms of the 1956 agreement, which Putin already put back on the table in 2001. Having failed to agree to a settlement in the 1990s when it was weaker economically, there are fewer incentives for Russia to do so now. On the other hand, Putin's reputation as a Russian patriot gives him greater room to maneuver on territorial issues than politicians from the liberal end of the political spectrum. During his first presidency, despite strong nationalist sentiments among the Russian population, Putin signed two border agreements with China. Furthermore, the visits to the islands by Russian officials that so incensed Tokyo in 2010–12 are more associated with Medvedev than Putin.

Since returning to the Kremlin in May 2012, Putin has taken action to improve Russo–Japanese relations. In August 2012, Moscow announced it would release records of Japanese prisoners of war (POWs) who died in Soviet camps (RIA Novosti 2012). At the APEC Summit the following month, Putin and Noda signed agreements to curb illegal crab fishing in Russian-administered waters in the Sea of Okhotsk (*Japan Times* 2012). Symbolizing the warming of bilateral relations, in July 2012 Tokyo gave the dog-loving Putin an Akita puppy, which Putin named "Yume" ("dream" in Japanese). In return, in February 2013, Putin sent a Siberian kitten named "Mir" ("peace" in Russian) to Akita Governor Satake Norihisa. Despite this "pet diplomacy" and other recent developments, Putin's domestic political situation makes a territorial settlement doubtful. At home, Putin's hold on power is weaker than during his first presidency. Anti-Putin protests since parliamentary elections in December 2011 have added to domestic political instability. In this climate, Putin is unlikely to risk further alienating public opinion by conceding territory to Japan.

Note

1 For clarity, I use the Japanese names of the four islands.

Bibliography

Asahi Shimbun (2011) "Maehara in for a Frigid Russian Welcome," February 9.

——(2012) "Hoppo Ryodo, Saishu Kecchaku Ni Iyoku 'Ukeire Kanou Na Dakyo Wo' Putin Shusho Kaiken," March 2.

Blagov, S. (2008) "Russia Struggles to Encourage Japanese Investments," *Eurasia Daily Monitor*, April 29, www.jamestown.org/single/?no_cache=1&tx_ttnews[swords]=8fd5893941d69d0be3f378576261ae3e&tx_ttnews[any_of_the_words]=sergei%20blagov&tx_ttnews[pointer]=11&tx_ttnews[tt_news]=33588&tx_ttnews[backPid]=7&cHash=4d5e589aef (accessed March 20, 2011).

Blanchard, J. (2010) "Economics and Asia-Pacific Region Territorial and Maritime Disputes: Understanding the Political Limits to Economic Solutions," *Asian Politics and Policy* 4: 682–708.

Bukh, A. (2012) "Constructing Japan's 'Northern Territories': Domestic Actors, Interests, and the Symbolism of the Disputed Islands," *International Relations of the Asia-Pacific* 12(3): 483–509.

Clark, G. (2005) "Japan-Russia Dispute Over Northern Territories Highlights Flawed Diplomacy," *Japan Focus*, April 7, www.japanfocus.org/-Gregory-Clark/2018 (accessed March 9, 2013).

The Economist (2011) "Broadsides from Broadsheets," February 7, www.economist.com/blogs/banyan/2011/02/japan_and_kuril_islands (accessed October 20, 2012).

Frolov, V. (2011) "Moscow Picking a Territorial Fight with Japan," *Russia Profile*, February 18, russiaprofile.org/experts_panel/32800.html (accessed October 15, 2012).

International Gas Union (2011) *World LNG Report 2011*, www.igu.org/igu-publications/LNG%20Report%202011.pdf (accessed October 13, 2012).

ITAR TASS (2011) "Suverenitet RF v Otnoshenii Kuril Ne Podlezhit Peresmotru—Kreml," February 7.

Japan Ministry of Defense (2012) *Defense of Japan 2012*, www.mod.go.jp/e/publ/w_paper/2012.html (accessed October 12, 2012).

Japan Times (2010) "Maehara Takes in Disputed Islands," December 5.

——(2012) "Noda Eyes Russia Trip in December," September 9.

——(2013) "Putin: Lack of Treaty 'Abnormal'," February 22.

JETRO (2013) "Japan's Monthly International Trade Report (January 2013)," Japan External Trade Organization, www.jetro.go.jp (accessed March 9, 2013).

Jiji Press (2010) "Russian-Held Isles Not Covered by Japan-U.S. Security Pact," November 3.

Kosyrev, D. (2005) "The Not-So-Wild East," *Russia Profile*, July 6, russiaprofile.org/international/a3976.html (accessed October 3).

Krastev, I. and Holmes, S. (2012) "An Autopsy of Managed Democracy," *Journal of Democracy* 23(3): 33–45.

Mack, A. and O'Hare, M. (1990) "Moscow-Tokyo and the Northern Territories Dispute," *Asian Survey* 30(4): 380–94.

Medetsky, A. (2009) "Russia and Japan Sign Nuclear Deal," *The Moscow Times*, May 13.

MEXT (2008) *Chuugakko Gakushuu Shidou Youryou Kaisetsu Shakai Hen*, www.mext.go.jp/component/a_menu/education/micro_detail/—icsFiles/afieldfile/2011/01/05/1234912_003.pdf (accessed July 20, 2012).

MOFA (2012) "Japan-Russia Foreign Ministers' Meeting between Foreign Minister Gemba and Foreign Minister Lavrov (Overview)," January 28, www.mofa.go.jp/region/europe/russia/meet1201.html (accessed February 22, 2013).

Nester, W. (1993) "Japan, Russia, and the Northern Territories: Continuities, Changes, Obstacles, Opportunities," *Third World Quarterly* 14(4): 717–34.

Nikkei Shimbun (2006) "Ryodo Mondai, Hoppo 4tou 'Menseki De Toubun' Aso Shi Kaiketsuan Ni Genkyu," December 14.

Owen, C. (2012) "Russia and Japan to Co-build LNG Plant," *Oil and Gas Technology*, September 4, www.oilandgastechnology.net/downstream/russia-and-japan-co-build-lng-plant (accessed October 12, 2012).

RIA Novosti (2011) "Russia Urges Japan to Renounce Far-Fetched Emphasis on 'Island Theme'," February 5, en.rian.ru/world/20110205/16246 8347.html (accessed February 26, 2012).

——(2012) "Russia to Release Japanese POW Records," August 28, en.rian.ru/world/20120828/175478168.htm (accessed October 30, 2012).

RT (2008) "Japanese Schoolbooks to Claim Russia's Southern Kuril Islands," RT.com, July 16, rt.com/news/japanese-schoolbooks-to-claim-russias-southern-kuril-islands (accessed October 24, 2012).

——(2009) "Trusting Relationship Unlikely to Solve Main Problem for Russia-Japan," RT.com, September 8, rt.com/politics/roar-russia-japan-relations (accessed October 24, 2012).

——(2011a) "Medvedev Orders Deployment of Weapons on Kuril Islands," RT.com, February 9, rt.com/politics/kuril-islands-medvedev-weapon (accessed October 10, 2012).

——(2011b) "Russia to Provide Extra Energy Help for its Neighbor in Trouble," RT.com, March 12, rt.com/news/russia-energy-help-japan (accessed October 25, 2012).

Togo, K. (2010) "Medvedev Signals Intention to Enhance Russian Presence," *Asahi Shimbun*, December 14.

Voice of Russia (2012) "Japan Drops Term 'Illegal Occupation' for South Kurils," March 2, english.ruvr.ru/2012_03_02/67308957 (accessed November 2, 2012).

Weir, F. (2012) "Putin Harnesses Russian Nationalism to Boost Presidential Bid," *Christian Science Monitor*, January 24, www.csmonitor.com/World/Europe/2012/0124/Putin-harnesses-Russian-nationalism-to-boost-presidential-bid (accessed July 12, 2012).

Weitz, R. (2011) "Why Moscow has Escalated its Territorial Dispute with Tokyo," *Pacific Focus* 26(2): 137–67.

Wiegand, K.E. (2005) "Nationalist Discourse and Domestic Incentives to Prevent Settlement of the Territorial Dispute Between Guatemala and Belize," *Nationalism and Ethnic Politics* 11(3): 349–83.

Williams, B. (2006) "Federal-Regional Relations in Russia and the Northern Territories Dispute: the Rise and Demise of the 'Sakhalin Factor'," *Pacific Review* 19(3): 263–85.

——(2010) "Dissent on Japan's Northern Periphery: Nemuro, the Northern Territories and the Limits of Change in a 'Bureaucrat's Movement'," *Japanese Journal of Political Science* 11(2): 221–44.

Yomiuri Shimbun (2006) "Nichiro Yuko Kobamu, Hoppo Ryodo Kokko Kaihuku 50nen," October 8.

——(2012) "Hoppo Ryodo Kosho, Zenshin Ni Kitai," March 5.

13 Okinawa today

Spotlight on Henoko

Alexis Dudden

The Ryukyu Islands—commonly referred to as Okinawa after the largest among the islands—have long found themselves and their people central to questions of Japanese state building, national identity, and sovereign control. Matsushima Yasukatsu, a leading member of the contemporary movement for Ryukyuan independence from Japan, underlines several points of departure for understanding the islands' history and their incorporation into modern Japan. He places equal weight on the Tokugawa era Satsuma clan's 1609 invasion of the islands and the Meiji government's 1879 annexation of them into the emerging Japanese empire. These histories notwithstanding, Matsushima stresses that Tokyo's decision to "discriminate" indiscriminately against Ryukyu islanders during World War II—despite having forced them to become subjects of the Japanese empire—and to "sacrifice the islands" outright at war's end has made them and their peoples' history a parallax for contemporary Japan's efforts at nationalized control over them (Matsushima 2012, i). Tokyo has repeatedly altered its claims vis-à-vis Okinawa and its people since 1945, which in turn makes the islands themselves appear to shift in meaning for Japan.

Even a short essay about contemporary Okinawa and its people must begin by making clear that these islands have been inhabited for tens of thousands of years. During excavation for a construction site in 2010–11 on the southernmost of the islands, workers uncovered fragments of rib shards among other pieces of human bone thought to be about 24,000 years old; local and national papers quickly declared them "the oldest in Japan" (*Yaeyama Mainichi Shimbun*, 10 February 2010; 11 November 2011). To be sure, the island of Ishigaki where the bones were found is legally defined as part of "Japan," yet claiming these ancient skeletal remains as "Japanese" is another matter. Complications with nationalizing the islands' people across time become clear at local history museums throughout the islands where displays consistently emphasize similarities between Okinawans and islanders in the northern Philippines in terms of ethnography and cultural practice. These islands are, of course, closer to Okinawa when compared to Tokyo or even Kyushu; moreover, the North Pacific's famous ocean current, the Kuroshio (Black Stream), flows from the south to the north throughout all of these islands, continuing to carry fish and boats along its path.

Equally important, even with formal annexation in 1879 into the Japanese empire, Okinawan islanders continued longstanding agricultural and fishing practices for their livelihoods through the end of the devastating Asia-Pacific War (1931–45). In 1944, one of the greatest historians of Japan in the modern era, E.H. Norman, wrote a brief report for the Canadian government detailing features of life throughout the Japanese empire that he viewed as critical for understanding and creating any successful future post-war policy planning for Japan. At the time of Norman's writing, it was still possible to emphasize the rudimentary nature of Okinawan life and also to describe the islands themselves as relatively undeveloped, something unimaginable today now that the islands hold such a central and militarized place in America's post-1945 world order.

In his report, Norman wrote: "[The Ryukyu Islands'] loss to Japan would not be of any serious economic consequence since the chief occupation of the islanders is fishing and Japan's best fishing grounds are in northern waters" (Norman 1944).

In simplest terms, in 1944, similar to 1879 or even 1609 for that matter, it was impossible to foresee what has become of Okinawa and Okinawans' way of life today.

Norman also addressed the question of who might control the islands after war's end. His observations suggest that protracted Allied domination—let alone purely American control—was not a consideration for even the most involved observer at the time of his writing (six months before the Allied invasion): "Although these islands have been administratively part of Japan since 1879, and their inhabitants are perhaps closer to Japan than China in language and custom, the Chinese still have a case to argue that they should be by right, Chinese" (Norman 1944).

Norman understood that although Japan had incorporated the islands into its empire during the early moments of its overseas territorial expansion, after Japan's defeat China could make legitimate claim to the islands in terms of the region's lengthy *pre*-Japanese imperial history; additionally, Norman's notice indicates that the Allies' post-war settlement with Japan would not collapse if Tokyo were to forfeit claim to Okinawa together with Korea and Manchuria (the plan that was already in the works). The reality, therefore, in 1944 for Norman's analysis that the islands were economically and strategically of minimal consequence to Japan proper brings into relief how profoundly American occupation of the islands *after* 1945 has changed them and their people forever.

At the end of the war, the Allies—particularly the Americans—occupied Japan in order to refashion the enemy into a peaceful partner. The Occupation technically lasted until 1952, and although this history is far too detailed to reduce to a few sentences, Okinawa's place in the mix would always be different. In important ways, even with the 1951 San Francisco Peace Treaty's restoration of sovereignty to Japan proper, the Ryukyu Islands (Okinawa) became differently controlled, as Article 3 of the treaty explained:

> Japan will concur in any proposal of the United States to the United Nations to place under its trusteeship system, with the United States as the sole administering authority, Nansei Shoto south of 29deg. north latitude (including the Ryukyu Islands and the Daito Islands), Nanpo Shoto south of Sofu Gan (including the Bonin Islands, Rosario Island and the Volcano Islands) and Parece Vela and Marcus Island. Pending the making of such a proposal and affirmative action thereon, the United States will have the right to exercise all and any powers of administration, legislation and jurisdiction over the territory and inhabitants of these islands, including their territorial waters.
>
> (Treaty of Peace with Japan, 1951)

The United States would officially "revert" Okinawa to Japanese administration and control in 1972, yet the overwhelming presence of American military personnel and weapons *continues* to render questionable the full dimensionality of this legal change. The statistics are well known yet always bear repeating; as of this typing, Okinawa comprises less than 1% of all Japanese territory—a scant 0.6%—yet 75% of the total number of US forces, civilian employees, and their dependants stationed in Japan live and work there, and all roughly 30,000 of them take up 20% of Okinawa's territory.

Today, most Okinawans work in jobs related to the islands' two major economies: tourism and the American bases (on the bases and off); a handful of islanders persist, however, in fishing and farming. Global changes to these traditional endeavors notwithstanding, during the second half of the 20th century the ongoing presence of the US military and its use of the islands and the islanders for American policy objectives in the region and the world has transformed them physically, structurally, and socially. In economic and environmental terms, daily life for Okinawans in Okinawa has entwined those ruling Japan—the islands have again been "Japanese" since 1972—into acting as agents of American bidding and, thus, fashion an entirely confused and compromised governance and claim over the nation's southernmost prefecture.

There are numerous ways to bring these conditions into relief; perhaps the most descriptive means, however, is through one example: the post-1945 tale of the small village of Henoko on Okinawa's east coast. The recent history of Henoko reveals a wide range of competing forces pitting the world's most powerful country in history—the United States of America—working in tandem with significant Japanese central government backing and a few local Okinawan politicians and businessmen against a small band of entrenched and knowledgeable resisters over the question of whether or not (and how) to build yet another new US military base on the island. As the resistance movement in Henoko approaches its second decade, its brief history makes it possible to understand, moreover, just how much is at stake for the future of all of Okinawa in terms of its past and present.

American bases, sexual assault, and quick fixes

In 1945 US troops moved into and occupied various Japanese bases in Okinawa and also began to construct new ones of their own. Ever since, repeated incidents of violence against locals—especially sexual violence—have defined the relationship.[1] Some observers underscore the significance of the US military's initial reworking of Japan's notorious wartime system of state-sponsored sexual slavery for its own purposes as soon as troops arrived on Okinawa (Molasky 1999; Kovner 2012). The American Occupation's Recreation and Amusement Association (RAA) in fact took almost its entire preliminary structural organization from the existing Japanese comfort women system, a euphemistic term that refers to the 200,000 Chinese, Korean, Philippine, Indonesian, Dutch, and other women and girls and young men forced into sexual servitude between 1938–45 for Japanese troops throughout the Asia-Pacific theater (Soh 2002).

Connecting early post-war American re-workings of this wartime system to their Japanese origins in no way downplays the violence inherent to any of its features. Rather, the continuation of this particular element of Japan's wartime behavior into the post-war functioning of Pax Americana in Okinawa makes more apparent how issues of sexual violence—which should still be understood as wartime sexual violence because American soldiers are active duty troops—became a consistent feature of Okinawan daily life from the middle of the 20th century on.

No one rape is worse than another; some, however, have the power to compel a large number of people into collective action against the crime. On September 4, 1995, three American servicemen—US Navy Seaman Marcus Gill and US Marines Rodrico Harp and Kendrick Ledet—all from Camp Hansen in the center of Okinawa island, rented a van, abducted a 12-year-old Okinawan girl, wrapped duct tape over her mouth and eyes and gang-raped her. Okinawans—and many others—declared that they had had enough. On October 21, 1995, 85,000 people gathered together to demand an end to the American abuse of Okinawa and Okinawans.

Following the girl's rape and the expanding anti-American protests in Okinawa, in November 1995 the commander of the United States Pacific Command, Admiral Richard C. Macke, gave a press conference intended to display American understanding and to placate protestors; his remarks, however, demonstrate a fundamental misunderstanding of the broader problems: "I think it was absolutely stupid. I have said several times: for the price they paid to rent the car (used in the crime), they could have had a girl (a prostitute)" (*The Virginian-Pilot*, accessed online, March 1, 2013).

Public outcry against Macke's "insensitivity" led to his forced early retirement and demotion to rear admiral. The penalty of losing two stars was a reduction in his pension from US$7,384 a month to $5,903 per month, still high by Okinawan standards

Tellingly, the US Navy's solution to what was chiefly seen as a PR gaffe was indicative of the US government's broader "fix" to come. In response to September 1995's horrendous crime and to the widespread protests against US troops' violence towards Okinawan civilians, the US government conceived a plan to reduce its footprint in Okinawa. Almost two decades later much of the plan has not been implemented, ensuring that the American military presence remains a source of outrage and protest today. In April 1996, a joint US–Japanese governmental commission announced that it would address Okinawans' anger by reducing the amount of land occupied by the American military in the center of Okinawa. This downsizing includes the Futenma Air Station, a large base in the middle of a densely populated urban area. There has been a helicopter crash at an adjacent university campus, and aside from fears about a

Figure 13.1 Picture of sit-in from *Okinawa Times*

more serious accident, nearby residents complain about the noise and environmental impact caused by routine operations.

Optimism that decades of protest and outrage over the American military presence in Okinawa—both in public and private—would finally yield positive change met with a discouraging new development. During the autumn of 1996 the public became aware of a significant provision in the new base agreement. The US planned to "give up" the Futenma base and shift operations to a *new* base planned offshore from the existing Camp Schwab near the small town of Henoko, on the island's eastern coast. On December 2, 1996 the US–Japan Special Action Committee on Okinawa (SACO) formally presented its proposal, revealing a new base extending out into the middle of Oura Bay.

Put simply, to address the seething, mass eruption of long-held resentments against the United States, officials decided to move some of the problems associated with American occupation writ large such as fighter jet and helicopter noise and accidents away from the most densely populated area of the island to a less populated area. The catch, however—as thousands of Okinawans immediately observed and against which they registered their abundant displeasure—is that the plan would necessitate the wholesale destruction of a pristine coral reef area and its surrounding waters. In short, the Henoko plan would annihilate a way of life, and the devastation would take place during peacetime and in full view.

With this so-called solution, the Americans and their Japanese counterparts (both in the central government in Tokyo and from Okinawa) made clear several things at once: first, they revealed their determination to avoid the fundamental problem of active duty troops living among civilians; on top of this, their proposal revealed how little those involved in the plan concerned themselves with Okinawan sensibilities. The plan to build a heliport near Henoko generated further outrage among Okinawans long burdened by American demands and betrayed by the Japanese central government's willingness to continue to sacrifice Okinawa and Okinawans in the name of preserving the security treaty—ANPO, as it is known in Japanese—at all costs.

Henoko

Standing at the water's edge in Henoko, the proposed base's costs become immediately clear. To begin with, the horizon line separating water and sky would disappear. Beneath the waterline, concrete slabs and iron rods would destroy a massive section of Oura Bay's coral reefs to undergird the helicopter launch and landing pads projected to run a mile and a half in length and a quarter mile wide. The 24-hour a day training missions would mean constant noise and jet fuel spills, all of which would devastate the habitats of countless reef and shellfish, a rare eelgrass ecosystem, and an endangered sea mammal, the dugong (a cousin of the manatee).

Even before the SACO officially announced the Henoko transfer, villagers sprang into action (Kikuno and Norimatsu 2010). Higa Seijun first organized fellow townspeople to preserve Henoko's way of life; their action transformed into a movement that has come to be known as the "Inochi o Mamorukai" (which literally translates as the "Society for the protection of life" and which encompasses multiple forms of life and livelihoods in its meaning) (McCormack and Norimatsu 2012). Villagers who had never considered themselves politically active joined the cause, including its oldest member, a 93-year-old woman known as Grandma Yoshi. Supporters initially demanded a special election, arguing that a decision of such importance merited a vote in an ostensibly democratic system. The December 21, 1997 mayoral race in the town of Nago—which has municipal jurisdiction over Henoko and its surrounding area—pitted pro- and anti-heliport causes against one another (the "pro" faction deriving largely from those employed in construction-related businesses throughout the islands which would benefit from building anything in a deeply rural area with chronic under-employment). In the election, defeating the powerful business and bureaucratic lobbies, 52% of voters voted for the candidate who opposed the proposed base. Yet, in ways that have long defined the anti-democratic maneuverings of all things related to American base issues throughout Japan—and which continue to do so—the central Japanese government forced the town's mayor to announce that Henoko would "accept the base" *despite* the majority vote to the contrary.

For the next seven years, protesters maintained a tent city protest on the beach while construction plans moved slowly ahead (including building big new roads through the hills leading across the island to the coastline area) (Heri Kichi Hantaikyo 2006). In April 2003, the political ground appeared to shift even further from opponents' aims. Protestors discovered that the government would go ahead with surveys and assessments regardless of democratic processes; in response, leaders of the Inochi o Mamorukai began to prepare a different action plan, meeting each Saturday at the beach to train in sea kayaking and other resistance techniques. On April 19, 2004 anti-base supporters staged a more visible non-violent sit-in on the Henoko dock that would block a survey boat's departure and began what would establish a more proactive and physical dimension to the protest movement at Oura Bay.

As the movement gained deeper traction and media attention, on August 13, 2004 an American military helicopter stationed at the Futenma base crashed into a classroom building of Okinawa International University. This incident had nothing to do with rape, but *again* underscored the daily instances of violence that Okinawans routinely endure because of the American military presence. By pure luck, school was not in session that day, and no one was killed. Nonetheless, another wave of large-scale protests against the US bases erupted to which Japan's political establishment—primarily in Tokyo—responded with the twisted logic that the crash demonstrated the need for a new base (the one proposed for Henoko) and that its construction must be sped up. Less than a month later, the Japanese government announced that Henoko's construction would begin forcibly if necessary. In other words, Henoko villagers and their supporters who were participating in their ongoing sit-ins would likely encounter physical harm and/or arrest. In response to this news, 400 people from all over Japan traveled to Henoko at their own expense to join the protesters.[2]

The numbers may sound small to some, yet they were far larger than the government-backed construction companies anticipated; fearing confrontation, Japanese surveyors received special permission from the US military command and launched their boats from nearby Camp Schwab and not from the public dock at Henoko. Protesters responded immediately with a peaceful flotilla strategy: an "in water" sit-in made up of sea kayaks and other small craft took root. Between September and December 2004, the struggle intensified with government-backed construction firms attempting to bore holes through the coral reefs to erect scaffolding on the one hand, and, on the other hand, protesters trying everything in their power to stop this.

By December 2004, several construction workers became reckless with their heavy equipment and disregarded the non-violent protestors' safety; a few members of the

Inochi o Mamorukai wound up in the hospital. News of their injuries outraged fishermen throughout Okinawa who were aware of the movement against a new base in Henoko, yet for various reasons had not yet joined, ranging from lack of time to lack of firm commitment to the Henoko cause (the small villages that continue traditional ways are, unsurprisingly, locally oriented regardless of individual beliefs). At this critical moment, "*uminchu*" (fishermen) from all over Okinawa appeared in Oura Bay, shifting the political ground in favor of the resistance by broadening the movement from protecting life in Henoko to protecting life in Okinawa.[3]

For nearly a decade now, a similar pattern has continued to shape this struggle in fits and starts, pitting those who would do the Americans' bidding and build the proposed heliport—today wholly transformed into a new "coastline plan" involving proposals for major military docks as well—against those who continue to live in tents on the beach and regularly take to their kayaks in protest to dispel surveyors and assessors on the other.

Henoko's back-story helps elucidate why this particular site of resistance and the people who keep it going have managed to ensconce themselves and their pleas while other similar movements have failed. To be clear, however, just because the supporters of the Inochi o Mamorukai have persisted for over 15 years does not mean that they will ultimately succeed in blocking the construction of the proposed heliport off of Camp Schwab. In September 2009, the Democratic Party of Japan (DPJ), the leading opposition party, ousted the Liberal Democratic Party (LDP), Washington's reliable and dutiful junior partner in managing the alliance. For a brief moment it appeared that the resistance movement in Henoko would actually achieve its democratically sought challenge as the DPJ Prime Minister Hatoyama Yukio made his opposition to the Futenma/Henoko bait and switch ploy known, agreeing instead with many Okinawans that any new base that the Americans wanted should not be built anywhere on Okinawa. Unfortunately for the protestors, Hatoyama's tenure was short and ineffectual, an object lesson in the costs of arousing Washington's displeasure. Two subsequent DPJ prime ministers reverted to established subaltern practice, acting as clients for the Americans and their designs. At the time of this writing in March 2013, American President Barack Obama and Japanese Prime Minister Abe Shinzo had recently met to affirm their over-arching commitment to building this new base. In simplest terms, the Henoko protest has made clear the difficulties that a small band of ordinary citizens face when challenging the Pentagon's power and agenda.[4]

In 2006, Okinawan photographer Ishikawa Mao and southern Japanese writer Urashima Etsuko collaborated on a book called *The Island is Rocking*: *An Okinawan Seaside Village Story*, which chronicles the protagonists of the resistance movement that has kept the heliport plan at bay now for nearly two decades (Urashima and Ishikawa 2006). Important in this mix is how Camp Schwab initially came to this quiet town. The Battle for Okinawa at the end of World War II was among the costliest series of bombardments and invasions that American troops visited on Japan. Some argue that in terms of civilian casualties and brutality, this front of the war was the worst. The scars and legacies of war are evident in the continued American military presence in Okinawa. American soldiers, sailors, and marines commandeered Imperial Japanese Army and Navy bases, and expanded them exponentially, making war daily life.

When the Asia-Pacific War came to Henoko, villagers remember the difficulties of fleeing into the hills to survive. Unlike the areas around the military bases in Futenma,

Kadena, Hansen among others on the other side of the central Okinawan hills, post-war life in Henoko began without Americans in its midst. Until 1959, that is. In 1959, with the Cold War in full swing, 6,000 US Marines arrived in this small village to establish the newly opened Camp Schwab base, which they carved into the hills with bulldozers and other pieces of heavy equipment, eventually extending its reach to the shoreline on the center of Okinawa's east coast. Overnight, the Americans brought yet another war to the surrounding village: Vietnam. By 1965, with the American campaign against Vietnam intensifying, Henoko's way of life transformed as fast as it could to keep up with the soldiers coming through for training en route to war and also for their rest and recreation leaves from the front lines. In local terms this meant new economies developed from construction and small businesses, especially bars and nightclubs, which also meant the arrival of non-locals to work in many of these jobs (from as far away as the southern Yaeyama islands and Miyako-jima).

Divisions flourished; the most visceral one came in the form of a line of razor wire rolled across the shoreline to make clear where Japan ended and the United States began. The balance of power could not have been starker: Americans would freely walk over the wire—on a short cut to town—while villagers were strictly forbidden from entering the "Property of the U.S. Marines" (as the sign explains). Annually, however, the barrier would come down on a special day called, "Christmas Children's Day," and villagers enjoyed a barbecue party with games and face painting at the beach with their American hosts, playing on the rocks and in the sand their grandparents took for granted.

Older people from the village who participate in the Inochi o Mamorukai movement to block construction of the proposed offshore base speak with regular consonance about their opposition: "The ocean let us raise our children. Selling it as a base will bring punishment from the gods" (Urashima and Ishikawa 2006, 45). This understanding of what is at stake appears on signs around the village, on placards people

Figure 13.2 Picture of new wall

bring to protests outside of Henoko, and on T-shirts; in short, the ocean made life possible. Recently the razor wire fence has morphed into an increasingly permanent structure, displaying the unease with which the heliport's proponents continue their cause.

During the past 10 years, this contoured pattern of struggle has endured between those who would do the Americans' bidding and build the proposed heliport and those who continue to live in tents on the beach and take to their kayaks in protest regularly to dispel surveyors and assessors. At the same time, once the resistance attracted "*uminchu*" from other parts of Okinawa and not just Henoko it changed the movement in tenor and depth. Predicting what will eventually transpire is neither possible nor fruitful; it is safe to say, however, that any confrontation might result in violence, making the nature of American demands on Okinawa and Okinawans seem more real to many throughout Japan with unpredictable reverberations.

Notes

1 The Internet offers many views on American basing in Okinawa as well as detailed maps and visual explanations of what the US forces stationed there do. One of the most informative is run by the group, "Close the Base" (closethebase.org/us-military-bases/).

2 Even with a group travel discount and an education discount, a trip for 10 people from Rikkyo University in Tokyo cost each participant roughly $1,200. By 2009 and again in 2012, the cost of airfare, car rental, and gas had increased markedly, bringing the cost of participation in the same activity to nearly $2,000. The sheer expense of such volunteer works means that the numbers of supporters on the ground—especially those who come from outside the small village—cannot tell the full story of commitment to the cause.

3 It is important to understand that "*uminchu*" means fisherman, but translates literally as man of the sea/people of the sea. Throughout the islands, Okinawans often use this term to name themselves in distinction from mainland Japanese whom they pejoratively call "*Yamato*" people, a name taken from the name for ancient Japan, which never had claim over the Ryukyu Islands.

4 The Henoko action has much in common with movements in the Marshall Islands, for example, in which locals seek accountability from the American military and government for spoiling their lands with nuclear testing.

Bibliography

Heri Kichi Hantaikyo (2006) *Heri Akushyon*, Naha, Okinawa: Nanyo Bunko.

Kikuno, Yumiko and Norimatsu Satoko (2010) "Henoko, Okinawa: Inside the Sit-In," *The Asia-Pacific Journal* 8(1:10), February 22.

Kovner, Sarah (2012) *Occupying Power: Sex Workers and Servicemen in Postwar Japan*, Palo Alto: Stanford University Press.

Matsushima Yasukatsu (2012) *Ryukyu Dokuritsu e no Michi*, Kyoto: Horitsu Bunkasha.

McCormack, Gavan and Satoko Oka Norimatsu (2012) *Resistant Islands: Okinawa Confronts Japan and the United States*, New York: Rowman and Littlefield.

Molasky, Michael (1999) *American Occupation of Japan and Okinawa*, New York: Routledge.

Norman, E.H. (1944) "Japan and the Japanese Empire: General Considerations," Canadian Department of External Affairs, Ottawa, September 22.

Soh, Sarah C. (2002) *The Comfort Women: Sexual Violence and Postcolonial Memory in Korea and Japan*, Chicago: University of Chicago Press.

Urashima Etsuko and Ishikawa Mao (2006) *Shima ga Ubareru: Okinawa, Henoko no Mura no Monogatari*, Tokyo: Kobunken.

Yaeyama Mainichi Shimbun (2010) February 10; November 11, 2011.

Part IV

Social dilemmas

14 Demographic dilemmas, women and immigration

Jeff Kingston

Japan's aging and declining population poses enormous policy challenges while casting a cloud over the nation's future prospects. One observer suggests that Japan is on demographic death row because the birthrate has remained low for so long (Magnus 2008, 35). This means that Japan has "locked in" certain future demographic realities that cannot be altered quickly by policy changes promoting an increased birth rate. While medical advances promise longer lives and a more active and healthy elderly, they don't really offer a demographic soft landing. An expanding elderly cohort may to some degree become more productive, but there is no magic pill or technology that can ensure they will not become a growing burden on pension and medical care systems while the number of taxpayers supporting those programs is shrinking. However, policy reforms can mitigate the fiscal and economic implications of a graying Japan.

Japan is one of the most rapidly aging societies in the world; from 1988 to 2007 the number of Japan's over 65s doubled. As of 2012, 24% of the population, numbering about 30 million, was over 65 years old and this was projected to reach 40% by 2055. Significantly, the number of workers supporting each retiree is shrinking from 10 in 1950 to 3.6 in 2000 and 1.9 by 2025, and there are fewer replacements in sight. According to the National Institute of Population and Social Security Research, by 2055 Japan's population will shrink 30% to 90 million.

The key elements of the demographic time bomb include Japanese women having fewer children, the retirement of the 7 million-strong baby-boom cohort (1947–49), and people living longer. Adding to the prevailing sense of malaise, since 2007 Japan's population is slowly declining. The combination of aging, low fertility and depopulation is creating a sense of urgency about the nation's future (Coulmas 2007). The implications are enormous, ranging from pensions and elderly care to a shrinking labor force and domestic market, economic stagnation, fiscal deficits and social cohesion, but the situation is not catastrophic, despite alarmist assessments (Campbell 2009). This chapter examines the prospects of promoting women's employment and increased immigration and whether such initiatives can help address the challenges of an aging society.

Fertility and work-life balance

Children younger than 15 constitute only 13% of the nation's 127 million people, compared to 20% in the United States. Japanese women are bearing fewer children; from a high of 4.3 babies in 1947, the total fertility rate—the average number of babies a woman will bear—dropped to a record low 1.29 in 2003, well below the number of babies needed (2.07) to maintain the current population. Since then the fertility rate has stabilized at about 1.37, but surveys indicate that even if people are able to have all the children they desire, the maximum fertility rate would climb only to 1.75.

Women are having fewer children mostly because it is very difficult to combine work with child rearing in Japan, while increasing numbers are delaying or forgoing marriage altogether. Unmarried rates for women aged 40 increased from 7.6% in 1995 to 14.1% in 2005, while the unmarried rates for those aged 30 increased from 14% in 1985 to 39.9% in 2005. As Htun discusses in Chapter 15, fertility is also low because a growing number of those who marry choose not to have children. As attitudes and social norms have changed, and lifestyles diversify, getting married and having children is no longer the default option it once was. Women who are now enjoying greater social and economic freedom wonder if having kids is really what they want, and consider carefully what they stand to lose by raising a family, especially given that their husbands continue to shift most of the child-rearing burden onto them.

Belatedly, firms and the government are implementing family-friendly policies aimed at providing the types of support women need to continue careers while raising families, but dual-earner couples still face difficulties in securing childcare and have trouble finding time to raise their families given long working hours. There are few signs that firms are adopting flexible work options that would make achieving a work-life balance more feasible. Moreover, the government has not given firms sufficient incentives to do so and also has not invested enough resources in creating a family-friendly social infrastructure, a neglect that forces many women to make a choice between careers or motherhood. Unlike in other leading industrialized nations, for women in Japan, careers and children are far too much of an either/or situation.

In 55% of married households, both spouses are working, marking a huge shift from the "breadwinner" model featuring a full-time housewife at home. In such two-income households, the lack of support from government and firms, combined with the absence of either spouse's parents, makes childcare a critical issue. Mothers and fathers can take childcare leave, with their jobs guaranteed, but they lose 40% of their income during their 14 weeks of paid leave.

Women cite the lack of childcare and the cost of raising children as the main reasons they are not having children. In some areas there are long waiting lists to get into public daycare programs, while private options are expensive and usually have inferior facilities. Nationwide, as of 2012, nearly 25,000 children were on the waiting lists of public daycare centers. The problem is more acute in urban areas, as Tokyo alone has 7,257 kids on the waiting list. In Suginami Ward in Tokyo about one half of the 3,000 applicants for public daycare in 2012 could not secure a slot. Prime Minister Abe promises to eliminate shortages of public daycare, but the government has promised this before.

In Japan, 62% of women drop out of the workforce when they have their first child, partly due to difficulties in securing daycare, but also because many see few incentives to stick with unpromising careers. In addition, due to prevailing values and norms, many mothers want to raise their children for the first three years of their lives. These women do not have the flexible work options available in many European countries that enable mothers to work reduced schedules, telecommute from home, or share jobs that make it much easier to balance work and family responsibilities. The problem is that it is extremely difficult for these women who quit their jobs to return to the workforce to similar full-time positions. This is primarily a problem of rigid corporate employment practices that emphasize continuous tenure and limited mid-career recruitment. It is also a reflection of gender discrimination that relegates working mothers to the labor force periphery; regular workers work regular hours according to employment practices that are geared towards married male workers who have a wife at home to take care of family responsibilities. Gender assumptions of employers are evident in the very common *tanshin funin* system that involves dispatching male workers to a firm's distant branch offices for a few years, living separately from their wife and any children who remain at home. There is an implicit assumption that the wife will take care of all household matters without any support from her husband, including childcare, making it difficult for wives in these circumstances to work full time.

When women are contemplating having a child, they are aware that this very probably means ending their careers unless they are public-sector employees or professionals (lawyers, doctors, accountants, etc.) who have credentials that give them privileged career tracks. Less privileged and credentialed women know very well that returning to work will mean a drop in pay, status, and responsibility. They also know that raising and educating children is very expensive, especially when one factors in the opportunity costs of abandoned careers.

For Japan, growing risk and instability in the job market is also translating into fewer children. For non-regular workers (part-time, contract, dispatched, temporary) with limited incomes and tenuous job security, getting married and having children is beyond reach, seen as something to which only people with "normal" lives and regular jobs can aspire. Given that in 2012 this "precariat" (low-paid workers without job security) represents 35% of the entire workforce, mostly young workers, the implications for the birth rate are quite serious. In 2011 the government found that ¥3 million (US$36,000) income is a crucial dividing line; below that income level, only 8% to 10% of men in their twenties and thirties were married while above ¥3 million, the proportion of married rose to 25%–40% percent, correlating with income (*Japan Times*, July 31, 2011).

Coping with crisis

The grim economic consequences of an aging society are potentially considerable. Fewer babies today mean fewer consumers, workers, and taxpayers tomorrow, translating into economic decline. The bulge of retirees at the top will depend on the taxes and premiums of fewer workers to fund their pensions, medical care, and other social programs targeting the elderly. The surge in demand for elderly care is raising government spending on medical care and pulling productive workers, mostly women, from the workforce to care for aging relatives. Tax increases and benefit cuts are imperfect and incomplete policy solutions.

The time bomb is certainly ticking away, but in many respects Japan has already been adjusting incrementally to a graying society. Since the early 1990s, the government has initiated a series of policy reforms that target the urgent problems of funding pensions, elderly care, and medical care costs. To be sure, the government is racing to catch up to various aspects of this unfolding crisis, but in terms of what governments around the world are doing and the scale of the problem, Japan is not in such dire straits.

The impact of a shrinking population and aging are gradual and predictable and thus manageable (Campbell and Ikegami 1998). There is an ongoing adjustment of policies and institutions in Japan driven by perceptions about what needs to be done, suggesting that fears about the consequences are overstated. For example, workers over 40 contribute to a nursing care insurance scheme introduced in 2000, the retirement age has been raised to 65, medical co-payments have been raised for those over 75 years of age who have a higher income, cheaper generic drugs are more widely used and in 2012 the government announced plans to double the consumption tax.

Alarmists also overlook the potential contributions of senior citizens. Many seniors in Japan continue working after retirement on reduced salaries because firms value their skills. The average mandatory retirement age has progressively climbed from 55 to 65, but raising this to 70, or eliminating it altogether, may happen in light of improved longevity and health. Retirees are a growing consumer market for niche products and services catering to their needs, spawning "silver" businesses ranging from leisure and education to health care and housing.

The government projects that social security spending will surge an eye-popping 42% between 2006 and 2015. Scary numbers along these lines are regularly invoked to create a sense of crisis that justifies and propels reforms. Certainly, Japan does face urgent problems in coping with the aging society, but it has a relatively good track record in dealing with an explosion in the numbers of elderly since the 1980s and thus the situation is not nearly as grim as the unnerving statistics and gloomy headlines suggest.

Medical care costs in Japan are massive and growing, but there are effective measures in place that contain costs. Japan spends less than half per capita of what the United States does on health care, but by most measures Japanese are considerably healthier. Between 1980 and 2003, while the proportion of the over-65 population in Japan rose from 9% to 19%, total health spending rose from 7% to 8% of gross domestic product (GDP). During the same period, the elderly population in the United States rose from 11% to 12% while health care spending nearly doubled from 9% to 17% of GDP (Campbell 2008a, 2008b, 34(1), 136–40). However, caring for a rapidly aging society is a massive policy challenge that is only partially funded by mandatory national nursing care insurance.

Caregiving

Japanese policy is consistent with global trends away from institutionalization towards greater emphasis on home- and community-based care. The guiding principle of these new plans is to encourage older people to live with a minimum of dislocation and a maximum of independence for as long as possible. Many elderly Japanese want to live independently at home if at all possible and over 90% of people aged 65 and over do so. With declining government support, however, combined with rising demand for such services and a shortage of professional caregivers, many families are in crisis, overburdened and overwhelmed by their caregiving obligations.

There remains, however, a strong inclination to rely on the family for caregiving as much as possible, with female relatives accounting for 85% of all caregivers. Some 35% of these female caregivers report giving up their job in order to nurse ailing elderly relatives. They are both obliged and inclined, by rearing and social expectations, to take on this onerous task, but many are getting too old for the job.

About one-half of family caregivers are aged 60 or over, meaning that much of elderly care is in the hands of the elderly. The Long Term Care Insurance (LTC) plan is aimed at providing nursing support for these primary caregivers depending on the care manager's assessment of need, periodically adjusted according to changes in the patient's condition. Even though this is a godsend to families enduring what the media dubs "nursing hell," many of the caregivers are themselves frail and even with nursing assistance are pushed beyond their limits, taking a toll on their health and reducing their capacity for caregiving. Moreover, changing norms, expectations, employment patterns, and gender roles are undermining this family-based caregiving model and it is unlikely that younger women will take on these tasks in the future to the same degree as their mothers and grandmothers have.

The government's current family-based caregiving model with supplementary professional support cannot last given trends in the familial support ratio, defined as the number of females aged 40–59 to the total population aged 65–84 (Ogawa *et al.* 2006). Given that primary caregivers are usually female relatives, the declining number of middle-aged women combined with the rapid growth in the over-65 population suggests the limits of this model. In 1990 the familial support ratio was 1.3, declining dramatically to 0.65 in 2010, and the future demographic potential for familial support is not promising. There are already increasing numbers of households without any caregivers; wife caregivers largely outlive their husbands, but as these widows grow frail they often do not have a relative on whom to rely. For them, at some point, assisted living and other institutional arrangements are necessary. However, the major implication is the surging demand for more professional caregivers. Who will take on this difficult, low-paid job? Could the answer come from overseas?

Foreign caregivers

Perhaps, but there is a tight global market for nurses and caregivers as aging societies elsewhere are also competing for the same limited pool of professionals and offer a better deal than Japan. The difficulties of mastering written Japanese, stringent qualification exams, and the distinct possibility of being sent home for failure to pass exams will hamper Japan's efforts to recruit and retain sufficient numbers of foreign caregivers.

Japan faces a serious shortage of nurses and caregivers as the number of elderly requiring nursing care is projected to total 7.8 million in 2025, a 1.7-fold increase from 2006. The government estimates that Japan faces a shortage of hundreds of thousands of caregivers and nurses, but has done little to alleviate this problem. The annual turnover rate for caregivers is more than 20%, and some half a million Japanese with licenses have given up working in the field; clearly many workers feel this is not a desirable job.

Japan's ad hoc approach to immigration reform is evident in Japan's Economic Partnership Agreements (EPAs) with the Philippines and Indonesia (Vogt and Achenbach 2012). These agreements embody the tinkering at the margins approach to the immigration issue, lacking any long-term vision while neglecting the interests of Japan and the migrant workers. These EPAs include provision for accepting 1,000 nurses and caregivers from each country over a two-year period to work in Japan for three to four years, but also set the bar very high for them to remain working in Japan beyond the trial period. These EPAs represent compromises hammered out between various ministries in Japan and with the partner nations to address Japan's massive staffing shortages for elderly care, but stop short of doing enough to alleviate the problem.

Japan agreed to accept up to 400 Indonesian nurses and 600 caregivers in 2008 and 2009 as "candidates" for government certification if they pass qualifying exams. In the event, only 104 Indonesian nurses and 101 caregivers, about two-thirds women, began work in 2008, reflecting problems of recruiting suitable candidates. In addition, there has been lukewarm interest because of concerns that the time and energy involved in becoming a candidate are not worth it given the high probability candidates will not pass qualifying exams and will be forced to return home after a few years.

Indonesian nurses must have two years' experience while caregivers are required to be graduates of institutions of higher learning or nursing school graduates certified by the Indonesian government. Candidates are given six months' Japanese language and vocational training and then work at hospitals and elderly care institutions. They receive the same salaries as Japanese staff and also get additional living assistance. Nurses are allowed to stay three years before taking national examinations, with three chances to pass, while caregivers have four years and only one chance to pass. Those who pass the exams will be given three-year visas and can renew these a maximum of three times. It is not encouraging that only two of the Indonesian nurses who took the exam in 2009 passed, prompting the government to offer subsidized supplemental language instruction. It turns out that by 2011, 63 out of the original 104 nurses who came in 2008 had returned home, citing language and other problems. In addition, they were discouraged by restrictions preventing them from providing the type of medical treatments such as drips and injections that they had been licensed to administer in Indonesia. Instead, the Indonesians are assigned tasks that do not require professional training such as bathing patients and table setting.

After five years of difficult negotiations, the initial 2009 target from the Philippines was 200 Filipino nurses and 300 caregivers, but only a total of 358 arrived, apparently reflecting the economic crisis in Japan and fewer than expected contract offers. Filipino caregivers must have graduated from a four-year vocational course (or nursing program) and be certified, while nurses are required to have three years of prior experience. Under the terms of the agreement, Filipinos who pass their licensing exams in Japan will be allowed to remain in Japan to practice their professions on an unlimited basis.

The basic problem is that this program is designed to fail and offers little immediate relief to the existing acute shortages of nurses and caregivers in Japan and also no long-term solution. The failure of this program, evident in the low pass rates, led the government in 2013 to give nurses and caregivers from both countries an extra year to prepare for their exams. In 2012, 36 of the 95 caregiver candidates passed the exam while only 47 of the 415 test takers passed the nursing exam.

Given Japan's rapidly graying population and rising demand for elderly care services, the small-scale EPA model suggests the government does not yet have an appropriate sense of urgency or pragmatism. Sending the nurses and caregivers home if they fail their exams is also a tremendous waste of investment by the employers in the workers, estimated at ¥30 million each over an initial four-year nursing visa. This is one of the reasons that employers have not extended as many contract offers as had been expected. The program also underutilizes the workers, most of whom are overqualified to perform tasks that are normally the work of hospital orderlies.

While opening the door to foreign nurses and caregivers remains a potential solution to growing elderly care staffing shortages, the politics of labor migration tap into a much broader set of anxieties related to immigration which we examine below.

Immigration

The rapid increase in the number of foreign residents in Japan during the Heisei era, doubling between 1990 and 2008 from 1.1 million to 2.2 million, has raised anxieties among Japanese about the future of their country, national identity, and how to manage the influx (Vogt 2013). However, non-Japanese represent less than 2% of Japan's population, a relatively small presence compared to foreign residents elsewhere (i.e. UK 5.0%, Germany 8.2%). Nonetheless, Japan as a mono-ethnic, homogeneous nation persists in the collective imagination even if there are some jarring signs of transformation evident in increasing international marriage and foreign enclaves.

In Japan, like most countries around the world, immigration is a controversial topic. Current debate about labor migration to Japan focuses on what kind of workers should be allowed in—i.e. only skilled workers or also unskilled workers, how many and from where, how long they should be allowed to stay and under what conditions (Roberts 2012). This discourse is shaped by widespread perceptions that foreigners often resort to crime, although national crime statistics show that in fact foreigners do not commit crimes disproportionate to their numbers. Advocates of opening the doors point to Japan's population decline, impending labor shortages, and the need for more tax-payers to keep the national medical and pension schemes solvent (*Nihon Keizai Shimbun*, September 28, 2009). Opponents insist on preserving the current degree of homogeneity and warn against the pitfalls of accommodating large resident foreign communities as are evident in Europe. These are not only jingoists trying to haul up the drawbridge; there also is concern that until Japan can put in place laws and regulations that protect the human rights of migrant workers, it should not extend them the welcome mat (Sakanaka 2009).

Immigration could be a key policy option in addressing labor shortages and the viability of social insurance schemes, but as we noted with foreign caregivers, there are no signs that the government will allow sufficient immigration to make much of a difference. To put this into perspective, the United Nations (UN) estimates that to stabilize Japan's population and avoid the consequences of a declining and aging population, Japan needs to accept 650,000 immigrants a year, a level well beyond what anyone in a position of power is contemplating (Haffner 2010).

Immigrants might also boost Japan's capacity to innovate and create new wealth with their influx of new ideas, language and cultural skills, global networks, and entrepreneurial spirit. However, as Cleveland discusses in Chapter 16, discriminatory attitudes persist and thus handicaps tapping the potential of immigration because the benefits are not appreciated. The recent influx of Chinese since the 1990s demonstrates just how valuable immigrants can be as they have leveraged their transnational networks to facilitate and contribute to burgeoning trade and investment links (Liu-Farrer 2011). Since 2007 Chinese have become Japan's largest foreign resident population (more than 600,000), while an additional 100,000 have become Japanese citizens. Many come as students and stay on after securing jobs with Japanese firms (Liu-Farrer 2012). Japan is one of the largest foreign investors in China and China is Japan's largest trading partner, creating openings for such transnational entrepreneurs. One key factor giving Chinese advantages over other immigrants like the *nikkeijin* (overseas-born ethnic Japanese, mostly from Brazil) is their greater degree of fluency in Japanese.

In certain sectors facing a shortage of skilled workers, such as IT, the government is allowing limited immigration. In 2012 the government initiated a new points system that targets foreigners with desired skills, achievements and level of income, but this fast-track permanent resident visa program will affect only about 2,000 people a year and only applies to those already living in Japan (*Asahi Shimbun*, December 28, 2011).

Japan also established a trainee program in 1993 that provides foreign workers to small and medium-sized enterprises with the stated goal of vocational training, although in reality this program provides low-cost, unskilled workers to Japanese companies. Overall, as of 2010, there were 190,000 trainees participating in a program that has attracted widespread criticism due to mistreatment of workers, unpaid wages and the absence of skill training (*The New York Times*, July 21, 2010). In July 2010 the trainee system was reformed and trainees are now subject to the labor standards law and must be paid the minimum wage during the three-year maximum duration of the visa. In addition, companies are no longer permitted to confiscate workers' passports. While these reforms mark a significant improvement on paper (and suggest what had been going on), trainees remain vulnerable and monitoring has been lax. As a result, poor working conditions persist and there are numerous cases of unpaid wages and other abuses. In 2013 the government acknowledged that monitoring has been ineffective in reducing abuses and that there has been little progress in achieving the ostensible goals of transferring technology and nurturing human resources in emerging economies (*Japan Times*, April 13, 2013). Despite bad press, this program survives (142,000 as of 2011, of whom 107,000 are from China) because it provides cheap, unskilled workers on a fixed-term, temporary basis.

The largest initiative for opening Japan's labor market targeted overseas-born ethnic Japanese, mostly from Brazil. Japan has long maintained a strict immigration policy barring unskilled labor, but in 1990, facing labor shortages, the government revised the immigration law and established a side door that maintained the ban in principle while enabling unskilled overseas ethnic Japanese workers to obtain work visas on the strength of their ancestral blood ties. The law allowed anyone whose parent or grandparent was a Japanese citizen to apply for a long-term resident visa. This visa allowed them to stay for three years and engage in any work, including unskilled jobs, and could be renewed indefinitely provided they kept a clean record. This *nikkeijin* exception was based on what is now regarded an erroneous assumption that Japanese blood would trump Latin American culture.

Now there are grave doubts about the merits of this ancestry "side door" as distinct *nikkeijin* communities have emerged that did not assimilate. The total number of permanent residents, those foreigners allowed to stay indefinitely, increased by 28% from 657,605 in 2000 to 911,362 in 2008, while the number of Brazilian permanent residents jumped more than 10-fold from 9,062 to 94,400 in the same period. Other *nikkeijin* married Japanese and, as of 2002, 34% of Brazilians resident in Japan held a spouse visa. Children born in Japan automatically get citizenship if one parent is Japanese.

As of 2009, Brazilians accounted for 317,000 of the estimated 370,000 *nikkeijin* residing in Japan, with Peruvians constituting the next largest group. Most worked in manufacturing, frequently in car parts production. This made *nikkeijin* vulnerable to the massive layoffs in the manufacturing sector during 2008–09, especially as the hard-hit automobile industry slashed orders from the subcontractors where many *nikkeijin* were employed. Suddenly many were out of work, local Brazilian schools and other services closed, and unlike in recent downturns, few expected a rebound soon enough to make waiting it out an option.

In response to this problem, in 2009 the Japanese government offered to pay *nikkeijin* airfares to return home, including their families. The government defended its policy by pointing to the bleak job prospects for the *nikkeijin*, many of whom lacked sufficient language skills to enter job training programs or apply for other jobs, while critics asserted that Japan was discarding these unskilled workers because they were no longer needed and have never fit in. Unlike in Germany where the government offers immigrants 900 hours of subsidized language and social integration training, the Japanese government did not offer remotely similar programs for the *nikkeijin*, or any other foreigners for that matter. The absence of language skills has kept many *nikkeijin* on the margins of society and trapped them in low-end assembly jobs with few opportunities for training or advancement.

While the situation of the Brazilians underscores the need for better social integration for migrants, in Japan their presence is also seen as an object lesson of the dangers of adopting immigration to address labor shortages and demographic decline. There are concerns that an influx of foreign workers might lead to undesirable social consequences.

The government justifies strict limits on immigration in terms of public opinion. This is as it should be in a democracy, but in Japan there are few instances where the Japanese government defers to public opinion over important policy issues. As Daniel Aldrich has argued, "Japanese leaders and civil servants envision public opinion as malleable; in this approach, the people's perspective should be changed to match the perspective of the administration rather than elevated as a guidestar which should be followed" (Aldrich 2012, 131). Thus, there is reason to be skeptical when Ministry of Justice officials invoke anti-immigration public opinion to justify their desired policy goal. Certainly, some Japanese harbor xenophobic attitudes, but does this mean that Japanese are staunchly anti-immigration?

The Prime Minister's Office conducted a survey in 2004 that shows that the Japanese public is not resolutely opposed to immigration (Prime Minister's Office 2005). When asked about allowing more foreign workers entry to address looming labor shortages, only 29.1% unequivocally opposed immigration. In this survey, respondents voiced anxieties about foreigners, especially crime and the need to spend money on social integration and social services, but the surprising result is just how un-adamant Japanese are regarding increased immigration. Even in remote rural Japan, foreigners are far more appreciated and welcome than one might imagine from government assertions (Faier 2009).

While Japanese may not be strongly opposed to more immigration, the Ministry of Justice remains so and it considers the risks of a large, permanent foreign community undesirable. This means that at most, there may be entry for slightly larger numbers of skilled workers, but unskilled workers will remain subject to discretionary regulation. Japan does remain dependent, however, on unskilled foreign workers taking on jobs that are unappealing to Japanese so the government will accommodate what is minimally needed in an ad hoc manner. Thus, the number of foreign workers in Japan will remain too small to have a significant impact on the overall labor market or boost consumption, fertility and social insurance revenues. So if immigration is not the answer to Japan's demographic dilemmas, what can be done?

Marginalized women

… women could actually save Japan.

(Christine Lagarde, Director of the International Monetary Fund, at Tokyo Press Conference, October 13, 2012)

The International Monetary Fund (IMF), focusing on the negative economic implications of an aging society in Japan, concludes that women could "save" the country, but only if the government and employers implement policies that reduce the gender gap in career positions and provide better support for working mothers (Steinberg and Nakane 2012). Some would argue that women already are saving Japan, taking on all sorts of responsibilities ranging from mother, wife and elderly caregiver to employee, volunteer and household finance minister. The IMF's focus is on how the aging population and shrinking labor force is depressing Japan's potential growth rate. Its report, *Can Women Save Japan?* argues that increasing women's labor force participation, especially in career-track jobs, could boost economic growth, but this requires overcoming two significant hurdles.

First, relatively few women land career-track jobs, constituting 12% of such new hires in 2010. Second, many drop out of the workforce after giving birth and do not resume working because they get inadequate support to do so and inflexible employment policies mean their careers have been derailed. Thus, many women are marginalized in the workforce and the skills and potential contributions of those who exit are squandered. Resumption of work after giving birth is usually on a part-time basis, meaning relatively low income. Thus, women have less money to spend and pay lower taxes, significant factors contributing to deflation and fiscal deficits.

Japan's Equal Employment Opportunity Law in 1987 has had little impact as the gender wage gap remains high and women constitute three-quarters of non-regular workers even though women on average have a higher level of educational attainment than men (Abe 2011). It is emblematic that full-time women workers earn 27% less than male counterparts, a wage gap almost double the 14% Organisation for Economic Co-operation and Development (OECD) average (MHLW 2011; OECD 2010). In most Japanese households both parents work because they need the income, but because women are shunted off to relatively poorly paid non-regular employment, many couples are struggling to make ends meet.

However, what is obvious to the IMF in 2012 is not happening on the ground and there are few signs that key adjustments are being made that could significantly bolster gender diversity in the workplace. As a result, women's potential contributions to the economy and society will be constrained owing to the absence of sensible reforms that would enable them to balance career and family responsibilities. It is very likely that women will remain under-represented in management and that glass ceilings and childbirth will continue to derail far too many careers because of rigidity in employment policy and practices.

Women perceive that they have limited prospects for a good career and thus few incentives to keep working. As a result, 74% of college-educated women quit their jobs voluntarily, more than double the rate in the United States (31%) and Germany (35%) (Hewlett and Sherbin 2011). The percentage of women who drop out of the workforce in their thirties remains high compared to the United States and Europe where women's labor force participation rates remain relatively steady even during child rearing years.

Government tax policies are also problematic as they push married women into part-time work because households stand to lose deductions if their income exceeds ¥1.03 million (about $10,000). In addition, long waiting lists for childcare and shortages of elderly caregivers mean that many women who want to work full time are unable to do so because they assume these responsibilities.

Clearly, the absence of supportive government and employer policies makes raising a family and pursuing a career too much of an either/or choice in Japan. For most married women having a family is combined with having a job, but rigid employment policies and inadequate life-cycle support for working mothers creates significant career obstacles. Most women want to work, and many households depend on them doing so, but too many careers are derailed and talents squandered due to policy failures that shunt working mothers into dead-end, low paid non-regular jobs. This is a costly self-inflicted wound that saps the vitality of the Japanese economy.

Policy drift and prospects

Limited prospects for substantial immigration suggests that Japan can ill afford to squander the potential of its women workers to the extent it now does, nor can it leave so many young people adrift. To improve its future prospects, Japan needs to establish an employment system that facilitates a transition from the periphery of non-regular work to regular work, improved work-life balance policies, more flexible working conditions, improved training programs for new employees and displaced workers, enhanced schooling to work initiatives, and the embrace of a working environment that taps into the diversity of life cycle needs and aspirations in 21st-century Japan. Alas, this is a list of what is not happening as reforms targeting improved conditions for the precariat, women, youth and immigrants appear inadequate. More likely is a muddling-through scenario of crisis-averting half-measures.

The socio-cultural consequences of Japan's rapidly aging population reverberate throughout society, changing how people think about their world and act in it. Coping with such cultural upheaval and adapting to the repercussions is never easy, but the prospects for mitigating the demographic crisis and adjusting to its consequences are reasonably good. Japan's prospects brighten to the extent that women, youth and immigrants can land better opportunities and the security and satisfaction this brings.

Bibliography

Abe, Yuko (2011) "The Equal Employment Opportunity Law and Labor Force Behavior of Women in Japan," *Journal of the Japanese and International Economies* 25: 39–55.

Aldrich, Daniel (2012) "Networks of Power," in Jeff Kingston (ed.) *Natural Disaster and Nuclear Crisis in Japan*, London: Routledge, 127–39.

Campbell, John (2008a) "The Health of Japan's Medical Care System: 'Patients Adrift?'" *Japan Focus* 2730, April 26.

——(2008b) "Review of David Wise and Naohiro Yashiro (eds), *Health Care Issues in the US and Japan*, Chicago: University of Chicago Press, 2006," *Journal of Japanese Studies* 34(1), 136–40.

——(2009) "Japan's Aging Population: Perspectives of 'Catastrophic Demography'," *Journal of Asian Studies*, Winter, 1401–6.

Campbell, John and Ikegami, Naoki (1998) *The Art of Balance in Health Policy: Maintaining Japan's Low Cost, Egalitarian System*, Cambridge: Cambridge University Press.

Chiavacci, David (2012) "Japan in the 'Global War for Talent': Changing Concepts of Valuable Foreign Workers and Their Consequences," *ASIEN* 124, July: 27–47.

Coulmas, Florian (2007) *Population Decline and Ageing in Japan: The Social Consequences*, New York and London: Routledge.

Faier, Lieba (2009) *Intimate Encounters: Filipina Women and the Remaking of Rural Japan*, Berkeley, CA: University of California Press.

Haffner (2010) "Immigration as a Source of Renewal in Japan," *Policy Innovations*, January 19, www.policyinnovations.org/ideas/commentary/data/000161 (accessed May 5, 2013).

Hewlett, Sylvia Ann and Sherbin, Laura (2011) *Off Ramps and On Ramps Japan: Keeping Talented Women on the Road to Success*, Center for Work-Life Policy.

Liu-Farrer, Gracia (2011) "Making Careers in the Occupational Niche: Chinese Students in Corporate Japan's Transnational Business," *Journal of Ethnic and Migration Studies* 37(5), May: 785–803.

——2012 "Ambiguous Concepts and Unintended Consequences: Rethinking Skilled Migration in View of Chinese Migrants' Economic Outcomes in Japan," *ASIEN* 124, July: 159–79.

Magnus, George (2008) *The Age of Aging: How Demographics are Changing the Global Economy and Our World*, New York: Wiley.

MHLW (2011) *White Paper on Working Women. Ministry of Health, Labour and Welfare*, www.mhlw.go.jp/stf/houdou/2r9852000002ea8h.html.

Nihon Keizai Shimbun (2009) "Population Crisis Questions National Strategy: Immigration Policy Inescapable," editorial, September 28.

OECD (2010) *Social Policy Division, Gender Brief*, Paris, www.oecd.org/els/social.

Ogawa, Naohiro, Retherford, Robert D. and Matsukura, Rikiya (2006) "Demographics of the Japanese Family: Entering Uncharted Territory," in Marcus Rebick and Ayumi Takenaka (eds) *The Changing Japanese Family*, London: Routledge, 19–38.

Prime Minister's Office (2005) *Immigration Attitude Survey*, www8.cao.go.jp/survey/h16/h16-foreignerworker/index.html.

Roberts, Glenda S. (2012) "Vocalizing the 'I' Word: Proposals and Initiatives on Immigration to Japan from the LDP and Beyond," *ASIEN* 124, July: 48–68.

Sakanaka, Hidenori (2009) *Towards a Japanese–Style Immigration Nation*, Tokyo: Japan Immigration Policy Institute.

Steinberg, Chad and Nakane, Masato (2012) *Can Women Save Japan?* IMF Working Paper 12/248, Washington, DC: IMF, October, www.imf.org/external/pubs/ft/wp/2012/wp12248.pdf.

Vogt, Gabriele (2013, forthcoming) "Foreign Workers," in James Babb (ed.) *Handbook of Japanese Studies*, London: Sage, chapter 14.

Vogt, Gabriele and Achenbach, Ruth (2012) "International Labor Migration to Japan: Current Models and Future Outlook," *ASIEN* 124, July: 8–26.

15 Reproductive rights in Japan

Where do women stand?

Tin Tin Htun

This chapter focuses on how state policies and society's perception of the reproductive functions of women have a strong impact on women's reproductive rights in Japan. Here we examine not only how the state encroaches on women's contraceptive choices and decisions about getting married and having a family, but also the relationship between social and cultural norms of family and motherhood and women's reproductive rights. Reproductive rights are, "the basic rights for all couples and individuals to decide freely and responsibly the number, spacing and timing of their children and to have the information and means to do so, and the right to the highest attainable standard of sexual and reproductive health. They also include the right of all to make decisions concerning reproduction free of discrimination, coercion and violence" (United Nations 1994, para. 7.3). Reproductive health and rights encompass sexuality, pregnancy and childbirth (reproduction), and should be addressed from the viewpoint of rights and health of individuals and couples, especially women, throughout their lifecycle (Ashino 2005, 11).

There is a heavy focus on abortion in scholarly and activist discourse regarding reproductive rights in Japan because it is undoubtedly a fundamental issue in debates over reproductive rights. However, the reproductive rights of women in Japan should be understood not only in terms of abortion and contraceptive use, but also in terms of general trends involving reproductive activities (birth rate, marriage and childrearing, sexual health, access to information and services related to reproductive health), and policies and legislation relating to family planning. As Cho (1997) argues, in reality the concept of reproductive rights is not a simple matter of individuals' choices and rights. Reproduction has social, cultural and political functions, and these functions have an especially critical impact on women. Since women's reproductive choices and activities are shaped by their legal, social, economic, and cultural context, it is important to assess how these factors shape the reproductive choices, practices, and rights of women in Japan.

Our analysis of women's reproductive rights in Japan considers the context of the falling birth rate, the high rate of abortion among younger women, the low rate of other forms of contraceptive, particularly the Pill, and the co-existence of a legal ban on abortion with the Maternal Protection Act allowing women to have an abortion under certain circumstances. In particular, we assess to what extent Japanese women have control over their reproductive activities by exploring how women's choices to have children or not are influenced by state policies and laws, gendered employment systems, and societal and cultural norms regarding family and motherhood.

Reproductive activities and choices of women in Japan today

The reproductive activities and choices of women in Japan follow a particular pattern, one based on the assumption that marriage is necessary to raise children properly. This pattern is a response to social and cultural norms of sexual behavior and having children. In Japan, infringements by the state and society on women's reproductive activities are manifested in the limited availability of contraceptives and in the poor education of women about methods of contraception and new advances in reproductive technologies. In addition, the strong association of marriage and motherhood both in terms of social expectations and policies further curtails women's reproductive options. In general, there is more concern in Japan with women's reproductive capacity and declining fertility than their reproductive rights.

The steadily decreasing birth rate is a longstanding national concern. In 1990, Japan encountered the "1.57 shock," when the total fertility rate of woman dropped to 1.57, below replacement level. In 2005, the fertility rate plunged to a nadir of 1.26, and as of 2012 the fertility rate was 1.39. One factor in the plunge is that the average age of first marriage for both women and men has increased. In 1970, the average age of first marriage for women was 24.2 and 26.9 for men, whereas in 2010 it was 28.8 for women and 30.5 for men. Both men and women are not only marrying later, but also more are opting not to marry (Gender Equality Bureau 2013). In 2011, 662,000 couples got married compared to over 1 million couples in 1970. The marriage rate (number per thousand) has dropped nearly half over 40 years from 10 in 1970 to 5.2 in 2011 (Statistics Bureau 2012). The declining marriage rate means a rising number of singles of both sexes, although these numbers are rising more dramatically for women, as getting married is no longer quite the default option it used to be. In 2000, 32.8% of men aged 30–34 and 19.1% of men aged 35–40 were single, while in 2010 these figures rose to 46.5% and 34.6%, respectively. For women, the increase in singlehood is even more striking: in 2000 13.9% of women aged 30–34 and 7.5% aged 35–39 were single, while in 2010 the number jumped to 33.3% and 22.4%, respectively (Ito 2011). As very few babies are born out of wedlock, the surge in singlehood is a major factor in the declining birth rate.

Although the overall marriage rate has dropped, "shotgun marriages" have increased and in 2009, 25.3% of first babies were born to couples that married after conception, compared to 12.6% in 1980. The rise of shotgun marriages is especially pronounced among younger women between the ages of 20 and 24. In 2009, 63.6% of first-born babies born to women in this cohort were premaritally conceived, up from 20% in 1980, while 81.5% of first births among teenage mothers were conceived premaritally (Ministry of Health, Labor and Welfare 2010). While shotgun marriages in Japan are increasing due to a relatively high number of unplanned pregnancies, abortion is by far the most common "crisis" response. There are so many unplanned pregnancies because couples rely on relatively unreliable means of contraception: condoms, the rhythm method and withdrawal.

Japan's overall abortion rate has declined from an average of 300,000 per annum in the early 2000s, to 202,106 in 2011 (Ministry of Health, Labor and Welfare 2011). However, the abortion rate of teenagers has been on the increase. The proportion of teenage abortions to the total has increased from 1.8% in 1975 to 13.7% in 2002. However, the highest number of abortions (47.1 per 1,000 in 2010) is in the 20–24-year-old cohort (Gender Equality Bureau 2013). The overall picture of reproductive activities indicates that the sexual behavior and fertility of women, particularly young women, has been changing. Although more women have become sexually active at an earlier age, they postpone marriage and child bearing until their late twenties. However, the increase in teenage abortions and the abortion rate among the early twenties cohort, as well as the increase in the number of babies born to shotgun marriages, suggests that young women have limited knowledge, choices and options to manage their reproduction effectively.

Recent surveys on the sexual behavior of young people reported a high rate of contraceptive use (Nishito and Sasaki 2012), but their increased abortion rate suggests that inadequate contraceptive use has led to increasing numbers of unintended pregnancies. Despite the fact that 60% to 90% of young people reported using condoms to prevent pregnancy, some studies also indicate that they may not be using condoms every time they have sex. It is also reported that young women tend not to take initiative in using contraception, leaving it up to men (ibid., 97). Although young people seem to understand the importance of using contraception, a survey on teen sexual health conducted in 2002–06 reported that 80% of teenage girls who had an abortion thought withdrawal and the rhythm method could effectively prevent pregnancy (Tachikawa Sogo General Hospital 2002–06). Young women's inadequate use of contraceptives and insufficient knowledge of contraceptive methods imply poor sex education and limited access to information on effective contraceptives. Furthermore, not taking the initiative in using contraceptive and entrusting men with the responsibility indicates lack of awareness of reproductive health rights.

This problem among younger women doesn't necessarily mean that the situation regarding reproductivity and contraception is any better among older cohorts (late twenties and older) in Japan. Limited contraceptive options are evident in married women's choice of contraceptives. A Health Ministry survey in 2008 reported that nearly 80% of married women in Japan relied on condoms, whereas only 2.2% used the Pill, 16.7% relied on withdrawal, and 3.6% practiced the rhythm method (Kato 2009). Compared to other developed countries, Japan has a distinctive pattern of contraceptive use—lower contraceptive use overall, predominant condom use, and very low use of medical methods such as the Pill, IUD (intra-uterine device), as well as female and male sterilization (Sato and Iwasawa 2006). To reiterate, widespread reliance on condoms, sometimes in combination with withdrawal and the rhythm method, often results in unplanned pregnancies and abortion. According to the government, in 2010 women in their late twenties, early thirties, and late thirties had a similar abortion rate, 45.2, 42.2 and 40.0 per 1,000 women, respectively (Gender Equality Bureau 2013). The Sixth Survey on Men and Women's Life and Awareness reported that despite the decrease in the overall abortion rate, the repeat abortion rate has increased (Japan Family Planning Association 2013). This indicates that although the abortion rate is decreasing, it is still a key birth control method for Japanese women to terminate unwanted pregnancies. Why do women choose abortion? This question cannot be answered just on the basis of individual women's choice or women's right to choose; rather, this question is best explored in the legal, social, cultural, and political context that makes abortion more available compared to other birth control options.

The legalization of abortion in Japan

The practice of abortion in Japan can be traced as far back as the Heian period (794–1192). In fact, abortion and infanticide were used in that period as family planning methods to cope with poverty, famine, and epidemics. Although abortion was considered immoral, it was not deemed a crime until the enactment of the Penal Code in 1880. The intention behind criminalization of abortion in Japan was to support national economic and military expansion by increasing the population (Maruyama 1995). The Penal Code, together with the Civil Code of 1898, legally established the *ie* (household) system that placed women under the total control of the male head of household. As such, women's essential duty was to serve her family and the state, and that meant, *inter alia*, bearing children. In 1907 the Penal Code was revised to impose stricter penalties for abortion and there were no exceptions, not even in cases of rape. This blanket ban had harmful consequences for women because it compelled many to endure the health complications of pregnancy and childbirth, and households had no means to limit family size, contributing to the scourge of poverty. Women seeking termination were forced to resort to unhygienic abortion and risked potentially serious health problems. Moreover, women who had illegal abortions were stigmatized since motherhood was their prescribed role (Kato 2009a). To strengthen the military and the labor force, women were pressured to have children. Indeed, the *ie* household system defined women's identity in terms of bearing children and continuing the family line while the government enjoined them to raise children to serve the emperor, making it a sacred duty. However, as Japanese militarism expanded in the early decades of the 20th century, the government became preoccupied with racial improvement and supported eugenic research.

Kato posits that pre-war state policies and practices regarding motherhood, abortion and eugenics focused on the state controlling women's bodies (Kato 2009a, 41–42). In 1940, Japan enacted the National Eugenic Law to prevent the birth of genetically inferior offspring and to promote the growth of a healthy population. Although the law prohibited abortion in accordance with the government's population expansion policy, it allowed voluntary and involuntary sterilization for people with hereditary diseases (Maruyama 1995, 133–34). However, it was not just the state that attempted to control women's bodies, as eugenic scientists proactively targeted women's bodies by performing eugenic surgeries, urging women to contribute to the national goal of racial improvement by bearing and raising healthy and strong children. In this sense, women's bodies were dedicated to, and sacrificed for, the nation.

After World War II abortion was legalized in 1948 during the US Occupation. There was an urgent need to control overpopulation amid food and housing shortages, and widespread economic distress. In fact, birth control activists managed to persuade a reluctant government to legalize abortion by citing eugenic reasons—protecting mothers' health by having smaller families would enable them to raise healthier children. The new law legalizing abortion was actually called the Eugenic Protection Law (Kato 2009a, 44). The stated purpose was to prevent the birth of "inferior descendants" and to protect mothers' life and health. The law allowed induced abortion not only for eugenic reasons, but also in cases involving rape, leprosy (Hansen's disease) or if continuation of the pregnancy or childbirth might endanger the health of the mother (Ogino 1994, 72). On the basis of the Eugenic Protection Law, people suffering from Hansen's disease were often forced into sterilization or abortion and in some cases without the consent of the patients (Ohashi 2003, 17). In 1949, the law was revised to allow abortions for "economic reasons." In 1952, the law was amended again to eliminate the need for approval from the local eugenic commissions, leaving the decision to the discretion of the attending physician, thus making abortion widely available to women (Maruyama 1995).

Critics of the Eugenic Protection Law point out that the legal restrictions embedded in the law amount to state assertion of control over women's bodies and constrain their rights and choices (Kato 2009a; Maruyama 1995). Although abortion has become widely available, a woman must obtain the approval of the physician performing the abortion and the consent of her male partner (if available). This restriction circumscribes women's right to decide whether they should have an abortion or not. Another restriction pointing to state control in this decision is the viability period, the period when the fetus is considered viable outside the mother's womb. Currently the viability period is set at 22 weeks, meaning abortion is only allowed within that period. The government determines the viability period and thus restricts the availability of abortions to women according to its criteria (Maruyama 1995, 150). The most glaring example of state control over women's reproductive rights is the coexistence of the Penal Code that criminalizes abortion and the Eugenic Protection Law that allows limited access to abortion. The Eugenic Protection Law was replaced with the Maternal Protection Law in 1996. While disability activists and feminist groups succeeded in pressuring the government to delete eugenic-related discriminatory clauses, abortion remains legally criminalized. The coexistence of these two laws, the former punishing women for abortion and the latter allowing women to have abortion under certain circumstances, establishes the state as the legal guardian of women's wombs, basically prohibiting abortion, but making exceptions at its discretion (see Kato 2009a; Maruyama 1995; Ohashi 2003).

The government's control over the reproductive rights of women is further evident in the attempt to restrict abortion by removing the exception for "economic reasons." In May 1972 the Ministry of Health and Welfare (MHW) proposed a revision to the Eugenic Protection Law aimed at rescinding justification of abortion on economic grounds. This was a blatant attempt to limit women's access to abortion. The MHW also introduced a selective abortion clause in cases where the doctor diagnosed a birth defect in the fetus. This was in reaction to the birth of deformed babies in the 1960s due to Thalidomide (a drug widely prescribed to ease morning sickness among pregnant women in Japan) and Minamata disease (due to mercury poisoning). The MHW's proposal was based on the assumption that a fetus with a defect or disability would cause unhappiness within a family. Preventing "unhappy births" through selective abortion was thus deemed a good welfare policy. The proposed revisions also called for establishing a counseling system for women regarding the proper age for marriage and for having a first child. This was a response to women's changing lifestyles and reflected the government's anxieties about women prioritizing their careers over marriage and childbearing (Kato 2009a, 59–61). The revision proposal failed due to fierce opposition from the women's liberation movement in Japan and sympathetic media coverage. Again in 1982, the government attempted to remove the economic reason clause to limit women's access to abortion, but failed. Women activists all over Japan mobilized against the proposed revision, arguing that the government was trying to increase the birth rate by using women's bodies without their consent (Kato 2009a, 128). Thus, women have been contesting the state's assertion of control over women and effectively organizing to protect their reproductive rights.

Advancements in reproductive technology, and government regulation of access, are an emerging arena of state infringement on women's reproductive rights. Although the government is encouraging women to give birth, new technologies are developing that reinforce the government's influence over women's choices (Kato 2009b). These technologies can provide pregnant women with more information about their fetus and thus facilitate selective abortion based on health indicators. Controversial new non-invasive prenatal testing that can detect chromosomal abnormalities such as Down's Syndrome in fetuses through blood testing is a case in point. Advocates in the disability community strongly protest such prenatal testing because it may lead to an increase of selective abortion of fetuses with genetic defects and reinforce discrimination against people with Down's Syndrome. On the other hand, it is widely known that there is a much higher possibility that fetuses of older mothers (> 35 years old) might have Down's Syndrome. This puts such mothers in a difficult position because the new test facilitates screening but they also feel confused and oppressed by the implications of what the test results can tell them about their prospective child. In some respects the medical community welcomes the new prenatal testing, but it is also divided over the screening procedure and beset by ethical concerns regarding the use of the test. The Japan Association of Obstetricians and Gynecologists has attempted to deal with these ethical concerns by issuing restrictive guidelines in 2013. These guidelines restrict availability of the test to pregnant women who are 35 years or older, and the simple procedure can only be performed initially at 15 designated medical institutions (Ito 2013). However, restricting access to the test based on these criteria takes the decision out of women's hands and limits their access to information that they might want to have in making their reproductive choices. The ongoing issue over who gets to decide about contraception and reproduction pits women against the medical community and government.

The Pill

The saga of the Pill in Japan, and the long delay in government approval, is emblematic of how the state and medical community have imposed restrictions on women's reproductive rights and ignored their interests. Double standards regarding women's sexuality, the state's demographic concerns and the medical community's self-interest explain why approval took over three decades.

The government repeatedly postponed approval of the Pill until June 1999, citing concerns about side effects and the impact on morality. The Pill had been used on a limited basis as an over-the-counter drug for treatment of menstrual disorders in the 1960s, but it is likely that some women used it as a contraceptive at that time. In 1972, the MHW withdrew the Pill from over-the-counter availability and thereafter a doctor's prescription was required. Although the Pill was not officially approved until 1999, the government did not prohibit physicians from prescribing it for reasons other than the treatment of menstrual disorders, so it was available for contraceptive use, but at doctors' discretion (Ogino 1994, 1999).

The first failure to gain approval of the Pill in 1965 was ostensibly due to concerns about the risk of side effects associated with the high estrogen dose Pill common at that time. Fear of women's sexual liberation was an additional reason for disapproval. In addition, gynecologists were keen not to lose income from performing abortions. In late 1986, due to lobbying by obstetricians and pharmaceutical companies, the government sought approval for a low estrogen dosage Pill, but again was stymied. This time, the reason for not approving the Pill was the prospect of lowering condom use and the risk of spreading HIV/AIDS. Another reason for not approving the Pill, probably the decisive reason, was the government's concern about the steadily declining birth rate. Again in 1997, there was another attempt to secure approval of the low dose Pill but this was derailed due to the alleged environmental risk caused by endocrines in the urine of women who take the Pill. Finally in June 1999, the Pill was approved, but only after the Health and Welfare Ministry hurriedly approved Viagra, the drug for treating male sexual impotence, in January 1999. This came without any domestic clinical trials and only six months after the initial application for approval. This fast-tracking of Viagra revealed a patriarchal double standard in Japanese society regarding sexuality, but the publicity shamed the government into finally approving the Pill (see Goto *et al.* 1999; Ogino 1999).

Feminists were long ambivalent about the Pill due to the potential health risks and this also slowed its approval. Some feminists also asserted that the Pill put too much of the burden of birth control on women. Some argued that condoms used in combination with the rhythm method or diaphragms could create better communication and cooperation between partners. There was also concern that the government's push for approval of the Pill, despite lukewarm demand by women, was ultimately aimed at restricting access to abortion, and yet another strategy for controlling women's bodies. However, after the 1994 Cairo Conference on Population and Development, the term "reproductive rights" was introduced in Japan, and feminists' position towards the Pill started to change. They asserted that it was the individual woman, not the state, who should make the choice based on information about the merits and demerits of the Pill. Although many women in Japan are still not in favor of the Pill even today, it has come to symbolize women's autonomy and right to self-determination (Ogino 1999). Unlike abortion, the Pill is not subject to legal constraints.

Counter-measures for falling birth rates: encouragement or pressure?

The persistent decline in the birth rate influences the Japanese government's position on birth control and abortion as the shrinking labor force and aging society have generated a panic about the declining birth rate. Fewer future taxpayers raise questions about the viability of social security and welfare for an aging population. Hirao (2007, 53) contends that the declining birth rate signifies Japanese women's decision to delay marriage or remain single. In addition, it reflects married women's decision about how many children they want to have. Surveys suggest that Japanese couples are having a smaller number of children than their desired number of children due to the high cost of raising them.

However, the government seeks to overcome couples' reluctance to have more children, as evident in "The Basic Law for Measures Against the Decreasing Birth Rate" and the "Law on Promoting and Fostering the Next Generation" promulgated in July 2003. The state's intrusion into women's lives was couched in terms of creating a family-friendly society in which people "can truly feel pride and joy" (ibid., 55). Hirao points out that the most striking aspect of the legislation is the emphasis on citizens' obligation to cooperate in reversing the declining birth rate. The government has prompted central and local governments to implement measures to support a family-friendly atmosphere at the workplace, but in doing so it is implicitly pressuring women to have more children. Sometimes the pressures are more explicit, as when Health Minister Yanagisawa Hakuo called women "birth-giving machines" and urged them to do their best to have more children (BBC News 2007).

The 2003 legislation especially targets women who choose not to have children or women who are unable to have children (Ashino 2001). Demonstrating how far the state is intruding in family matters, the law contains detailed measures for helping infertile women/couples and refers to increasing the birth rate as a shared "national responsibility" (Ashino 2005, 12). It is even more revealing that the government has provided special subsidies for fertility treatments since 2004, while women still have to pay for contraception and abortion expenses as they are not covered by health insurance.

Hirao argues that these policies to raise the birth rate fail to address the gender structure that leads to women delaying marriage and childbearing (Hirao 2007, 55–56). It is important to note that the various measures aimed at easing shortages of daycare facilities, providing childcare support services, and creating a favorable environment at work so that women can achieve a work-life balance have failed to raise the birth rate. The policy failures on boosting fertility can be understood in the wider context of gender discrimination and the varied disincentives women face in deciding to have children. The overall tax and pension system, for example, discourages women from working full time by providing tax breaks and dependant allowances for non-working and part-time working spouses (wives) whose income is under ¥1.03 million a year. Wives who maintain this dependant status are also enrolled under their husbands' social security, but have to pay for themselves if they exceed the income ceiling. These features of the tax and social security system in Japan thus provide strong incentives to women to limit their earnings and remain financially dependent. One consequence is that 55% of women work as non-regular workers (part-timers, temporary workers, working at home) (Gender Equality Bureau 2013). This means that the majority of women workers are in low-paid jobs with no fringe benefits and career prospects. Above all, they are not entitled to paid maternity leave and family-friendly benefits stipulated by the government's pro-birth measures. This reduces household income while increasing a sense of insecurity, critical factors in considering why women opt for small families. Although female regular workers are entitled to family-friendly benefits, a persistent M-shaped labor force participation pattern of women workers in Japan indicates that these women stop working upon becoming pregnant and only re-enter the workforce after they finish childrearing, but mostly on a non-regular basis. Employers do not accommodate women's lifecycle needs and thus careers are systematically derailed. However, the M-shaped pattern of the female labor force participation also indicates that there are problems on the home front as well: women get little help with family and childcare responsibilities.

Japanese fathers rank lowest among counterparts in other advanced industrialized nations in terms of time spent on childcare and housework (33 minutes per day for childcare only and one hour including housework) (Gender Equality Bureau 2013). Similarly, the number of first-time Japanese fathers taking childcare leave was only 2.36% in 2011, while it was 87.8% for first-time Japanese mothers. On the whole, it is women who have to leave the workforce or choose to work as non-regular workers to reconcile work and family life. This pattern prevails among married couples in Japan. The choice of women staying home to take care of children and family is mainly influenced by pragmatic reasons (work rules, tax, social security, cost of childrearing). However, this pattern reinforces the gendered role division at home, with men as "breadwinners" and women as caregivers. For a majority of Japanese women, pursuing a career comes at the cost of raising a family and vice versa, because it is very difficult to combine work and household responsibilities (Tachibanaki 2010). Thus, women's reproductive rights in terms of the number, spacing and timing of having children are severely restricted by inadequate government measures, by a work environment that is not particularly mother-friendly, and by a gendered division of housework and childcare at home.

The impact of societal norms for family and motherhood on women

It is not only gendered institutional and legal systems and policies that influence women's decisions about having children. Societal and cultural norms of family and motherhood in Japan also play a critical role. Birth and childrearing outside the confines of marriage is deemed inappropriate and as such very limited. According to the International Survey of Low Fertility Societies (2005), more than 70% of Japanese people consider marriage as a solution in case of an unplanned pregnancy (Hertog and Iwasawa 2011, 1683). Only 2% of births occur out of wedlock in Japan and this number has hardly changed over the years, while shotgun marriages are on the rise. Japanese women opt for shotgun marriage or abortion in response to unplanned pregnancy rather than bearing children out of wedlock, because a family is deemed crucial for raising children, even if the father is not an ideal partner. If the father is already married, or refuses to get married, women view abortion as the reasonable and responsible solution (Hertog and Iwasawa 2011). Thus, societal norms and attitudes regarding family, reinforced by the male breadwinner model, strongly influence women's reproductive choices in Japan. Furthermore, these norms and systems focus on heterosexual women and couples, and exclude the reproductive rights of lesbians, gays, bisexuals, and transgender (LGBT) couples, since Japanese law prohibits same-sex marriages or civil unions (Hongo 2008).

Although Japanese women in general want to become mothers, they are also apprehensive about raising children. They are very much aware of societal and cultural expectations regarding a mother's role in childrearing. Motherhood as it is conceived in Japan places great value on selfless devotion (Ohinata 1995, 205). In practice this means mothers in Japan are expected to sacrifice their time and energy to raise "high-quality" children in ways that men are not, and judged in terms of how their children turn out. Although women internalize the cultural norms of motherhood by giving priority to the family and raising children, they also feel ambivalent about childrearing (Hirao 2007). Certainly children are seen as a source of joy, but women also feel apprehensive about raising children and not being able to do what they want to do. This apprehension about properly carrying out a mother's expected role in Japan influences single women's perceptions about marriage and family, making them wonder if it is worth sacrificing their career prospects and whether they can meet the heavy expectations. As such, cultural norms of motherhood may not have a direct impact on the reproductive choices of women, but they can cast a shadow over women's reproductive choices.

Conclusion: women and reproductive rights

Women's reproductive activities and choices in Japan are shaped by the government's policies regarding family planning, employers' practices, and social and cultural norms related to family and motherhood. The issues of reproductive health/rights, apart from feminist activists and disability activists involved in the reproductive rights movement, are not widely understood or featured in public discourse in Japan. Although reproductive health/rights are mentioned in the Plan for Gender Equality 2000, a legal framework to realize these rights has not yet been developed. Abortion is legal under very limited circumstances, but it is not recognized as a fundamental constitutional right (Murayama 1995, 147). In fact, women's legalized right to abortion does not constitute recognition of women's rights or self-determination, since the state determines the criteria that circumscribe that right. Although the Eugenic Protection Law granting limited access to abortion was revised with the Maternal Protection Law in 1996, this has not had a significant impact on promoting women's reproductive health and rights because women are still subject to punishment for abortion under the Penal Code. Since the state determines access to abortion at its discretion, it continues to exercise control over women's bodies. Restricted access to abortion, poor sex education and limited availability of information on contraceptive choices and advances in reproductive technologies limits women's control over their reproductive activities. The medical guidelines issued in 2013 restricting expecting mothers' access to simple prenatal screening to determine the heath of the fetus underscores the extent to which women's right to decide is curtailed.

Due to the falling birth rate, and the stark implications of a shrinking and aging population, women are under government pressure to have more children. The legislation and policy packages introduced to address the low birth rate promote the assumption that it is a woman's duty to bear children. Such an assumption is also implicit in employers' policies and reinforced by cultural and social norms. The government wants women to make the "right choice" (having children) and is trying to make it easier for them to do so, but it does not offer an equal amount of assistance or encouragement to those who want to make the "wrong choice" and limit or not have children. For example, the government targets women and couples who are having infertility problems by providing subsidies to cover infertility treatment. In contrast, women who wish to use oral contraceptives or have an abortion must pay for this themselves, since these options are not covered by health insurance. The Japanese state thus emphasizes women's role in terms of their reproductive function, while limiting women's right to determine reproductive choices free from government pressures and strictures.

Feminist activists in the reproductive movement have argued that the reproductive rights of women should be problematized in the larger context of gender inequality, particularly within the context of social norms and institutional systems that perpetuate gender inequality and a gendered status quo. The gendered social security and tax systems in Japan that encourage men to be breadwinners and women to be home makers have a direct impact on women's decision to bear children down to the number, spacing, and timing of having children. These systems promote assumptions regarding marriage, family, mothering and childrearing that work to constrain women's reproductive choices. In Japan, women's struggle to realize and practice their reproductive rights remains a work in progress as gendered practices and systems remain resilient in the face of pressures for social reform.

Acknowledgment

I would like to thank Jeff Kingston for his input and editing.

Bibliography

Ashino, Yuriko (2001) "A Modern Version of 'Breed and Proliferate'? Problems in the Bill for Counteracting the Declining Birth Rate," *Women's Asia 21 Voices from Japan* 7, spring: 22–24.

——(2005) "Ten Years after the Cairo Conference: What Should Japan do about the Issue of Reproductive Health and Rights?" *Women's Asia 21 Voices from Japan* 14 (winter): 11–13.

BBC News (2007) *Japan Women Called Child Machines*, January 27, news.bbc.co.uk/2/hi/asia-pacific/6306685.stm (accessed March 8, 2013).

Cho, Hyoung (1997) "Fertility Control, Reproductive Rights, and Women's Empowerment in Korea," *Asian Journal of Women's Studies* 3(1), March 31, acws.ewha.ac.kr:8081/acws/m6-2.html (accessed February 23, 2013).

Gender Equality Bureau (2013) *Women and Men in Japan 2012*, www.gender.go.jp/english_contents/index.html (accessed February 24, 2013).

Goto, Aaya, Reich, Michael and Aitken, Iain (1999) "Oral Contraceptives and Women's Health in Japan," *JAMA* 282(22), December 8: 2173–77.

Hertog, Ekaterina and Iwasawa, Miho (2011) "Marriage, Abortion, or Unwed Motherhood? How Women Evaluate Alternative Solutions to Premarital Pregnancies in Japan and the United States," *Journal of Family Issues* 32: 1674–99.

Hirao, Keiko (2007) "Contradictions in Maternal Roles in Contemporary Japan," in Theresa W. Devasahayam and Brenda S.A. Yeoh (eds) *Working and Mothering: Images, Ideologies and Identities*, Copenhagen: NIAS Press, 51–83.

Hongo, Jun (2008) "Gay Scene: Tolerance, Legal Limbo," *The Japan Times*, December 23.

Ito, Masami (2011) "Matchmakers in Wings as Singles Rise," *The Japan Times*, November 1, www.japantimes.co.jp/news/2011/11/01/reference/matchmakers-in-wings-as-singles-rise/ (accessed March 22, 2013).

——(2013) "New Prenatal Test in High Demand but Limited to Risk Cases," *The Japan Times*, March 28: 1, 3.

Japan Family Planning Association (2013) *Dai 6 Kai Danjyo no Seikatsu to Ishiki ni Kansuru Chosa* (The sixth survey of men and women's life and awareness), www.koshu-eisei.net/upfile_free/20130118kitamura.pdf (accessed March 22, 2013).

Kato, Mariko (2009) "Abortion Still Key Birth Control," *The Japan Times*, October 20.

Kato, Masae (2009a) *Women's Rights? The Politics of Eugenic Abortion in Japan*, Amsterdam Press, www.oapen.org/search?identifier=340104 (accessed February 14, 2013).

——(2009b) "Selective Abortion in Japan," *The Newsletter* 52 (winter), old.iias.asia/files/IIAS_NL52_2021.pdf (accessed February 15, 2013).

Maruyama, Hiromi (1995) "Abortion in Japan: A Feminist Critique," *Wisconsin Women's Law Journal* 1, spring: 131–60.

Ministry of Health, Labor and Welfare (2010) *Jinkō Dōtai Tōkei Tokushu Hōkoku* (Special report on vital demographic statistics), www.e-stat.go.jp/SG1/estat/GL08020103.do?_toGL08020103_&listID=000001071104& requestSender = search.

——(2011) *Report on Public Health Administration and Services*, www.mhlw.go.jp/english/database/db-hss/dl/rophas_2011_year.pdf.

n.a. (n.d.) *International Conference on Population and Development*, www.choiceforyouth.org/information/treaties/international-conference-on-population-and-development (accessed February 23, 2013).

Nishito, Tomoko and Sasaki, Kumiko (2012) "The Present Situation of Sexuality among Youth and Sexuality Education: A Literature Review," *Osaka Medical College Faculty of Nursing* 2, March: 95–102, www.osaka-med.ac.jp/deps/dns/pdf/zasshi/14.pdf (accessed March 20, 2013).

Ogino, Miho (1994) "Abortion and Women's Reproductive Rights: The State of Japanese Women, 1945–91," in Joyce Gelb and Marian L. Oalley (eds) *Women of Japan and Korea*, Philadelphia: Temple University Press, 69–94.

——(1999) "You Can Have Abortions, but No Oral Contraceptive Pills: Women and Reproductive Control in Japan," *Asian Journal of Women's Studies* 5(3), September 30, acws.ewha.ac.kr:8081/acws/m6-2.html (accessed February 5, 2007).

Ohashi, Yukako (2003) "Misguided Maternal Protection Law," *Women's Asia 21 Voices from Japan*, September 11: 16–18.

Ohinata, Masami (1995) "The Mystique of Motherhood: A Key to Understanding Social Change and Family Problems in Japan," in Kumiko Fujimura-Fanselow and Atsuko Kameda (eds) *Japanese Women: New Feminist Perspectives on the Past, Present, and Future*, New York: The Feminist Press, 199–211.

Sato, Ryuzaburo and Iwasawa, Miho (2006) "Contraceptive Use and Induced Abortion in Japan: How is it so Unique among the Developed Countries?" *The Japanese Journal of Population* 4(1): 33–54, www.ipss.go.jp/webj-ad/webjournal.files/population/2006_3/sato-iwasawa.pdf (accessed February 24, 2013).

Statistics Bureau (2012) "Statistical Handbook of Japan 2012," www.stat.go.jp/english/data/handbook/c02cont.htm (accessed March 22, 2012).

Tachibanaki, Toshiaki (2010) *The New Paradox for Japanese Women: Greater Choice, Greater Inequality*, Tokyo: International House of Japan.

Tachikawa Sogo General Hospital (Teens Sexual Health Project) (2002–06) *Sei o Torimaku Kankyō to Sei Kōdō no Jitsujō—Sanfujinka Gairai Ankēto (2002—2006-nen) no Kekka kara* (Facts about the environment and surrounding sexual behavior-obstetrics outpatient survey results from 2002–06), www.t-kenseikai.jp/tachisou/teens/opinion1.html (accessed March 20, 2013).

United Nations (1994) *Programme of Action*, International Conference on Population and Development, Cairo, September 5–13.

16 Hiding in plain sight

Minority issues in Japan

Kyle Cleveland

Japan has a race problem. While it is a developed democracy with an increasingly vibrant civil society, boasting an affluent consumer economy and increasing tolerance of alternative lifestyles, minorities continue to languish on the margins of society with few civil rights and limited prospects for integration as officially recognized citizens. These contrary impulses between diversity and exclusion have characterized the nation for at least a century, and highlight the regressive political policies that sustain racial inequality.

The overarching ideology of racial homogeneity that has legitimated this state of affairs remains firmly implanted in the national psyche, and is evident in the pronouncements of conservative politicians such as the popular former Governor of Tokyo Ishihara Shintaro and Prime Minister Abe Shinzo, who have invoked racially loaded language to justify the colonization of Korea (including the forced conscription of Korean "comfort women" into wartime brothels), dismissed the atrocities associated with the Rape of Nanking (1937–38) and remained obstinately unsympathetic—even belligerent—to the claims made by the victims of Japan's wartime policies. It is tempting to dismiss such race-infused nationalism as characteristic of a Japan that no longer exists, distinct to elderly politicians who are out of touch with the realities of modern society, whose nostalgic, reactionary views have been supplanted by more progressive attitudes commensurate with the diversity that is readily evident. However, these sentiments are not the shrill cry of fringe right-wing Uyoko nationalists, but are voiced by mainstream, popularly elected politicians whose insensitive and racist comments do not apparently harm their political prospects; after making these statements they were reelected and remain in power.

Japan's international relations continue to be undermined by these views, which are not merely the episodic venting of ill-advised personal animosity, but rather express a coherent worldview, a political ideology in which Japanese conservatives still assume a position atop a presumed racial hierarchy over and against its former colonial victims with whom it now attempts to cultivate economic exchange and negotiate frayed diplomatic relations. It is within the context of these historical disputes that Japanese nationalism takes on racial dimensions (Diene 2006). Japanese nationalism and racism converge at the myth of Japanese homogeneity, the archaic worldview that all Japanese derive from a common bloodline that is racially pure and unadulterated by foreign influence. Despite claims to antiquity, this myth is largely a post-war reactionary construct that exonerates Japan of wartime responsibility by claiming that Japan's imperialism was an heroic effort to bring all of Asia under the sphere of Japan's prosperity and to remake those countries in Japan's image (Lie 2008). The rationale for this was racist: because non-Japanese Asians were viewed as being uncivilized, immature and incapable of making advances without Japan's guidance, a fundamental reordering of these societies was seen as a justifiable—even benevolent—necessity.

Japan's imperialist history casts a long shadow over its international relations, serving as a vehicle for positioning Japan at the pinnacle of Asia, and thereby relegating its former enemies to their proper place in the regional hierarchy (see Chapter 10). In his seminal work on race in the Pacific War, the historian John Dower has demonstrated that even though Japan was critical of the United States for hypocritically maintaining the legal segregation of the races even as it fought wars of "liberation" against the Axis powers, Japan also promoted its own version of Manifest Destiny (Dower 1986, 8). Contemporary Japanese political rhetoric uses this history as a touchstone for nationalist claims. When Ishihara bluntly refers to Asian minorities as "sankokujin," a derogatory label that literally means "third-country foreigners," he is referring to ethnic Chinese, Taiwanese and Koreans brought to Japan in the early 20th century. Similarly, when PM Abe offers devotion at Yasukuni, where revisionist nationalistic narratives in the Yushukan war museum justify Japan's wartime actions and dismiss atrocities in the city of Nanking as minor infractions by undisciplined troops, he revisits these ideological notions and updates their relevance to Japan–China relations, with predictable results.

Japan is unique today in that it maintains racially laden nationalistic views despite their political implications and in the face of historical and genetic analyses that have long made these notions untenable. However, by the onset of World War II, such master-race theories of cultural superiority based on notions of racial purity had become inscribed in the worldviews of Western nations as well, providing ideological rationales for British colonialism, German anti-Semitism, and American exceptionalism. These culturally distinct versions of racial difference were inspired by the late 19th-century eugenics movement, an influential paradigm of scientific racism that used flawed readings of Darwin's theories of evolution and Mendelian genetics to support beliefs in racial purity (Morris-Suzuki 1998, 357). As the principles of scientific racism became widespread, they provided rationale for immigration policies that restricted the influx of the so-called inferior races on the one hand, while providing ammunition for imperialist conscription of "uncivilized" lands on the other.

In Japan the basic principles of race-based stratification remain pertinent and politically influential. These racial assumptions are encoded in Japan's political policies in Asia and prove useful to politicians as a strategic provocation that reinforce notions of cultural superiority while once again putting its Asian neighbors in their "proper place." Such grand narratives are useful to state-level actors, but they are not generally subscribed to by the general public, who may entertain vague notions of cultural superiority, but do not conceive of these issues in coherent political terms. Public opinion polls suggest more ambivalence than truculence about Japan's wartime past while support for and opposition to Yasukuni Shrine visits, for example, vacillates considerably. The legacy of race-based nationalism casts a long shadow across Japan and is important for understanding Japan's regional politics and international relations, but it only partly explains racism as it is expressed and experienced throughout society at an inter-personal level.

Partisan politics, passive public

When right-wing nationalists direct their ire towards foreigners, the meaning is clear: the object of contempt is directly addressed and the sentiment unambiguously derisive.

Yet alongside these explicit, negative attitudes that are lobbed by politicians like weapons in the cultural war of words, the vast majority of Japanese neither voice strident views nor openly advocate policies that are punitive in nature and explicitly discriminatory. In his analysis of multi-ethnic Japan, John Lie (2001, 172) takes up the issue of Japanese racism, and concludes that while stereotypes derived from Japan's colonial rule continue to inform Japanese attitudes toward other Asians (especially Koreans and Chinese), at worst most Japanese are passive racists. Among the general public, whose views seldom rise to direct confrontation, it is difficult to ascertain if a lack of overtly hostile racist views in the public domain represents a stifling of unvoiced beliefs firmly held to the breast, or if they are not there in the first place. This possibility—that things are exactly as they appear and a lack of overt expression means that there is no underlying racism—is an interesting proposition, but this would only be convincing if the larger society were free of pervasive racial inequalities.

Scholars have long noted the multi-faceted nature of racism. Prejudicial attitudes apparently arise from and express underlying feelings of insecurity and hostility, but the relationship between belief and action is imprecise and difficult to measure. Whereas racist attitudes may point toward discrimination, they may not be acted on, either because there is no opportunity to do so, or because there are negative consequences if the discrimination is not condoned (Jencks 1993). Without a direct linkage to discriminatory action to demonstrate intent, racist attitudes may remain implicit, expressed in such indirect and symbolic ways that their true intention is indecipherable not only to those scrutinizing these attitudes, but to those who hold such views (Lawrence 1987). Whether unconscious or incoherent, attitudes are notoriously illusive and malleable. People's attitudes evolve through their life experiences, and are subject to manipulation by prevailing political ideologies but may lie dormant and unvoiced until provoked by especially evocative events that align with agendas that may be racist in consequence, but are driven by partisan agendas that are not necessarily racial in nature (Wright 1995).

Racial attitudes, even if conscious, are contentious when they are brought to light and given voice, which serves to suppress views that are out of synch with norms of civility. Contemporary Western societies tend to police public speech by imposing standards for "politically correct" communication, holding people—public figures especially—accountable when they dare deviate from this expectation. In societies in which racist views have been subjected to scrutiny and are ridiculed as vestiges of a past that has been discredited, openly hostile and racist views are taken as evidence of ignorance by the subject voicing them, or as archaic ideologies biased by agendas that are seen as repugnant when democratic values hold sway. Under these conditions, the threat of public ridicule may prevent overt racial animosity from being voiced as it has effectively been censored by public opinion, if not proscribed by law.

In Japan, by contrast, racist views are seldom openly expressed except in public arenas. Given the lack of public censure, this is not politically problematic, and so does not appreciably weigh on state-level actors. In the domain of interactional dynamics, the lack of aggressively asserted racism in Japan—or any strident political view for that matter—may be analogous to "politically correct" censorship, but instead of a dampening down of offensive views because they violate values of democratic inclusion, this silence may be the result of societal norms that discourage potentially divisive views from being raised, irrespective of the substantive content of such views.

One area where this is evident is in the relative lack of political activism in areas associated with race. In the last couple of decades, there has been progress, with Japanese minorities finally being granted recognition they had previously been denied by the national government. Following protracted and bitter disputes over land rights in Sapporo, and in response to lobbying by the Ainu Association of Hokkaido (AAH), this indigenous Japanese minority was able to secure concessions by the mid-1980s to protect their land and cultural traditions. With support from United Nations Working Group on Indigenous Populations, who pressured the Japanese government to adhere to human rights protocols, in 1997 the Ainu were finally granted official recognition by the Japanese government with the establishment of the Ainu Culture Law, which effectively overturned the 1899 Ainu Protection Act, which had prescribed assimilation into Japanese society and denied them fundamental civil rights for a century. Effectively leveraging international pressure to their advantage, in 2008 the AAH compelled the Japanese Diet (national parliament) finally to acknowledge the Ainu as an indigenous population, and officially recognize their distinct language, religion and culture (Howell 1994).

Alongside the Ainu, Japanese minorities that most evoke the history of Japanese racism are outcaste groups that historically have suffered the most severe oppression and discrimination among Japanese minorities (Neary 1997). As Japan's "untouchables," these groups, comprising "Hinin" (literally, non-human) and "Eta" (literally, an abundance of filth), were officially established in the Edo era (1603–1867) as outcastes due to their association with death (burial of bodies, animal slaughter and leather working), and impurity according to Buddhist precepts (Groemer 2001). By the Meiji period, with the dissolution of the feudal caste system, these groups were brought together under the term "Burakumin" (literally, village or hamlet people), in acknowledgement of their position on the margins of society. With the rise of activist groups such as the Burakumin Liberation League in the 1950s, incremental gains, ranging from financial aid to anti-discrimination initiatives, were made in the 1960s and 1970s, and by the 1980s prefectural governments had established Human Rights Promotion Centers to promote Burakumin rights alongside other marginalized groups.

The hard-fought gains that minorities have achieved in the last generation represent real progress, but they were not the result of a societal-level debate on the meaning and significance of race as it is embodied in the experience of these discriminated minorities, nor were they the result of political activism by those who do not have a direct stake in the issues that affect these minorities. In Japan, minority politics are the province of minorities. The political gains by minorities in Japan are a testament to their tenaciousness in the face of governmental intransigence and political apathy among the general public. As demoralizing as this may be for those concerned with racial equality, the lack of engagement among the general public on these issues has less to do with race than it does with the nature of public politics in Japan.

Interactional dynamics of Japanese racism

The interactional dynamics of Japanese society become relevant in the form, if not the substance, of racial claims. Anthropologists (Hall 1990) have argued that in "high-context" societies such as Japan, beliefs are often left implicit and are not articulated, but are inscribed in the situational context where their reality is taken for granted (Lebra 1976). Under such conditions, they need not be overtly expressed, since they are already implicitly acknowledged and considered banal facts not worthy of debate. In contrast, "low-context" societies such as the United States require explicit communication for people to make themselves understood, as the cultural distance between divergent nationalities, religious worldviews, political orientations, and socio-economic classes demands that people stake their claim by asserting their point of view.

The logic that underlies this dichotomy holds that high-context societies such as Japan are homogeneous in nature, and that citizens are so effectively socialized that they share a collective consciousness, a set of values that are almost universally held and taken for granted without opposition. Any close reading of Japanese history would undermine this ideal type interpretation. In comparison to other countries Japan may appear to have collective identity as a defining cultural trait, but in the modern era it is certainly more diverse than the rhetoric of inclusiveness would maintain.

Notions of Japanese cultural distinctiveness do not take into account how state-level policies that sustain racial ideology operate across multi-racial societies as a means of managing racial conflict and furthering political interests (Hanchard and Chung 2004, 334). When viewed through this lens, even if cultural practices are distinctive, the political processes through which they are applied operate by similar principles and result in common outcomes. Japan has a multitude of cultural characteristics that shape racial practices in distinctive ways, but what really matters is how this results in social inequality, and in this regard Japan's discrimination in housing, education, and employment are hardly unique.

The distinction between high-context and low-context societies is more of a useful heuristic to see how Japan does *not* deal with racial inequality rather than how it *does*. The point here is that with a longstanding racialized ideology having established the foundation for how people conceive of their status on the hierarchy of cultural difference, these views only emerge in a coherent way when they are attached to particular political policies under conditions of conflict. Under normal conditions, they remain inchoate ideas that lie dormant in the collective consciousness and do not coalesce as overt and coherent views except when needed as a rhetorical strategy of provocation, to put the other party in their proper place (Wright 1995). With this in mind, we can see why Japan's geopolitical relations in Asia are continually unsettled by the harsh rhetoric of Japanese politicians. Provocative comments may only be episodic, but they serve as a reminder that Japan has not really contemplated the impact of its actions on its former colonial subjects, and generations later still doggedly adheres to notions of cultural superiority.

Because of the cultural tendency to avoid provocative and radical views, Japanese society discourages racist views from being voiced, but not because they are offensive and out of synch with egalitarian values. Rather, an other-directed orientation that avoids confrontation and offense serves to flatten out racial beliefs to the extent that they cannot stand out and be seen as overt expressions of racial animosity. This makes it difficult to ascertain what people actually believe, and it raises methodological problems for the study of how racial beliefs are translated into social policy: how can we empirically measure something that may be there, but is hidden behind a façade of civility, or is even unconscious to those holding the beliefs? An obvious solution to this dilemma would be to move away from how people express themselves in racial terms to examine how minorities position themselves in relation to the way they are actually treated. In this way, scrutiny would not fall exclusively on actors and their presumed motives, but rather on how racism affects the lives of minorities in Japan.

Japanese minorities: hiding in plain sight

In a society that values conformity, cultural practices evolve that require it, with the penalty of discrimination serving as a mechanism of enforcement. Japanese racial minorities remain a comparatively "invisible minority" who are hiding outside the scrutiny of mainstream Japanese. Both as a means to assimilate and secure privileges that might otherwise be denied them, and in order to avoid invidious discrimination, some Japanese minorities attempt to "pass" as non-minority Japanese. In an effort to avoid the consequences of revealing their outcaste status, the Burakumin escape public censure by passing as non-minority Japanese, a practice that is compelled as much as it is a voluntary choice. Until recently elite families would conduct a perverse form of due diligence by hiring private detectives to determine if a prospective spouse is of Buraku descent, and major Japanese corporations would blacklist Burakumin names from lists of prospective hirees. These practices are now illegal, and it is estimated that approximately 70% of Burakumin marry a non-Burakumin, but old habits die hard: in recent years nationalist bloggers on social media such as MIXI and 2-Channel have identified majority Burakumin neighborhoods, revealing Burakumin-linked names and exposing them to harassment and discrimination.

The rise of social media has offered opportunities for minorities to promote their causes, and to extend their social networks to those with whom they share a common experience of social marginalization. Social media offers a means of conveying experience outside intensive face-to-face direct association into the free-floating networks of virtual communities that are bound by common interests rather than common cultural origins. This emerging paradigm has the potential to be a welcome progressive force in Japan: it provides opportunities for marginalized people to express themselves, and conceivably could be a way out of the social isolation that has led to their disengagement from civil society. However, the blogosphere also provides anonymity and the corresponding lack of accountability that may enable more strident views to be expressed than would be allowed in direct face-to-face interaction. In this universe of shared virtual experience there is no check against belligerency, and one consequence of this is that groups that are protected in mainstream cultural discourse and the public realm are subject to attack. Racism flourishes in this environment in viral forms that defy social control.

Mainstream media is more circumspect, both because of the aforementioned cultural inclination to avoid controversial issues (especially when they touch on issues that are fundamentally related to the complexities of Japanese identity), and because broadcast codes now reflect the rights of minorities and how they can be publically characterized. For a period of several years in the late 1990s, I hosted a bi-monthly program in Tokyo on Inter-Fm 76.1 radio. Over the course of this program, "International Forum," we addressed various issues of interest to the international community in Tokyo, and for one of the episodes we discussed minority rights in Japan. As we discussed the status of the Burakumin, the sound engineer shut the mikes, rushed into the studio and declared: "you can't call them Burakumin." As the topic under discussion was the Burakumin Liberation League, we were confused why a label that is used by the main civil rights organization of this group could not be spoken on the public airwaves, on a radio program that was founded to reach the foreign community after the 1995 Kobe earthquake. The reason offered—that this was a "*sabetsu kotoba*" (a discriminatory term)—was complicated by the engineer's edit of the recorded broadcast. After carefully splicing out the offensive term using a sound editing software program, he turned to us in the recording booth and said "good: they will think you are talking about Koreans."

At Temple University's Japan Campus in Tokyo, where I teach courses in race and ethnicity, I once had a Korean student learn in the course of the semester that he was not actually Japanese. When the student discussed issues we were studying in class at home, his father revealed his Korean ancestry, explaining that when he and his Japanese mother were first married he assured her that he would raise their children as "real" Japanese so they would not have to face discrimination as ethnic Koreans. The fact that this practice continues to exist is testimony to the weight of racial categories on the lives of minorities in Japan: in their study of ethnic discrimination in Japan, Lee and DeVos (1981) found that 70% of Zainichi Koreans hid their heritage and attempted to pass as non-ethnic Japanese, and this practice continues today. However, in the 21st century, an increasing number of younger Zainichi are naturalizing because there are many practical advantages of citizenship and they do not feel as compelled as their elders to assert their ethnic identity.

The suppression of deviant identities in Japan comports with the passivity of most Japanese on racial issues. In both cases the threat of public disclosure dampens overt expression, and this withdrawal from the public arena prevents social inequalities from being addressed head-on. Under the threat of public rebuke, racial minorities are inhibited from asserting their rights, lest they pay the price of social exclusion. This trend does not hold, however, for ethnic minorities such as the Ainu, who have demanded acknowledgement of their rights as Japanese citizens, despite their heritage of having been forcibly conscripted into the Japanese nation-state in the Meiji era. In Hokkaido, the Ainu have established cultural preservation centers where their heritage is celebrated, a byproduct of political gains that secured legal recognition by the Japanese government on more fundamental issues such as being officially recognized as an indigenous minority.

In similar ways, Okinawans have vigorously fought for their rights against the political interests of the Japanese state. Having initially come under partial Japanese control in 1609 (at which time it also maintained a tributary obligation to China), the former Ryukyu Kingdom was officially annexed in 1879. As Okinawa was forcibly assimilated into Japan, with Japanese language and culture practices being imposed on what was previously an autonomous kingdom with a distinct culture, China and Japan continued to assert territorial rights until the Pacific War, after which the United States took control of the islands (Rabson 1996). The wartime experience of the Okinawans was tragic: in one of the most brutal campaigns of the entire war, one quarter of the civilian population were killed, and Okinawa remained under US control until sovereignty was returned to Japan in 1972, with the presumption that US military bases remain. As an occupied land, now beholden to the interests of both the United States and Japan, Okinawa has tried in vain to reclaim its autonomy, with massive public protests against the US military. The US base structure occupies approximately one fifth of the island, where 75% of US military bases in Japan are located. There have been numerous incidents of crime and violence against Okinawan citizens, a longstanding source of contention that Japan has failed to address effectively (Johnson 1999).

Okinawa is a highly visible exception to the Japanese practice of pushing minority issues underground, not only because of a strong political activism, but also because

Okinawans, despite their partial assimilation, maintain distinctive cultural characteristics. Many mainland Japanese consider Okinawa to be an exotic locale and although they may not appreciate its complex history, understand that it was once a separate kingdom, with its own language and culture. However, Okinawa remains the poorest of Japan's 47 prefectures, and its inability to compel the Japanese state to recognize its interests and reorganize its relationship to the United States demonstrates a lack of autonomy and influence in national affairs (see Chapter 13).

Another visible exception to the Japanese practice of denying minorities not only their rights but acknowledging their very existence, involves the Nikkejin, Japanese emigrants and their descendents abroad. With support from the Japanese government, under the terms of a bilateral treaty with Brazil concluded in 1907, tens of thousands of Japanese went to work in Brazil's coffee plantations and eventually became the largest population of Japanese outside Japan (there are about 1.5 million people of Japanese descent in Brazil). Nikkejin suffered exploitive work conditions and were subject to assimilation policies in Brazil, and elsewhere, that denied their cultural heritage. While many remained in Brazil, over 300,000 eventually returned to Japan from the late 1980s, seeking jobs and a chance to reconnect to their Japanese heritage. This migration was facilitated by the Japanese government, which passed an immigration law in 1990 that provided special working visas for the dekasegis (a term for overseas ethnic Japanese who have migrated back to Japan) to address labor shortages (see Chapter 14).

Despite initial hopes that the Nikkejin would more readily assimilate than other foreign migrant workers, they have largely maintained their Brazilian ethnicity despite being "racially" Japanese, a recipe for exclusion, as they fall between the categories of being a foreigner and a "real" Japanese (Roth 2005). Moreover, with weak language skills, most Nikkejin tend to work in assembly-line jobs in manufacturing or what are known as 3K jobs—"Kitsui, Kitanai and Kiken" (hard, dirty, dangerous) work that Japanese tend to avoid. Due to their association with these low-level jobs, and because they do not pass as Japanese due to their Brazilian ethnicity, the Nikkejin have suffered both class-based and ethnic discrimination (Tsuda 1998).

In contemporary Japan, the status of Korean and Chinese minorities was established through, and marked by, Japan's wartime imperial policies. Following the Japanese annexation of Korea in 1910, hundreds of thousands of Koreans were forced into menial labor (chiefly coal mining and construction) in Japan, alongside Burakumin and Okinawans at the lowest tier of the labor market, and were often confined to ghettos contiguous to those of these minority populations (Lie 2008, 5). Anti-foreigner sentiment culminated in a mob lynching days after the 1923 Kanto earthquake of thousands of ethnic Koreans (and a lesser number of Chinese), who were accused of poisoning wells and disturbing public order (Ryang 2007). In World War II, ethnic Koreans suffered enforced migration, near slave-like treatment working in factories to support the war effort, and tens of thousands were recruited as "comfort women" to provide sexual services to the Japanese military. The shared past with China is equally divisive.

After defeating China in the first Sino–Japanese War (1894–95), Japan was able to wrest control of Formosa (Taiwan) and Korea from China, and in the second Sino–Japanese War (1937–45) invaded China and inflicted millions of deaths and casualties. Issues related to these wartime atrocities continue to fester, as contemporary Japanese political discourse denies or minimizes the nature and magnitude of these historical events. Public opinion polls continue to demonstrate that Japanese hold anti-Chinese attitudes: for instance, a 2013 BBC/Globescan poll addressing rising concern over China's increasing power found that 70% of Japanese surveyed said China's trade practices are unfair, and 88% (the highest among 26 countries polled) held negative views of China's rising military power. As previously noted, these views are associated with state policy and may not map onto interactional dynamics at a personal level. For individual beliefs to affect state politics, there has to be a coherent connection between the interests of political leaders and their constituents, a questionable proposition in Japan, where ruling elites pursue their agendas with the passive acquiescence of a politically apathetic public. Despite problems at the government level, however, Chinese have become the largest foreign contingent in Japan.

Conclusion

Ultimately, in order to account for the complexities of history as it is embodied in contemporary society, we must look beyond the proffered beliefs of individuals to the institutions that they inhabit and the social structures that constrain their behavior (Bonilla-Silva 1997). In Japan, racial attitudes vary dramatically, and are poor approximations of racial ideology. We see evidence of them—if only a glancing view—in the passive exclusion of foreigners at an interpersonal level, but in societal institutions, racially based policy is readily evident. For example, the Japanese Koseki (Family Registry) system, institutionalizes non-citizen status by allowing local authorities officially to validate a spouse's marital status at their discretion (Chapman 2008, 435). The implications of these policies include the inability of foreign parents to secure visitation rights to their children after divorce because, *inter alia*, as of 2013 Japan has yet to adopt the terms of the 1996 Hague Convention on Protection of Children.

In Japan, racial discrimination remains largely unchallenged and often unrecognized, a problem viewed as happening somewhere else. In the last couple of decades there has been progress, with Japanese minorities finally being granted recognition that had previously been denied by the national government. However, there are good reasons why many non-Japanese continue to feel marginalized in a society where not belonging is a crucial disadvantage.

Bibliography

Bonilla-Silva, Eduardo (1997) "Rethinking Racism: Toward a Structural Interpretation," *American Sociological Review* 62(3): 465–80.

Chapman, David (2008) "Tama-chan and Sealing Japanese Identity," *Critical Asian Studies* 40(3): 423–43.

Creighton, Millie (1997) "Soto Others and Uchi Others: Imagining Racial Diversity, Imagining Homogeneous Japan," in Michael Weiner (ed.) *Japan's Minorities: The Illusion of Homogeneity*, Routledge, 211–38.

Diene, Doudou (2006) *Racism, Racial Discrimination: Xenophobia and All Forms of Discrimination: Mission to Japan*, Economic and Social Council, United Nations, daccessdds.un.org/doc/UNDOC/GEN/G06/103/96/PDF/G0610396.pdf?OpenElement (accessed November 10, 2012).

Dower, John (1986) *War Without Mercy: Race and Power in the Pacific War*, New York: Pantheon Books.

——(2012) "Race, Language and War in Two Cultures: World War II in Asia," in *Ways of Forgetting, Ways of Remembering: Japan in the Modern World*, New Press.

Groemer, Gerald (2001) "The Creation of the Edo Outcaste Order," *Journal of Japanese Studies* 27(2): 263–93.

Hall, Edward T. (1990) *The Hidden Dimension*, Anchor.

Hanchard, Michael and Chung, Erin Aeran (2004) "From Race Relations to Comparative Racial Politics: A Survey of Cross-National Scholarship on Race in the Social Sciences," *Du Bois Review* 1(2): 319–43.

Howell, David L. (1994) "Ainu Ethnicity and the Boundaries of the Early Modern Japanese State. Past and Present," *Journal of Contemporary History* 31(142): 69–93.

Iwasawa, Yuji (1986) "Legal Treatment of Koreans in Japan: The Impact of International Human Rights Law on Japanese Law," *Human Rights Quarterly* 8(2): 131–79.

Jencks, Christopher (1993) *Rethinking Social Policy: Race, Poverty and the Underclass*, Harper Perennial.

Johnson, Chalmers (1999) *Okinawa: Cold War Island*, Japan Policy Research Institute.

Lawrence, Charles R. (1987) "The Id, the Ego, and Equal Protection: Reckoning with Unconscious Racism," *Stanford Law Review* 39(2): 317–88.

Lebra, Takie (1976) *Japanese Patterns of Behavior*, University of Hawaii Press.

Lee, Changsoo and DeVos, George (1981) *Koreans in Japan: Ethnic Conflict and Accommodation*, Berkeley: University of California Press.

Lie, John (2001) *Multiethnic Japan*, Harvard University Press.

——(2008) *Zainichi Koreans in Japan: Diasporic Nationalism and Postcolonial Identity*, University of California Press.

Morris-Suzuki, Tessa (1998) "Debating Racial Science in Wartime Japan," *Osiris* 13(2): 354–75.

Neary, Ian (1997) "Burakumin in Contemporary Japan," in Michael Weiner (ed.) *Japan's Minorities: The Illusion of Homogeneity*, Routledge, 50–78.

Rabson, Steve (1996) "Assimilation Policy in Okinawa: Promotion, Resistance, and 'Reconstruction'," *Japan Policy Research Institute*, www.jpri.org/publications/occasionalpapers/op8.html.

Roth, Joshua Isaiah (2005) "Political and Cultural Perspectives on 'Insider' Minorities," in Jennifer Robertson (ed.) *A Companion to the Anthropology of Japan*, Blackwell Publishing Ltd, 73–88.

Ryang, Sonia (2007) "The Tongue That Divided Life and Death: The 1923 Tokyo Earthquake and the Massacre of Koreans," *The Asia-Pacific Journal: Japan Focus*, September, japanfocus.org/-Sonia-Ryang/2513.

Tsuda, Takeyuki (1998) "The Stigma of Ethnic Difference: The Structure of Prejudice and 'Discrimination' Toward Japan's New Immigrant Minority," *Journal of Japanese Studies* 24(2): 317–59.

Wright, Lawrence (1995) "Cold Wars, Evil Empires, Treacherous Japanese: Effects of International Context on Problem Construction," in Joel Best (ed.) *Images of Issues: Typifying Contemporary Social Problems*, Aldine Transaction, 313–36.

17 Mental health and therapy in Japan

Conceptions, practices, and challenges

Sachiko Horiguchi

The aim of this chapter is to provide a critical overview of conceptions and practices in the realm of mental health and therapy in Japan. In order to do so we examine the Japanese mental health care system and how it has evolved with a particular focus on the development of psychiatry and clinical psychology. We also analyze cultural conceptions of mind and body in Japan and the role of indigenous therapies that highlight the pluralistic nature of the Japanese mental health care system. Finally, we examine recent anthropological studies on contemporary mental health challenges in Japanese society, suicide and *hikikomori* (youth social withdrawal), and their relevance to larger issues and concerns in contemporary Japan.

Treatment of mental illness and psychiatry in Japan

Treatment of mental illness has a long history in Japan, but the expansion of Japanese psychiatry into everyday life developed only from the late 19th century. In his overview of the history of treating mental illness in Japan, Reynolds (1987, 110) suggests that herbs, hot baths, moxibustion, pine needle fumigation, fasting, acupuncture, bloodletting, ingestion of the blood of poisonous snakes, etc., were used psychotherapeutically from early times. Special diets, fasting, meditation and rest were offered at specialized Buddhist temples, while shamanism has also been practiced in Japan since prehistoric times (Lebra 1982). By the early 20th century, common treatments for mental illness included hypnosis, autohypnosis, breathing exercises, prayer, suggestion, bed rest, physical exercise, lifestyle training, work therapy, travel, massage, and various religious exercises.

It is widely acknowledged that a unified "bodymind" conceptualization in East Asian medicine contrasts with the Cartesian dualism in Western thought that assumes a distinction between mind and body (Lock 1982, 220). Lock also finds that in Japan, even where social and psychological components in the disease causation are acknowledged, the physical manifestations of an illness are the focus of treatment. Somatization, or psychological distress expressed in the form of somatic symptoms, is viewed as a means of expressing dissent (see Lock 1987, 1988; Reynolds 1976).

Japanese conceptualization of psychological issues is expressed in words such as *kokoro* (heart), *seishin* (spirit), *hara* (abdomen), and most importantly, *ki* (energy flow), which highlight the inter-relationship of somatic and psychic variables in the popular domain. Doi (1973) introduced *kokoro* as one of the gate-keeping words in studies of Japanese self (Ryang 2004, 181–82). Moeran (1984, 263) argues that *kokoro* is a keyword in Japan's internal cultural debate, representing at one level the triumph of irrational "feeling" over rational "mind," while also challenging the narrowness of the Cartesian concept of "mind" (Moeran 1984, 261). *Seishin* refers to one's inner spiritual fortitude and self-discipline; Japanese believe that such strength and inner harmony can be cultivated through physical training (Moeran 1984, 255). Confucian and Buddhist ideals are found in *seishin*, and it is understood as representing the strength of group as well as individual spirit. Related to *seishin* is the importance placed on *hara* (abdomen) in Japan. Lock (1982, 225) notes that in the Edo period, a man with *hara* was believed to be able to transcend his physical limitations. As with the concept of *ki* and *kokoro*, many everyday phrases with the term *hara* are related to the expression of emotion (e.g. *hara ga tatsu*, or *hara* stands up = angry), or convey the idea that *hara* is the emotional center of the body (e.g. *hara-guroi-hito*, or a person with black *hara* = evil-hearted person (Lock 1982, 225–26)).

Ki (*qi* in Chinese) is intrinsic to Japanese thought, the idea that not only all living things but also the world, and the cosmos itself, are filled with this life energy (Kitanaka 2012, 25). *Ki* is considered invisible and intangible, something that can be felt in the movement of wind and in breathing. As something that is constantly circulating, *ki* can alter and be altered by both external and internal forces. According to Doi, *ki* (mind or spirit) is related to emotion, judgment, self-consciousness, and will. He defines *ki* as "the movement of the spirit from moment to moment" (Doi 1973, 97). The cultivation of *ki* management is seen as essential to achieving a calm, balanced, and healthy state (Lock 1980, 76).

Doi (1973) points out that in Japan, illnesses can be linguistically divided into three major types: those that are "from *ki*" (*yamai wa ki kara*) produce physical manifestations in the body; illnesses "of *ki*" (*ki no yamai*) produce predominantly psychological/emotional symptoms and include depression, obsession, neurosis, and hypochondria; and finally, illnesses in which "*ki* has changed" (*kichigai*) refer to psychotic problems.[1] *Ki* is closely associated with the pre-modern conception of *utsu*—a term currently used to refer to depression; as Kitanaka (2012, 255–56) explains, when pre-modern Japanese talked about *utsu*, presumably it was *ki* itself that was stagnating in the physiological sense, while the same *ki*—causing blockage in the human body—was thought to give rise to a psychologically depressed state. According to Doi (1973), as long as *ki* is simply off balance and not actually changed, it is possible to restore health through therapy. This has led to the idea that health and illness are a matter of balancing *ki* energy, resulting in a limited conceptualization of mental illness (Ozawa-de Silva 2006, 12).

Kitanaka (2012, 31) suggests that during the Edo period, *ki* began to lose its corporeality and instead came to be used as a psychological term merely indicating mood or feeling. Unlike Chinese who have largely retained the traditional meaning of *qi*, as a notion that unites mind and body, Japanese have begun to see *ki* as a psychological notion, stripped of its former relationship to the body. For modern Japanese, except in traditional medicine and martial arts, *ki* denotes little more than the mind or feeling (Doi 2000).[2] This distinction between mind and body forms the basis of biomedicine and psychiatry in contemporary Japan that began to take hold during the Meiji modernization (1868–1912).

Kitanaka (2012, 40–53) examines the transformation of Japanese psychiatry in three phases, each leading to the expansion of psychiatry into everyday life. The first phase was from the 1870s to 1930s, when the Japanese state introduced psychiatry as a force for modernization. This was a period when the view that mental illness was a biological disease displaced the earlier notion in the Edo era that insanity was caused by a discord of *ki*. Psychiatry was institutionalized as a tool of exclusion and stigmatization of those deemed a threat to the new social order (Kitanaka 2012, 40–42). The Law of Confinement and Protection of the Mentally Ill, enacted in 1900, permitted home confinement of the mentally ill and emphasized the responsibility of the family to provide protective supervision, although the principal aim was to sanction confinement of the mentally ill in mental hospitals (Kuno and Asukai 2000, 362–63). Kure Shūzō, professor of the School of Medicine in Tokyo Imperial University, is deemed the "father of psychiatry" in Japan. He established Kraepelinian German neuropsychiatry and he and his colleagues contributed to psychiatry's dissemination by actively engaging the state and private sectors as well as media, particularly in discussions of abnormality and pathologies of modern life (Kitanaka 2012, 44–45).

The second expansion of psychiatry started in the 1950s and continued through the 1960s, a period marked by expanded institutional care in a growing number of private mental hospitals. This promotion of institutionalized care sparked a longstanding anti-psychiatry movement that started in the late 1960s (Kitanaka 2012, 40, 48). In the immediate post-war period, the American psychoanalytically oriented model of "mental health" was briefly popularized, but leading psychiatrists steeped in the German tradition soon re-established neurobiological psychiatry as the core of Japanese academic psychiatry.[3] In response to the collapse of the *ie* (family) system under the new Civil Law (1947) and the outlawing of private detention under the 1950 Mental Hygiene Law, there was a "shortage" of public psychiatric institutions; in consequence the number of private hospitals offering institutionalized care suddenly increased. As Kuno and Asukai (2000, 362–63) suggest, the revision of the Mental Hygiene Law in 1965 introduced the provision of community-based mental health services, but an assault on American Ambassador Edwin O. Reischauer in 1964 by a mentally disturbed 19-year-old led to expanded confinement and state surveillance of the mentally ill. Psychiatric institutions continued to expand, but as international criticism mounted, an anti-psychiatry movement emerged in Japan's academic psychiatric community. This movement gained popular support following media reports in 1984 about the murder of two patients by staff in a psychiatric hospital, the so-called "Utsunomiya scandal." The Utsunomiya scandal caught the attention of the United Nations Commission on Human Rights and led to a major revision of the Mental Health Law in 1987 (Imamura 2012, 75; Oketani and Akiyama 2012, 87–89). This revision aimed at the protection of human rights for people with mental illness, and at provision of rehabilitative services to promote community integration of the mentally ill. However, transition to community care has remained slow due to the profit-driven nature of privately run mental hospitals which comprise the majority of psychiatric institutions in Japan.[4]

The third period started in the 1980s and continues to the present, characterized by growing interest in mental health, especially related to the workplace and economic distress (Kitanaka 2012, 52). The revision of the Fundamental Law for People with Disabilities in 1993 entitled the mentally ill to receive social welfare provisions as "disabled." Following this revision, the Mental Health Law was further revised and renamed the Mental Health and Welfare Law in 1995. This re-named law introduced the *seishin-shōgaisha-hoken-fukushi-techō* (health welfare handbook for the mentally disabled), which was designed to facilitate their access to social welfare programs. These revisions further promoted the deinstitutionalization, normalization, and rehabilitation of the mentally ill (Kitanaka 2012, 52; Komine 1996). The governmental certification of psychiatric social workers started in 1998, and in the revision of the Mental Health and Welfare Law in 1999 community living support centers, home care service, and short-term residential programs were added to the list of community-based programs that are eligible for public funds (Kuno and Asukai 2000, 363). The Mental Health and Welfare Law has been revised every five years, and in 2014 the article stipulating family responsibility for treatment of mentally ill relatives is to be abolished (*Yomiuri Shimbun* 2013). Alongside this interventionist trend of progressive measures has been the aggressive promotion of antidepressants by the psycho-pharmaceutical industry. Moreover, the dissemination of DSM-III (the *Diagnostic and Statistical Manual of Mental Disorders*, published by the American Psychiatric Association) has promoted re-Americanization of Japanese psychiatry. Although criticism against DSM remains among Japanese psychiatrists, the neo-Kraepelinian paradigm and descriptive approach adopted since its third edition is appealing to the neurological understanding of mental illness taken by Japanese psychiatrists steeped in the Kraepelinian tradition (Kitanaka 2012, 53). Despite some progressive developments, however, mental health care in Japan remains characterized by long-term in-patient care with low levels of staffing at private mental hospitals (Tsuchiya and Takei 2004, 88). This approach relies on high levels of drug dosage and poly-pharmacy (Imamura 2012, 75–77) while doing little to counter prevailing stigma against mental illness (see Ando and Thornicroft 2012).

Two recent significant movements are trying to curb this stigmatization and promote a more progressive treatment regime. First, the National Federation of Families of the Mentally Ill played an active role in anti-stigma campaigns, most notably in changing the terminology for schizophrenia from *seishin-bunretsuō* (mind split disease) to *tōgōshicchōshō* (dysfunction of integration) in 2002 (Ito 2012, 45). Second, the Bethel House founded in 1984 in Urakawa-cho, Hokkaido, has attracted public attention as a model for community-based care for people with schizophrenia and other psychiatric disorders (Imamura 2012, 79–82). Through its businesses and running of unique events such as the yearly "Delusion and Hallucination Festival" (where schizophrenic patients with the best delusion and auditory hallucination are awarded), the Bethel House has been successful in reintegrating its members into Japanese society and reducing stigma (see Nakamura 2013).

Expansion of clinical psychology and its problems

Psychology has become popularized in Japan over the last two decades, and yet, as a professional institution, it has remained relatively marginalized under the dominance of psychiatry in the Japanese mental health care system. Both psychiatrists and psychologists treat mental health issues, but while psychiatrists are trained and state-certified as biomedical doctors, psychologists are trained in psychology departments and are not state-certified or allowed to prescribe medication. The *rinshō-shinri-shi* (clinical psychologist) qualification basically requires that the person study in approved universities (148 of them as of 2013) for six years, including two years' postgraduate study, and pass the annual clinical psychology exams. There have been over 2,000 applicants for the exam annually since 2003, quadruple the number of applicants in 1995 (Nihon Rinshō-shinri-shi Shikaku-nintei Kyōkai 2013). As a result, universities in Japan are either setting up or expanding clinical psychology departments to help offset overall declining student enrollment. Working as a school counselor (institutionalized in 1995 by the Ministry of Education) is the most common option for *rinshō-shinri-shi*, but it is unstable employment usually entailing one-year contracts, and many clinical psychologists work part time for several employers to make a living.

The establishment of clinical psychology in Japan owes much to Kawai Hayao's influence (Kitanaka 2003, 240). Kawai has published over 230 books and frequently appears on TV and other media, thus popularizing Jungian psychology. As mentioned above, clinical psychology was extensively introduced from the United States beginning in the 1950s at a time when Japan was reinventing itself in many ways and often looked to American models. In 1964, the Japanese Association of Clinical Psychology (*Nihon Rinshō-shinri-gakkai*) was established, but collapsed in 1969 amid dissension over the association's attempt to establish a national licensing system (Kitanaka 2003, 241). Kawai and his colleagues then played a pivotal role in subsequently establishing a successor organization, the Association of Japanese Clinical Psychology (Nihon Shinri-rinshō-gakkai) in 1982. Through numerous publications, Kawai and other Jungians widely popularized Jungian readings of Japanese personhood. For example, Kawai (1988), through his work on folklore and clinical practice, has employed the Jungian notion of the "Great Mother" and focused on the maternal values deeply embedded in Japanese society (Kitanaka 2003, 241–42). The Association of Japanese Clinical Psychology successfully established a licensing system in 1988, and since then the field of clinical psychology has expanded and diversified, with 26,329 certified clinical psychologists as of 2012. Although there have been longstanding efforts to establish a government-authorized system for licensing clinical psychologists, this has not yet happened. As a result, psychotherapy carried out by clinical psychologists is not compensated under the national health insurance system, putting many psychologists in a financially vulnerable position (Kitanaka 2003, 244–45).

Despite ongoing tensions, psychiatry and clinical psychology both provide mental health care for people in distress, and comprise part of a larger system of mental health care in Japan. Before going on to discuss mental health challenges faced by Japanese society, I would like further to re-contexualize psychiatry and psychology as part of a larger pluralistic health care system that Japan has long enjoyed by examining so-called indigenous mental therapies in Japan.

Pluralism of Japanese medicine and Japanese indigenous therapies

The Japanese medical system is often characterized as pluralistic in nature (Lock 1980, 257; Ohnuki-Tierney 1984). This pluralism persists despite the dominance of biomedicine in the Japanese medical system as promoted in the post-war national health insurance system. Alternative therapies such as *kanpō* (traditional Japanese medicine of Chinese origin), acupuncture and moxibustion, *seitai* (body correction), and *shiatsu* (acupressure), are strongly embedded in Japanese culture, and remain a widespread therapeutic option for coping with distress (Ohnuki-Tierney 1984, 212).[5]

Morita Ryōhō and *Naikan* are Japanese indigenous therapies that lie at the nexus of religion and psychotherapy. Morita Masatake, a psychiatrist based at Tokyo Jikei University School of Medicine, promoted *Morita Ryōhō* (Morita therapy) in the 1920s for the treatment of *taijinkyōfu-shō* (phobia of interpersonal relations), primarily involving fear of eye-to-eye contact. *Morita Ryōhō* involves two steps of "absolute bed rest" and gradual adaptation to one's outer reality through everyday physical work in groups. First, the patient undergoes bed rest, during which he/she is not allowed to communicate with others, to read books, to watch TV, or to listen to music. The patient is expected to achieve a sense of no-self (*muga*) through this therapy. In the second step, the patient performs daily tasks such as cleaning the house or taking care of the plants in groups. The goal of this step is to accept things as they are (*aru-ga-mama*), including one's weaknesses (Ohnuki-Tierney 1984, 81–82; Reynolds 1976, 109).

Another well-known indigenous Japanese therapy, *Naikan* (literally meaning looking into oneself) is a particular kind of introspection based on a fixed method of re-collection and self-reflection established by Yoshimoto Ishin, an ex-businessman and pious Shin Buddhist in the 1940s. During the *Naikan* session that continues for seven days, clients rise at 5:00 or 6:00 in the morning, and until 9:00 in the evening, they sit behind paper screens set in the corners of the room. They are only permitted to leave for the toilet and bathing, and they take meals in the same room behind the screens. Clients are asked to recall their past and are visited every two hours by the *Naikan* practitioner for an interview (Ozawa-de Silva 2006, 5–6). This highly ritualized procedure aims to achieve two goals, which are the discovery of guilt and gratitude. The client is asked to look at himself/herself vis-à-vis his/her relationships with others from three perspectives: care received (usually beginning with an examination of his/her relationship with his/her mother), care reciprocated, and troubles caused. The role of the *Naikan* interviewer is to make sure that the client follows instructions and reflects successfully on his/her self-examination.

Whilst many believe that Buddhism and Confucianism influenced Naikan (Ozawa-de Silva 2006), and Zen influenced *Morita*, Murase (1982, 324) argues that they are both rooted in Shintoism. More importantly, Murase (1982) also argues that both *Naikan* and *Morita* are oriented towards a rediscovery of the core values of Japanese society, which can essentially be expressed by the idealized term *sunao* (honesty). *Sunao* connotes disingenuousness and innocence of childhood, and implies the harmonious and natural state of mind vis-à-vis oneself and others. *Sunao* entails ideals of Japanese personhood, often characterized by its emphasis on interdependency and situational, multiple selves in contrast to the Western conception of the individual (Rosenberger 1994). I now turn to emergent mental health challenges facing Japan, with a particular focus on suicide and *hikikomori* (youth social withdrawal).

Mental health challenges in contemporary Japan

Suicides and the gendering of depression

Scholars and media alike have often pointed to the historical roots of cultural legitimacy of suicides in Japan (Kawanishi 2009, 33–34) and lack of religious prohibition against the act of suicide. In the feudal period, *seppuku* (literally stomach cutting, a form of ritual suicide practiced by samurai) was considered an honorable deed. *Shinjū* (double suicide by lovers) was romanticized as the ultimate expression of love, and *oyako shinjū* (parent–child suicide) was portrayed as an act of love and responsibility toward the child. Such symbolic aestheticization and idealization of suicides endured even after modernization, as represented in the annual broadcasting of the legendary drama of *Chūshingura* (a suicide pact between samurai), school-recommended modern novels featuring suicide, like well-known novelist Natsume Sōseki's *Kokoro*, or sympathetic responses from the public to the suicide of the post-war literary giant Etō Jun in

1999. This reflects a persistent view of suicide as the ultimate expression of personal will, or what Japanese often refer to as *kakugo no jisatsu*, or "suicide of resolve." This is in contrast to the view of suicide as a pathological act caused by depression (Kitanaka 2008, 153).

In light of Japan's rising suicide rates, such "traditional" explanations are increasingly being challenged within psychiatry and indeed in public discourse (Kitanaka 2008, 2012, 107–28). Japan has suffered from over 30,000 cases of reported suicide every year since 1998, an epidemic often attributed to the combination of financial distress caused by prolonged economic stagnation and the aforementioned cultural legitimacy of suicides in Japan (Kawanishi 2009, 24, 33–34; Ozawa-de Silva 2008, 522–23). This has prompted the state to adopt new suicide counter-measures, and the Basic Act on Suicide Prevention was enacted in 2006 (Ito 2012, 38). A series of lawsuits concerning overwork suicide (see Kitanaka 2012, 155–73) has not only prompted the Ministry of Health, Labor and Welfare to adopt new criteria for diagnosing suicide that expanded the domain of "pathological" suicide, but also given psychiatrists a platform to alert the public about the link between suicide and depression and thereby medicalize depression. However, at the same time, as Kitanaka's (2008, 2012) ethnography of clinical practice illustrates, psychiatrists retain ambivalent attitudes toward pathologizing suicide and limit their biomedical jurisdiction by treating only what they regard as biological anomalies. They carefully avoid the psychological realm in treating their patients, instead attempting to persuade them of the biological nature of suicidal impulses, although they acknowledge how the boundary between "pathological suicides" and "suicides of resolve" is blurred in the clinical setting. One ironic consequence of this medicalization of suicide "may be that psychiatrists are reinforcing the dichotomy between normal and pathological, 'pure' and 'trivial', suicides, despite their clinical knowledge of the tenuousness of such distinctions and the ephemerality of human intentionality" (Kitanaka 2012, 86). Thus, the medicalization of suicide scarcely seems poised to "supplant the cultural discourse on suicide that has elevated suicide to a moral act of self-determination" (ibid.).

The demographics of suicides in Japan since the late 1990s indicate that men in their forties and fifties are at highest risk (Kawanishi 2009, 35–36).[6] This corresponds to the stereotypical image of "the model *salaryman*" committing *karoshi* (death due to overwork), which has been recognized as a Japanese social issue since the late 1980s (Kawanishi 2009, 38–39). These *salaryman* workers face strong expectations to contribute to their companies through long hours of unpaid overtime, but for many this workload is excessive and undermines their health, both physical and mental. According to Kitanaka (2012, 129–49), the resulting paradigm of men afflicted with work-induced depression has created a master narrative in popular discourse—which is distinctly lacking in the case of depressed women who struggle to build a trusting relationship with (typically male) doctors in clinical encounters. This male-centered discourse on depression in Japan is peculiar, given that depression has long been represented in the West as a *female* malady (Kitanaka 2012, 129).

Another peculiarity of Japanese suicides is the recent emergence of Internet suicide pacts (Ozawa-de Silva 2008). Contrary to the sympathy accorded to suicides committed by "overworked *salarymen*," the mass media tends to portray Internet group suicides, a new form of *shinjū*, as irresponsible, thoughtless acts, and those who engage in them are seen as too weak-willed to die on their own (Ozawa-de Silva 2008, 520). However, Ozawa-de Silva (2008) analyzes postings on suicide-related websites to assert that Internet suicides are characterized by severe existential suffering, a loss of a sense of the "worth of living" (*ikigai*) among Japanese youth, as well as profound loneliness and lack of connection with others. This problem of isolated youth is most symbolically represented in the "problem" of *hikikomori*, which is explored in the following section.

Hikikomori ***at the intersection of mental health and illness***

Hikikomori, literally meaning "withdrawal," came to be discussed as a social problem afflicting Japanese youth from the late 1990s. This was largely through the efforts of psychiatrist Saitō Tamaki who coined the term, and the media-induced "moral panic" sparked by reports of crimes allegedly committed by *hikikomori*. In response, the Ministry of Health, Labor and Welfare has developed guidelines (Ministry of Health, Labor and Welfare 2003, 2010) that established *hikikomori* as a mental health issue to be dealt with at public health centers and mental health welfare centers. At the level of general media discourse, *hikikomori* has often been represented as an ethnicized, gendered and classed phenomenon (Horiguchi 2012). First, it is generally believed that *hikikomori* is unique to contemporary Japanese society. This is symbolized by the assertion made by Saitō (2001, 124–33), the main figure in the *hikikomori* debates, that the existence of *hikikomori* represents an ongoing example of *Nihonjin-ron* or theories about Japanese uniqueness. Saitō drew on Doi's well-known theory of *amae* (dependency), known to define the Japanese psyche and the positive value given to interdependency in Japan, to explain why Japanese parents allow their *hikikomori* children to stay with them. This does not mean that *hikikomori* as a phenomenon is unique to Japan, but rather the uniqueness lies in the existence of the cultural category of *hikikomori* itself. Regarding gendering, there is a media consensus that there are more male than female *hikikomori* cases, a phenomenon also reflected in official surveys (Cabinet Office 2010). Again, this does not necessarily mean that in reality there are more male cases, but rather reflects the higher probability that male cases are reported (Shiokura 2000, 168). Furthermore, *hikikomori* is presented as a middle-class phenomenon, meaning that it is a problem for most families nationwide since most Japanese view themselves as middle class (Shiokura 2000, 239–40). However, in recent years researchers and practitioners have found a strong link between *hikikomori* and poverty, raising questions about whether *hikikomori* and their families should be eligible for social welfare provisions.

Competing discourses on definitions of *hikikomori* as well as causal explanations made for *hikikomori* encompass a range of biological, psychological and social issues. The ambiguity of the term *hikikomori* has allowed for a variety of interpretations, and governmental institutions, practitioners, psychiatrists, and journalists promote diverse definitions (see Horiguchi 2012). Furthermore, because of the range of issues *hikikomori* encompasses, non-academic as well as academic commentators have provided varying causal explanations, while various interested individuals and organizations have institutionalized various forms of support and advocacy mechanisms, constituting what is often called the "*hikikomori* industry." Commentators and advocates interested in educational issues tend to focus on educational problems, particularly in relation to longstanding problems of school non-attendance (*futōkō*) and bullying (*ijime*). Others focus on the psychological issues, in relation to traumas and dilemmas in communication and provide communication-oriented support programs.[7] Others analyze *hikikomori* in terms of deteriorating labor conditions (Furlong 2008), linking it with the problems of *freeters*, NEETs (a term imported from the UK referring to youth "not in education, employment, or training"), and youth unemployment issues, arguing for more extensive employment support and a broader social safety net. *Hikikomori* is also often connected to issues associated with the nuclearization of the Japanese family, and professional help and peer support for families is provided in the public sector as well as through civil groups (Horiguchi 2011).

Although *hikikomori* is generally defined as a non-psychotic problem, in practice, it has lain at the borderline between mental health and illness or of normality and disability. Psychiatrists responsible for devising the most recent guideline (Ministry of Health, Labor and Welfare 2010) categorized it under the DSM classification of mental disorders (see above), and suggest how *hikikomori* may mask psychosis, or how it should better be understood as one form of developmental disability (*hattatsu shōgai*),[8] rather than social pathology. Furthermore, some psychiatrists maintain that *hikikomori* is a necessary process in human life, hence should not be problematized in any way (Horiguchi 2012). Interviews conducted between 2010–12 by the author with psychiatrists, psychologists, counselors, lay supporters of *hikikomori*, as well as those who have experienced *hikikomori* and their families, reveal wide variations in conceptualization of *hikikomori*, and varying ideas about the extent to which *hikikomori* should be supported or treated by psychiatry. Whether or not medicalization of *hikikomori* will continue remains to be seen, but similar to the aforementioned dilemmas psychiatrists have faced in treating suicidal patients, psychiatrists as well as lay practitioners remain ambivalent about whether it merits any form of intervention.

Conclusions

Through an historical overview of the evolution of Japan's mental health care system and the challenges it faces, this chapter provides a nuanced understanding of the construction of Japanese identities at various levels. This chapter also illuminates how Japanese cultural conceptions of personhood (situational and other-oriented in nature) and the Japanese view of mind and body as a unified entity, underlie Japanese ideas about health/illness/death, and animate its pluralistic medical system. Our examination of the establishment of Japanese psychiatry and psychology and their expansion into everyday life offers a glimpse into ways in which Western ideas and practices have been translated into Japanese society, particularly in the post-1945 period. This process features the involvement of various key institutions and individuals, and how discourses on Japanese uniqueness (*Nihonjin-ron*) are negotiated and contested in that process. Popular and clinical discourses on recent mental health challenges such as suicide and *hikikomori* highlight a masculine bias and the shifting roles of the family and work in Japan. We also see that movements to alleviate stigma against mental illness or various measures taken to address these mental health issues exemplify how ideas about normality/abnormality are historically constructed and challenged. Every society develops its conceptions of the boundary between normality and abnormality, and ideal selfhood, which form the basis of identities–individual, local, as well as national. It is through critically examining changing ideas and practices of mental health and therapy in a given society at all these levels that we are better able to understand these conceptualizations.

Notes

1 The previous term for insanity was "*tabure*" (deviation from others), which was treated by various forms of religious chanting meant to drive the bad spirit away. Such beliefs gave way in the Edo era (1603–1868) to the notion of *kichigai* as defined by doctors who came to redefine it as a loss of balance in interpersonal relations as well as in natural elements within an individual's body (Kitanaka 2012, 29; Oda 1998).

2 This does not mean that Cartesian dualism has taken strong hold in contemporary Japan. One example that represents the prevailing idea of mind–body holism is the proliferation of psychosomatic medicine in Japan. *Shinryō-naika* (psychosomatic medicine) treatment was introduced in the early 1960s by Dr Ikemi, a medical practitioner who was influenced by research on psychosomatic illnesses in the United States. Kitanaka (2012, 72) notes that *shinryō-naika* attempted to overcome Cartesian dualism by emphasizing the intimate relationship between mind and body. Although similar attempts are evident in the West, what makes Japanese psychosomatic medicine unique is the way that doctors approached the problem by focusing on the body (as Japanese traditional doctors would), rather than on the mind (as psychotherapists would), based on the belief that inducing changes in the body will help heal the mind.

3 Psychoanalysis was introduced in the 1910s but has never become popular as a mode of treatment (see Kitanaka 2003, 240). Scholars (see Ohnuki-Tierney 1984, 81–83; Murase 1982) attribute this to the other-orientation of Japanese personhood, suggesting that the emphasis on self-examination and introspection in psychoanalysis based on the Western conceptualization of the individual self does not suit the Japanese, whose sense of self is situational and defined through how others might see them.

4 Among the in-patients, over 70,000 are considered "*shakaiteki-nyūin*," or social hospitalization, which refers to those whose symptoms are settled but remain in hospital because of the lack of a community care system. Japan has had the highest number of psychiatric beds per capita among Organisation for Economic Co-operation and Development (OECD) countries (OECD 2012).

5 Ozawa-de Silva (2006, 2008) points to the *iyashi* (healing) boom Japan has experienced since 1995, where increasingly Japanese sought spiritual healing in not only traditional religious practices but also in commodified forms such as books, music, incense and aroma, plants and so on.

6 It should be noted that suicide is the leading cause of death in Japan for those under the age of 30 and there has been a significant increase in the number of suicides among youth (Ozawa-de Silva 2008, 520).

7 This corresponds to longstanding characterization of Japanese people as prone to fear of interpersonal relations (*tajinkyōfu*) (see above), and the newly emerging characterization of youth as having difficulty in face-to-face communication with others.

8 The *hattatsu shōgai* category is a uniquely Japanese categorization of a variety of disabilities associated with children, such as ADHD, learning disabilities, or high-functioning autism (including what is commonly known as Asperger syndrome), but excluding intellectual disabilities. This category came to be widely known from the 1990s.

Bibliography

Ando, Shuntaro and Thornicroft, Graham (2012) "Attitudes to Mental Illness in Japan and Britain," in Ruth Taplin and Sandra J. Lawman (eds) *Mental Health Care in Japan*, London and New York: Routledge, 113–41.

Cabinet Office (2010) *Wakamono no Ishiki ni kansuru Chōsa* (*Hikikomori ni Kansuru Jittai Chōsa*) *Hōkokusho* (*Gaiyoban*) (A report on a survey on youth consciousness [empirical survey of *hikikomori*] summary), www8.cao.go.jp/youth/kenkyu/hikikomori/pdf/gaiyo.pdf (accessed May 1, 2013).

Doi, Takeo (1973 [1971]) *The Anatomy of Dependence*, trans. J. Bester, Tokyo: Kōdansha International.

——(2000) "Noirōze, Ki no Yamai, Kichigai" (Neurosis, illness of Ki, insanity), in *Doi Takeo Senshū* 6 (Collected works of Doi Takeo vol. 6), Tokyo: Iwanami Shoten.

Furlong, Andy (2008) "The Japanese *Hikikomori* Phenomenon: Acute Social Withdrawal among Young People," *Sociological Review* 56(2): 309–25.

Horiguchi, Sachiko (2011) "Coping with *Hikikomori:* Socially Withdrawn Youth and the Japanese Family," in Allison Alexy and Richard Ronald (eds) *Home and Family in Japan: Continuity and Transformation*, London and New York: Routledge, 216–35.

——(2012) "*Hikikomori:* How Private Isolation Caught the Public Eye," in Roger Goodman, Yuki Imoto and Tuukka Toivonen (eds) *A Sociology of Japanese Youth: From Returnees to NEETs*, London and New York: Routledge, 122–38.

Imamura, Yayoi (2012) "How Mental Hospitals Treat their Patients, and Programmes for Rehabilitation into the Community," in Ruth Taplin and Sandra J. Lawman (eds) *Mental Health Care in Japan*, London and New York: Routledge, 73–82.

Ito, Hiroto (2012) "Mental Health Policy and Services: Where We Stand," in Ruth Taplin and Sandra J. Lawman (eds) *Mental Health Care in Japan*, London and New York: Routledge, 36–56.

Kawai, Hayao (1988) *The Japanese Psyche: Major Motifs in the Fairy Tales of Japan*, Dallas, TX: Spring.

Kawanishi, Yuko (2009) *Mental Health Challenges Facing Contemporary Japanese Society: The "Lonely" People*, Folkestone: Global Oriental.

Kitanaka, Junko (2003) "Jungians and the Rise of Psychotherapy in Japan: a Brief Historical Note," *Transcultural Psychiatry* 40(2): 239–47.

——(2008) "Diagnosing Suicides of Resolve: Psychiatric Practice in Contemporary Japan," *Culture, Medicine, and Psychiatry* 32: 152–76.

——(2012) *Depression in Japan: Psychiatric Cures for a Society in Distress*, Princeton, NJ: Princeton University Press.

Komine, Kazushige (1996) "Seishin Hoken Fukushihō eno Kaisei," *Kokoro no Kagaku* (Science of the mind): 67.

Kuno, Eri and Asukai, Nozomu (2000) "Efforts Toward Building a Community-based Mental Health System in Japan," *International Journal of Law and Psychiatry* 23(3/4): 361–73.

Lebra, William (1982) "Shaman-client Interchange in Okinawa: Performative Stages in Shamanic Therapy," in Anthony Marsella and Geoffrey White (eds) *Cultural Conceptions of Mental Health and Therapy*, Dordrecht, The Netherlands: Kluwer, 303–16.

Lock, Margaret (1980) *East Asian Medicine in Urban Japan*, Berkeley: University of California Press.

——(1982) "Popular Conceptions of Mental Health in Japan," in Anthony Marsella and Gregory White (eds) *Cultural Conceptions of Mental Health and Therapy*, Dordrecht, Holland: Kluwer, 215–34.

——(1987) "Protests of a Good Wife and Wise Mother," in Edward Norbeck and Margaret Lock (eds) *Health, Illness, and Medical Care in Japan: Cultural and Social Dimensions*, Honolulu: University of Hawaii Press, 130–57.

——(1988) "A Nation at Risk: Interpretations of School Refusal in Japan," in Margaret Lock and Deborah Gordon (eds) *Biomedicine Examined*, Dordrecht, The Netherlands: Kluwer Academic, 377–414.

Ministry of Health, Labor and Welfare (2003) *Jūdai/nijūdai wo chūshin toshita "Shakaiteki Hikikomori" wo meguru Chiiki-seishin-hoken-katsudō no Guideline* (Guidelines of intervention in local mental health activities for "*shakaiteki hikikomori*" mainly among teenagers and those in their twenties) (complete version), Tokyo: Kokuritsu Seishin/Shinkei Centre, www.mhlw.go.jp/topics/2003/07/tp0728-1.html (accessed May 1, 2013).

——(2010) *Hikikomori no Hyōka/ Shien ni kansuru Guideline* (Guidelines for evaluation and support of *hikikomori*), www.ncgmkohnodai.go.jp/pdf/jidouseishin/22ncgm_hikikomori.pdf (accessed May 1, 2013).

Moeran, Brian (1984) "Individual, Group and *seishin:* Japan's Internal Cultural Debate," *Man* (N.S.) 19(2): 252–66.

Murase, Takao (1982) "*Sunao*: A Central Value in Japanese Psychotherapy," in Anthony Marsella and Geoffrey White (eds) *Cultural Conceptions of Mental Health and Therapy*, Dordrecht, The Netherlands: Kluwer, 317–29.

Nakamura, Karen (2013) *A Disability of the Soul: An Ethnography of Schizophrenia and Mental Illness in Contemporary Japan*, Ithaca, NY: Cornell University Press.

Nihon Rinshō-shinri-shi Shikaku-nintei Kyōkai (2013) *Rinshō-shinri-shi Shikaku Nintei no Jisshi* (Implementation of the certification of clinical psychologists), www.fjcbcp.or.jp/nintei_1.html (accessed May 1, 2013).

Oda, Susumu (1998) *Nihon no Kyōkishi* (Records of madness in Japan), Tokyo: Kodansha.

OECD (2012) *OECD Health Data*, Paris: OECD, www.oecd.org/health/health-systems/oecdhealthdata2012.htm (accessed May 1, 2013).

Ohnuki-Tierney, Emiko (1984) *Illness and Culture in Contemporary Japan*, Cambridge: Cambridge University Press.

Oketani, Hajime and Akiyama, Hiromi (2012) "National Federation of Families for the Mentally Ill in Japan: Historical and Future Perspectives," in Ruth Taplin and Sandra J. Lawman (eds) *Mental Health Care in Japan*, London and New York: Routledge, 83–97.

Ozawa-de Silva, Chikako (2006) *Psychotherapy and Religion in Japan: The Japanese Introspection Practice of Naikan*, London and New York: Routledge.

——(2008) "Too Lonely to Die Alone: Internet Suicide Pacts and Existential Suffering in Japan," *Culture, Medicine, and Psychiatry* 32: 516–51.

Reynolds, David (1976) *Morita Psychotherapy*, Berkeley: University of California Press.

——(1987) "Japanese Models of Psychotherapy, in Edward Norbeck and Margaret Lock (eds) *Health, Illness, and Medical Care in Japan: Cultural and Social Dimensions*, Honolulu: University of Hawaii Press, 110–29.

Rosenberger, Nancy (ed.) (1994) *Japanese Sense of Self*, Cambridge: Cambridge University Press.

Ryang, Sonia (2004) *Japan and National Anthropology: A Critique*, London: Routledge and Curzon.

Saitō, Tamaki (2001) "'Hikikomori' no Hikaku-bunkaron" (Comparative cultural debates from the perspective of "*hikikomori*"), *Chuō Kōron* 1401: 124–33.

Shiokura, Yutaka (2000) *Hikikomori*, Tokyo: Village Center Press.

Tsuchiya, Kenji and Takei, Nori (2004) "Focus on Psychiatry in Japan," *British Journal of Psychiatry* 184: 88–92.

Yomiuri, Shimbun (2013) "Seishin Shōgaisha no Koyō Gimuzuke Kaiseihō Seritsu" (Revised law requiring employment of the mentally disabled enacted), *Osaka morning edition* June 14, 2013.

Yoshida, Y. and Komiyama, S. (2003) "Hikikomori 100-man-nin jidai no Shinkoku" (The seriousness of an era of one million *hikikomori*), *Yomiuri Weekly* January 5–12, 89–92.

18 Violence in schools

Tensions between "the individual" and "the group" in the Japanese education system

Robert Aspinall

On January 8, 1980, Ohira Mitsuyo, a 14-year-old second-year junior high school student in Hyogo prefecture, attempted suicide by cutting open her stomach with a knife. Her life was saved when passers-by found her and called an ambulance. During her first year of junior high school, she had transferred to a new school mid-way through the year, meaning that she entered her homeroom class as a newcomer after it had already formed into a strong social group. Almost immediately she was subject to pitiless bullying by the class that was orchestrated by, in her words, "the leader of the 'bad' girls in our homeroom" (Ohira 2002, 26). At first, the bullying took the form of ostracism, followed by obscene graffiti carved into her desk, a bucket of water being poured over her in the toilets and dumping of her belongings into the trash. She endured this and in her second year was able to make three friends with whom she was able to share some intimate details about her life. However, these friends divulged this secret information, including a private medical condition and the name of a boy she had a crush on, to some other girls, who used it to torment and ridicule Ohira. "I looked at the faces of my three 'friends' one by one. All three wore a very peculiar smile: a triumphant leer. In all my life I had never seen such a hideous smile" (Ohira 2002, 52). Betrayed by her only friends, Ohira was reduced to suicidal thoughts: "if I tell my parents what happened today, they'll tell the people at school. Then I'll be a 'rat' again and even worse things will happen. I've reached the limit. I can't take any more … the only thing to do is die" (Ohira 2002, 53–54). After her suicide attempt she was hospitalized for a while and then forced to return to the same school where the bullying became even worse than it had been before. On top of this she had to cope with the intense shame her actions had brought to her parents and family. Unable to endure the misery of school life, Ohira dropped out and entered a life of delinquency, finding acceptance and friendship in a group of thugs and small-time crooks.

This is just one story among thousands of a young life destroyed by school bullying. In Ohira's case, with the help of a family friend, she was able to escape a life on the margins of society and turn her life around. She successfully completed her education, studied law at home, and in 1994 passed the notoriously difficult bar exam. As a lawyer she involved herself in juvenile cases, and wrote an inspirational book to encourage others who were going through the hell of school bullying (Ohira 2002). In 2004 she went on to further success, being appointed deputy mayor of Osaka city. Sadly, most cases of severe school bullying do not have this kind of happy ending. Studies of bullying in Japan have shown that one feature of the Japanese classroom that exacerbates the situation is the unwillingness of others to intervene on the side of the victim because they do not want to risk also being picked on. For Ohira, this was one of the worst parts of her experience—that even her "friends" would betray her to the bullies. A full understanding of the phenomenon of bullying cannot be attained without addressing the ways in which group conformity is learned in classrooms and clubs.

Group conformity can have many positive dimensions. There can be no question that one of the reasons for the success of the Japanese education system in teaching the vast majority of children to master the basics of numeracy, literacy and science, lies in the order that prevails in the vast majority of school classrooms up and down the country. How else could Japan's boys and girls stuck in typically large class sizes of up to 40 students, out-perform their competitors in Europe and North America in so many standardized tests? However, is violence in schools the price that must be paid to maintain these orderly classrooms, and scholastic achievement, either in the form of student-on-student violence or teacher-on-student violence? The well-known Japanese proverb "the nail that sticks up will be hammered down" (*deru kugi wa utareru*) refers both to the conformity and the violence implicit in this view of the Japanese classroom. This chapter will first examine the ways in which children learn how to conform to the group in Japan, and then move on to an analysis of bullying and corporal punishment, and the ways in which both of these problems have been addressed by those on the Left and the Right of the political spectrum from the 1980s up to the present day.

The socialization of young Japanese children into the group

A common notion among Western authors writing about Japan is that one of the defining characteristics of "Japaneseness" is loyalty to the group. During the 1970s and 1980s, Western—particularly American—scholars and journalists visiting Japan noted the loyalty of workers to their companies and cited this as a competitive advantage Japanese industry had over the West. The Japanese education system was described by these foreign observers as being central to the socialization of such cooperative and loyal workers. One example of this genre is a 1986 book by Benjamin Duke, the title of which, *The Japanese School: Lessons for Industrial America*, neatly encapsulates the concern of many in the West about the role of education in both the rise of Japan and the relative decline of Western industrial competitiveness. According to Duke, the nurturing of Japan's productive work force begins in the elementary school classroom.

> The first grade *kumi* [class] represents the beginning of the formal process of group training, Japanese style, that is, developing ties that bind the individual to his group to achieve the ultimate goal, group harmony. It is, in every sense, the initial stage in school in the long task of preparing the future Japanese worker for the harmonious adjustment of employer-employee relationships characteristic of labor relations within Japanese industry.
>
> (Duke 1986, 25)

The way in which this harmony was achieved also caught the interest of Western scholars. At the elementary school level direct supervision by the teacher is often less important than peer supervision. "Rather than controlling the students themselves, teachers often delegate authority, roles and responsibilities to class members" (Okano and Tsuchiya 1999, 59). Continuous participation by all members of the class in all activities including classroom cleaning and the distribution of food at lunchtime is given great emphasis. Unruly, uncooperative and even violent behavior has to be managed within the group—something that can startle Western observers of a Japanese pre-school or elementary classroom (Tobin *et al.* 2009).

The strong emphasis placed on group harmony is directly linked to two more values that are held in high esteem at all levels of the Japanese education system: the notion of equality within the group, and the idea that effort is the primary determinant of academic achievement (Aspinall 2006). The notion of equality requires that all children in the class must take it in turns to assume positions of responsibility (such as the classroom monitor in charge of keeping the blackboard clean, etc.). The emphasis on effort rather than innate ability means that children are very rarely made to repeat a grade, and are never advanced ahead a grade whatever their academic performance. Children who have mastered a particular task more quickly than their peers are encouraged to help those in their group who are still struggling. Rapid advancement for some talented youngsters is not a priority in comparison with the need for all members of a group to join together to cooperate and help one another.

Group harmony and *amae* for the pre-school and elementary school child

Of course group harmony is a value that is fostered in the home as well as the school. It is universally acknowledged that *amae* is a key concept in considering differences between Western and Japanese values. Takeo Doi, a Tokyo psychiatrist trained in psychoanalysis in the United States, popularized this concept in the 1970s (Doi 1971). According to this theory, giving oneself to the promotion and realization of the group's goals imbues the Japanese with a special psychological satisfaction. Most scholars who write in English on Japanese education and childrearing have found it useful to retain the Japanese term *amae* and not try to translate it. This is not because they agree with Doi that the concept represents something unique to the Japanese psyche, but because of the lack of an appropriate equivalent word in English. Words like "dependency" or "indulgence" are not adequate because of their pejorative connotations. As the expert on pre-school education Lois Peak writes, "to an American, indulgence means overlooking commonly understood limits of behaviour to gratify excessive desires or special requests" (Peak 1991, 41). She contrasts this with a Japanese mother's understanding of *amae*: "though *amae* also entails gratifying such desires and requests, within the Japanese family it is not an abrogation but a reaffirmation of commonly accepted rules of behaviour. By showing *amae* to family members, a Japanese child is following culturally appropriate rules for demonstrating trust and affection within intimate relationships" (ibid.).

Crucially, Peak found that this indulgence of selfish behavior within the family was not extended to the school. One of the key functions of the Japanese pre-school and elementary school is the teaching of appropriate behavior *inside* the home and *outside*. In the home, children can relax and express their feelings freely—even to the extent of expressing selfish desires. Outside the home, children have to learn *shūdan seikatsu*, how to live in a group—a place where one must necessarily suppress one's own desires for the good of the collective. Some scholars have observed that parents look to teachers to provide the strict discipline during school hours that they feel unwilling or unable to apply at home (Miller 2009, 241). However, by placing a positive stress on the notion of *dependence*—the exact opposite of the American ideal of *in-dependence*—both school life and home life support the forging of strong group bonds from the earliest age.

Secondary schools and group conformity

Class groups, especially homeroom classes, continue to be a vital arena for the forming and strengthening of group bonds when children graduate from elementary school to junior high school at the age of 12. School clubs also start to play an essential role in nurturing feelings of group loyalty and harmony. On the other hand, ethnographic research has found that membership in groups that are not sanctioned by the school is frowned upon. American anthropologist Gerald LeTendre found that "membership in independent clubs, groups or even cliques was strongly controlled. Students were free to participate in such groups outside of school but could not openly display membership in such groups through clothing or adornment" (LeTendre 2000, 156).

One vital area of continuity between primary and secondary schools in Japan is that children more than teachers enforce conformity and obedience to rules. Clubs, which are usually subject to fairly lax supervision by adults, are essential arenas for the socialization of young Japanese. They are places where children learn the structure of obligation and hierarchical responsibility in senior–junior (*sempai–kōhai*) relationships. First year members of clubs are delegated menial tasks like making the tea, cleaning up and carrying the bags of their *sempai* (White 1994, 94–95). They understand that they have to go through this kind of initiation if they are to earn the right to move on to greater responsibilities when their time comes. Junior club members also learn the correct use of *keigo*, the polite language that is required when junior and senior members of any group in Japan converse. Loyalty to the club is essential, and attendance at all club activities goes without saying for the duration of the student's time at the school. Thus—in complete contrast to school club activity in Western countries—Japanese secondary school students usually join only one club during their entire school career.

School violence: the literal "hammering down" of dissenters and misfits

Adolescents everywhere are subject to various psychological forces that enforce conformity to group norms. Their journey from childhood to adulthood is accompanied by a growing sense of awareness of where they stand within the complex net of social relations that surround them. There are positive forces of acceptance and belonging for those who conform, complemented by negative forces of ostracism and isolation for those who break group rules. At the extreme end of the range of negative forces, of course, lies physical violence. This can come from teachers (in the form of corporal punishment) or peers (in the form of bullying). In this section we will deal with these two forms of violence in turn as they apply to Japan.

Corporal punishment or *taibatsu* was made illegal in Japan in 1947 under Article 11 of the School Education Law, but the law has effectively been ignored in practice with many teachers openly saying that physical punishment of children is effective and justifiable. Even in cases of severe injury or death resulting from physical assaults by teachers against children, punishments have been lenient, with teachers defending their actions by saying that they had the educational interests of the child at heart. One of the most notorious cases in recent years involved Totsuka Hiroshi, the head of a special yacht school (set up to deal with emotionally disturbed children). This facility was known for a very strict disciplinary regime that was implicated when two young people died and two went missing between 1979 and 1982. Totsuka, however, defended the reliance on violent methods, saying that "corporal punishment is part of education." The judge disagreed and sentenced Totsuka to six years' imprisonment, but he resumed teaching at the school in 2006. Since then the Totsuka Yacht School has experienced a number of student suicides. Many Japanese agree with Totsuka's belief in the efficacy and necessity of corporal punishment, even if it is illegal. A *Yomiuri Shimbun* public opinion poll conducted in February 2013 found that 47% of respondents said they would tolerate corporal punishment by teachers and sports coaches, so it is not surprising that such practices still appear widespread.

In January 2013, a second-year student of an Osaka senior high school committed suicide a day after being physically punished by his basketball coach. The coach explained that he had been trying to "motivate" the boy (*Yomiuri Shimbun*, January 11, 2013), and that his methods had helped the team achieve great success. Like many traditional-minded coaches of boys' teams, he claimed that he was determined to be tough on the boys "in order to make men out of them" (*Yomiuri Shimbun*, January 6, 2013). Many parents of children at the school agreed with his harsh methods and submitted a petition to the Osaka board of education calling for the coach to be treated leniently (*Yomiuri Shimbun*, February 18, 2013).

While the media was extensively reporting on this suicide case, a separate controversy about corporal punishment in sports erupted. On January 29, it was publically revealed that 15 top female judo athletes had sent a joint complaint to the Japan Olympic Committee (JOC), claiming they had been harassed and beaten by coaching staff in the run up to the 2012 London Olympic Games. They had earlier complained to the All Japan Judo Federation (AJFF), but had met with a wall of silence. Once the scandal entered the public sphere Sonoda Ryuji, the head coach of women's Olympic judo, was forced to resign and the sports minister proposed that each sports association set up new committees to look into the violent treatment of athletes by their coaches. It is clear that the minister's actions were at least partly an exercise in damage control as foreign media coverage of the judo team abuse put Tokyo's bid to host the 2020 Olympics at risk. The physical abuse of even elite Olympic athletes illustrates just how widespread tolerance of corporal punishment is within Japan's sporting culture. Nobody familiar with Japanese athletics could credibly feign surprise at the allegations, but everyone knows that such practices are out of step with international norms and the Olympic ethos.

The issue of bullying is much discussed in the Japanese media, and periodically the coverage can escalate to the point of a moral panic.[1] There have been three peaks of reported incidents of bullying, including suicides caused by bullying (sometimes referred to as "bullycide" by victims' advocacy groups), that have prompted such moral panics and have occurred at roughly 10-year periods since the 1980s (Yoneyama 2008, 2). The first of these moral panics followed a series of seven student suicides in 1984 and nine in 1985 (Morita *et al.* 1999, 313). The resulting media outrage prompted the Ministry of Education to start collecting data on bullying cases from 1985 onwards.

These national surveys on bullying in Japan show that there is a tendency for bullies and victims to be classmates. One study, following the second media panic in the 1990s, found that 20% of bullies were "close friends" of the victim (Morita *et al.* 1999, 322). Surveys have also shown that a common form of bullying is ostracism, with bystanders usually being very reluctant to intervene to help the victim (ibid.). Yoneyama Shoko, a scholar of comparative education, goes so far as to say that "Japanese *ijime* distinctively differs from bullying in other societies, however, in that it is *always* collective"

(Yoneyama 1999, 164, emphasis in original). This may be an over-statement, although comparative research confirms the impression that "bullying by large and often female groups is disproportionately common in Japanese schools" (Greimel and Kodama 2011, 37).

The progressive critique of school violence in Japan and efforts to reform the system

Some critics of Japan's education system, including Yoneyama Shoko, have argued that corporal punishment and bullying are not examples of "things going wrong" but actually inevitable features of the structure of the system and essential for its maintenance. Referring to findings from the 1980s that "teachers often take the lead in group punishment of those they consider misfits," journalist Karel van Wolferen observed "the teacher abetting the bully is almost paradigmatic of how the System works" (van Wolferen 1993, 120–21). The "system" referred to here is van Wolferen's term for the giant social and economic control mechanism that dominates all areas of life in Japan, and is the subject of his controversial book *The Enigma of Japanese Power*. Writing a few years after this, Yoneyama ascribes Japanese bullying to "over-conformity" or "over-socialization" (Yoneyama 1999, 166). She also finds clear evidence of teachers participating in bullying and claims this is one sign of "the authoritarian mode of human interaction which is dominant in Japanese schools" (Yoneyama 1999, 168). According to Yoneyama, this authoritarian mode of classroom interaction—whether the bullies are teachers or students—can be directly linked to the suffocating control the Ministry of Education exercises over all levels of the school system. In her view, bullying and other forms of violence in schools fulfill the function of creating generation after generation of docile and conformist citizens who are programmed to obey authority. Future citizens of Japan are taught at an early age the dire consequences of failing to "fit in" and conform to group norms. The adult authority figure (the teacher), the student authority figure (the *sempai*) and the immediate peer group (the homeroom class or club) all play a vital part in making sure that every member of society learns the importance of conformity before they leave school.

Since the 1980s, voices from many quarters have been raising concerns about the extent to which the emphasis on conformity and obedience had gone too far and was not only doing harm to individual children, but also having adverse economic consequences by stifling creative thinking (Neary 2002, 215). In response to these calls, the Ministry of Education introduced a wide range of reforms in 2002 under the label of *yutori kyōiku*. These reforms were designed to allow time for more creative educational projects while reducing some of the pressures of a rote memorization, exam-driven approach to education (Tsuneyoshi 2004). The reduction in the compulsory part of the curriculum led to accusations of "dumbing-down," a sentiment that induced another kind of moral panic when international test scores published in 2004 seemed to show that Japanese children were dropping down world rankings of scholastic achievement. A close analysis of the actual statistics revealed that in most subjects, Japanese students' scores had not declined at all, but their positions in the global league tables had "dropped" because of the inclusion of new countries and territories that did not take part in the previous surveys. Nevertheless, the highly misleading nature of the media's reporting of this invented crisis helped to bring an end to the *yutori kyōiku* reforms, and provided a spur to the conservative backlash (Takayama 2008).

The conservative response to the problem of school violence

Conservatives in Japan tend to respond to the moral panics about bullying and other kinds of violence in schools by blaming the lack of moral education and the emphasis on individual freedom in the post-war system (Schoppa 1991, 49). Like conservatives in other advanced capitalist nations, they see the modern school system as over-emphasizing freedom and individuality, and under-emphasizing responsibility and discipline. Japanese conservatives also draw a connection between teaching traditional moral values and nurturing love of nation. Pride in one's nation, according to this view, is closely linked with self-esteem and respect for one's fellow countrymen.

Liberal Democratic Party (LDP) leader Abe Shinzo, one of the strongest proponents of this "patriotic panacea" view of educational reform, established the Education Rebuilding Council during his first term as prime minister in 2006–07. Against the backdrop of the third media panic in the 2000s about school bullying and violence, Abe used this Council to push through a reform of the Fundamental Law of Education (Yoneyama 2008, 15). His so-called patriotic education reform replaced the 1947 Occupation-era law with one that requires schools to instill a sense among students of, "respect for [Japan's] tradition and culture and a love for the home and country that have served as a cradle for them."

The Education Rebuilding Council did not survive Abe's fall from grace in 2007 when he resigned as prime minister. However, when he returned as prime minister in December 2012, the Council was re-established as the Education Rebuilding Implementation Council. The deliberations of this council coincided with what may come to be seen as the fourth moral panic about violence in schools. Following the "bullycide" of a second-year junior high school boy in Otsu, Shiga Prefecture in October 2012, and a clumsy, failed cover-up by the local Board of Education, the mass media reported a new wave of serious cases of bullying and inadequate responses by relevant authorities. This was unfolding at the same time that the media was featuring the scandal of the abusive basketball coach (mentioned above).

In response to the media panic, Abe directed his Education Rebuilding Implementation Council to compile proposals for anti-bullying legislation and for stricter measures against corporal punishment. The new Council suggested requiring the inclusion of moral education as an independent subject in the curriculum, reviving a proposal made by its previous incarnation back in 2006–07. The debate over moral education has been the source of great controversy throughout the post-war period during which teachers' unions and other progressive organizations have opposed making it a school subject in its own right (Schoppa 1991, 152). The Japanese Left has always been concerned that this would open the door to a government mandated moral code being taught to the nation's youth as in the decades leading up to and during Japan's military aggression from 1931–45. Opponents depict moral education as a recipe for instilling a war-mongering hyper-nationalism. Advocates of making moral education an independent school subject, including the conservative *Yomiuri* newspaper, argue that it would help prevent bullying by nurturing "students' natural human inclination to be considerate of other people's feelings" (*Yomiuri Shimbun* editorial, March 1, 2013).

When it comes to corporal punishment, conservatives are often ambivalent about the law since they believe that *taibatsu* is necessary to promote proper values and discipline. Sports coaches with a reputation for toughness seek to inculcate *konjō* ("fighting spirit" or "willpower") and *seishin* ("spirit") when training their teams (Miller 2009, 246–47). These are values dear to the heart of most conservatives, and thus over-enthusiastic coaches often step over the line between strict discipline and physical violence with impunity.

There are signs, however, that this tolerance for a certain amount of corporal punishment may be waning. In the case of the basketball player in Osaka who committed suicide after being beaten, the mayor of the city, Hashimoto Toru, strongly condemned the coach's actions and apologized to the parents. Hashimoto, a high-profile conservative, admitted that he once condoned physical punishment by coaches, but subsequently changed his mind because of doubts that such methods are effective. However, public sentiments backed the coach, so on Adult's Day 2013 he backtracked, telling the crowd of new 20 year olds that in some cases *taibatsu* might be justified.

Miller asserts that the traditional authoritarian style of coaching in Japan is gradually "giving way to and being challenged by 'scientific' coaching methods which emphasize the teaching of skills (*gijutsu*), reliance on self-discipline and a 'thinking' approach to sports" (Miller 2009, 247). However, old-school methods remain deeply embedded in Japan's sports culture and there is widespread support for the coach and his methods.

The political debate about "groupism" and individuality

Serious efforts to put an end to corporal punishment and reduce bullying in schools are clearly part of a trend to stress the importance of the individual vis-à-vis the group. Anthropologist Peter Cave has traced the discourse about "individuality" in Japanese education back to the Meiji period when the modern education system was in its infancy (Cave 2007, chapter one). He argues that the "question of whether or not more individuality is needed in education is related to the issue of selfhood in Japan, which has often been seen as stressing the group over the individual" (Cave 2007, 13). Those who are arguing for more individuality, whether they are on the Left or the Right of Japanese politics, are therefore not merely asking for a modified curriculum or revamped classroom management, but are calling for fundamental changes to the Japanese notion of self. This may go a long way to explaining the great difficulties reformers have had in getting reforms implemented.

One of the most important organizations promoting a reform agenda in the modern era has been Prime Minister Nakasone's Ad Hoc Council on Education (Rinkyōshin). It issued four highly influential reports between 1985 and 1987. In its first report, "stress on individuality" (*kosei jūshi*) was laid down as the first principal of educational reform (Cave 2007, 17). This resulted in a proposal for a revised national curriculum in 1989 that emphasized pupils' interest and motivation rather than just knowledge and understanding. Many educators on the Left, however, were suspicious of the Nakasone/LDP agenda. They believed that the reforms represented a strategy for introducing neoliberal market principles into education along with intensified academic selection rather than promoting individuality.

Teachers were divided over how to deal with the Rinkyōshin's reform proposals. They were faced with the challenge of placing a greater emphasis on individuality while at the same time maintaining their commitment to egalitarianism. The granting of greater choices to students carried the implicit risk of increasing inequality within the education system, anathema to many union members. The issue was so controversial that it was one of the causes of the split in the Japan Teachers Union (Nikkyōso) in 1989, as some union leaders backed many of the reforms while others resisted them all (Aspinall 2001, 55–56).

The new discourse on children's rights

In parallel with Rinkyōshin's emphasis on individuality, another discourse was emerging to challenge traditional views of the role of the individual in Japan's education system. This was the discourse about the rights of the child. The 1947 Constitution introduced the concept of individual rights to Japanese law, but as political scientist Ian Neary points out, "neither those in senior positions in Tokyo nor the leaders of local communities had much familiarity with ideas of rights. Far more familiar was the idea that individuals and groups should set aside their selfish desires and work for the good of the community and the state" (Neary 2002, 16). If the concept of rights for adults was unfamiliar to many Japanese at first, the concept of rights for children was completely alien. Children continued to be taught, at home and in school, the values of group conformity, social hierarchy and proper family roles.

Before the 1970s, political arguments about education in Japan had never brought up the subject of children's rights per se. During the 1980s, however, international developments in this area forced Japanese educators to face up to novel concepts. The United Nations (UN) Convention on the Rights of the Child came into force in 1990 and was ratified by Japan in 1994. It is based upon the so-called "three 'p's": children's needs for a balance of "provision," "protection" and "participation." Classical liberal theory on human rights distinguishes between positive rights (the right to be given something, like education, housing, employment, health care), and negative rights (the right to be left alone by the state and by others in one's own private sphere where one can hold one's own political and religious views and express them without fear of censure). Thus, the right to provision clearly is an example of the former, and the right to protection and participation could combine both positive and negative rights. For example, the protection of an individual child requires the action of parents, guardians and/or the state, but at the same time the purpose of protection is to allow the child to grow into a free-thinking individual, confident that their views will be tolerated by society.

Both the Japanese Left and the Japanese Right have been much more comfortable advocating positive rights than negative rights for children. The Ministry of Education could claim genuine achievement, for example, in getting over 90% of boys and girls to stay in full-time education until the age of 18. The numbers going on to higher and further education are also impressive, and Japan boasts very good results in science and mathematics when compared to other nations. The progressive opposition complains about imposition from above in the education system—for example, the government's enforcement of respect for the national flag and anthem—but values the teaching of group-centered ideals in the classroom. Left-wing and other progressive teachers want to teach children the values of sharing and selflessness as well as group solidarity. Both Left and Right, therefore, are dedicated to the protection of children (defending their positive rights), but both sides are ambivalent about the concept of negative rights when applied to children. The *yutori kyōiku* reforms aimed at nurturing these rights, for example, by promoting freedom of choice and more creativity, but this agenda generated a backlash across the ideological spectrum favoring a more structured and disciplined education.

Conclusion

In the business newspaper *Nikkei Weekly* an influential businessman, Inamori Kazuo, was asked why Japan had failed to produce companies to rival Apple, Microsoft and Google (September 10, 2012). He replied that the environment in Japan is very bad for venture firms: "as the saying goes, the nail that sticks up gets hammered back down." He links this with the "strong group mentality" of the Japanese people. This is presumably the same "group mentality" described by Benjamin Duke at the start of this chapter. When Duke did his research in the 1970s and early 1980s, in an era when American fears about a rising Japan animated public discourse, Japanese education was envied and the group mentality was seen as a strength of the Japanese economy. Since the asset bubble burst at the outset of the 1990s, these erstwhile virtues are usually portrayed as significant handicaps.

The school is one of the key places where children learn how to conform to the rules and expectations of the group, and has been the focus of long-running controversies as well as short-lived moral panics about what the proper relationship between the individual and the group should be. The Japanese proverb about the nail being hammered down if it dares to stick out has become something of a cliché, but the violent nature of the imagery invoked is particularly apt to those who experience the physical violence that is sometimes directed at those who do not "fit in" for one reason or another. Some critics have argued that these victims are the collateral damage that is the inevitable result of a rigid system, and have pushed for a more relaxed curriculum, more flexibility and more choice. The return to power in December 2012 of the LDP and Prime Minister Abe Shinzo, however, heralds a different direction for educational reform with a stress on order, discipline and a more thoroughgoing moral education (as defined by ministry-approved textbooks). Only time will tell whether this reduces bullying and corporal punishment, or whether the blindness to the nexus of these forms of violence will persist.

Note

1 "Moral panic" is used here in the sense outlined by Stanley Cohen when he describes how "[a] condition, episode, person or group of persons emerges to become defined as a threat to societal values and interests [and] its nature is presented in a stylised and stereotypical fashion by the mass media" (Cohen 2002, 1).

Bibliography

Aspinall, Robert W. (2001) *Teachers Unions and the Politics of Education in Japan*, Albany: State University of New York Press.

——(2006) "Using the Paradigm of 'Small Cultures' to Explain Policy Failure in the Case of Foreign Language Education in Japan," *Japan Forum* 18(2): 255–74.

Cave, Peter (2007) *Primary School in Japan: Self, Individuality and Learning in Elementary Education*, London and New York: Routledge.

Cohen, Stanley (2002) *Folk Devils and Moral Panics*, Abingdon: Routledge.

Doi, Takeo (1971) *The Anatomy of Dependence*, Tokyo: Kodansha.

Duke, Benjamin (1986) *The Japanese School: Lessons for Industrial America*, New York and London: Praeger.

Greimel, Elfriede and Kodama, Makiko (2011) *Bullying from a Cross-cultural Perspective: A Comparison between Austria and Japan*, Hiroshima University Institutional Repository, ir.lib.

hiroshima-u.ac.jp/metadb/up/kiyo/AA1244667X/JEducSci_4_29.pdf (accessed March 21, 2013).

LeTendre, Gerald (2000) *Learning to be Adolescent: Growing up in U.S. and Japanese Middle Schools*, New Haven and London: Yale University Press.

Miller, Aaron (2009) "*Taibatsu*: 'Corporal Punishment' in Japanese Socio-cultural Context," *Japan Forum* 21(2): 233–54.

Morita, Yohji, Haruo, Soeda, Kumiko, Soeda and Mitsuru, Taki (1999) "Japan," in P.K. Smith *et al.* (eds) *The Nature of School Bullying*, London and New York: Routledge.

Neary, Ian (2002) *Human Rights in Japan, South Korea and Taiwan*, London and New York: Routledge.

Ohira, Mitsuyo (2002) *So Can You*, trans. John Brennan, Tokyo: Kodansha International.

Okano, Kaori and Tsuchiya, Motonori (1999) *Education in Contemporary Japan: Inequality and Diversity*, Cambridge: Cambridge University Press.

Olweus, Dan (1999) "Norway," in P.K. Smith *et al.* (eds) *The Nature of School Bullying*, London and New York: Routledge.

Peak, Lois (1991) *Learning to Go to School in Japan: The Transition from Home to Preschool Life*, Berkeley, CA: University of California Press.

Schoppa, L.J. (1991) *Education Reform in Japan: A Case of Immobilist Politics*, London and New York: Routledge.

Takayama, Keita (2008) "The Politics of International League Tables: PISA in Japan's Achievement Crisis Debate," *Comparative Education* 44(4): 387–407.

Tobin, Joseph J., Hsueh, Yeh and Karasawa, Mayumi (2009) *Preschool in Three Cultures Revisited*, University of Chicago Press.

Tsuneyoshi, Ryoko (2004) "The New Japanese Educational Reforms and the Achievement 'Crisis' Debate," *Educational Policy* 18(2): 364–94.

van Wolferen, Karel (1993) *The Enigma of Japanese Power*, Tokyo: Tuttle.

White, Merry (1994) *The Material Child: Coming of Age in Japan and America*, Berkeley, CA: University of California Press.

Yoneyama, Shoko (1999) *The Japanese High School: Silence and Resistance*, London and New York: Routledge.

——(2008) "The Era of Bullying: Japan Under Neoliberalism," *The Asia-Pacific Journal* 1(3:09), December 31.

19 Hidden behind Tokyo

Observations on the rest of Japan

John Mock

This chapter extends the reader's gaze beyond the metropolitan core (Tokyo–Osaka) that dominates the English-language literature on Japan. It is important to understand rural, small town and smaller city Japan because most Japanese do not live in the core and most of the land area of the Japanese archipelago lies outside the boundaries of Japan's urbanized confines. There is a very different dynamic in rural and small town Japan, where there has been a dramatic level of depopulation and aging and economic stagnation. In contrast, the metropolitan core is still growing, and looks prosperous and modern in spite of two decades of economic stagnation. This chapter features the "other" Japan, the one hidden behind the metropolitan core, by examining changes in land use, demography, the rural and small town economy, transportation, communications and architecture. The relative neglect of this topic is striking because regional Japan is both idealized as a repository of "traditions" and values while also denigrated as backward. The declining "other" has been subjected to extensive government policy interventions, but as I argue here, these frequently have been misguided. I also analyze how "other" Japan is an interesting arena of identity politics in a nation that has experienced massive socio-economic convulsions in the post-World War II era.

Population distribution

Looking at Japan in very broad terms, the metropolitan corridor stretches from Kanto to Kansai or Tokyo/Saitama/Chiba to Osaka/Kobe. Both ends are massive metropolitan sprawls with multiple civic entities. In the middle is the enormous Nagoya industrial area. However, even riding the shinkansen (the high speed "bullet train") from Tokyo to Osaka (right through the heart of the conurbation), it is evident that much of the landscape is more sparsely settled and all along the route one sees virtually uninhabited mountainous areas. Outside of this metropolitan corridor, there are few large urban nodes and they are spaced more widely apart. In between are substantial regional cities and between those are a large number of fairly small cities.

In terms of scale, metropolitan Tokyo (including Yokohama/Kawasaki) has about 35 million people, a bit less than 25% of the total population of the country. Metropolitan Osaka is home to another 10 million, while Fukuoka and Sapporo metropolitan areas have populations of about 2 million. Sendai, Hiroshima and several other "regional cities" have about a million residents each. The next tier, which includes a lot of prefectural capital cities, ranges from about 200,000 to 600,000 residents. To be considered a "city" (*shi*) in Japan, a civic unit must have a minimum of 30,000 people, but there is no density requirement. For example, in the last round of administrative consolidation (*gappei*) in 2005, "cities" like Kita Akita City in central Akita Prefecture, about 400 kilometers (km) north of Tokyo, were formed by consolidating four very sparsely populated townships, themselves the result of an earlier consolidation in 1955. Kita Akita City does have just over the 30,000 population minimum, spread out over a land area of 1,152 square km (km^2) (see Figure 19.1). The population density is 31.1 people/km^2 compared to more than 14,000 people/km^2 in the central 23 wards of Tokyo and 2,627 people/km^2 for the three prefectures (*Itto Sanken*) of the metropolitan area (Japan Statistics Bureau n.d.).

Demographers use the term "densely inhabited district" (DID) instead of city because of precisely this confusion. In this usage, a DID has a population of more than 5,000 residents, but a density of at least 1,000 people/km^2. Obviously, Kita Akita City does not come anywhere near this definition since about 92% of its area is forest. All of the population (and all of the connecting roads, farms, fields and everything else) are in the remaining 8%. This gets further complicated by the Japanese use of the term *inaka*, often translated into English as "rural" to mean everything outside of the metropolitan core, even very large cities such as Sapporo and Fukuoka, which are clearly not "rural."

Using Akita as an example of one of the less populous prefectures, it is interesting to note that while incomes in Akita are much lower, costs—particularly land costs—are also much lower and dwellings are much larger, while household size is bigger than the national average. There is also a higher suicide rate in Akita. Finally, subverting national assumptions about the backwardness of "other" Japan, the National Achievement Test, in which elementary school fifth graders are compared across the nation, Akita regularly places first.

Historical context

By the outbreak of World War II in 1941, Japan's population had surged from around 30 million in 1868 to 70 million, with about 21% living in relatively big cities. With the end of the war, roughly 8 million Japanese, military and civilian, who were scattered across Japan's Asian empire, were repatriated. This repatriation was primarily to rural Japan because of war devastation in urban areas and lack of food in Japanese cities. From about 1955, as Japan's surging economy generated jobs in urban areas, many small towns, rural areas and even small cities experienced a declining population, even as the overall Japanese population continued to increase up until 2007.

During the Allied Occupation, the government carried out an agrarian land reform that targeted the high incidence of rural poverty by redistributing land from landlords to the previously landless sharecropping cultivators. This reform affected some 4.5 million small-scale farm households, catapulting them out of poverty. In this period of pre-mechanized wet rice agriculture, holdings averaged a bit less than 2 acres, the amount of land a farm family was able to work without additional help. While enormously beneficial, this reform also had the detrimental effect of promoting very small-scale farming at a cost to productivity and viability.

During the Japanese "miracle" of rapid economic growth during the 1950s and 1960s, young people were pulled into the industrial belts around the major cities along the Tokyo-Nagoya-Osaka metropolitan axis, a massive migration that was exacerbated by national, regional and prefectural policies that promoted urbanization and resulted in a narrow concentration of economic activity. The "pull" from the small cities, towns

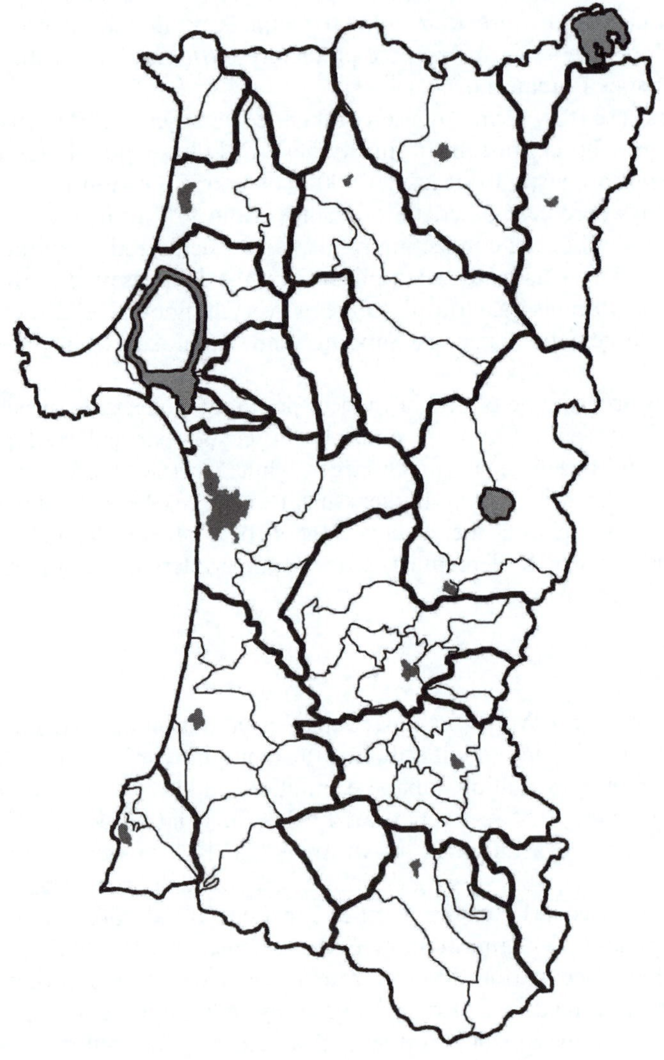

Figure 19.1 Consolidation in Akita Prefecture
Note: The light lines are the pre-consolidation boundaries, the dark lines are the post-consolidation boundaries, the grey irregular shapes are DIDs.

Table 19.1 Statistical overview, Tokyo, Akita and national average

Category	*Tokyo*	*Ranking*	*Akita*	*Ranking*	*National Average*
Density: persons/km^2	5,751	#1	99	#45	343
Unemployment rate	4.7%	#18	5.7%	#7	5.1%
Living space/dwelling (m^2)	63.94	#47	139	#2	–
Commercial land cost/m^2	¥1,551,400	#1	¥39,000	#47	¥156,857
Residential land cost/m^2	¥323,300	#1	¥19,200	#47	¥55,351
Prefectural income per capita	¥4,851,900	#1	¥2,310,600	#42	¥3,068,900
Life expectancy (male)	79.82	#14	78.22	#46	79.59
Life expectancy (female)	86.39	#22	85.93	#39	86.35
Suicide (male)/million	26.8	#46	63.46	#1	34.00
Suicide (female)/million	13.17	#19	22.99	#1	12.95
Male doctors/million men	452.24	#12	384.12	#30	383.70
Female doctors/million women	158.19	#1	62.67	#38	85.04
Total physicians/million	303.71	#2	213.63	#34	230.40
Murder/million	0.349	#40	0.416	#38	0.530
National achievement test	64.7	#7	69.2	#1	63.1

Source: (Statistics Japan, the rankings are based on 47 prefectures)

and rural areas was primarily economic and social. Not only were there relatively well-paid jobs, but it was also considered modern and fashionable, even for middle school graduates, to head for the big city. This process, starting in about 1955, quite literally drained young people from the fringes and rural heartland of Japan into the big cities.

21st-century Japan

In his introductory book on Japanese society, Yoshio Sugimoto points out that while Americans and many other outsiders have an image of the "average" Japanese worker as being a young to middle-aged man who is a permanent lifetime employee of a large company, the "real" average Japanese worker is a middle-aged woman working as a part-time employee in a small company (Sugimoto 2010, 1). In a very broad sense, one could make the same point about Japan as a whole. Many outsiders (and not a few "insiders") think of Japan as a terribly crowded urban metropolis, essentially equating downtown Tokyo with "Japan." Such urban chauvinism is not unique to Japan (e.g. the New Yorker's view of the United States featuring the Manhattan skyline against the backdrop of a flat and generally undifferentiated landscape), but is everywhere misleading.

So while there is value in looking at the "famous" part of Japan, the great cities and the well-known historical sites, it is also worth noting that these highlights bypass most of Japan, the "other half," in effect. Most Japanese, about 60%, live in smaller cities, small towns or even the truly rural countryside. Further, most of Japan, probably about 80% of the land area is fairly sparsely populated—a far cry from the ubiquitous image of crowded Tokyo commuter trains.

Non-metropolitan Japan

In much of Japan, the overwhelming majority of areas are both losing population and rapidly aging (see Figures 19.2, 19.3 and 19.4, with Akita as an example of

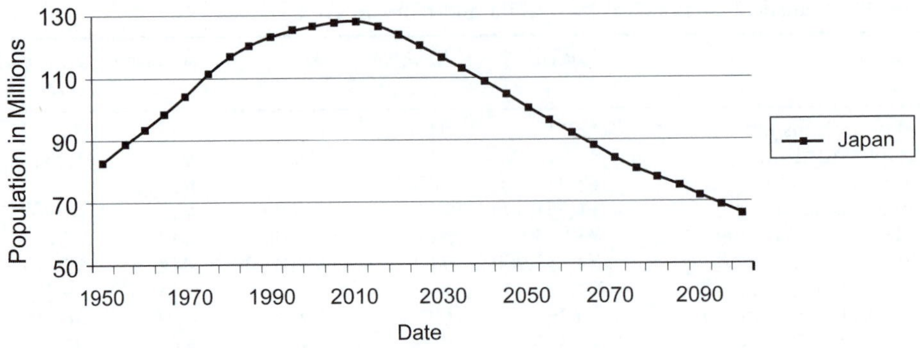

Figure 19.2 Population of Japan: historic and projected

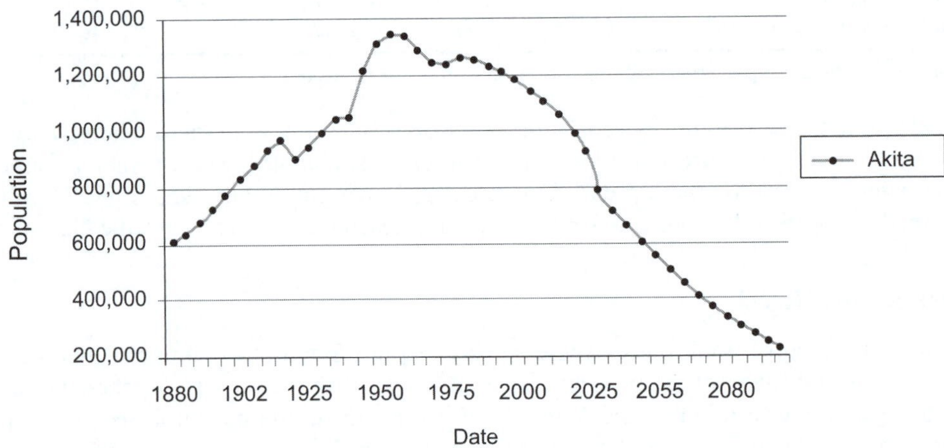

Figure 19.3 Population of Akita: historic and projected

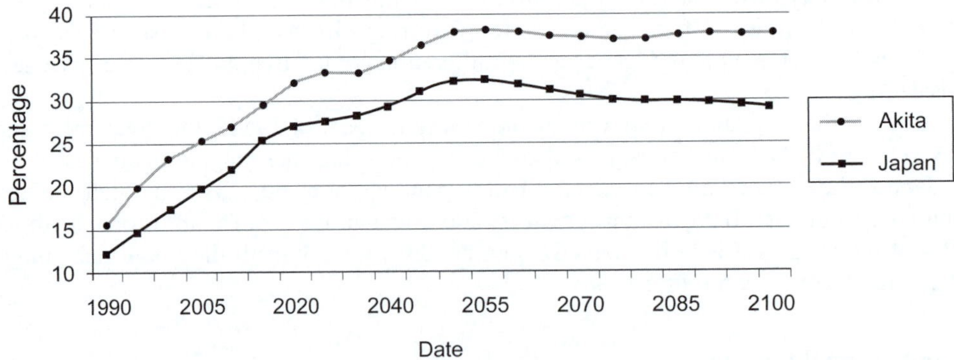

Figure 19.4 Aging population of Japan and Akita, % of 65+

non-metropolitan Japan). The overall population of the country is decreasing with a birthrate far below replacement rate and minimal migration into the country. Due to net urban migration, the less densely populated spaces are losing population while the more densely populated areas are gaining population. Further, rural out migration involves mostly younger people, leaving behind higher concentrations of older people in the less populated areas. For a variety of reasons, including changing agricultural practices and governmental policies, the economies of non-metropolitan Japan are quite weak and prospects for substantial improvement are limited.

Given this general overview, however, one must note that there are major differences among the various parts of non-metropolitan Japan. The Japanese archipelago, a collection of more than 30,000 islands, mostly volcanic and tectonically active, has an enormous range of different geographical and environmental characteristics.

Obviously, in a short essay like this, it is impossible to examine these variations in detail, but it is useful to explore some general themes and see how specific areas fit.

Much of Japan, by area and population, is outside of the DIDs. As noted above, non-metropolitan Japan is depopulating and aging the most rapidly (see Figure 19.4). There are several reasons for this, such as stagnation and declining prospects in agriculture, fisheries and forestry; rise of educational levels; governmental policies at various levels that pull young people into cities; job opportunities; and widespread perceptions about the "uncoolness" of rural life endlessly reinforced in the mass media.

Agriculture, fisheries and forestry: Agriculture

These three areas come under the rather tight control of the central government ministry, currently called the Ministry of Agriculture, Fisheries and Forestry (MAFF). At the end of World War II and really up to the beginning of the 1970s, Japanese agriculture was still largely not mechanized. Part of this had to do with technical difficulties, adapting tractors, for example, to work in wet rice fields and coming up with a mechanical means for transplanting rice seedlings. In the 1970s, tractors suitable for "rototilling" wet rice fields and "walk behind" mechanical translators, capable of planting two rows at a time, were introduced. The tractors were relatively expensive and farmers' cooperatives tended to buy them and share their use among their members. This was also true of rice drying machines that were collectively maintained.

Over the next two decades, up until the 1990s, the technology improved with modern "riding" rice transplanters capable of planting four to six rows at once, small combines that can harvest in dried rice fields (still fairly soft ground) using caterpillar treads (the early versions bagging the rice, while later versions can transfer directly into trucks without bagging) and other innovations like laser devices for making rice fields perfectly flat (necessary for even flooding). Further, with increasing incomes gained from non-agricultural employment, farmers were more likely to own their own tractors, transplanters and drying machines.

The result of these innovations was to increase massively the capital outlay needed to engage in rice farming and, at the same time, substantially decrease the amount of labor needed. This declining need for labor along with the decrease in rice subsidies, forced family members to seek non-agricultural employment. The peak need for labor, during planting and harvesting seasons, can be met by non-agriculturally employed family members taking a day or two off in the spring and again in the fall.

The countryside, therefore, looks very different than it used to, particularly in the very common mountainous areas (approximately 75% of Japan has a slope of 15° or more). Where Japan had a "groomed" look in the early 1950s—the *satoyama* ("village mountain") look that evokes nostalgia among the elderly—the current situation is quite different. In the past, relatively dense, if small, hamlets were clustered in the valleys with the habitations very close to each other, surrounded by rice fields and some dry fields interspersed with some fruit trees. The inhabitants intensively worked not only the fields, wet and dry, but they also utilized the surrounding area, called the *satoyama* (里山 literally "hamlet mountain," or "village mountain") even if the area was not really a mountain; pastoral remoteness was the key feature. Wood for fuel and building purposes was taken from the forests. Grassland was maintained by frequent burning to prevent the succession of brush and trees. The grass was cut and used as fertilizer in the rice fields. Even further away, *sansai* (山菜 "mountain vegetables") were gathered to supplement the diet.

The current habitation pattern is quite different. First, there are far fewer people and those who remain are quite a bit older, in many cases limiting their physical activity. Second, the whole pattern of agriculture has changed. Whereas in the past, hillsides were burned and the grass cut and brought to the rice fields as fertilizer, now chemical fertilizer is widely used, often purchased at the local JA (Farm Cooperative). Similarly, firewood (or locally made charcoal) is no longer the primary fuel. Kerosene can also be ordered from the JA and delivered to the front door. Thus, the forest has returned (or been replanted, see below) and the open spaces and commons have not been maintained.

Third, with improving transportation systems, particularly better road networks and the acquisition by farmers of their own trucks, commercial fruit farming has become more common. Fourth, while *sansai* are still prized and the gathering of *sansai* is done with great enthusiasm in much of mountainous Japan, and sold at a huge mark-up at fancy supermarkets and department stores in Tokyo, the vegetable material gathered is no longer an essential part of the diet, but rather is considered to be "good for health" and a dietary supplement in a more affluent society. Gathering *sansai* has gone from being an important part of the subsistence diet to a foraging "hobby" with the exception of "professional" *sansai* collectors.

The net result is that land use is far less extensive than it was in the past. Not only has the population become much smaller, and much more aged, but there is also much less land in use. This means that more than 90% of the area of some townships has no human habitation. Much of this has been reforested, mainly with *sugi* (Japanese cedar) something of a rural revenge on city dwellers as great plumes of cedar pollen (*kafun*) are swept into the lowland urban areas, causing widespread pollen fever. In less mountainous areas, there are empty fields and in much of rural Japan, empty houses are common. In what was Ani machi, now part of Kita Akita City, the percentage of abandoned houses doubled from 6% to 13% between 1996 and 2005.

In the non-mountainous areas, those that have not been overwhelmed by urban sprawl, the situation is somewhat similar, but not as extreme. There are, however, empty fields and in many towns, even in the flatlands, a lot of empty houses. The economics and demographics of agriculture are such that it simply is not sustainable in its current form. Japan grows more rice than it usually consumes. Therefore, the government has reduced the amount of land allocated to rice by limiting subsidies, but there is still usually a surplus. In addition, as part of international trade agreements, Japan purchases some rice from other countries, most of which is used for industrial purposes or given away to poorer countries as food aid. The net result is that the tiny farms simply do not produce sufficient income to support a family. Overwhelmingly, Japan's farms are run on a part-time basis with most farming households depending on other sources of income. Future prospects look bleak as the average age of farmers has crept into the late sixties and there are very few young farmers. Farming is not "cool" and it is very difficult to make it a full-time sustainable occupation or to find a wife. With a declining and aging population, there is a strong incentive for consolidation of small plots, but uncultivated fields tend not be put on the market because it is viewed as an unfilial selling-off of the patrimony. Thus, even if a young person wants to be a farmer, and has sufficient capital to purchase land, it is extremely difficult to acquire large, economically viable plots of land.

Lilliputian plots prevent productivity increases that could enhance the competitiveness of Japanese farming in the face of increasing international pressures to open the agricultural market as discussed by George Mulgan in Chapter 2. This is partly a legacy of the Occupation-era land reform following World War II and partly the policy failures of MAFF and the stifling influence of JA. Land reform tied successive generations of (mainly) oldest sons to farms that have become economically non-viable (hence the movement to additional non-agricultural employment). Combined with the very conservative nature of MAFF, changes in agricultural practices—one might almost say even elementary rationalization of agriculture—became, and remains, essentially impossible. The result is the current situation with the massive overproduction of rice that is too expensive to be sold on the world market, underproduction of fruit and vegetables, and the inability of the country to grow anything like enough food to feed itself; food self-sufficiency is about 40% but this could be increased substantially.

Fisheries

The fisheries industry is clearly a critical component for coastal Japan. As with agriculture, in the early post-war years, fisheries and aquaculture were largely not mechanized, but the processes of mechanization had already started because many of the technical aspects had already been worked out elsewhere. Also like the agricultural sector, fisheries and aquaculture participants were largely locked into cooperatives and held under the firm hand of MAFF, ensuring that the fishing industry essentially became less and less economically viable. The maintenance of tiny, unsustainable ports and the lack of consolidation of ports or processing plants has undermined the economic viability of the industry, although aquaculture seems to be much more sustainable than fisheries. The depletion of fish stocks through over-fishing continues and threatens the future of local fisheries. Conservation measures have achieved some marginal successes such as the re-establishment of *hatahata*, a coastal fish, in Akita, but this is a rare exception.

Many coastal communities are poor because fisheries-related income is insufficient and there has been limited success with diversification measures. It is these communities that face the risk of extinction and thus they have been eager to attract any business that could reverse their declining fortunes. As Aldrich points out in Chapter 6, the nuclear power industry has targeted such vulnerable communities by offering them inducements to host nuclear reactors. Such hosting communities were reassured that the reactors posed no risk, but now the 150,000 people displaced by the three meltdowns and hydrogen explosions at Fukushima better understand the risks—as do the prefecture's farmers and fishermen who have lost their livelihoods because nobody wants to eat what they are selling due to radioactive contamination of a large swath of land and ocean around the damaged power plant. These displaced and ravaged communities get little consolation from the Fukushima nuclear plant operator's belated admission that the accident could have been avoided if it had acted responsibly and adopted appropriate safety countermeasures. They were expendable.

Forestry

Forestry is the area suffering the most from misguided MAFF policies. During World War II, Japan deforested its mountains (and those of Korea, incidentally) in an effort to sustain the war effort. After World War II, thus, there was a rather desperate need for reforestation. In the post-World War II period, labor was very inexpensive and the decision was made to clear the remnants of the mixed hardwood and conifer forests and replant with *cryptomeria* (*sugi*, "Japanese cedar"). *Sugi* is a tree that is a fairly good building material, particularly for relatively small structures like individual houses. It is fairly soft and very easily worked, aromatic and aesthetically very pleasing. It also grows quite quickly, reaching maturity in only a few decades. It naturally grows in bottom-land, in the damp soil in valleys, not up on hillsides. However, the decision to plant *sugi* on hillsides as well resulted in an enormous number of monoculture *sugi* plantations where the relatively fragile trees are subject to high winds resulting in considerable damage. *Sug*i cultivation also requires substantial labor to trim the lower branches which allows it to grow straight.

In the post-war period, this made some sense because of the rather urgent need for reforestation but as the decades have passed, serious consequences have appeared including the almost total destruction of the forestry industry in Japan. To just run through the difficulties quickly, first, *sugi* needs substantial labor to produce good building timber. While immediate post-war labor was inexpensive, labor in Japan is now among the most expensive in the world. It is now cheaper to ship in building materials from North America and even Scandinavia than to use domestic *sugi*. In addition, very few young people have any interest, despite a dearth of alternatives, to work in forestry-related employment. It is not easy work.

Second, there are ecological difficulties with *sugi* plantations replacing native hardwoods and conifers. *Sugi* does not produce food for animals (like oak or beech, which produce nuts), although it does provide cover and nesting areas. Thus the variety of animals and plants living in the Japanese mountains, once very numerous, has been greatly reduced and there has been a marked increase in conflict between humans and bears (although that conflict has a number of other related causes). In addition, *sugi* is not self-regenerating in areas like hillsides. In the past, the *zokibayashi*, the mixed hardwood forest, would usually re-grow after cutting with new shoots growing out of the cut trunks. In fact, this "coppicing" technique produces more wood than individual trees, but is not usually employed with *sugi*. What would be optimal would be a mixed hardwood coppice forest.

Third, while many of the *sugi* plantations are technically owned by individuals or collectively by villages or towns, MAFF has had enormous influence in deciding whether or not to harvest particular stands of *sugi*. As mentioned earlier, one of the perceived advantages of *sugi* is that it grows quickly. However, this is now a disadvantage, as some of the *sugi* plantations have become too old to be useful as building material. Fourth, along with everything else, *sugi* produces enormous amounts of pollen every spring and many people suffer from mild-to-severe allergic reactions to *sugi* pollen. Finally, given mountain villages of largely elderly inhabitants, there is a real danger of villages being overshadowed and eventually swallowed by the *sugi* plantations (Knight 2006).

Several decades ago MAFF could have started to replace *sugi* with a mix of native hardwoods and conifers, taking into account the red pine blight that has been a major problem in Japanese forests. However, no such program has been undertaken and, in fact, MAFF seems to resist any such attempts. The official philosophy of MAFF is fairly obvious: preservation of resources and production of food and building material. However, many observers argue that as a very large and intrusive national bureaucracy, the primary motivation appears to be the preservation and expansion of the "territory" under its control (cf. George Mulgan 2000, 2005, 2006). Given institutional inertia and an inclination to preserve the status quo and serve existing vested interests, MAFF discourages innovation. The argument is that the national ministries are inherently unable to adapt well, are primarily interested in maintaining their own power and find little value in actually dealing with the major problems that confront it or that are a consequence of their own misguided policies. It reflects a structural inability to initiate reform, a path dependency that allows problems to fester. Thus, like agriculture and fisheries, forestry seems to be locked into a "no win" situation with an uninspired bureaucracy set in its ways, an aging population, no successors, and no really economically viable product. Meanwhile, severe ecological consequences ensue.

Education

Another major shift has been a huge overall increase in levels of formal education. In the early 1950s, a middle school diploma (six years of elementary school, three years of middle school) was considered sufficient to leave school and move into the work force. Technically, this is still true, with compulsory education only extending through middle school. However, nearly 99% of youth graduates from some form of high school and there is considerable hand wringing about a high school diploma being insufficient for employment. Japan only provides about half the necessary high school seats in public institutions, requiring the other half of high school-age students to attend private schools that are very expensive, especially in relation to rural incomes. Partly as a result of land reform (and the increase in rural family incomes), there has been a big increase over the past half century in the levels of formal education. Currently about half of high school graduates go on to two- or four-year university courses while the remaining half get some other form of post-secondary education such as training programs or *semmon gakko* ("specialty" schools).

This shift in the level of formal education levels has two major effects. The first is the process of going on to high school. Almost all of the high schools are located in DIDs, meaning students living far away from the DIDs must either endure a very long daily commute or actually move to the DID to attend high school. Using Akita as an example (see Figure 19.5), it is clear that almost all of the high schools (the small black squares) are in the DIDs (the irregular shapes). The few high schools not in DIDs are low-level agricultural or commercial high schools. This tilt toward DIDs is further

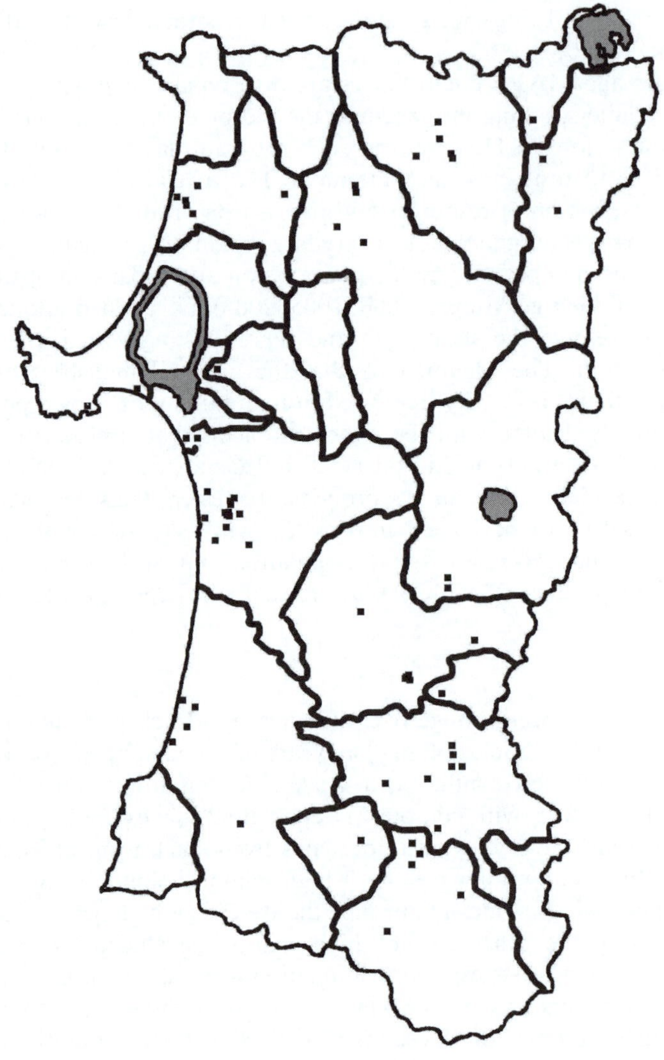

Figure 19.5A High school and DID distribution in Akita
Note: black squares are high schools

Figure 19.5B High school and DID distribution in Akita
Note: irregular grey areas are DIDs

evident in the concentration of tertiary educational institutions, including all of the high-status universities, in large cities or the metropolitan center. There is, in effect, no such thing as a "university town" in Japan; all universities have "urban" campuses. Thus the placement of high schools and tertiary institutions literally pulls young people out of rural areas and into the cities.

There has also been a rise in student expectations as they expect that increased educational levels will translate into good jobs. Rural Japan, partly because of government policies, offers little in the way of occupational choices and there is a major difference in incomes; Tokyo salaries are a bit more than double those in Akita. Tokyo is ¥4,851,900 per person while Akita is ¥2,310,600/person (Statistics Japan n.d.). Certainly there are significant cost of living differences, particularly rent, but for young people the lure of city life transcends pecuniary considerations and is worth the price of escaping what they dread most—the perceived dead-end, fish-bowl life in the countryside

Both at the national and the prefectural level, government-sponsored ventures, like innovative start-up venture capital companies, are concentrated either in the metropolitan center or in prefectural capital cities. This means that even if young people want to live in the countryside, it is very difficult for them to use their education in an appropriate way. There is also a clear implication that "smart" people go to cities, while the more unfortunate stay in the countryside.

It is also important to understand that in rural areas, the previously vibrant local towns are dying. The shopping streets in many fairly large towns have experienced prolonged hard times and many shops are closed, creating what has become known as *shutta-gai*, stretches of downtown commercial districts where the shutters of shop fronts are permanently closed. With the deterioration of the agricultural base of the countryside, the movement of secondary industries into regional cities, the metropolitan core or offshore, and the concentration of newer "information industries" (sometimes called quaternary industries) almost completely into the metropolitan core, the "urban" function of towns and small cities has disappeared. The result is a concomitant loss of population and all the problems of a fundamentally depressed economy. Scenic areas and hot spring areas can rely on tourism, but for most of rural Japan the collapse is profound and irreversible.

Public works

The mainstay of central government support for rural Japan is embodied in the *doken kokka* (construction state) entailing massive spending on public works, some of which may be marginally useful, while others are pure pork barrel and some are environmentally harmful. This is basically the fiscal steroids of the rural economy, funneling contracts to local construction firms and creating an addiction to public works jobs. This is the reality of "cash and carry" rural politics as local political bosses do their part in promoting this "workfare" and in exchange get the "support" necessary to win elections. In reality the local construction firms "outsource" (*marunage*) the jobs to large construction companies based in cities so that the big money is recycled back to the center. Public works are also a means of political control, bribing voters and threatening them with cuts in allocations if they vote incorrectly (against the Liberal Democratic Party—LDP). Some observers also argue that the *doken kokka* prevents the emergence of sustainable local businesses while others blame it for extensive destruction of the natural environment, including covering hillsides and coastlines in concrete, erecting unneeded dams, and building roads and bridges to nowhere.

Thus, there is a cycle of government projects ostensibly helping rural areas that are really designed to mobilize votes for the conservative LDP. The relevant bureaucrats, particularly those of the MAFF and Ministry of Land, Infrastructure and Transport, are in turn rewarded by a legal form of graft called *amakudari*, the "descent from heaven," where they retire from the bureaucracy and are hired, at very high salaries, by the industries they once supervised. This inherent conflict of interest makes the bureaucracy pro-business at the cost of the public interest.

Being "cool"

It is difficult to live in Japan and not notice the constant denigration of "country bumpkins," even as the countryside's natural beauty is extolled. Oddly, former bumpkins wax on about their *furusato* (hometown) and the general population imagines that the "real" Japan, whatever that is, remains resilient in the countryside, and in fact, many Japanese choose to live outside the urban regions even if they have other options. If fact, some people go to great lengths to avoid living in the metropolitan centers. However, there is an explicit and unexamined sense of urban superiority that is no more noticeable than when a former rural denizen returns to the hometown to lord it over those who have been left behind, literally and figuratively.

The romance of the *furusato* as an artifact of extremely rapid urbanization in the 1950s is celebrated twice a year, at *oshogatsu* ("New Year") and *Obon* (the "Festival of Light" in August), when urbanites jam train stations and highways as they flock to meet relatives, former schoolmates and honor ancestors. Of course, as these are extended holidays, the international airports are also busy as rural ties loosen and affluent travelers decide that they might have more fun in Paris or Bali. The government has flailed away on a variety of *furusato* revival plans, mostly white elephant projects, while local entrepreneurs and officials try to figure out what they can offer that affluent Japanese want; *jibiru* (craft beer) is one of the few success stories. Sustainable businesses and industries remain a hope rather than a reality.

Essentially, the larger the population, the "cooler" a place is. Thus, Tokyo is by far the "coolest" place to live and the constant media babble insists that this is where smart young people should go for a happening lifestyle. Osaka is almost as cool, and really the only rival to Tokyo, economically, socially or even linguistically. Big "outside" cities like Sapporo, Kitakyushu, Kyoto, Hiroshima, Nagoya and Sendai are not nearly as cool, but way cooler than smaller cities and towns. The cool quotient keeps diminishing in gradients as the towns get smaller, but nothing is less cool than the boondocks, even if they may be a pleasant place to live or raise a family, because these places exist at the fringes of the mainstream media frame. The hip logic is that only eldest sons who cannot escape, and the really uncool, will remain in rural areas.

Further, if they do, not only will they stay uncool, but they might stay unmarried. First sons may enjoy the advantages of primogeniture, but remain more encumbered by filial obligations and "locked in" to a lifestyle of declining appeal. Eldest sons in rural areas are increasingly marrying non-Japanese women, mainly from the Philippines, but also from Taiwan, China and Thailand. In Akita, the largest "foreign" minority is Chinese men who work in various industries on a short-term basis. However, the second largest "foreign" minority are Filipinas who have married into Akita families

Figure 19.6 Snow can be a complicating factor outside of metropolitan Japan
Source: (Photograph by John Mock)

and who, even though they rarely become Japanese citizens, are usually "permanent" residents (unlike the Chinese men). Small towns and villages even have formalized international introduction services to facilitate this process, with delegations going back and forth. While this has clearly helped "internationalize" the countryside, it also indicates that young Japanese women are now "outsourcing" rural marriage and looking to escape the burdens of "traditional" life and the limited opportunities and financial penalties that entails.

Aesthetics

Even though Japanese architects win many international prizes, much of Japan suffers from a deterioration of architectural quality and the lack of preservation of traditional habitation. In fact, there appears to be an effort to destroy as much of the past as quickly as possible and replace it with the amazingly unattractive. Much of non-metropolitan Japan is becoming a rather unattractive sprawl of shopping centers, semi-pre-fabricated homes and tacky business fronts, many of them tied to the metropolitan center. The Bulgarian architect Milena Metalkova-Markova writes:

> As a result of lack of policies on preservation and the strong drive of local residents to become "modern" by abandoning the traditional style of housing (often trying to catch up with industrialized urban Japan and avoid at all costs the risk of

> being called "backwards", "bound to the past" or "old-fashioned"), the (rural) townscape today is a chaotic agglomeration of uninspiring buildings within a picturesque natural landscape, presenting a serious challenge to any revitalization measures.
>
> (Mock and Metalkova-Markova 2006, 35–36)

This tends to make the countryside a sort of "low-rent" version of the urban core. While there is a sentimental nostalgia about the disappearance of thatch-roofed houses outside of the "ye old village" heritage sites, they are a fire hazard. More importantly, the cheap labor, expertise and availability of thatching material that once made these a logical choice are no longer available and thus this "quintessentially Japanese" symbol of pastoral beauty has become prohibitively expensive.

While there is much to lament about rural depopulation and the decaying, but lasting scars inflicted on the countryside by the *dokken kokka*, "mall-ification" and abandoned human habitat, there is an environmental upside. Ecosystem recovery will not be a recreation of what existed before, but it may be environmentally much healthier and aesthetically less grating, than what existed at the demographic peak.

The future

Peter Matanle and Anthony Rausch (2011), with the Shrinking Regions Research Group, have done a massive study of regional Japan and categorize efforts toward the future as being various combinations of redevelopment, repopulation, recovery and reinvention. The approach taken thus far, at all levels of government, has mainly focused on redevelopment and repopulation. These initiatives have been largely unsuccessful. To the extent that there has been success, it is almost always based on listening to, and empowering, local people and communities. Local knowledge and local initiative with regional and even national support, has—in isolated cases—led to recovery. Following this model, rather than the current centralized model, is a more likely path to success.

While tourism may be economically sustainable in some areas, it is not the answer for all of rural Japan's economic and demographic problems. Further, it is overwhelmingly obvious that tourism brings consequences that many rural areas simply do not want and apparently many areas are actively hostile to developing tourism. Even in those areas eager to welcome more tourists there is often a stunning lack of capacity to deal with foreign tourists and cater to their needs. World Heritage sites like Chusonji in remote Tohoku have adapted and attract large numbers of Chinese visitors, but this is the exception and not the rule.

Essentially, Matanle and Rausch argue that "regional Japan" is an incredibly complex and rich set of areas and that these different areas need to be examined and acted upon according to their individual needs and resources, not with some sort of "one size fits all" solution. They have four specific suggestions: first, while tourism may be successful in some areas, in most areas local industrial development is needed; second, municipal governments and other "players" in regional Japan should look to develop professional brand-creation and brand-management capacity, "with the aim of extracting added value from their inherent cultural and natural assets" (Matanle and Rausch 2011, 432); third, significant immigration is unlikely, so regional planning should assume very much reduced populations; and fourth, there is a need for more research into potential positive outcomes of shrinkage especially involving reductions of human pressure on the environment.

Bibliography

George Mulgan, Aurelia (2000) *The Politics of Agriculture in Japan*, New York: Routledge.

——(2005) *Japan's Interventionist State: The Role of the MAFF*, New York: Routledge.

——(2006) *Power and Pork: A Japanese Political Life*, Canberra: Asia Pacific Press.

Japan Statistics Bureau (n.d.) *Statistics*, Ministry of Internal Affairs and Communications, Statistics Bureau, www.stat.go.jp/data/kokusei/2000/guide/2-01.htm#pos4.

Kelly, William W. (2006) "Rice Revolutions and Farm Families in Tohoku: Why is Farming Culturally Central and Economically Marginal?" in Christopher Thompson and John Traphagan (eds) *Wearing Cultural Styles in Japan: Concepts of Tradition and Modernity in Practice*, Buffalo, NY: SUNY Press.

Knight, John (2006) *Waiting for Wolves: An Anthropological Study of People-Wildlife Relations*, Honolulu: University of Hawai'i Press.

Matanle, Peter and Rausch, Anthony S. (2011) *Japan's Shrinking Regions in the 21st Century: Contemporary Responses to Depopulation and Socioeconomic Decline*, Amherst, New York: Cambria Press.

Ministry of Internal Affairs and Communication (n.d.) *Housing Survey*, www.stat.go.jp/english/data/jyutaku/results.htm.

Mock, John (2006) "The Social Impact of Rural-Urban Shift: Some Akita Examples," in Christopher Thompson and John Traphagan (eds) *Wearing Cultural Styles in Japan: Concepts of Tradition and Modernity in Practice*, Buffalo, NY: SUNY Press.

Mock, John and Metalkova-Markova, Milena (2006) "Social and Cultural Impact of Depopulation in Central Akita," in Ikuo Kawakami, John Mock, Yukiko Sugita and Munehiko Asamizu (eds) *Japan's Globalization*, Tokyo: Kumpul Publishers.

Sugimoto, Yoshio (2010) *Introduction to Japanese Society*, third edition, Cambridge: Cambridge University Press.

Part V

Reforming Japan?

20 Seeking to change Japanese society through legal reform

Matthew J. Wilson

Bolstered by its rapid modernization and societal advancement, Japan has emerged over the past half-century as a world leader. The country enjoys one of the highest standards of living in the world. Its high life expectancy, literacy, per capita income, safety, level of convenience, and overall freedom surpass most countries. Japanese public officials are generally known for their integrity, and enjoy a high level of public trust. Consequently, Japan is renowned for its innovative ideas, advanced technology, overall stability, and quality of life. In fact, emerging countries study and even model their economic and legal systems after Japan as they look to its ideas, economic prowess, and incorporation of foreign influences.

Notwithstanding its achievements, Japan's importance has been discounted since the turn of the century due to its ongoing economic ills and political stagnation. After decades of unparalleled commercial growth and success on the global stage during the latter half of the 20th century, Japan entered an extended period of economic uncertainty known as the "two lost decades." In the early 1990s, Japan's so-called "bubble economy" burst, causing stock prices to plummet, property values to crash, and its economy suddenly to stall (Ito and Mishkin 2006). In search of a solution to combat economic stagnation effectively, policy makers turned to the law. To retool itself and prepare for the future, the government decided to revamp Japan's legal system and bring it closer to the people.

The traditional role of law in Japan and societal reforms

Legal systems and the law influence all segments of society. The law defines important social norms, establishes priorities, and settles the boundaries of acceptable behavior. It influences relationships, politics, and economic activity. Not only does the law incentivize certain behavior, but it also requires recognition and respect. The effectiveness of law essentially depends on either voluntary compliance or enforcement through sanctions, penalties, or extralegal means. Legal systems comprising processes and institutions such as courts, legislatures, and administrative agencies are essentially tasked with articulating, recognizing, and enforcing the law. Effective systems enforce the law in a fair manner while protecting individual rights, ensuring justice, and facilitating public understanding of the process. With globalization and the proliferation of cross-border activities, the role of law has expanded in importance causing many countries to reassess their legal institutions, policies, and principles over the past several decades. Japan is no exception.

Japan has traditionally limited the role of law and the visibility of its legal institutions particularly in comparison to Western nations (Kato 1987). Absent extraordinary circumstances, a typical Japanese citizen would have had little, if any, occasion to come in direct contact with the judicial system. Litigation and crime are less common in Japan than other countries. The cultural pervasiveness of honor, shame, and conflict aversion combined with the emphasis on societal harmony and apologies generally mean that the law and formal legal mechanisms often take a back seat to informal means of conflict resolution. Some have even postulated that the Japanese will sacrifice individualistic aspirations in favor of the preservation of group harmony, and that the typical Japanese citizen will avoid legalist approaches when resolving conflicts arising from personal relationships, social ordering, and commercial dealings (Parker 1988). Upon closer examination, however, systemic barriers have played a major role in discouraging the use of Japan's legal system (Haley 1978). Institutional impediments to justice have historically included excessive court filing fees, lengthy and non-congruous trials, antiquated procedural rules, lack of discovery, low damages awards, limited private causes of action, and an insufficient number of judges and attorneys, particularly outside of metropolitan regions (Wilson 2005).

Although the role of law has often been discounted, legal reforms have historically played a major role in facilitating change in Japan. In the early seventh century, China's Buddhist and Mandarin courts shaped the foundations of the modern Japanese state (Anderson and Masuura 2012). In the mid-1800s, Japan quickly turned to legal reforms to withstand challenges from the Western world, protect itself from unequal treaties, and propel society forward (Oda 2009). Reforms included the adoption of a Western-style constitution in 1889 based on the Prussian model, civil and criminal codes modeled after those in France and Germany, the Diet (Japan's national legislature), and a cabinet system. After the conclusion of World War II, policy makers again employed the law to transform society. When Japan accepted the Potsdam Declaration in 1945, the Supreme Commander of the Allied Powers ("SCAP") assumed control of the country. Overwhelmingly American in its composition, SCAP strived to demilitarize, democratize, and reconstruct the country. To achieve these goals, SCAP turned in large part to legal reform. The first major step was drafting a new constitution. Still unchanged to this day, the Constitution anointed the popularly elected Diet, instead of the emperor, as the supreme body of state power. It expressly limited governmental powers, recognized greater individual rights, and separated church and state. The Constitution declared that sovereignty rested with the citizenry, and sought to equalize the rights of all individuals. It also established a system of checks and balances among the legislative branch, executive branch, and judiciary, which maintained the power of judicial review as a means of guaranteeing individual rights. During the SCAP occupation, Japan also enacted major employment laws that gave workers enhanced rights, new securities laws, an anti-monopoly law, a code of criminal procedure, and education laws that emphasized peace, justice, and respect for individuals.

The new era of revolutionary legal reforms

The socio-economic crisis that ensnared Japan in the final decade of the 20th century again fuelled significant reforms to established laws, policies, and legal institutions. Instead of relying on minor fixes, Japanese political discourse in the mid-1990s shifted towards promoting deregulation, administrative reform, and increased citizen engagement. During Japan's post-war era of unabated economic growth, bureaucratic intervention and administrative regulation were regarded as key ingredients to the country's success. Industry and government often collaborated on research, development, and sales particularly in sectors important to Japan's growth. Companies did not necessarily turn to lawyers for assistance or the judiciary for redress. Rather, they directly engaged in discussions with governmental agencies that almost always required permission to proceed with any major economic activity. Bureaucratic discretion was powerful, and complying with informal administrative guidance was a prerequisite for success. This formula seemed to stall, however, when the "bubble economy" burst and failed to recover. As a result, many started viewing bureaucratic involvement as stifling and demanded substantial change.

In looking for ways to overcome Japan's festering economic problems, policy makers resolved to shift the mindset of a society known for its excessive regulatory control to one that was more globalized, democratized, and open. In theory, fewer regulations would stimulate innovation, encourage competition, create jobs, and reduce dependency on public works projects and other governmental assistance. The goal was enabling free commerce while allowing the courts to address violations of the law. In essence, the reforms would "reposition the public as actors, not bystanders, in governance" of the country, and the public would shift from "governed objects" to "governing subjects" (Justice System Reform Council 2001). Once the laws and regulations were more transparent and open, there was hope that the citizenry would become more engaged in the legal system.

What started as a limited discussion about reducing governmental involvement to stimulate the economy quickly evolved into a wholesale re-evaluation of Japan's political, economic, and legal structure. In the decade from 1996 through 2005, law makers initiated a cascade of legislation that surpassed significantly the original proposals by reform advocates. These legal reforms targeted companies, financial institutions, the legal system, and entire citizenry.

To advance legal reforms, the Diet passed Law No. 68 of 1999, effectually creating the Justice System Reform Council (JSRC) or Shiho Seido Kaikaku Shingikai at the behest of Prime Minister Obuchi Keizo (1998–2000). Faced with a sense of crisis, the JSRC was tasked with looking at structurally reforming Japan's legal, political, and administrative systems. It was also charged with clarifying "the role to be played by justice in Japanese society in the 21st century" (Justice System Reform Council 2001), and proposing measures that would realize a justice system that is easy for the people to use, facilitates public participation, strengthens the legal profession, and improves the judicial infrastructure.

Unlike past discussions regarding legal and civic reforms, which were limited to justice system insiders, Japan reached out to a more diverse group to examine existing systems and recommend changes. The 13 JSRC members, all approved by the Diet, consisted of members of the legal profession (a former judge, former prosecutor, and practicing attorney) as well as legal academics, professors from non-law fields, leaders from industry, a consumer advocate, a labor leader, and a famous novelist (Saegusa 2009). This composition enabled a fundamental re-examination of the justice system.

Between July 1999 and June 2001, the JSRC convened 63 meetings, solicited public input, and promoted transparency by releasing meeting minutes and an interim report (Katsuta 2010). They also intensively studied foreign legal systems for possible reform models. On June 21, 2001, the JSRC issued its final report recommending changes to the legal system (Justice System Reform Council 2001). True to form, Japanese law reformers sought to honor traditions while looking to improve policies and systems through the integration of ideas from abroad. The report called for 13 major changes to Japan's legal system and advanced a more user-friendly justice system that facilitated greater access to legal assistance, promoted public participation, and reinforced the administration of justice. The specific goals underlying the report arose from three pillars of fundamental reform, namely: (1) a legal profession "rich both in quality and quantity"; (2) a popular base in which citizens' trust in the legal system is enhanced through their participation in legal proceedings; and (3) a justice system that "shall be made easier to use, easier to understand, and more reliable." According to the JSRC, this could be accomplished by significant revisions to legal education, the legal profession, public access to the justice system, and fundamental laws such as the civil and commercial codes.

Japanese law makers quickly and uniformly adopted most of the JSRC's recommendation reforms without significant political infighting. One such reform was the Justice System Reform Promotion Act of 2001. Consequently, the Japanese Cabinet established the Office for Promotion of Justice System Reform (OPJSR) to facilitate reform and take the lead in enacting relevant legislation. Within its first few years, the OPJSR advanced and the Diet passed dozens of major reforms including, among others, civil litigation reforms designed to accelerate lawsuits, improve procedural processes, and improve public access; modifications to the criminal justice system by streamlining pretrial proceedings, expediting trials, and improving the court-appointed defense counsel system; and substantial changes to the dispute resolution system (Wilson 2010a, 2010b). Another key aspect of the reforms related to the creation of specialized courts. Understanding the impact of intellectual property (IP) on the Japanese economy and society, the reformers felt that the judiciary should assume an even greater role in protecting IP rights. As such, Japan created the Intellectual Property High Court in April 2005 to hear appeals on patent rulings made by the district courts and Japanese Patent Office. Arguably, however, the reforms with the greatest impact arose from modifications to the legal profession and introduction of public participation in the criminal justice system.

Efforts to create a legal profession that is rich in quality and quantity

Reforms targeting the quantity and quality of the legal profession were historic. In 2001, prior to the reforms, Japan had only 18,243 *bengoshi* or licensed lawyers. As of 2012, Japan had increased its lawyer population to 32,088, which translated to approximately one attorney for every 4,100 people (Japan Federation of Bar Associations 2013). By comparison, the United States has nearly 1.25 million licensed lawyers, or about one attorney for every 273 people (American Bar Association 2013). Due to the scarcity of lawyers in Japan, these professionals were primarily responsible for litigation-related matters, while non-lawyers engaged in legal activities typically handled by Western lawyers such as commercial transactions, corporate matters, intellectual property, employment, bankruptcy, probate, and others. Japanese lawyers were overwhelmingly concentrated in the Tokyo and Osaka metropolitan areas. In fact, many rural areas had little or no local access to legal assistance. As of 1999, 72 out of the 203 districts courts had either no lawyer or just one lawyer in their districts (Saegusa 2009). The limited number of licensed attorneys was problematic on other levels too. On a global scale, Japanese companies encountered more conflicts with foreign companies. However, they were significantly disadvantaged without an adequate number of Japanese attorneys capable of advising them on cross-border matters. Domestically, Japanese businesses also needed more lawyers to handle increasingly complex non-litigation matters. This need was compounded with Japan's shift to deregulation.

To become a licensed attorney in Japan, one has always had to pass the national bar examination (NBE or *shihou shiken*). Before the recent legal reforms, NBE applicants were not required to hold a law degree, or even a university degree for that matter (West 2007). Administered only once per year, the NBE was extremely competitive, as the government set the pass rate at 3% or lower (Saegusa 2009). For those few applicants who passed the NBE, it normally took over five attempts before succeeding. Between 1960 and 1990, only approximately 500 applicants were allowed to pass the NBE on a yearly basis. From this point until the recent reforms, the number of successful test takers gradually increased until it reached 1,000 in 1999.

Once an applicant passed the NBE, the Japanese Supreme Court provided specialized legal education and practical training over a two-year period through its Judicial Training and Research Institute (JTRI). During this period, the government paid a stipend to all JTRI students. Staffed by present and former judges, prosecutors and lawyers, the JTRI provided uniform education through common curriculum, practical training, and apprenticeships in the courts, prosecutor offices, law firms, and corporations. JTRI training focuses almost solely on litigation-related matters such as how to conduct a trial, proffer evidence, and interrogate a defendant. At the end of the JTRI experience, attendees became judges, prosecutors, or lawyers.

JTRI training was completely separate from university education up until the legal education reforms in 2004. Individuals desiring to pass the bar exam typically turned to private "cram schools" that focused exclusively on teaching how to pass the bar exam (West 2007). In many instances, individuals aspiring to be attorneys spent more time in cram schools than studying in a formal university environment. Despite an immense expenditure of personal time, money, and energy, the overwhelming majority never passed the bar examination. Not only could this talent have been constructively devoted to other areas of society, but also the cramming system meant that test takers had a very narrow focus and failed to grasp learning techniques adequately beyond memorization.

At the university level, Japanese legal education was primarily an academic affair devoid of substantial analytical or skills training. Although approximately 45,000 undergraduate and graduate students pursued legal studies at 93 institutions of higher education at any one time, these universities did not provide bar exam preparation or practical legal training. Instead, undergraduate law departments taught general theory and legal principles, while graduate studies focused on raising legal scholars. Instruction was provided primarily through theoretical and doctrinal lectures. In essence, university law departments served as training grounds for white-collar workers, business leaders, and government bureaucrats. While such instruction instilled many in the general workforce with some legal knowledge, it was not a substitute for formal legal training.

Expecting that the country would experience a quantitative and qualitative demand for legal services due to the wave of legal reforms and global economic influences, the JSRC proposed monumental changes to the process for educating and licensing lawyers. Some academics and practitioners worried that there would not be enough jobs for the increasing number of lawyers. Others were concerned about maintaining high standards. Largely ignoring these worries, the Diet passed the Act on Education in Law School and Connection with the Bar Examination in 2002. This legislation re-conceptualized the legal education system by calling for the establishment of graduate-level professional law schools which would integrally connect legal education with a significantly higher pass rate on the national bar examination and a one-year stint of apprenticeship training through the JTRI. In the reformers' minds, these new law schools would enable Japan to nurture a new generation of high-quality lawyers equipped to meet societal needs and conquer the challenges of the 21st century. However, due to concerns about maintaining standards, the new bar exam limited applicants to only three attempts within a five-year period.

On the legal education front, the Ministry of Education, Culture, Sports, Science, and Technology (MEXT) prepared standards and a model curriculum for the new professional law schools. Ironically, in an environment of reduced governmental involvement, MEXT would heavily regulate the law schools and control the number of students, number of professors, and graduation requirements. MEXT could also set the model curriculum and influence course content. Because the new law schools were intended to train future lawyers, the government felt a need to maintain internal controls. At the same time, Japanese reformers had honed in on the US model of professional legal education for direction. Those tasked with designing the new system, some of whom had experienced American law schools at first hand, were impressed by the US legal education system and the outcomes produced with the three-year juris doctor degree. US law schools were known for producing high-quality lawyers and strict evaluation standards. Using the US model, the new Japanese law schools embarked on a mission to expand the curriculum and pedagogy. They also set out to reduce student-teacher ratios, integrate licensed practitioners into the faculty, and offer practical skills courses.

In moving forward, Japanese legal education faced the challenge of implementing new ideals and methodologies. American-style education was a significant departure from past Japanese practice, and the implications of implementing such a system were not widely discussed or broadly understood in advance of the reforms. Also, Japanese schools needed to deal with the unique challenge of integrating students with an undergraduate law degree into classrooms that included students having no legal background. One partial solution allowed law faculty graduates to complete law school on an expedited two-year track. However, this was an imperfect solution.

Similar to the American legal system, the reformers also felt it necessary to raise the NBE pass rate both to increase the size of the legal community and ensure the success of the new law schools. The JSRC recommended that Japan raise the NBE pass rate to around 70% or 80% and that 3,000 applicants be allowed to pass the bar exam each year. In essence, this would enable the lawyer population to more than double to 50,000 by 2018. By raising the pass rate, universities would theoretically eliminate any undue emphasis on the NBE. They could comfortably expand the curriculum beyond core bar exam-focused courses and integrate specialized materials and experiential activities such as legal aid clinics into the curriculum.

Unfortunately, Japan's legal education system reform and changes to its bar examination fell short of expectations. Initially, there was much hope and excitement. In 2003, MEXT accepted applications from universities meeting the established standards for the new law schools. Despite speculation that only 12 to 20 universities would apply for permission to create a new law school, MEXT received over 70 applications. In April 2004, 68 new professional law schools, subsequently expanded to 74, opened their doors, accepting 5,800 students. Many students quit their jobs or otherwise altered their life plans to enroll. With these enrollments and an eventual target of 3,000 NBE passers each year, the maximum possible pass rate would be slightly over 50%. This was significantly below the target suggested by the reformers.

In 2006, the first NBE for the new professional law school students took place, and the initial pass rate was close to 50%. Thereafter, the NBE pass rate dropped every year until it leveled off at around 25% in 2011. Over 2,100 applicants passed the bar exam in 2012—more than any time in the past. Although the number of successful NBE test takers is much higher than the pre-2006 rate, fewer individuals are willing to invest three years and the substantial monies necessary to obtain a juris doctor degree due to the relatively low pass rate. The three-time cap on taking the NBE further discourages potential applicants. As such, within the first eight years under the new legal education system, the number of law school applicants dropped about 80%. With fewer students applying to law schools, a growing number of schools reduced their enrollments. By 2011, Japanese law schools admitted only 3,620 students, down by 2,200 students from 2006. The situation for 20 law schools was so dire that some admitted fewer than 10 students in their entire first-year class.

One wonders whether Japan's experiment with professional law schools and the new bar exam was doomed from the start. The expanding lawyer pool and reformed legal education system faced opposition from practicing attorneys and governmental bureaucrats. Within the first few years of the new bar exam and opening of law schools, critics started questioning the overall quality of the new lawyers and new law schools. Global economic turmoil starting in 2008 also negatively affected the availability of legal jobs, which also generated more calls to scale back planned increases in the lawyer population. Former methods of licensing lawyers also reemerged in 2010 in the form of a "preliminary exam system" that allows non-law school graduates to take an exam to determine whether they have the knowledge equivalent to law school graduates. This system was purportedly designed for working individuals and those who cannot afford law school. All applicants passing the preliminary exam may take the national bar exam up to three times within five years. In 2011, however, the pass rate for the first preliminary exam was less than 2%.

Notwithstanding, the new system has taken root and had positive effects. Newly licensed lawyers appear to be finding their way by opening new law offices and seeking employment in corporate settings. As of 2013, nearly 800 Japanese lawyers were working in corporate legal departments, up significantly from 64 in 2001 (Brennan 2013). Those unable to find steady employment in metropolitan areas have started branching out to under-represented rural areas in search of business. Furthermore, the precipitous drop in law school applicants will likely streamline the law school system. The survivors will likely be those law schools with high bar pass rates. In 2012, 60% of all successful exam applicants came from the top 10 law schools. In contrast, over half of the law schools had fewer than 10 successful bar exam applicants, and several law schools even had none. It is anticipated that the strong law schools will prosper, while the weaker schools will merge or cease operations.

Japan's expansion of public participation in its justice system

Another one of the most significant reforms came with the introduction of public participation into the judicial process. Reformers viewed the judicial system as an engine for propelling fundamental societal change. Accordingly, Japan targeted certain aspects of the criminal justice system for this purpose. It was believed that lay judge participation in criminal trials would essentially function as one of the key pistons in the engine.

For over six decades, the Japanese justice system had largely been the exclusive province of the legal profession, in which professional judges were tasked with handling all criminal trials, civil trials, and any appeals. During the 15-year period leading up to World War II, Japan briefly experimented with criminal jury trials without success. Despite some debate immediately after the war about reinstituting jury trials as part of democratic reforms, this concept was dismissed. As a result, tribunals comprising one or three professional judges conducted criminal and civil trials. The judge-only system worked well in many respects, and the judiciary was widely respected. On the other hand, justice was slow as courts conducted trial sessions at the average rate of one session per month. Others worried that justice was incomplete. For example, judges handling criminal trials relied heavily on written materials, particularly an investigation dossier compiled by the government prosecutor. Naturally, prosecutors structured dossiers to ensure convictions, and notwithstanding objections from defense counsel, judges generally accepted these dossiers into evidence with little reservation. Also, Japanese prosecutors were required only to disclose the statements that they intended to introduce into evidence at trial, enabling them to withhold exculpatory materials or statements harmful to their case. In this context, Japan's criminal conviction rate fluctuated between 99.5% and 99.9%. In the unlikely event that the tribunal found the accused innocent, the government had the right to appeal.

Japan transformed its criminal justice system through the Act Concerning Participation of Lay Assessors in Criminal Trials ("Lay Judge Act") on May 21, 2004. This Act authorized the creation of the lay judge or quasi-jury system known as the *saiban-in seido*. By design, this law purposefully limited lay participation to involvement in certain serious criminal cases only. With little attention or public debate, the Diet accepted the JSRC's recommendation and quickly enacted this law specifying that the lay judge trial process would start five years later.

Japan's lay judge system is the product of considerable preparation. Although it borrows and mixes concepts from various countries, Japan adopted this system based on its own needs. Identical to jury systems in common law countries such as the United States and United Kingdom, Japanese citizens are selected from voter registration lists for compulsory participation in a single trial. Unlike these countries, Japan's lay judge system does not contemplate an all-citizen panel, however. Rather, like civil law systems such as the Schöffe lay judge system in Germany or the échevin system in France, ordinary Japanese citizens participate in trials as "lay judges" while sitting alongside professional judges. In Japan, the new lay judge tribunals consist of six lay judges serving alongside three professional judges in contested criminal trials involving crimes such as homicide, robbery resulting in bodily injury or death, bodily injury resulting in death, unsafe driving resulting in death, arson, kidnapping, abandonment of parental responsibilities resulting in the death of a child, and other serious cases involving certain rape, drug, and counterfeiting cases. A majority vote is sufficient for the tribunal to reach a verdict, except that at least one professional judge must concur in the majority's conclusion to convict the defendant.

The lay judge system itself was constructed to facilitate active citizen participation and cooperation between professional judges and lay judges. To create a recipe for fair and just results, the professional judges contribute their legal expertise and the lay judges share their respective knowledge and experience. At trial, the lay judges theoretically possess authority equivalent to that of the professional judges, in that they both determine facts and participate in sentencing. Notwithstanding, the professional judges are solely responsible for interpreting legal and procedural matters due to the lay judges' lack of formal legal training.

By advocating the inclusion of citizen participation in serious criminal trials, the reformers sought to empower the citizenry to develop a greater civic consciousness and become more involved in public affairs. In theory, lay judge participation would help facilitate a more democratic society by infusing a broader range of backgrounds and experience into the justice system and imparting a sense of empowerment. It would thus reduce the chasm between the public and the law, one that undermined the judiciary's legitimacy, while encouraging the citizenry to move away from its excessive dependency on the government, and better position Japan for a more prominent role in global affairs. Up until this point, Japan had been the only Group of Eight nation without a system allowing substantive public participation in trials. Hamada Kunio, former Japanese Supreme Court Justice, expressed his belief that the experiment with citizen participation would foster independent thinking and enable Japanese citizens to become more "capable of formulating their opinion in international scenes" (Fujita 2009).

The lay judge system did not necessarily arise due to discontent with the legal system. In general, Japanese judges and legal professionals have always been widely respected and regarded as highly intelligent. Although certain interest groups such as the Japan Federation of Bar Associations (JFBA) had campaigned for jury trials as early as the 1980s, the government and public typically ignored such calls. By the time the JSRC was contemplating reforms, though, citizen confidence in the Japanese criminal justice system had started eroding. Some people criticized judges for their poor fact-finding and over-reliance on prosecutors. The media and other groups scrutinized a string of high-profile wrongful convictions caused by forced confessions (Wilson 2010a, 2010b). Additional criticism had also emerged regarding time-consuming trials, indifference to crime victims, and the isolation of the judiciary. Reformists hoped that citizen participation would eliminate these problems, infuse sound common sense into the judicial process, and increase prosecutorial accountability (Justice System Reform Council 2001).

Japan expended massive resources in implementing and operating the lay judge system. Prosecutors and defense attorneys were trained extensively in jury advocacy skills and techniques. The government and JFBA spent over US$50 million educating and promoting the system to citizens through billboards, print advertisements, television programs, DVDs, Japanese *manga* and *anime* (cartoons and animation), a mascot, mock trials, symposia, YouTube videos, and other means. Additionally, courtrooms were remodeled to accommodate nine judges (six lay judges and three professional judges) sitting on the bench, and deliberation rooms were constructed with sensitivity given to the lay judges' comfort. Yearly operational costs of the lay judge system include tens of millions of dollars for lay judge compensation and travel-related expenses. Lay judges and alternates receive about ¥10,000 ($100) per day for their services, while citizens who undergo selection screening receive a maximum of ¥8,000 ($80). Resources have also been invested in mitigating burdens on lay judges. For example, lay judges traumatized by the criminal proceedings have free access to psychological counseling.

Despite Japan's sizeable investment and its interest in bringing the justice system closer to the public through the lay judge system, opponents of the new lay judge system initially argued that citizen participation was an expensive exercise in futility (Dobrovolskaia 2007). They pointed to the troubles engulfing jury systems around the world and questioned why Japan would adopt a judicial mechanism that was apparently withering in other countries. Critics contended that Japan had wasted millions of dollars implementing a system without significant public debate that also faced considerable public skepticism and ran counter to Japanese legal traditions. There was also concern that lay judges would lack proper training, suffer from insufficient knowledge, and rely too heavily on emotion. Moreover, opinion polls preceding the implementation of the lay judge system consistently showed widespread public reluctance to participate.

Within the first three years of full operation, however, the lay judge system succeeded on many levels. Professional judges now deliberate alongside lay judges to reach collective decisions about verdicts and sentences. Overwhelmingly, citizens serving as lay judges describe their experience as positive or extremely positive despite their initial reservations about serving (Shinomiya 2010). Lay judges almost uniformly feel that their civic service provides an unparalleled opportunity to think seriously about important societal issues. In turn, these positive experiences alleviated many public concerns. Furthermore, judicial transparency and accountability have increased dramatically. The trial process itself has moved from a lengthy, disjointed, and largely opaque system conducted primarily based on written documents over the course of several months (if not years), to a more transparent and cohesive trial process focused on oral testimony given during hearings over the course of consecutive days. Prosecutors and criminal defense attorneys have gained considerable practical training in jury trial advocacy techniques, and now embrace their new roles as advocates. The accused have also benefited from a more translucent environment, in which prosecutors disclose more information in advance of trial in comparison with past practice.

Despite its achievements, the new lay judge system is not perfect and Japan needs to seek ways to refine the system further. The extraordinarily high conviction rate, which continues to exceed 99.5%, gives rise to questions about fairness. The uneven distribution of power between prosecutors and defense attorneys in terms of financial resources and training opportunities is disconcerting. Valid concerns exist about the new right of victims and their families to question witnesses, provide statements, submit recommended sentences, and give closing statements at trial to the lay judge panel before the determination of guilt. Also, the presence of professional judges in the deliberation room combined with the strict secrecy restrictions prohibiting lay judges from speaking freely about the trial deliberations are potentially troubling. Although the judiciary has purportedly taken steps to minimize the possibility of professionals dominating their citizen counterparts, there is still high potential for undue influence (Kamiya 2012). Additional worries have emerged that rigidity and time concerns may sometimes trump fairness and comprehensiveness. For example, a court typically determines the verdict announcement date even before the trial begins. To meet this target, thorough examination can take a backseat to honoring timelines.

Conclusion

Japan's recent monumental legal reforms have generally brought welcome change. They have yielded positive results in the courtroom, classroom, and marketplace. The reforms have also elevated the role of law, transparency, and global norms. Although it is still early in the process, the legal system is now more accessible to the public, trials are easier to understand, and democratic processes have been expanded. As a result, the citizenry appears to have gained a greater appreciation of public governance. As the country moves forward, Japan will need to resist the inescapable calls to scale back the reforms if they are to take effect fully. Instead, Japan should consistently look for ways to consolidate, improve and sustain the momentum of reforms in ways that render the judiciary more responsive to the needs of 21st-century Japan and thereby enhance its integrity and relevance.

Bibliography

American Bar Association (2013) *Lawyer Demographics*, www.americanbar.org/content/dam/aba/migrated/marketresearch/PublicDocuments/lawyer_demographics_2012_revised.authcheckdam.pdf.

Anderson, Kent and Matsuura, Yoshiharu (2012) "Japanese Law Reform: Balancing Old and New," *East Asia Forum*, December 7.

Brennan, Tom (2013) *Japan's Lawyers Heading In-House*, January 1, www.americanlawyer.com/PubArticleAL.jsp?id=1202580575361&Japans_Lawyers_Heading_InHouse&slreturn=2013030 61728 58.

Dobrovolskaia, Anna (2007) "An All-American Jury System Instead of the Lay Assessor (Saiban-in) System for Japan?" 24 *J. Japanese L.* 57.

Fujita, Akiko (2009) *Japan Gets Ready for New Jury System*, Voice of America, July 1.

Haley, John (1978) "The Myth of the Reluctant Litigant," 4 *J. Japanese Stud.* 366.

Ito, Takatoshi and Mishkin, Fredric (2006) *Two Decades of Japanese Policy and Deflation Problem*, Chicago: University of Chicago Press.

Japan Federation of Bar Associations (2013) *White Paper on Attorneys.*

Justice System Reform Council (2001) *Recommendations of the Justice System Reform Council: For a Justice System to Support Japan in the 21st Century.*

Kamiya, Setsuko (2012) "Lay Judges Present Ideas to Make System Better," *Japan Times*, January 21, www.japantimes.co.jp/text/nn20120121f2.html.

Kato, Masanobu (1987) "The Role of Law and Lawyers in Japan and the United States," *B. Y. U. L. Rev.* 627.

Katsuta, Takuya (2010) "Japan's Rejection of the American Criminal Jury," 58 *Amer. J. Comp. L.* 497.

Oda, Hiroshi (2009) *Japanese Law*, 3rd edition, Oxford: Oxford University Press.

Parker, Richard B. (1988) "Law, Language, and the Individual in Japan and the United States," 7 *Wis. Int'l L.J.* 179.

Saegusa, Mayumi (2009) "Why the Japanese Law School System Was Established: Co-optation as a Defensive Tactic in the Face of Global Pressures," 34 *Law & Soc. Inquiry* 365.

Shinomiya, Satoru (2010) "Defying Experts Predictions, Identifying Themselves as Sovereign: Citizens' Responses to Their Service as Lay Judges in Japan," 43 *Social Science in Japan* 8.

West, Mark (2007) "Making Lawyers (and Gangsters) in Japan," 60 *Vand. L. Rev.* 439.

Wilson, Matthew J. (2005) "Failed Attempt to Undermine the Third Wave: Attorney Fee Shifting Movement in Japan," 19 *Emory Int'l L. Rev.* 1457.

——(2007) "The Dawn of Criminal Trials in Japan: Success on the Horizon? 24 *Wis. Int'l L. J.* 835.

——(2010a) "Japan's New Criminal Jury Trial System: In Need of More Transparency, More Access, and More Time," 33 *Fordham Int'l L. J.* 487.

——(2010b) "U.S. Legal Education Methods and Ideals: Application to the Japanese and Korean Systems," 18 *Cardozo J. Int'l & Comp. L.* 295.

21 Parochialism

Japan's failure to internationalize

Robert Dujarric and Ayumi Takenaka

Japan is an international economic giant, but remains closed in many respects. During most of the Tokugawa era (1603–1868), *sakoku* (closed door) was the law of the realm. Today, the country remains secluded in many ways. Its "gross national cool" may give it a marginal international caché, but it is a global economy without a globalizing society.

One indicator is foreign direct investment (FDI). FDI fosters globalization. It brings expatriate staff and allows locals to find employment at home with foreign organizations, often a first step to an overseas assignment. However, FDI accounts for only 4% of Japan's national income, vs. 23% for the United States and 27% for Germany (UNCTAD 2013). FDI statistics are imprecise but the gap is so wide that there is no doubt that Japan is an outlier among large mature market economies.

Demographically, Japan is also an exception. Only 1.7% of its residents are foreign, of which about 19% are Japan-born Koreans (Ministry of Justice 2012). Foreigners are 0.9% of the labor force in Japan, vs. 9.4% in Germany and 14.7% in Sweden. Germany and Sweden, like Japan, never had large and long-lasting empires, but unlike Japan, they now have a significant number of workers from several continents.

Corporations do not release employee breakdowns by nationality, but following discussions with experts and a survey of available data, there is no doubt that headquarters of Japanese corporations, compared to those of other countries, have only small numbers (at most) of foreigners in managerial positions. The few exceptions prove the rule. The most famous one was Carlos Ghosn. A Brazilian-born French citizen, he ran Nissan, but only after French car maker Renault bought control of the company.

Overseas, Japanese are dramatically under-represented in international organizations. At the United Nations (UN), Japan's financial contributions should give it 202–73 spots in the professional ranks, rather than the 65 who hold such positions (2011 data, private communication, former UN Official 2012). A broader measure of UN employment indicates that there are more than twice as many French than Japanese and more than 60% more Germans and Italians than Japanese, even though Japan contributes more to the budget and is more populated (United Nations 2009). Relative to Japan's huge economy, Japanese are rare in the ranks of the World Bank, the International Monetary Fund (IMF), and big nongovernmental organizations (NGOs). In the corporate world, non-Japanese businesses employ very few Japanese nationals outside of their Japanese subsidiaries (see also Carroll 2010).

Moreover, insularity is rising. Younger Japanese are less keen on living overseas than their parents were. Today's Japanese want domestic safety, not foreign adventure

(Furukawa and Minahan 2012, 76). A Japanese diplomat told us that even in the Foreign Ministry, junior officials were not eager to be stationed outside Japan (we address these issues at greater length later).

Introverted Japanese universities

Some 132,000 foreign students in Japan represent a remarkable increase from 50,000 10 years earlier (UNESCO Institute for Statistics 2008), but they hail almost solely from East Asia, more than half from China alone. Most ambitious, rich, and/or talented Asians prefer US or British Commonwealth institutions despite Japan's proximity. Japan attracts a disproportionate number of students to private, second-tier colleges at the undergraduate rather than doctoral level (OECD 2008). Signs are that Asians studying in Japan are frequently there due to their failure to enter prestigious institutions at home or to attend schools in the Western, Anglophone world. Many are drawn by Japanese government scholarships, whereas the United States and the United Kingdom do not need these incentives. With the exceptions of those in scientific fields where Japan excels, and Japanology itself, Japan was not their preferred destination. Based on research in Dalian, China, Vanessa Fong reports that although, "Japan was considered the most convenient, lowest cost, and easiest option, it was usually not the top-choice" (Fong 2011, 46). This appears to apply to many Asians.

Japanese aiming for the best jobs in the public and private sectors congregate in a handful of undergraduate faculties (*gakubus*, similar to the "faculties" of continental Europe) in fewer than 10 universities nationwide. These *gakubus* remain nearly exclusively Japanese in terms of both students and faculty. Tokyo University Law Faculty is the most prestigious non-scientific one. Out of 1,013 students, only 12 were from abroad (Tokyo University 2012). Clearly, Japan's best and brightest are not gaining much international exposure during their university years. By comparison, close to 20% of the students at Harvard University are not from the United States (Harvard University 2013—2011–12 data), as are many instructors. Over 40% of the students at Paris' elite Institut d'études politiques (IEP-Paris, Sciences-Po) are not French, and many classes are taught in English (IEP-Paris 2013; see also Descoings 2007). At the University of Oxford 24% of students are not domiciled in the European Union (EU), and 11% are from the EU but not the UK (University of Oxford 2013). Overall, the *Times Higher Education* (THE) ranks Japanese universities slightly below South Korean and Chinese ones in international outlook and well below schools in the West (THE 2013).

A telling piece of data is that 70% of Tokyo University's undergraduate students confess to being unable to communicate in a foreign language (*Toyo Keizai*, July 30, 2011, 24). This is astronomically high for the top-ranked institution in a rich non-English-speaking country with close ties to the United States and the Commonwealth. At Todai, as Tokyo University is known, only 4% of the undergraduates have studied abroad (ibid.), and as of May 2011 only 0.4% of them were actually studying outside Japan (*Toyo Kezai*, December 24–31, 2011, 172).

Consequently, Japan is training the next generation of the elite in seclusion. By comparison, the Yale College Center for International and Professional Experience class of 2011 had 1,294 graduates. According to the University, 315 had taken part in Yale overseas educational programs, 100 had been involved in non-Yale study abroad opportunities, and hundreds of others had received fellowships for study or work outside of the United States. Almost 60% experienced some form of university-sponsored or -supervised activity outside of the United States (Yale University 2013, 3). Though Ivy League universities still send relatively few students on long study abroad stays, they have made enormous strides in internationalizing in the past two decades.

Overall, US study abroad programs rose from under 100,000 students participating in the mid-1990s to 154,168 in 2000–01 and 273,996 in 2010–11 (Institute for International Education 2013). From 2003 to 2009, the percentage of French students outside of their country went up by 35% (Parlier 2010). In contrast, in the decade to 2008, Japanese venturing outside of their country declined by more than 10%.

Another comparison regarding students in the United States with Germany, Europe's largest economy, and France, a country that internationalized later than Germany, is telling. In 2000–01 there were 9,800 Germans and 6,877 French studying in America compared to 46,872 Japanese; 11 years later there were 9,347 from Germany and 9,232 from France while the number of Japanese had fallen to 19,966 (Institute for International Education 2013). At three very selective institutions, Columbia, Harvard, and Massachusetts Institute of Technology (MIT), German numbers went up significantly in the first decade of the 21st century. By contrast, in 1998–99 there were 705 Japanese enrolled at these universities, but only 339 in 2011–12. In the two decades from 1991, Canadians, Germans, and Britons grew in numbers at Harvard, while the number of Japanese fell from 179 to 94 (Harvard University 2013). Declines in the seven years to 2012 are also evident for Japanese at Yale and the University of California–Berkeley. That the relative percentages of Japanese vs. Chinese students should evolve makes sense since China is at a different stage of development, but the contrast with "old" European economies is striking.

These "brand name" US universities are the training ground of the globalized managerial classes. The Japanese who attend them are generally in fast-track corporate and government jobs. Thus, the trend indicates that the next generation of the Japanese establishment will be a more insular one while the rest of the world is moving in the opposite direction. Other studies indicate that young Japanese engineers are now more likely to stay at home than study abroad (Normile 2010).

Overall, only 1.4% of Japanese study abroad, including those who study on a short-term basis or during vacations. This amounts to 60,225 individuals, according to 2008 figures (UNESCO Institute for Statistics 2008), compared to 101,913 South Koreans, even though South Korea's population is less than half the size and not as rich. Even accounting for Japan's declining population, the numbers are stagnating while trends in international education are growing in other nations.

Additionally, the Japanese educational and employment systems afford few opportunities to spend vacations overseas in summer jobs, internships or exchange programs. Taking a gap year is risky. Japanese employers dislike "non-linear" CVs that differ from the norm of secondary school followed immediately by four uninterrupted years of college leading straight to a respectable job.

Equally important is the dearth of Japanese teaching overseas. We looked at several renowned English-speaking universities in economics, engineering, physics, chemistry, math, business, and finance.[1] These are global disciplines where moderate English proficiency is often sufficient. Out of 1,306 faculty members, only six were Japanese (plus four with limited Japanese background), whereas over 60 were from other parts of Northeast Asia. Of the 110 doctoral candidates, many of whom serve as teaching assistants, coming from Northeast Asia (China, Taiwan, South Korea, and Japan) only nine were Japanese. Although not perfectly accurate, these figures reveal a low Japanese profile. It is noteworthy that a survey we conducted of three leading economic journals from 2010 to 2012, *RAND*, *Econometrica*, and *AEA* (American Economic Association), shows that Japanese authors are seriously under-represented relative to the rest of East Asia in authorship.

"[F]ew Japanese scholars participate in global networks where leading scholars, irrespective of their nationalities, cooperate" (Ito and Kurihara 2010). If more Japanese taught overseas, they would link Japanese academia with the outside world. Moreover, if there were more "transnational" Japanese professors, it would be easier to get Japanese to study abroad, as well as foreigners to attend Japanese universities.

Bastions of insularity

Education and the labor market reinforce insularity. Prestigious universities have alumni groups in large corporations (*Toyo Keizai*, October 22, 2011, 95–97). These old boys' (OB) networks are key not only in securing a job, but also in finding a good marriage partner and establishing oneself as a respected member of society. OB connections originate in universities, corporations, and ministries that are for all practical purposes exclusively Japanese. Unlike an Oxbridge or Stanford connection that has global utility, as there are alumni from all over the world, a Todai or Keio (one of Japan's top private universities) one is a currency that is only legal tender in Japan. A long career with Western multinationals will generate useful connections worldwide, but OBs of Japanese big business are less likely to have ties with foreigners.

Japanese returning from overseas frequently complain that they lost out to friends who remained in-country. Old boys know that Japan is the best place to maintain their networks through work, golf outings, and dinner parties. This applies, for example, to Japanese officials in international organizations. They say they pay a price for having left the central bureaucracy, whereas in some countries a stint in global institutions is a career accelerator when returning home.[2] Corporate executives argue that spending two years as a young manager on a company-sponsored foreign MBA (master's degree of business administration) may be less productive career-wise than staying with one's employer in Japan,[3] and young scientists believe that those who do not leave Japan do better than those who undertake research overseas (Normile 2010).

Young Japanese fare better if they attend an elite *gakubu* at home and secure a respected and safe position in big (Japanese) business, the civil service, the media, or academia. Seeking recognition in Japan, gaining domestic credentials, and cultivating Japanese affiliations is the logical choice. National credentials are always essential, but in Japan they are almost the only ones that matter, whereas in other countries a mix of local and foreign ones is better.

An additional reason for this seclusion is the lack of lateral mobility. The best jobs go to those who join an employer for the long term upon graduation from college. There has been an increase in lateral hiring, but it remains fairly rare in big business. Leaving a secure post with a good Japanese employer to move abroad is risky, as return to Japan is hard and opportunities in foreign-owned or newly established ventures are a small segment of the labor market.

Moreover, one question is whether even Japanese who were educated or worked overseas for a long time want to return to Japan. Mobile global talent is ambitious. Opportunities for quick promotion are rare in Japan except for entrepreneurs. It is harder for an excellent staffer in his thirties in Japan to get the sort of upward mobility that he could expect in other countries. This management philosophy is not without merit, but is disheartening for enterprising employees.

In the rest of Asia, the returns on a foreign education and work are higher. These countries, like early Meiji Japan, are at a stage where there is a premium on acquiring knowledge and experience in more advanced nations (Auslin 2011). Moreover, being less stable than Japan and/or facing more immediate security threats, their citizens like the idea of having an exit strategy.

Japan's success gives it the power to set its own standards. A US$5.9 trillion economy is a big market, making it easy for regulators, or social norms in general, to establish "Japan-only standards" (what some call the "Galapagos Syndrome," i.e. Japan having a unique ecology found nowhere else). Nearly everything is not only translated but also adapted to fit Japanese tastes. Thus, even if they work for foreign multinationals in Japan, Japanese are the product of an insular society and ill-prepared for life overseas.

In academia, Japanese scholars are sufficiently numerous to nurture a rich ecosystem of learned societies and journals. Researchers from smaller or poorer nations, however, are forced to join the international academic community.

Economic reasons also explain inward-looking trends. Japanese corporations have restructured in the past decades by changing employment policies. As in other countries, this has led to more precarious jobs with less security, and for many a lower salary, but without flexible labor markets. Young Japanese are focusing on landing harder-to-find "lifetime employment" positions at home in big corporations and government service. Thus students stay in Japan due to the fear of missing the boat (*Facta*, April 2012, 57).

Moreover, in liquid labor markets, employees need marketable skills, such as IT expertise or finance, that can appeal to another employer. In Japan, the lack of inter-firm mobility for good positions puts a premium on company-specific talent, such as understanding the inner workings of the corporation and firm-wide personal contacts. Therefore, pursuing overseas educational opportunities is less valuable as they help develop specific portable skills but will be detrimental in strengthening one's position within the company.

In the "bubble years" of the 1980s, foreign study made it possible to travel, learn something, and have a good time. Now that the economy is stagnant, leaving students and their parents with less money and the labor market more competitive, it is seen to be a costly distraction. In contrast, in most other countries, it is a ticket to end up on the winning side of the rat race.

Japan, Inc.'s push for globalization

The Japanese establishment—or "Japan, Inc."—sees the dangers of insularity. Corporate Japan needs overseas profits to compensate for a shrinking domestic population. Japanese conglomerates actively took advantage of a favorable exchange rate following the 2008 financial meltdown to engage in foreign acquisitions. Japan thus needs a larger cadre of internationalized Japanese and foreigners who can be integrated into a Japanese corporate environment.

As a result, fostering "globally competent human capital" is a frequently heard phrase. Big business says it wants to hire more foreigners and to impart a dose of cosmopolitanism to its Japanese "salarymen." The symbol of this drive is Rakuten, Japan's largest Internet retailer. Founder and CEO Mikitani Hiroshi (Harvard MBA) made English the official language. Businesses are emphasizing linguistic and cosmopolitan/multicultural skills (*Daily Yomiuri*, January 25, 2011). Others express interest in hiring more foreigners. The Cabinet Office even has a Global Human Capital Development Council (*Facta*, April 2012, 57).

Japanese universities have taken up the flag of globalization, but it remains at half-mast. Some offer more classes in English to attract foreign students and faculty. In some cases degrees can be completed solely in English, but these are not as prestigious as the "traditional" ones that are taught in Japanese. The Association of National Universities announced in 2013 that it wanted to double the number of English-language courses offered to 24,000 by 2020 and to double the proportion of foreign students to 10% by the same date (*Japan Times*, March 10, 2013). A government-sponsored "Global 30" aims to globalize the top universities (but has now been scaled down). Todai's Global Leadership Program also aims to groom students for foreign study and internships abroad (*Yomiuri Daily* 2012). In 2008 the government proposed to bring in 300,000 foreign students by 2020, and eased visa policies for foreign graduates desiring to extend their stay. Other possible reforms in the works include, in the case of a top-ranked universities, moving the academic year from the current Japanese system of starting in early April and graduating in March to the September-entry/May–June graduation format of the North Atlantic schools.

Obstacles to globalization

Globalization, in its cultural, educational, and other intangible forms, is Western. It is not the old Victorian-era imperialism but is patterned on the norms of the cosmopolitan Anglophone metropolises of London, New York, Silicon Valley and, in Asia, the British-born Singapore and Hong Kong.

The growth of economic power outside of the Euro–North American zone does not invalidate this fact. Many of the new economic actors, such as Brazil, Mexico, Turkey, Israel, Russia, are wholly or partly included in the broader Western cultural sphere. Others, such as India and South Africa, have retained much of the administrative, educational, and cultural legacy of European colonialism. Even Communist Party-ruled China sends its brightest and wealthiest to be trained in the West (Overholt 2008, 111). In many areas the reforms of the past 30 years have made China more Western.

Japan, unlike China, operates under European code law and a constitution drafted by Americans, but in many key respects, it remains non-Western. It was never colonized by the West, unlike South and Southeast Asia. Nor has American influence been as profound as in South Korea and Taiwan. In China, the upheavals of the century that preceded Deng Xiaoping's reign forced the Middle Kingdom's autocrats to open up the country more radically to foreign influences and investment than Japan has had to do since the 1880s.

Japan also lacks other ties that bind most Asian nations to the West. There are no Japanese counterparts to Hong Kong, Taiwan and Singapore, which serve as an invaluable bridge to help Chinese navigate the West. There are none of the huge Christian congregations of American ancestry found in South Korea (of all the Northeast Asian societies, Japan's is the one with the smallest fraction of followers of

Western faiths). China, India, Pakistan, South Korea, Taiwan, the Philippines, and Vietnam also have large diasporas in the North Atlantic nations and Australia that are bridges to the West.

From 1870 through the 1960s, only about 1 million emigrated from Japan, mostly to the Americas. By 1965 when the United States, and later Australia, lifted racist restrictions, Japanese were prosperous enough to prefer to stay home. Ethnic Japanese in the New World now belong to the second and subsequent generations. They are often intermarried and frequently with no or only limited ties with Japan. Their potential as a connector between Japan and other lands is small, in contrast to other Asians, many of whom are recent migrants with a foot in two societies.

In the case of universities, there are issues specifically related to the education industry. The Education Ministry has significant management authority over them. However, unlike the Ministry of Economy of Trade and Industry (METI), the Finance Ministry (MOF), the Ministry of Defense (MOD), and of course the Foreign Ministry (MOFA), it is involved in few international activities. With some exceptions, its officials do not need to interact with foreigners, negotiate treaties and agreements, or travel beyond the confines of the island nation. As such, it is unsuited to globalizing Japanese education. In addition, relatively few Japanese university program managers and administrators, who are key to any university's globalization drive, are experienced in working with the outside world.

Moreover, Japanese universities lack centralized managerial control. They are "feudal" organizations where vested interests and "veto players" deprive the president and his staff of the power to fight inertia (Hall 1998, 91). In such a context, plans for sweeping reforms end up as inadequate half-measures.

One way of globalizing universities is to recruit foreign students and professors, but it is hard to attract outside talent. The barriers to entry are high since it is hard to function effectively without a good understanding of Japanese and, more importantly, of Japanese customs and operating procedures. There are also barriers to exit since Japan expertise is not highly valued outside of the country, Japan being *sui generis* and very different from the rest of Asia. Studying in Japan or a posting there is often not the best choice for someone looking to move on to other places later on. For example, a business weekly noted that foreign students ask if a degree from Tokyo University will allow them to get a job at Samsung (*Diamondo*, September 29, 2012, 41–44). Those seeking global credentials in the Asia-Pacific should fly to Hong Kong, Singapore, or Australia. Similarly, for a dynamic young academic, even the best Japanese universities do not compete with the big-name Western schools, and those in Hong Kong and Singapore, as a springboard for international visibility in most disciplines.

Beyond the realm of academia, globalization in corporate Japan is fraught with obstacles. American multinationals can find North American-educated English speakers from the five continents who are used to or at least aware of American norms, but hiring foreigners entails a real "cultural revolution" for Japanese businesses which cannot fill their organizations with foreigners familiar with Japan (see Nakamoto 2009).

Organizations, like computers, run on a software operating system (OS) based on procedures and values that reflect those of the society. The Japanese OS is forged in a school system that aims to nurture loyal subjects and docile workers (Yamamura 1997, 68). Schooling in Japan is primarily a "moralizing and socializing organization, and secondarily a teaching institution" (McVeigh 1998, 129) that prepares those who will work in Japan.

Since Japanese know little about the outside world and few outsiders are able to function in a Japanese environment, internationalizing the workplace creates a dilemma for Japanese businesses. It is not clear that Japanese manufacturers could maintain their well-deserved reputation if half of their staff ran on Japanese OS and the other half on some sort of globalized OS. As Watanabe Masahiro argues, profitable Japanese businesses are 100% Japanese (*Toyo Kezai*, March 2, 2013, 50–55). Successful Western multinational companies have executives and senior managers from all over the world, but in the end, they run on what we could call a "Western OS." The most recent attempt at globalizing corporate Japan was the acquisition by Nomura Securities, a very Japanese institution, of assets of the US investment bank Lehman Brothers in 2008. A few years later, this transaction is generally viewed as having failed, partly—but not solely—due to the difficulty in merging two incompatible corporate cultures.

The *Toyo Keizai* weekly developed a matrix showing jobs for which there was a Japan premium, i.e. those where insider knowledge of the society limits competition from foreigners, and those where this premium is low (*Toyo Keizai*, August 27, 2011). With a few exceptions, such as computer programming, the Japan premium is very high for jobs that require a university degree (and many that do not). Almost all of these positions demand an excellent command of Japanese and a familiarity and willingness to follow Japanese rules. This means that the vast majority of professional positions in Japan today are unsuited for foreign nationals. Therefore globalizing corporate Japan is extremely difficult.

Besides these obstacles, there are broader social consequences to globalization that will foster hostility to it in Japan. Japan has a cultural homogeneity that is unique in the non-Western world. In other Asian countries there is a chasm between Western-oriented elites and the masses. In Japan, however, the upper class, like the rest of the population, is the product of the domestic educational and cultural systems.

Globalization usually fuels the "denationalization" of the elites who become culturally disconnected from their homeland (Guilluy 2010, 46–58). The political risks are visible in the rise of radical populist parties in many countries amidst the eurozone crisis, where anger at the denationalized elites is palpable, but this has not happened in Japan because all citizens are very "national." In addition, acquiring this "cosmopolitan social capital" is not cheap (see Bourdieu 2002 [1984], on social capital). It entails frequent language study trips, years of study abroad, overseas internships, etc., that only wealthy parents can fund, generating further concerns about economic inequality.

Protecting insiders

As soon as the price of globalization becomes clearer, the enthusiasm of many of its proponents tends to fade.

In a globalized Japan, senior but mediocre academics would face global competition. Students exposed to foreign experiences would return questioning the quality of the instruction in Japan. They would also challenge other aspects of Japanese society, such as entrenched gender inequality and a preference for seniority. They could lose respect for their bosses, whose credentials are solely domestic.

Protecting credentials is important to all privileged castes and guilds. For example, Todai introduced an English-instruction BA program called Peak, but Japanese in Japan who have worked hard to learn English will be barred from entrance. Applicants must have been educated outside of Japan for most of their pre-university schooling (Tokyo University 2013, 3). Thus Peak may turn out to marginalize foreigners and Japanese raised overseas from the mainstream core of the Japanese elite, thereby protecting the prestige of "real" Todai degrees.

In the 1980s some Westerners criticized Japan, at that time a rising economic juggernaut, for not playing by the rules of economic liberalism. These so-called "revisionists" took to task the established experts on Japan, labeled the "Chrysanthemum Club," for not criticizing the country (Packard 2010). Ivan Hall argued that Japan ran an "intellectual closed shop" (Hall 1998, 7) and accused Japan, Inc. of restricting foreign scholars' access while Japanese were returning home with intellectual property gleaned from American laboratories (Hall 1998, 127). Other "revisionists," such as Clyde Prestowitz (1988), van Wolferen (1989), James Fallows (1994), were inspired by Chalmers Johnson's analysis of Japan's political economy *MITI and the Japanese Miracle* (Johnson 1982), which called on Americans to wake up to Japan's allegedly unfair practices.

Regardless of the validity of these views, which have been mostly invalidated by developments in the past two decades, today's non-globalization is not part of some nefarious strategy to take advantage of gullible Americans. It is the product of forces within Japan that are recognized by many Japanese analysts and business leaders as hurting the economy but are strongly embedded in its past and present. Path dependence (North 1990) makes it very hard to overcome the various institutional, social and cultural barriers to globalization

Conclusion

Crane Brinton explains in *The Anatomy of Revolution* (Brinton 1953) that the elite must lose faith in the legitimacy of existing institutions for a revolution to succeed. Today's Japanese Establishment still believes in the system, though not as strongly as 30 years ago. The collapse of the Tokugawa destroyed long-held beliefs, making early Meiji Japan "singularly open to new ideas" (Craig 2009, 145; see also Kunitake 2009), but in Heisei Japan the system is still robust. Many prominent Japanese pontificate about the desirability of globalization without winning many converts. Unfortunately, globalization is dangerous for mono-cultural, monolingual, parochial men. Therefore, their commitment to globalizing Japan is hampered by self-interest and their own lack of understanding of the non-Japanese world.

The status of women illustrates the difficulty of globalizing Japan. Japanese women are estimated to account for 10% of the Japanese managerial labor force compared to 30% or more in many other developed countries (Steinberg and Nakane 2012, 18; see also Hewlett and Sherbin 2011), and are far more under-represented in executive positions than females in many other Asian nation and the West (McKinsey & Company 2012, 4). Some argue that if Japan were to utilize its educated women fully, gross domestic product (GDP) would increase by 15% (Matsui *et al.* 2010).

Despite the cost of this failure, progress in empowering women has been minimal. The cause is not some unique Japanese cultural trait, but the interlocking educational, corporate, political, and social mechanisms that have created a path-dependence mechanism that is hard to alter. The issue of (non-)globalization is equally embedded in interlocking processes that make it hard, though not impossible, to forge a new path.

Moreover, the selection process to reach the decision-making levels of the Japanese political, bureaucratic, media, and business worlds weeds out those endowed with the pioneering spirit even more than in most societies. Promotions put more emphasis on seniority than in other countries, thereby increasing the likelihood that those at the top will be risk-averse managers. This process started in the later Meiji period. With the institutionalization of the university system and exam-based bureaucratic state, "an intellectual aristocracy began to be transformed into the closed structure of a bureaucratic oligarchy" (Ward and Dankwart 1964, 164; Smethurst 2009).

Unlike the 1860s, Japan today is not a realm where the regime is on the verge of total collapse. In the long run, isolation will have increasingly negative economic consequences, but those in power do not yet see the threat as sufficiently urgent to do anything about it before they retire.

Notes

1 Economics: Chicago, Chicago Graduate School of Business (GSB), Columbia, Princeton, London School of Economics (LSE). Finance: Insead, Chicago GSB, Harvard Business School (HBS), Wharton, Princeton. Business: Harvard, Wharton. Physics: Caltech, MIT, Stanford. Electrical engineering: Caltech, Columbia, Cornell, MIT, Stanford. Chemistry: Caltech, MIT. Math: Caltech, MIT. Data gathered in June/July 2012.
2 Private email from a former UN official, 2012.
3 Private conversation with Japanese banker, March 15, 2013.

Bibliography

Auslin, Michael (2011) *Pacific Cosmopolitans: A Cultural History of U.S. Japan Relations*, Cambridge, MA: Harvard University Press.

Bourdieu, Pierre (2002 [1984]) *Questions de sociologie*, Paris: Les Editions de Minuit.

Brinton, Crane (1953) *The Anatomy of Revolution*, London: Cape.

Carroll, William (2010) *The Making of a Transnational Capitalist Class: Corporate Power in the 21st Century*, London: Zed Books Publishing.

Craig, Albert (2009) *Civilization and Enlightenment: The Early Thought of Fukuzawa Yukichi*, Cambridge, MA: Harvard University Press.

Descoings, Richard (2007) *Sciences Po: école ou université internationale*, Paris: Entretien Avec Esprit.

Fallows, James (1994) *Looking at the Sun: The Rise of the New East Asian Economic and Political System*, New York: Pantheon.

Fong, Vanessa (2011) *Paradise Redefined: Transnational Chinese Students and the Quest for Flexible Citizenship in the Developed World*, Stanford, CA: Stanford University Press.

Furukawa, Hinori and Minahan, Brian (2012) *Nihon de shigoto ga takunattme gurobaru kigyo de hatarakuru jin ni naru hon* (How to prepare yourself to work in a global company), Tokyo: Chukei Publishing.

Guilluy, Christophe (2010) *Fractures françaises*, Paris: François Bourin Editions.

Hall, Ivan (1998) *Cartels of the Mind*, London: Norton.

Harvard University (2013) *Harvard Worldwide*, March 5, www.worldwide.harvard.edu/iws/facts/index.jsp (accessed March 5, 2013).

Hewlett, Sylvia Ann and Sherbin, Laura (2011) *Off-Ramps and On-Ramps Japan: Keeping Talented Women on the Road to Success*, New York: Work-Life Publishing.

IEP-Paris (Institut d'études politiques) (2013) *Sciences Po dans le monde*, March 5, www.sciencespo.fr/node/109 (accesssed March 5, 2013).

Institute for International Education (2013) *International Students: All Places of Origin*, March 9, www.iie.org/Research-and-Publications/Open-Doors/Data/International-

Students/All-Places-of-Origin/1950-2000, and www.iie.org/Research-and-Publications/Open-Doors/Data/International-Students/All-Places-of-Origin/2010-12 (accesssed March 9, 2013).

——(2013) *Open Doors Data*, March 10, www.iie.org/Research-and-Publications/Open-Doors/Data/US-Study-Abroad/All-Destinations (accessed March 10, 2013).

Ito, Hajime and Kurihara, Jun (2010) *A Discourse on the New Kai'entai: A Scenario for a Revitalized Japan. Politico-Economic Commentaries*, Tokyo: Cambridge Gazette.

Japan Times (2013) "Colleges to Double Foreign Students," March 10.

Johnson, Chalmers A. (1982) *MITI and the Japanese Miracle: The Growth of Industrial Policy, 1925–1975*, Stanford, CA: Stanford University Press.

Kunitake, Kume (2009) *Japan Rising: The Iwakura Embassy to the USA and Europe 1871–1873*, New York: Cambridge University Press.

Matsui, Kathy, Suzuki, Hiromi, Eoyang, Christopher, Akiba, Tsumugi and Tatebe, Kazunori (2010) *Japan: Portfolio Strategy Womenomics 3.0: The Time is Now*, Tokyo: Goldman Sachs Publishing.

McKinsey & Company (2012) *Women Matter: An Asian Perspective Harnessing Female Talent To Raise Corporate Performance*, Sydney: New Media Australia Publishing.

McVeigh, Brian (1998) "Linking State and Self: How the Japanese State Bureaucratizes Subjectivity through Moral Education," *Anthropological Quarterly* 71(3), Washington, DC: Catholic University of America Press.

Ministry of Education, Culture, Sports, Science and Technology (MEXT) (2008) *Career Advising for Foreign Students and the Profile of Foreign Faculty at Japanese Universities*, Tokyo.

Ministry of Justice (2012) *Toroku gaikokujin tokei* (Statistics on foreign migrants in Japan), www.immi-moj.go.jp/toukei/ (accessed February 14, 2013).

Nakamoto, Michiyo (2009) "Cultural Revolution in Tokyo," *Financial Times*, August 18.

Normile, Denis (2010) "Will Homebody Researchers Turn Japan into a Scientific Backwater?" *Science*, December 10: 1475.

North, Douglass C. (1990) *Institutions, Institutional Change and Economic Performance*, Cambridge: Cambridge University Press.

Organisation for Economic Co-operation and Development (OECD) (2008) *The Global Competition for Talent*, Paris: OECD.

Overholt, William (2008) *Asia, America, and the Transformation of Geopolitics*, New York: Cambridge University Press.

Packard, George R. (2010) *Edwin O. Reischauer and the American Discovery of Japan*, New York: Columbia University Press.

Parlier (2010) "Les étudiants français champions de la mobilité Erasmus," *Le Monde*, June 1.

Prestowitz, Clyde V. (1988) *Trading Places – How we are Giving Our Future to Japan and How to Reclaim It*, New York: Basic Books.

Smethurst, Richard (2009) *From Foot Solider to Finance Minister: Takahashi Korekiyo, Japan's Keynes*, Cambridge, MA: Harvard University Press.

Steinberg, Chad and Nakane, Masato (2012) "Can Women Save Japan?" IMF Working Paper WP/12/248, October, Washington, DC: IMF.

THE (*Times Higher Education*) (2013) *World University Rankings*, March 9, www.timeshighereducation.co.uk/world-university-rankings/2012-13/world-ranking/region/asia (accessed March 9, 2013).

Tokyo University (2012) *Student Numbers*, March 3, www.u-tokyo.ac.jp/stu04/e08_02_j.html (accessed March 5, 2013).

——(2013) *Peak*, February 10, peak.c.u-tokyo.ac.jp/app2013/PEAKAppGuidelines2013entry.pdf (accesssed February 10, 2013).

UNCTAD (United Nations Conference on Trade and Development) (2013) *UNCTAD Stat*, unctadstat.unctad.org/UnctadStatMetadata/Classifications/Tables&Indicators.html (accessed February 1, 2013).

UNESCO Institute for Statistics (2008) *Global Education Digest: Comparing Education Statistics Across the World*, Montreal.

——(2009) *Global Education Digest: Comparing Education Statistics Across the World*, Montreal.

United Nations (2009) *Gender Distribution of All Staff*, December, www.un.org/womenwatch/osagi/pdf/Nationalities2010/NationalityTotals_Summary_2008–20093.pdf (accessed March 8, 2013).

University of Oxford (2013) *Full details of domicile*, March 10, public.tableausoftware.com/views/Studentstatistics-UniversityofOxford/Nationalitydomicile?embed=yes&:tabs=yes_=yes (accessed March 10, 2013).

van Wolferen, Karel (1989) *The Enigma of Japanese Power*, New York: Alfred A. Knopf Publishing.

Ward, Robert and Dankwart, Rustow (eds) (1964) *Political Modernization in Japan and Turkey*, Princeton, NJ: Princeton University Press.

Yale University (2013) *Yale College Center for International and Professional Experience*, March 5, www.yale.edu/yalecollege/international/welcome/pdf/2011_report.pdf (accesssed March 5, 2013).

Yamamura, Kozo (1997) *The Economic Emergence of Modern Japan*, Cambridge: Cambridge University Press.

Yomiuri Daily (2012) “University of Tokyo Plans ‘Elite’ Linguistic Education,” July 13.

22 What's behind what ails Japan[1]

David Leheny

Apparently American bosses love to be contradicted in front of their clients by their own summer interns. Or at least this is what one might glean from a May 2012 *New York Times* article about the problems young Japanese educated abroad face on the Japanese job market. The author interviews several Japanese—including some foreign-born—with degrees from prestigious American and British universities, finding that they faced what seemed to be significant disadvantages on the Tokyo job market. In the stories provided, these include apparent age limits on new recruits, differences in interviewing styles (including a possibly gendered rejection of one woman who laughed too much during her interview), and, mostly puzzlingly, apparent Japanese corporate frustration with one Yale-educated advertising intern who, in very polite language, would correct his bosses in meetings when they made mistakes about social media and technology.

As journalism, of course, it is a horrible piece of work, not because it makes Japan look bad—after all, it is hardly the job of *The New York Times* or any other paper to make a country look good, though the *Times* does seem over the years to have a special affection for stories about what ails Japan (Zipangu 1998)—but rather because of the absence of any meaningful consideration of how we know this to be a serious or distinctive problem. After all, while the article refers to the fact that there are large numbers of Korean students in the United States (who, we are led to surmise, will not face problems on the Korean job market, though there is no evidence provided to support this), there is nothing about the likelihood that an American with a degree from a foreign university (particularly one other than Oxford or Cambridge) would find difficulty finding work in a major American firm. The article certainly provides no comparable case in which a voluble intern (foreign-educated or otherwise) was rewarded for interrupting his bosses during a meeting with clients in an American boardroom. One would be hard-pressed to guess from the article that while the Japanese government has displayed increasing alarm at the declining number of Japanese students studying abroad (e.g. MEXT 2008), American universities are themselves also worried that study abroad has stalled and that new incentives are needed to entice American students to spend a term or a year overseas (McMurtrie 2012).

That is, to the extent the story works—as it seems to, given the number of positive comments it received on *The New York Times* website as well as favorable attention from other websites—it is not because of what is inside the story but rather what is outside of it: a view that Japan is too closed, that Japan is economically struggling, that these problems are probably related, and that the nail that sticks up in Japan (particularly when in a board meeting, and sticking up involves embarrassing one's bosses) gets hammered down (if, by hammered down, we mean not getting invited to many more meetings and not receiving a long-term job offer). Forced to explain why a half-Japanese, half-American candidate educated at, say, Yale actually would be far more likely to find a job with a top Japanese firm in Tokyo than she would if, say, she had a degree from the University of Tokyo and tried to get a job on Wall Street with a top American firm, presumably most *New York Times* readers would simply point out that American universities are superior to their Japanese counterparts, not that there is anything closed-minded about American employers. In other words, the critique can be persuasive only because of what people already assume to be true about Japan.

This is what we are supposed to do as scholars: to think critically, and to teach our students how to do the same, but doing so has to require an excavation of the assumptions we bring into our critiques or that even motivate our critical engagement, to confront the usually unspoken alternatives and imaginaries that lie in the background of our intellectual pursuits. It is not to put the spotlight on the analyst rather than on the subject—whether Japanese employment markets or anything else—but rather to recognize that the analyst is implicated to some degree in the analysis. So in considering critical perspectives on Japan, my goal in this brief chapter is to examine three potential sources of critical views of Japan: tensions between particularity and universality, commitments to different forms of international engagement, and views of changing international norms. I do not aim to say that critical perspectives drawn from these directions are wrong or misplaced; at different times, I have engaged in all of them. My point, rather, is when these assumptions and preoccupations remain unstated, they make it harder to see how our critiques are often contingent and partial, shaped by larger intellectual and political concerns that may change over time. I also think that more analytical self-awareness would make arguments drawn from these critical perspectives more broadly persuasive.

The other modern

As the first non-Western nation to have achieved economic and industrial modernization, Japan long represented open-ended promise. For many Japanese "pan-Asianists" in the 1920s, Japan's success presented a unifying Asian alternative to Westernization (and Western colonialism), even if Chinese and Korean nationalists living under Japanese imperial control seem to have been less enthusiastic about the argument (Aydin 2007, 154–60). In the immediate post-war era, Japan's role as a capitalist alternative to the economic success stories of the Soviet Union and other socialist nations helped to fix Japan's growth as an essential part of America's Cold War strategy. In these versions, Japan could provide hope largely in the form of a different story, one juxtaposed with the idea that one had to adopt Western ideas in order to modernize or, alternatively, that a non-Western cultural background might prevent a country from modernizing robustly.

Interrogating studies of Japan from the 1950s–70s, Amy Borovoy (2013; see also Borovoy 2012) argues that Japan, by dint of its non-Western background, offered a crucial tool to intellectuals of the era: a "laboratory" for exploring the possibilities of modernization. While modernization theory is a broad category, with roots among 19th-century social theorists, notably Emile Durkheim and Max Weber, its American variant in the 1950s and 1960s focuses substantially on the idea traditional societies would be altered in relatively predictable ways by patterns of economic development, with social, political and cultural implications (Stephenson 1968; see also Inkeles 1969). One critical account (Bernstein 1971, 142) used Japan's Meiji-era modernizers as the pre-eminent examples of political elites the model of which might be emulated by others, particularly with the wide presumption that Japan's rapid and economic transformation might pull it "up" to the civilizational level of the West. Indeed, while modernization theory has probably always had at least as many critics as proponents, it remains a kind of cornerstone of much of the language of international development. Virtually all experts in the field espouse and even celebrate cultural tolerance, but other ideas embedded in assumptions about modernization—women's rights, transparent governance, respect for diversity—tend to set hard limits on what is acceptably traditional and what is not. We might value cultural diversity, but it is more difficult to defend female genital mutilation.

It was these teleological assumptions about cultural change—that more "modern" people will think and behave in a certain way, as opposed to more backward and "traditional" people—that helped to animate the work of a generation of scholars working on Japan. As Borovoy notes, Robert Bellah, in his classic 1957 account of Tokugawa religion, aimed to find indigenous roots for economic transformation that might parallel Weber's focus on a Protestant work ethic, and argued that Japan's particular form of rationalization/modernization took the form not primarily of increased individualism but rather of loyalty to hierarchical structures, from family to nation (Borovoy 2013). This emphasis on durable cultural difference allowed simultaneously an interest in economic development while also allowing the idea of modernization to shed some of the ethnocentric ideals of Westernization. Thus, in Borovoy's analysis, Bellah's work both fits within the teleological rubric of modernization theory while also carving out new terrain for exploring important differences in Japanese culture.

It also allowed Bellah's work to fit within an emerging genre, at least as popular in Japanese as in English, of studies about the essential differences in Japanese culture. While Ruth Benedict's early post-war study *The Chrysanthemum and the Sword* remains in some ways a foundational text, it was for many supplanted by studies by Japanese authors, like Takeo Doi's *The Anatomy of Dependence* as well as Chie Nakane's *Japanese Society*, which provided holistic accounts of how Japanese think and act, basing the claims on everything from childhood experiences to the reproduction of patterns of hierarchy and deference. These ideas, too, are widely criticized—we respect intellectual diversity, but no one wants to be identified as a *nihonjinron* (discourses of Japaneseness) thinker—but have at various times been embraced in powerful institutions. One such was the International Research Center for Japanese Studies which, on its establishment in the 1980s, was initially headed by key figures like the philosopher Umehara Takeshi, a scholar associated with the investigation (and, some argued, the aggrandizement) of Japanese uniqueness.

Nihonjinron, like modernization theory, is now far better known for its critics than proponents (in English, see Dale 2012 [1998]; in Japanese, see Oguma 1995). The durability of the genre, even in attenuated form, might speak to a demand for national uniqueness that one could attribute to an international system of distinct, sovereign states (Leheny 2011), but proponents also represent a potential source of at least one direction for critical perspectives on Japan: that of the lost nation, the one that has struggled continually with the threat of being obliterated by a modernizing path that destroys tradition. Indeed, much of the cultural work of late-modern Japan has been the construction and preservation of an earlier Japan (Ivy 1995; Robertson 1988; see also Borovoy 2012 on Doi's negotiation of pre-war conceptions of community with post-war social democratic ideals of care).

This "invention of tradition," to use a concept developed by Eric Hobsbawm and Terence Ranger (1983), is of course hardly unique to Japan, but Japan's early position as a non-Western modernizer perhaps uniquely endowed it with relevance to mainstream political and social debate. Even today, while scholars, Japanese and foreign alike, would likely dismiss such efforts, books that extol the distinctive (and, crucially, non-Western) virtues of the Japanese are big business. One of the most visible among recent contributions is mathematician Fujiwara Masahiko's (2005) bestselling *Kokka no hinkaku* (Dignity of a nation). While full of discussions about what makes Japan such a wonderful country, it is not just the work of a cheerleader, like politician Asō Tarō's 2007 book *Totetsumonai Nihon* (Japan the tremendous). It is instead a quietly angry work that explicitly juxtaposes Japan's traditional culture and values with the Western ideas that have invaded and in some ways suppressed them. Fujiwara, for example, includes an unusual survey of Japanese history that elucidates Japanese actions by connecting them either to the *bushidō* (samurai/warrior code) that ostensibly defines Japanese culture, or to practices of imperialism and unethical violence that Japan learned from the West.

He also builds, if carelessly, on the critique that Japanese philosophers like Watsuji Tetsurō have made of Western rationalism. In Fujiwara's hands, the argument sits easily alongside the claim that often accompanies critiques of putative American demands for neoliberal reform: that Japan adopt market-oriented, political-economic mechanisms that privilege individual rationality, risk taking, and productivity. He is not, however, primarily interested in economics, but rather in the differentiation between a coldly rational/logical/individualistic America and a warmly intuitive/social/communitarian Japan, one which more or less negates anything that Westerners might have to say about Japan. Arguing that "pure logic will make the world fail" (*ronri dake de wa sekai ga hatan suru*), Fuijwara goes on an extended discussion of what is wrong with pure rationality and logic. Most of it fails, naturally enough, to stand up to any sort of deep scrutiny, but generally relates to the idea that there are moral premises that cannot simply be reduced to logical deduction. He further claims that logic itself is unable to deal with true complexity. It is a far cry from, say, Kant's *Critique of Pure Reason*, not to mention anything Watsuji ever wrote, but in some sense, Fujiwara has anticipated the challenge. As he puts it, "these are things that I wouldn't expect Westerners to understand" (*kore wa ōbeijin ni wa nakanaka rikai dekinai yō desu*) (Fujiwara 2005, 65).

One might dismiss this as simple nationalism, but it is worth considering the form that this nationalism takes. That is, it is not simply a statement that Japanese culture is better than others, that Japanese values trump others, or so forth, though these ideas would fit relatively comfortably in his book and in many others in the broad *nihonjinron* genre. It is rather that there is a true, real Japan that persists with some fluctuations alongside the modernization that Japan has so proudly achieved. While at some points this purported maintenance of a traditional culture through modernization has been a source of some national or at least administrative pride, with Japanese officials celebrating Japan's ability to act as a translator between traditional Asia and the modern West (Zarakol 2011), it has also served ambiguously in a powerful dual capacity. Japan can serve simultaneously as a symbol that modernization can take many forms while also reminding observers of the traditional culture—even if it is itself a modern invention—constantly at risk of being lost in the pressure to modernize. So it is worth considering the possibility that assumptions about the culture-crunching mission of modernization themselves at least contribute to one particular possible critical perspective on Japan: that it is always on the verge of losing something, always on the verge of being less than it was before.

War, peace, security

If Japan's wartime behavior were justified ideologically within Japan at least in part by the modern challenge that Japan posited to Western modernization, Japan's seeming post-war about-face helped to mark a very different era. Under the US Occupation, Japan adopted a constitution that partly built from Japan's own political institutions but adopted a number of crucial democratic guarantees and, of course, its most notable feature: Article 9:

> Aspiring sincerely to an international peace based on justice and order, the Japanese people forever renounce war as a sovereign right of the nation and the threat or use of force as means of settling international disputes. (2) To accomplish the aim of the preceding paragraph, land, sea, and air forces, as well as other war potential, will never be maintained. The right of belligerency of the state will not be recognized.

The article was politically useful to officials in both Tokyo and Washington. While stopping short of enforcing a wholesale change in Japanese leadership, it represented a clear break from Japan's wartime government. The emperor could still play a role (if now only symbolic), and many Japanese officials, including some who had been jailed as war criminals by the Occupation, could reclaim places in public life, particularly through the conservative political parties that ultimately coalesced into the Liberal Democratic Party (LDP) in 1955.

Since then, Article 9 has become a hallowed example of the elasticity of text and its meaning: first in the creation of the "Self-Defense Forces" (in place of "land, sea, and air forces") in 1954; the extension of the US–Japan security treaty (1960); the collaborative drafting of contingency military plans with the United States (1963); the cabinet's acceptance of a National Defense Program Outline, detailing specific roles, functions and plans for the improvement of defense (1976); the abandonment of the "1% ceiling" of defense spending as a percentage of Japan's gross domestic product (GDP) (1987); the creation of a law to support Japan's participation in peacekeeping operations overseas (1992); the dispatch of Japanese ships to support the American effort against al-Qaeda and the Taliban in Afghanistan (2001); and a Japanese contingent to take part, starting in 2004, in the occupation of Iraq following the US-led invasion in 2003. This has led to a paradox. Japan, with one of the world's largest military budgets and with an unquestioned ability to defend itself from conventional military attack (after all, only the United States could credibly threaten Japan with a non-nuclear attack, and even then only at a dear price for the US military), is also shaped in part by a series of antimilitarist claims that limit the state's ability to make rapid shifts in its force posture or overseas commitments.

For many on the Japanese Left—and for their supporters overseas—Article 9 represents the best of what Japan could offer: a sturdy commitment to pacifism and a rejection of violence as a means for resolving international issues. Combined with elaborate reminders of the violence wreaked upon Hiroshima and Nagasaki through the use of atomic bombs, Article 9 has been a potent symbol of Japan's special responsibility—as the victim of nuclear weaponry—to stand against warfare in the future.

It has been galling, therefore, that Japan's expanding security roles, even if glacially paced by the standards of Japanese hawks and the American military, have been driven by Japan's security relationship with the United States. This meant that while Japanese troops took part in neither the Korean War nor the Vietnam War, Japan's support was certainly expected by the United States, provoking Japanese antiwar organizations in the 1960s, like Beheiren, to view their mission in almost metaphysical terms (Tsurumi 1969; Marotti 2009; Lind 2009, 531). This was not a struggle over what (certainly limited) role Japan should play in supporting American military initiatives in Vietnam, but rather a wholesale critique of the country Japan had become. With its leftists initially purged by the US occupation, then supplanted in electoral popularity by a conservative ruling party with clear connections to the wartime government, Japan had become, in this view, a mere shadow of what it was supposed to represent. Indeed, the increasing visibility of Vietnam War photos, many taken by renowned Japanese photographers like Ichinose Taizō and Sawada Kyōichi, helped to ensure a link to the famous images of post-bombing Hiroshima and Nagasaki. Once again, the United States was raining destruction on the peoples of Asia, but this time, Japan was its willing handmaiden through its logistical support (US bases in Okinawa) and "recreation" zones for soldiers on leave.

Indeed, this has been the central dilemma for many Japanese progressives, particularly as infatuation with communist governments—whether the USSR, China, or North Korea—declined in the later years of the Cold War: the possibility that Japan's largely non-militarist security depends on Japan's complicity in extraordinary levels of military violence carried out by its closest ally. However, it has also been a problem for Japanese conservatives, many of whom argue steadfastly in favor of constitutional revision to eliminate the despised and emasculating Article 9, but differ over whether Japan's foreign policy should be so closely tethered to the country that ostensibly forced Japan to accept the article, not to mention a "masochistic" narrative of wartime history in the first place.

Japan's security stance, while in some ways offering much to please most Japanese during long stretches of the post-war period, was also ripe for the production of more attractive alternatives. For many on the Left, there was the Japan that would stand firm against pressure for remilitarization, standing as a beacon of peace and development in a world that desperately needed both. For many on the Right, there was a prouder, stronger Japan, one willing to define and to defend its own interests while instilling healthy patriotism into younger generations that had been instructed, through peace-oriented education and by leftist teachers, that Japan's history was a bad one, not a great one.

These images have helped in some ways to mobilize sympathetic treatments for both perspectives by outside analysts. Long a critic of Japanese rearmament efforts, the renowned historian Gavan McCormack has argued, for example, that Japan has been profoundly reshaped by the American alliance, and in a manner that has directed it toward a more expansive military role and even toward the exploration of nuclear armament (McCormack 2007). In contrast, former US Deputy Secretary of State

Richard L. Armitage emphasized after the March 11, 2011 earthquake and tsunami disaster that the US military had been proud to come to Japan's defense, before suggesting that a strong Japan would be one even more committed to the relationship:

> Though I very much appreciate the comments and thanks from everyday Japanese about Operation Tomodachi, let me assure you, Americans are not looking for your gratitude. This was our duty. We did our duty … Before we talk about where the U.S.–Japan relationship and alliance will go, the question you [Japanese] should ask yourselves is: "What kind of nation do you want?" Are you going to be a top-tier nation? Or are you going to be content with second-tier status?
>
> (Armitage 2011, 46, 51; the point would be repeated in a subsequent report, Armitage and Nye 2012).

That is, there is another, better Japan: one committed to its pacifist constitutional principles, not deformed by American pressure; or one that is a stronger and more respected member of the international community largely because of its willingness to share in the burdens of American leadership.

Indeed, any quick survey of the literature on Japanese security politics will immediately reveal hundreds of scholarly articles, op-ed pieces, or the like. Often these are by conservative American and Japanese writers who emphasize global responsibility and leadership, or Left-leaning Japanese or foreign critics (like myself) who call attention to efforts at constitutional revision and rearmament, frequently mapping these onto concurrent efforts to whitewash atrocities in Japan's wartime behavior or to provide only the most optimistic possible assessments of US diplomacy and international engagement. Whatever the intentions of these pieces, they often carry with them the implicit statements of what that better Japan would look like, and it is worth at least considering, as people engage in debates about security policy, both why we have come to imagine that this better Japan might be possible, as well as the political and cultural assumptions that these images help to reveal.

Norms

One of the most potent rallying cries that those conservatives dedicated to rearming Japan have had at their disposal is the fact that not having a real military (however one would describe the Self-Defense Forces) is somehow abnormal. After all, China, both Koreas, not to mention every other power in the Asia-Pacific seems entitled not only to maintain military forces but also to deploy them if they deem necessary. West Germany's membership in the North Atlantic Treaty Organization (NATO) since 1955—the same year the LDP took power—had embedded it in myriad multilateral military institutions, giving it a security footprint that Japan ostensibly lacked. After all, what kind of real country lacked even the power to enter into a negotiation for collective self-defense? Even at the level of pure symbolism, the parliamentary opposition from Left-leaning parties to the re-adoption of the *Kimigayo* as national anthem and *Hinomaru* as national flag had left Japan in the unusual position of having neither, until Prime Minister Obuchi Keizō championed legislation in 1999 giving them official status. The long shadows of wartime legacies and taboos, whatever else one might say of the merits of Japan's pacifism and rejection of painful symbols of its imperial past, left Japan in an unusual position globally.

Unusualness can be politically costly. Theorists of international norms—or standards of behavior that are supposed to adhere to state actors—have made the case that there are powerful incentives driving states to participate in the increasingly ubiquitous accoutrements of statehood. Everyone has a flag, everyone has an anthem, not to mention a legislature (even in authoritarian countries where the legislature rubber stamps executive decisions), a K–12 education system (even where such systems are tragically underfunded and poorly attended), a Ministry/Department of Foreign Affairs, and a national science board. Many of these organizational forms are dictated in part by the structure of advanced industrial nations that tends to replicate the powerful international institutions that manage engagement counterparts, so that being part of international agreements on labor, education or development requires the establishment of comparable state offices. If a country does not have a foreign minister, who does it send to meet other foreign ministers? If it does not have a counterterrorism office, who attends international counterterrorism conferences (Leheny 2003, 6–8)?

These norms are more than constitutive features of states. They are also regulatory, in that they are designed to shape state behavior in line with transnational expectations. States do not commit genocide, and they do not torture—or if they do, they must deny it. States are expected to commit to the protection of human security, to women's rights, environmental conservation, and other progressive causes. Much of the research on international norms has focused on the role of "norms entrepreneurs," often politically progressive transnational organizations that push for bans on land mines, or on whaling, or on the commercial sexual exploitation of children. That is, as officials of states face pressure to sign up to international agreements dictating that they must help to protect children, women, the environment, victims of war, and so forth, they are in part responding to the pressure that comes from an international community when certain states can be regarded or described as aberrant or abnormal.

Indeed, much of the critical work on Japan, particularly from political science over the past two decades, has come from challenges to Japan's status vis-à-vis clear international norms. The story is a relatively common one. A transnational movement—often but not always starting in Northern or Western Europe—works with international organizations to get a problem onto the international agenda, and encourages governments to sign a convention or treaty that commits them to the abolition of some public bad or to the promotion of some public good. However, Japan is often dilatory, facing criticism from its counterparts for behavior that is backward, insular, or simply selfish.

The most obvious example is, of course, whaling (Hirata 2004). Japan is one of a small number of countries that still engages in whaling, and is the loudest international proponent of its maintenance, outraging many environmentalists but reflecting, according to Japanese officials, both Japanese custom as well as Japanese scientific awareness that many species of whales are not endangered. The story here is a relatively clear-cut one, in that there is strong (even emotional) international pressure for Japan to abolish its suspiciously "non-commercial" scientific whaling, and a vocal Japanese government that seemingly offers generous development assistance packages for small and poor members of the International Whaling Commission (IWC) in exchange for their votes in favor of Japanese positions.

However, there are other examples that usually follow a somewhat different pattern, with the Japanese government pulled—usually a bit late—into some international agreement. For example, Japan's shaky commitments to the rights of refugees (e.g. Flowers 2009) and to other immigrants (Gurowitz 1999) show that international norms may work, but face special barriers in Japan due in part to political institutions that privilege ethnic homogeneity. Japanese movements themselves, particularly feminist organizations, have been crucial in pushing for legal reforms that have connected Japan, even if later than its counterparts, to developing international regimes involving children's rights, women's rights, protection from domestic violence, and the like (Chan-Tiberghien 2004; Iida 2004; Leheny 2006). In these cases, Japan frequently comes across as perhaps more dithering than uniformly truculent, and the studies tend to present the domestic activists as being particularly laudable for their willingness to stand up for important principles in the face of local opposition.

It is interesting that attention to international norms has been so common among those writing in English about Japan's international politics. On its face, this may simply reflect, again, that Japan is different, or closed-minded; certainly it is not terribly hard to find voices inside and outside of Japan willing to say just that. However, it is also worth considering the speed with which studies of international norms, which really began to gain ground in the 1990s, became visible in political science in general, and so widespread in studies of Japanese politics. After all, many of the early writers on international norms were themselves members of social movements—for environmental protection, against apartheid, for women's equality—and this theoretical perspective allowed at least a means through which to assess (and, in some cases, to celebrate) the impact of these endeavors. Particularly in the wake of a Cold War that had ended surprisingly peacefully, and with an absence of other obvious international relations issues to dominate the field, there was a moment in the 1990s (before 9/11, before the Arab Spring, before most International Relations theorists seriously engaged the rise of China) when such norms could sit comfortably alongside trade agreements and European Union development as major topics for research. Particularly with a Japan that no longer seemed to pose an economic threat to the United States or to other countries, and with an increased number of younger Japan specialists who had themselves spent time in Japan and come to various conclusions about its commitment to progressive values, there were clear opportunities for the melding of political and intellectual interests in productive ways.

None of this is to say that research on international norms and their impact on Japan is inappropriate or misplaced, but the cumulative weight of these studies tends to position Japan as a constant laggard or reactionary on global issues, positions that can usually be confirmed with a quote from a Japanese activist who bemoans his or her own country's antediluvian ways (the same way, for example, an American opposed to the death penalty might speak about penal culture in Texas) or from a Japanese Right-winger who angrily tells activists to respect tradition. Yet the seemingly constant unidirectionality of norms—from Northern/Western Europe to the rest of the world—might also lead one to examine whether the promotion of norms as a viable political strategy is reserved for some nations rather than others. It might further prompt consideration of how earlier efforts at "raising consciousness," building "epistemic communities," and denoting global problems have themselves shaped the views of the researcher. One need not believe that it is wrong to protect children from sexual exploitation or that countries should not offer asylum to refugees to inquire about how certain positions get increasingly taken for granted as part of the iconography of what states do, or what they are supposed to do.

Indeed, some of the best scholarship on norms does almost exactly this. While firmly maintaining their commitments to the insights of gender studies, for example, Carpenter (2003, 2006) and Kinsella (2011) each react critically to gendered notions of combatants and soldiers, and to the unintended consequences of efforts to "protect women and children" as norms of warfare and peacekeeping. Similarly, Subotic (2009), while enormously critical of Serbian behavior during the Balkans war, shows that truth and reconciliation commissions mandated by international norms can be used by local political entrepreneurs for goals that have little to do with truth and even less to do with justice. Norms, that is to say, become elements of political debate and activity on their own, and do not simply draw dividing lines between the good and the bad, the progressive and the backward.

Conclusions

Critical studies of Japan that build from theories of international norms have made major contributions to our knowledge of Japan, of politics, and of international relations. Critical studies of Japan that have reacted to the over-reach of modernization theory as well as to the debates surrounding Japan's pacifist constitution have, of course, been at least as valuable. Indeed, those of us doing research on Japan and teaching about Japan have a professional responsibility to voice critical perspectives, whether we think of this as speaking truth to power or simply trying to ensure that we teach our students to think carefully, to evaluate evidence fairly, or to keep their minds open.

However, critiques should never begin and end with the object of critique itself. Indeed, a critical perspective requires at least some openness to the idea that one's own preoccupations and views will likely shape the analysis. My goal is not to suggest that authors prattle on endlessly about their own positionality, but rather to suggest that there are intellectual and political contingencies that shape how we are likely to approach Japan. They therefore demand scrutiny, in terms of what may lie behind our decisions to challenge or to mimic *nihonjinron*, to excoriate or to celebrate the Abe Cabinet's emphasis on the US-Japan alliance, or to ask why Japan never seems quite up to speed with international norms of behavior. Even when our analyses may be on solid ground, without some kind of critical engagement with our own assumptions, we may be making arguments that feed all too easily into relatively unconsidered statements about what ails Japan and how to "save" it.

As a college professor in the United States, I would love to have more Japanese students in my classes, and would love Japanese employers to reward them for taking my classes and earning a degree from my university. I would, if shown convincing evidence, be extremely glad to believe that this would solve some of Japan's problems, perhaps by creating a better-educated or more global workforce that would help to re-energize Japanese entrepreneurs, spur growth rates, and assist in some ways in broad economic growth. However, I would also want to be wary of making an argument that fits so well with my own interests and predispositions, at least without considering how much I would want a summer intern sitting next to me during my lectures, and correcting me publicly (however politely) on those, I hope, rare occasions when I get something wrong.

Note

1 The author thanks Amy Borovoy and Jeff Kingston for their insightful comments on earlier drafts of this essay.

Bibliography

Armitage, Richard L. (2011) "Our Duty," in Bryce Wakefield (ed.) *Japan and the United States after the Great East Japan Earthquake: Report of the 3rd Japan–U.S. Joint Public Policy Forum*, Washington: Woodrow Wilson International Center for Scholars, 46–55.

Armitage, Richard L. and Nye, Joseph S. (2012) *The U.S.–Japan Alliance: Anchoring Stability in Asia – A Report of the CSIS Japan Chair*, Washington: Center for Strategic and International Studies.

Asō Tarō (2007) *Totetsumonai Nihon* (Japan the tremendous), Tokyo: Shinchōsha.

Aydin, Cemil (2007) *The Politics of Anti-Westernism in Asia: Visions of World Order in Pan-Islamic and Pan-Asian Thought*, New York: Columbia University Press.

Benedict, Ruth (1946) *The Chrysanthemum and the Sword: Patterns of Japanese Culture*, Boston: Houghton Mifflin.

Bernstein, Henry (1971) "Modernization Theory and the Sociological Study of Development," *The Journal of Development Studies* 7(2): 141–60.

Borovoy, Amy (2012) "Doi Takeo and the Rehabilitation of Particularism in Postwar Japan," *Journal of Japanese Studies* 38(2): 263–95.

——(2013) "Robert Bellah's Search for Meaning: The National Body as Community," paper presented at Princeton University Workshop.

Carpenter, R. Charli (2003) "'Women and Children First': Gender, Norms, and Humanitarian Evacuation in the Balkans 1991–95," *International Organization* 57(4), autumn: 661–94.

——(2006) *Innocent Women and Children: Gender, Norms and the Protection of Civilians*, Surrey: Ashgate.

Chan-Tiberghien, Jennifer (2004) *Gender and Human Rights Politics in Japan: Global Norms and Domestic Networks*, Stanford: Stanford University Press.

Dale, Peter N. (2012 [1998]) *The Myth of Japanese Uniqueness (Routledge Revivals Series)*, London: Routledge.

Doi, Takeo (1973) *The Anatomy of Dependence*, trans. John Bester, Tokyo: Kodansha International.

Flowers, Petrice R. (2009) *Refugees, Weapons, and Women: International Norm Adoption and Compliance in Japan*, Stanford: Stanford University Press.

Fujiwara Masahiko (2005) *Kokka no hinkaku* (The dignity of a nation), Tokyo: Shinchōsha.

Gurowitz, Amy (1999) "Mobilizing International Norms: Domestic Actors, Immigrants, and the Japanese State," *World Politics* 51(3): 413–45.

Hirata, Keiko (2004) "Beached Whales: Examining Japan's Rejection of an International Norm," *Social Science Japan Journal* 7(2): 177–97.

Hobsbawm, Eric and Ranger, Terence (eds) (1983) *The Invention of Tradition*, Cambridge: Cambridge University Press.

Iida, Keisuke (2004) "Human Rights and Sexual Abuse: The Impact of International Human Rights Law on Japan," *Human Rights Quarterly* 26(2): 428–53.

Inkeles, Alex (1969) "Alex Inkeles Comments on John Stephenson's 'Is Everyone Going Modern'," *American Journal of Sociology* 75(1), July: 146–51.

Ivy, Marilyn (1995) *Discourses of the Vanishing: Modernity, Phantasm, Japan*, Chicago: University of Chicago Press.

Kinsella, Helen (2011) *The Image before the Weapon: A Critical History of the Distinction between Combatant and Civilian*, Ithaca: Cornell University Press.

Leheny, David (2003) *The Rules of Play: National Identity and the Shaping of Japanese Leisure*, Ithaca: Cornell University Press.

——(2006) *Think Global, Fear Local: Sex, Violence, and Anxiety in Contemporary Japan*, Ithaca: Cornell University Press.

——(2011) "The Other Rashomon Story: International Norms and Continuing Constructions of Japaneseness," in Alisa Gaunder (ed.) *Handbook of Japanese Politics*, London: Routledge, 361–71.

Lind, Jennifer (2009) "Apologies in International Politics," *Security Studies* 18(3): 517–56.

Marotti, William (2009) "Japan 1968: The Performance of Violence and the Theater of Protest," *American Historical Review* 114(1): 97–135.

McCormack, Gavan (2007) *Client State: Japan in the American Embrace*, London: Verso.

McMurtrie, Beth (2012) "Growth in Study Abroad Approaches Standstill," *Chronicle of Higher Education*, November 12, chronicle.com/article/Growth-in-Study-Abroad/135716/ (accessed February 24, 2013).

MEXT (2008) "*Heisei 20nendo daigaku kyōiku no kokusaika kasoku puroguramu (chōki kaigai ryūgaku shien) no kōbo ni tsuite*" (About invitations for the program to accelerate the internationalization of university education (support for long-term study abroad)), www.mext.go.jp/a_menu/koutou/kaikaku/koubo/07112206.htm (accessed March 16, 2013).

Miyaoka, Isao (2004) *Legitimacy in International Society: Japan's Reaction to Global Wildlife Preservation*, New York: Palgrave Macmillan.

Nakane, Chie (1972 [1970]) *Japanese Society*, Berkeley: University of California Press.

Oguma, Eiji (1995) *Tan'itsu Minzoku Shinwa no Kigen: "Nihonjin" no Jigazō no Keifu* (The myth of the homogenous nation: a genealogy of the meaning of Japaneseness), Tokyo: Shin'yōsha.

Robertson, Jennifer (1988) "*Furusato* Japan: The Culture and Politics of Nostalgia," *Politics, Culture, and Society* 1(4), summer: 494–518.

Stephenson, John (1968) "Is Everyone Going Modern? A Critique and a Suggestion for Measuring Modernism," *American Journal of Sociology* 74(3): 265–75.

Subotic, Jelena (2009) *Hijacked Justice: Dealing with the Past in the Balkans*, Ithaca: Cornell University Press.

Tabuchi, Hiroko (2012) "Young and Global Need Not Apply in Japan," *The New York Times*, May 29, www.nytimes.com/2012/05/30/business/global/as-global-rivals-gain-ground-corporate-japan-clings-to-cautious-ways.html (accessed May 16, 2013).

Tsurumi Yoshiyuki (1969) "Beheiren," *Japan Quarterly* 16(4): 444–48.

Zarakol, Ayşe (2011) *After Defeat: How the East Learned to Live with the West*, Cambridge: Cambridge University Press.

Zipangu (ed.) (1998) *Japan Made in USA*, New York: Zipangu.

Index